THE INDIAN STATE
AND
POLITICAL PROCESS

About the Book

An attempt has been made to analyse the story of many Indias which co-exist within One Indian State and they also participate in democratic-electoral process at the national, regional and local levels from Kashmir to Kanaykumari. Further, the analytical exercise undertaken in this volume tries to link the external and internal dimensions of the Indian State and democratic political process because dialectics of a society cannot be analyzed and explained by isolating it from other societies around the world. The Grand Transition of India and its social dialectics have been explained by linking the negative and the positive developments of the last sixty years i.e. from Jawaharlal Nehru to Sonia Gandhi phase of politics. The main focus of the study is to 'demystify' the contradictory reality of democratic capitalist state of India.

About the Author

C P Bhambhri, currently 'Distiguished Scholar' of Jawaharlal Nehru University, New Delhi, has been Professor and Dean of the School of Social Sciences. He also has been a Visiting Professor to McGill University, Canada and Dar-Es-Salaam University, Tanzania. He is a prolific writer who has published in international and national academic professional Journals and has also intervened through newspapers articles.

THE INDIAN STATE AND POLITICAL PROCESS

C.P. BHAMBHRI

SHIPRA

Rs. 1250; US$ 47.00

ISBN: 978-81-7541-374-0

First Published in India in 2007

The Indian State and Political Process

Published by:
SHIPRA PUBLICATIONS
LG 18-19, Pankaj Central Market,
I.P. Ext., Patparganj, Delhi-110092, India
Tel.: +91 11 2223 5152/6152
E-mail: info@shiprapublication.com
www.shiprapublication.com

Preface

The Indian State, including Political Process, has been analysed by examining close linkages between Class, Capital and State. It is not only Karl Marx, Fernand Braudel has also informed that 'Capitalism only triumphs when it becomes identified with the state, when it is the state.' The historical development of capitalism and the maturing of capitalist mode of production and social relations of production has clearly shown that capital and state are completely integrated and it has led to a social situation where the state has successfully hegemonized the whole society with a view to appropriate surplus value for private profit by suppressing and exploiting the underclass and every strata of the labouring classes.

The Indian state has been building capitalism and the capitalist classes have grown in strength because of their close linkages with political and bureaucratic decision-makers. The success story of close relationship between state and capital can be substantiated on the basis of transnationalization of the Indian Capitalists. The Big Business in India is actively involved in foreign capitalist markets as sellers and buyers of industries. It cannot be a one way traffic because Indian capitalists cannot invest in other 'capital' markets unless they are willing to 'open' their market to Foreign Direct Investors and Financial Institutional Investment. A very interesting phenomenon is at work because 'capital deficit' country has become not only a 'recipient of capital', it has also become an 'exporter of capital'. India has voluntarily and consciously opted to integrate itself with finance-capital led imperialist globalization and the reason for the growing integration of India with global-imperialist world Order is that the leading exploiting classes are willing to act as junior partners of global capitalism. What is the impact of integration of the Indian State with global capitalism? Eric Hobsbawm has warned that national identities in the Age of Global-Imperialist Capitalism is 'doomed to the dustbin of history'. George Soros in his latest book *'The Age of Fallibility: Consequences of the War on Terror'* (2006) observes that "Since the capital move around freely, nation states can no longer attract or regulate capital. And that creates uncertainty. It also increases differences between the rich and the poor, which creates political unrest. So it is an imperfect system." Joseph E. Stiglitz in his latest book *'In Making Globalization*

Work" warns that "There is growing disparity between the richest countries and the poorest countries, and growing inequalities within most countries around the world." The Indian ruling classes led by the Indian State have volunteered to become junior partners of the New Imperialist System in spite of the fact that Soros or Stiglitz and many others have given enough warnings to a peripheral developing country's Indian state and its leading classes. An analysis of the Indian state substantiates the argument that national bourgeoisie of yesterday is dead and 'collaborating bourgeoisie' is blindly following the new path of capital accumulation for private profit irrespective of its consequences for the whole society.

The growing social disaffection among the exploited and oppressed labouring classes is reflected in their active participation in democratic-electoral process of India. The power of vote in the hands of powerless and struggling citizenry has given birth to a 'mixed situation'. If on the one hand, the oppressed are finding solutions through their participation in democratic-electoral process, on the other, thirteen states of India are facing 'violent challenge' from socially disaffected and oppressed who have been condemned as Naxalites or Maoists. Not only this. India's Transition to capitalism is not smooth because the Indian bourgeoisie is not ready to take on the inherited economic and social categories of the past. Karl Marx had alerted that past never dies, it has to buried and fought against because it gets reproduced in different forms. The Indian capitalist classes want short cuts to '*Transition*' and they are not interested in disturbing the foundation of inherited feudal-landlord social order. If on the one hand, dominant social forces are not interested in disturbing the foundation of inherited social order, on the other, all the inherited social categories of the past like caste or religion or any other primordial loyalty have been appropriated and patronized by the ruling classes to manage and manipulate Indian democratic-electoral process. The story of India is that many Indias are co-existing within one India and macro-analysis of these many India within the framework of one India has been undertaken to understand the complexities and contradictions of a society in Transition. The story of India's Transition to Capitalism is 'exceptional' because capitalism which emerged in the western capitalist countries went through an 'undemocratic', 'authoritarian' and 'imperialist' stage of historical development. The challenges of Transition were not faced in a democratic milieu by the emerging capitalist social order in the West, and India is facing gigantic problems of Social Transition along with the ongoing process of democratic-electoral system. This story has been described here.

C.P. Bhambhri

Contents

1

Introduction

The centrality of state in the organisation of a modern society has been well recognised even by the evangelical neo-liberal imperialists and every group of religious fundamentaligius. Not only this. Every attempt to displace and dislodge the state by market fundamentalists has proved a non-starter and the global custodian of neo-liberal economic ideology like the World Bank in its *World Bank Development Report of 1997* has abandoned its own project of private economic management in a report on '*The State in a Changing World*.'[1] Jude Howell, in his essay on '*Reflections on the Chinese State*', while reviewing the literature on the State in the post-Cold war 'reform period' of global economic integration, has informed us that in the plethora of literature on State, the following categories have been discussed, examined and identified. They are: (a) 'the entrepreneurial state'; (b) 'the corporatist state'; (c) 'the regulatory state'; (d) 'the dual development state'.[2] (e) 'the rent seeking state etc. etc.' Judge Howell concedes the 'centrality of capitalist economy to the definition of the developmental state' but he hesitates to admit that all the above variations of the state mentioned by him are applicable to capitalist states whether of the developed or the developing capitalist societies. Peter Evans, an important theorist of Bourgeois social sciences, has written about an 'embedded autonomy' of the state which is 'relatively autonomous of particular interest pressures and groups' and Evans has further elaborated that "It is an autonomy embedded in a concrete set of social ties which bind the state to society and provide institutional channels of the continual negotiation and renegotiations of goals and policies."[3] Perry Anderson in his review article of Herve Juvin's book, quotes the author who has stated that "What communism set out to do, and disastrously failed to achieve, capitalism is in the process of realising". Juvin went further and stated that "The market economy…, was the bearer of the project of the west; born under the sign of reason, mistress of universalism and of individuation".[4] While Perry Anderson maintains that "Neo-liberalism is unsupportable", Jeffry A. Fieden, a historian of capitalism, maintains that "The history of the modern world economy illustrates two points—First economies work best when they are open to the world. Second, open economies work best when their governments address the sources of dissatisfaction with global capitalism."[5] The upshot of above description is that in all capitalist countries, the state is integrally involved in the processes of capital accumulation by private capitalists and the theorists of capitalist state are at great pains to build an aura of mystique around the role of state in the management of capitalist social relations and even the concept of 'embedded autonomy of the capitalist state' by Peter Evans is not able to conceal the reality of close and intimate linkages between the state and capitalist economy. Further, the bourgeois theorists have been compelled to define the nature and essence of political process which exists in their democratic societies. The same theoretical mystification of political process is indulged by the bourgeois theorists on the lines of their attempt to mystify the essence of the capitalist state. Peter Evans has brought the cat out of the bag when he states that the "state is relatively autonomous of particular interest pressures and groups." Political process in capitalist democracies is co-terminus with the interplay of multiple and competitive particularistic interest pressures or organised pressure groups. Pressure groups compete in politics for the promotion of their interests and public decision-makers of the capitalist states are continuously engaged in bargaining with these contending and competing groups in society. A few bourgeois theorists have got irritated with the 'iron grip of these pressure groups' over political decision-makers and managers of the capitalist state. Political process in a democratic capitalist society operates around the principles of free market economy where competition and bargaining among multiple market actors gets resolved by arriving at an 'equilibrium' among the competing groups. To sum up, the study of state and its relationship with actual democratic political process demands that the state should be considered as a neutral 'arbiter' and a referee while dealing with multiple and competing demands of pressure groups in democracy. This is the essence of bourgeois social theory of state and its relationship with political process in a capitalist society.

Karl Marx brought an epistemological rupture with dominate theoretical framework of liberal, democratic, capitalist societies and he argued that the state in capitalist societies is neither neutral, nor impartial and not at all an 'arbiter' of competing multiple pressure groups and he rejected the philosophical and sociological grand theoretical tradition of his Age by providing an 'alternative' paradigm of study of society based on the method of social dialects and materialistic interpretation of history of human societies. The Theory of History is linked with the theory of

State by Marx because 'the state' – is the 'legal and political superstructure' of the material structure of society because "Marx…held that the character of the superstructure is explained by the nature of the base, and that the latter is explained by the nature of productive forces". David Held sums up the Marxist socialist political project around 'the power of capital, labour and the state'.[6] To conclude, Karl Marx summed up. 'The state and the structure of society are not, from the standpoint of politics, two different things' Marxist approach to the study of politics or political process is to integrally relate 'state with the structure of society' and politics has to study and examine the relationship between 'capital, class, and state' because state which is the other name of politics does not hang in the air. The State and political process can be studied only by locating the nature of classes and class power by identifying the concrete social reality of specific society like India. Social and political relations are conditioned and determined by material structures of society existing in a particular society at a specific moment of history of that society. This approach is followed here to study the state and political process of India beginning with 1947 to 2006.

II

American social science, practiced by Indian scholars, made an entry point in the newly liberated countries of Asia, Africa and Latin America and scholars from the United States suggested that the approach to the study of newly decolonised societies should be around a theoretical framework of 'Modernisation'. The line of argument of the 'Modernisation theorists' was that old traditions of the ancient society of Asia, Africa and Latin American have now come face to face with Modern institutional values which are associated with the whole baggage of modernity in the Western countries. How has this interaction between 'Tradition' and 'Modernity' actually functioned in concrete situations? Further, the Western social scientists also exported their "Theory of social change because the crux of the issue in newly decolorised societies was the actual process of change". Talcott Parsons, an American sociologist, has maintained that 'social change is an ongoing process' and in history, there is no 'war of all against all'. Karl Popper, a philosopher, has suggested that social change is gradual and piece meal process. Thus, the dominant western modernisation theorist have argued that there can be moments of crisis "but human societies can arrive at their own levels of social equilibrium in the phase of social change." Gabriel Almond, Samuel Huntington and Francis Fukuyama and others have been struggling to find out the institutional arrangement for the maintenance of 'Political an social order' in societies which are experiencing large-scale social changes. Francis Fukuyama has even written 'A manifesto for strong state institutions' for economic development of developing countries in the Twenty-First Century.[7]

The very title of an edited volume by Clifford Geertz '*Old Societies and New States*' sums up the approach of study followed by western social scientists on the study of newly decolonised societies. The western historians had also engaged themselves in the studies of modern age and John Rapley has summed it up by stating that 'What killed off the European Middle Ages was capitalism.'[8]

The western social science on 'Modernisation of Developing Societies' abandoned their own history of 'Transition' or a 'Great Divide between Feudalism and Capitalism' and the attention was focused on the changes of the social superstructure without relating such changes with the changes in the material foundations of society. To sum up, western theoretical framework was applied by Indians for the study of Indian politics and society in a dehistoricised manner and symbols of traditional society were examined by applying them to the study of modern processes of nation and state building in developing countries. The best summing up of this approach was by Rajini Kothari who wrote "Caste have been politicised and politics has been influenced by caste". Indian scholars, like their western counterparts, did not elaborate the theory of modernity which was in reality the doctrine of bourgeois modernity. Bourgeois modernity was equated with western system of democracy either of the variety of 'free market economy' or of the 'welfare capitalist democratic state system'. Thus equation of 'bourgeois modernity' with western system of 'democracy' was the real ideological plank of the modernist theorists, and Indian scholars applied this theoretical framework for the study of Indian democracy. John Kay writes that 'Democracy itself is a market place in political leadership. Representative democracy acknowledges the need for political leadership and authority, but insists that the ideas which leaders implement and authority they exercise, is regularly contested.[9]

Concrete studies on Indian democracy were undertaken by bourgeois social scientists on the basis of yardsticks provided by western bourgeois modernity theorists.

(1) Has Indian democracy become competitive during the last sixty years? The answer to this question is in the positive because free political party competitive system based on active voters' participation has become a reality of Indian participatory democracy.

(2) Have the elected and defeated political parties accepted the

verdict of the voters in elections to the Lok Sabha and State Assemblies? India has witnessed 'alternation' of elected governments on the basis of verdict of the voters. Indira Gandhi vacated the seat of power in 1977 when the voters not only rejected her personally, they also punished her for imposing an Emergency Regime from 1975 to 1977.

(3) Have the institutions of democracy provided the system of checks and balances to contain the emergence of undemocratic and anti-democratic tendencies among the elected representatives of the people? Indian democracy is engaged in a struggle to find a proper equilibrium among the institutions for governance and the misuse and abuse of power by the elected representatives is under public scrutiny and free press and civil society groups have also become quite active in exposing the misdeeds of democratically elected representatives. It is a long struggle because the institutional balance of power always gets disturbed because different centres of power have always competed against one another to arrogate more powers for themselves.

(4) How has the constitutional schema of reconciling democracy with pluralism in India operated during the last about sixty years? Every western democracy is involved in a struggle to maintain a proper balance among competing political, cultural and religious groups in a multi-cultural society. India has a long way to go to reconcile the logic of participatory democracy with the conflicting demands of multiple and diverse social and cultural groups. Of late, the great challenge to the constitutional schema of "maintaining the values of democracy along with the demands of cultural diversities has been under siege by the challenge posed by the religious fanatics and extremists".

(5) What has been the impact of democratic process on processes of social change in India? The theory of 'gradualism' as suggested by western bourgeois theorists has been employed for the study of political and social change in India. The most important impact of universal adult franchise system has been felt by the voters whose levels of political and social consciousness have grown and Indian voter of the Twenty-First Century has come to realise the power of ballot. Political empowerment of the oppressed and suppressed castes especially the Indian Dalits has taken place on the basis of his power to vote. To sum up, Indian democracy has fulfilled the main requirements of bourgeois democratic theorists and formal and representational democratic system has emerged during the last

sixty years of the actual functioning of democratic process in the country. A long list of defects of Indian democracy has been frequently put forward by the so-called 'liberal democratic theorists' who are always clamouring for the 'reform of the system'. The major distortions of democratic process, as pointed out by writers, are 'criminalisation of politics', and the increasing role of 'money power', 'muscle power' and 'the rigging of elections'. Liberal democratic theorists are always looking at symptoms and symbolism of democracy and they do not investigate the reality behind the observable facts and they do not make any distinction between the 'apparent and the real' while studying society. This is the basic flaw of liberal democratic theorists, whether of the west or of India.

III

Marxist intellectual political project is concerned with the study of 'the power of capital, classes (exploiting and labouring classes) and the state' because any study of politics of a capitalist country, whether developed or in the process of becoming capitalist, is incomplete without establishing a rational linkage among 'Class, capital and State' including relationship between 'State and Market'. A knotty question is that in spite of the fact that "Capitalism is not only superior and different from all earlier systems of modes of production", it has also to deal with the inherited social relations and structures of the past. Marx was clear that the 'new mode of production is born out of the womb of the old' but past, in multiple social forms, persists and refuses to disappear even when new capitalist modernity is getting born. What is the nature of 'social transition' in such a society including India? It has been argued that India is culturally unique and socially and historically 'exceptional' and in spite of the emergence of capitalist modernity, the stranglehold of the 'past' traditional social structures and identities still continue and newly emerging capitalist social relations have not been able to break the backbone of the past. While the notions of Indian historically determined 'uniqueness' and 'exceptionalism' deserve to be clearly rejected, historically inherited specificities of India on the eve of independence have to be identified because politics does not hang in the air or in clouds.

On the eve of Independence, India decided to reconcile many contradictory and conflicting tendencies in its Constitution. India had inherited highly authoritarian, feudal, princely social order which was based on the principle of absolute inequality in society and the Constitution, on the other hand, established a democratic political system on the basis of 'universal adult franchise'. How could constitutionally guaranteed 'equality among citizens' operate in a society which operated on the basis of material and cultural structures of 'inequality'? The principle of universal adult franchise was adopted by the Constitution-makers for a society which was completely authoritarian and exploitative.

Further, colonial rule had not only 'arrested the growth of economy', it had also created distortions in the total productive process of colonised India. Feudal landlordism along with more than 625 princely states co-existed with emerging capitalist mode of production because the 'colonial rent seeking state' did not allow the process of contest between inherited feudalism and emerging capitalism. Hence on the eve of independence, India had inherited a material structure of antagonistic modes of production consisting of landlordism, feudalism and emerging capitalism and this kind of material base of society was expected to operate on the basis of democratic political superstructure. How could feudal princely states be allowed to co-exist with elected representative democratic political system? How could peasantry accept feudal and absentee landlord system of economic exploitation and also participate in any form of democracy? How could capitalist class 'accumulate' for growth in a society of parasitism of the feudal and absentee landlords? India launched a grand experiment of democratic governance while anti-democratic and authoritarian structures were still intact on the eve of Independence. Indian democratic state had to grapple with not only domestic archaic social, cultural and material arrangements of social organisation, a free democratic country was born in a global situation which was hostile to freedom and democracy in India. If on the one hand, India was engaged in a full-fledged war with Pakistan on Kashmir, on the other, Peasantry of Telegana had revolted against the state which was seen to be comparadore, neo-colonial and pro-imperialist. On the eve of independence, India also faced secessionist movements which had refused to accept any territorial control by the Indian State. This was the context in which post-Independence leadership was expected to establish a 'centre of power' which was democratic, secular, pluralist and federal. It deserves to be clearly stated that all decolonised countries had to face both domestic and external challenges in the way of establishing a 'centre of power', and India could not be exception to this general rule of global hostilities against the developing countries. While keeping in mind both the internal and external hostilities, the post-Independence leadership tried to maintain 'autonomy' of the emerging democratic state.

This 'autonomy' of the state has been eroded under the impact of New Economic Policy project undertaken by the Indian ruling and governing classes. India of the 1990s has taken a big shift away from the post-Independence tradition of maintaining the 'autonomy of the centre of power' both from internally powerful and exploiting social classes and externally from international pressures and dictates of the capitalist states of the west. This erosion of the autonomy of the state in the 1990s has created a crisis situation for the governing classes which are facing serious challenges from the exploited groups because the Indian state has abandoned the agenda of re-distribution and equality based social order. Powerful exploiting social classes have entered into collaboration with the global centres of developed capitalism and the Indian state has accepted an instrumentalist role for itself. An authority on capitalism has a warning for the Indian globalisers and economic liberalisers. Jeffry A. Frieden observes "Globalisation needs supportive governments, and supportive governments need domestic political support. International economic affairs depend on political backing from powerful countries and from powerful groups in those countries. The integrated world economy before 1914 rested on government actions to sustain it; when these policies became unpopular, they could not be maintained, and with them fell the international economic order. Today's global economy also depends on the domestic political underpinnings of national policies".[10] If the high priest of capitalism like Frieden is maintaining that 'political support' is essential for globalisers and liberalisers, and unfortunately for the ruling classes the Twenty-First Century has begun with an erosion of political support for the Indian ruling classes because the fully integrated 'state, classes and capital' has created a situation of serious social discontent. Political class, which is an external face of the exploiting ruling classes and a state which has become an 'instrument of class rule and class power', is unable to carry conviction with the exploited underclass and political parties are not able to get electoral verdict because of their unpopular policies. The state in such a situation of growing social discontent is increasingly becoming repressive and coercive political class of India. The state is reviving religion to shift away the public opinion from serious economic and political crisis prevailing in India. Daniel Bell, a high priest of conservatism, had suggested that 'unfettered individualism' of exploitative capitalism leads to the 'return of the sacred' i.e. religion in society.[11]

This is precisely the prevailing situation in India where religion or the 'sacred' has been revived in a big way and political class is patronising such religious revivalism to provide an alternative to highly discontented 'wretched of the Earth'. This is the new reality of politics and it has come to occupy a very important space and democratic elections are maneuvered on the basis of emotive issues link religion. If religion-based politics of the1990s is challenging the secular foundations of the Indian Republic, the new economic policy of globalisation, liberalisation and privatisation is not able to motivate the whole Indian society because political class of the 1990s is not able to offer anything worthwhile to the majority of the poor. The practitioners of the New Economic Policy have completely abandoned the agenda of social equality and the redistribution of wealth. How can the slogan of economic growth per se offer any cohensive social and national agenda for the whole society? The New Economic Policy of the 1990s is socially 'exclusive' and it has created a social situation in which individuals or fragmented groups have been involved in their own struggles for the maximisation of profit and benefits. It is only in India but in every country which has adopted the economic model of the market economy and opened up its developed markets to international finance capital, has been facing the crisis of growing unemployment and social inequality. Ralph Dahrendorf, representing the view point of bourgeois social science stated in the 1960s that "inequality of status and wealth is thus a 'natural' state of human society, and acts as an important sources of incentive for people towards betterment.' Such a view was challenged and questioned by Nehru who proclaimed his commitment to socialism in which the state was to actively promote equality among unequal citizens. Philip Nel has stated that "...no one is disputing that within-country inequality has increased for most countries of the world during the most recent phase of globalisation".[12] Is someone listening? Not only this. Nel is giving a warning to "growth-oriented free market economy believers that "Crucially, having a high level of inequality makes it difficult for a country to translate economic growth into pro-poor growth."[13]

NOTES AND REFERENCES

1. World Bank, New Delhi, Oxford University Press, 1997.
2. Judge Howell, 'Reflections on the Chinese State' in '*Development and Change*' 37(2), pp. 278-79, 2006.
3. Peter Evans, 'The State as Problem and Solution: Embedded Autonomy and Structural Change' in S. Haggard and R.R. Kaufman (eds.), *The Politics of Economic Adjustment,* Princeton: NJ Princeton University Press, 1992, p. 163, also see pp. 139-81.
4. Perry Anderson, 'The World Made Flesh': *New Left Review*, 39, May-June 2006, pp. 136, 138.
5. Jeffry A. Frieden, *Global Capitalism: Its Fall and Rise in the Twentieth Century*, New York: WW Norton & Company Inc. 2006, p. 476.
6. David Held, 'Global Social Democracy' in Anthony Giddens (Ed.): *The Progressive Manifesto: New Ideas for the Centre-Left*, Polity Press: Cambridge 2003, p. 144, see pp. 137-72.

7. Francis Fukuyama, State-Building: Governance and World Order in *The Twenty-First Century*, London: Profiles Book Limited, 2004.
8. John Rapley, 'The New Middle Age', *Foreign Affairs*, Vol. 85, No. 3, May/June 2006, p. 98, also see pp. 96-98.
9. John Kay, 'The Embedded Market' in Anthony Giddens (Ed.), *The Progressive Manifesto*: *New Ideas for the Centre-Left*, Cambridge: Polity Press, 2003, pp. 44-45.
10. Jeffry A. Frieden, *Global Capitalism: Its fall and Rise in the Twentieth Century*, New York: W.W Norton of Company Inc. 2006, p. xvii.
11. Daniel Bell, *Cultural Contradictions of Capitalism*, 1976.
12. Philip Nel, 'The Return of Inequality', *Third World Quarterly, 2006*, Vol. 27, No. 4, p. 694, see pp. 689-706.
13. Philip Nel, 705.

2

Jawaharlal Nehru: The Foundational Phase

The retreating colonial state partitioned the country and transferred power to the leaders of all-India national Congress in India and the Muslim League in Pakistan, and these two countries emerged on the international map with Dominion Status on August 15, 1947. The Indian nationalist leadership recognised this fact of Dominion Status and Jawaharlal Nehru, the first Prime Minister of free India, clearly stated that the real journey for the establishment of Sovereign Democratic Republican state has just begun and many more steps will have to be taken to achieve the goal of 'Purna Swaraj' or complete Independence of the country. Nehru, in his famous speech 'Tryst with Destiny', stated that "Now the time comes when we shall redeem our pledge, not wholly or in full measure but substantially." The reference by Nehru in his 'speech' was to the ongoing process of Constitution making for India. The Constituent Assembly had held its first session on 9 December 1946, and the Draft Constitution, as prepared by the Drafting Committee, was presented to the Assembly President on 21 February 1948. Dr. B.R. Ambedkar moved a resolution that the 'Constitution' as settled by the Assembly, be passed. The Constitution was adopted on November 26, 1949 and after signatures of the members of the Constituent Assembly, the new Republic's Constitution was proclaimed on January 26, 1950. The Dominion Status of India ended with the adoption of the Constitution and the challenging task of laying the firm foundations of a modern, democratic, secular, federal Republic of India was undertaken in right earnest by the nationalist leadership. It deserves to be clearly understood that the task of laying down 'foundations' of a modern independent state is never an easy one and this has the reason that Jawaharlal Nehru faced many difficulties and problems in dealing with issues of state-formation in India. Nehru had to shoulder major responsibilities of sate-formation because he was much more than 'first among equals' while performing his obligations as Prime Minister. Nehru was not only one of the tallest leaders of anti-colonial struggle for independence, as Prime Minister from August 15, 1947 to May 27, 1964, he remained in full command of his government and the Congress party. It is essential to catalogue the major steps taken by the Nehru government during his fourteen years of power for dealing with the complex issues that faced the country after independence.

(a) Partition of India and the challenges which emerged during the early years of partition.
(b) Integration and Democratisation of more than 560 princely states into the Union of India.
(c) The holding of first Lok Sabha and State Assembly elections in 1951-52 on the basis of universal adult franchise.
(d) India-Pakistan war on Jammu and Kashmir from 1947-48 and post-ceasefire problems in the Security Council of the United Nations.
(e) Appointment of Fazal Ali Commission on the Reorganisation of States and discussions and decisions in 1955-56.
(f) The launching of Five-Year Plans for Economic Development of the country.
(g) Foreign policy of Non-Alignment and friendship with all countries and in keeping away from two power blocs of the cold war phase of politics. Nehru had emerged as the real leader after the Lok Sabha elections of 1952, 1957 and 1962.
(h) Nehru received set back: India-China Border Dispute 1962.
(i) Nehru breathed his last on May 27, 1964.

Nehru provided the framework for the domestic and foreign policies with a goal to create a 'relatively autonomous state' on the basis of policies of economic planning and non-alignment and peaceful co-existence with every country. Economic Planning was launched to accelerate the rate of growth of Indian economy to overcome inherited backwardness and poverty of the country. Nehru preferred the system of state-led and state-directed strategy of economic growth by following a model of 'mixed economy' with commanding heights for the public sector enterprises. The system of economic planning was equated with socialism and in reality Nehru laid down the foundations of state capitalism where private sector enterprises co-existed with enterprises controlled by the State and in Nehru's words "public sector occupying the commanding heights."

Nehru should be studied in a proper historical context because his contribution to the making of a modern, democratic, federal, secular and welfare state can be analysed and evaluated only by keeping in mind the challenges faced by every newly decolonised and liberated country from the colonial rule. Nehru laid down the foundations of a "relatively autonomous state which was based on democratic legitimacy" and he took great pains to spread the message of democracy during his extensive election campaigns; during the Lok Sabha elections of 1952, 1957 and 1962. Nehru could attempt to establish a relatively autonomous state and dominate over powerful social class forces because he mobilised the Indian voters and got his political strength from voters of India. Democracy acted as a countervailing force for restraining the desire of powerful social class forces which wanted to control and dominate over the state. This is the real meaning of Nehru's contribution to Indian democracy.

Only one illustration about Nehru's firm commitment to democracy can be provided by narrating the story of Reorganisation of States which was piloted by him. The post-Independence national leadership was faced with a Herculean task of creating a new political map for providing a shape to the completely shapeless British Provinces and 562 princely states, which had agreed to sign an Instrument of Accession in favour of India.

People's representatives have to speak and understand the language of their own voters and unlike the alien British rulers, elected representatives have to be accountable to their electorate and furthermore a common language of the elected and the voter is the only bond which provides a link between the parliament and the people. The implementation of the principle of language–based democracy in a multi-lingual country was a gigantic task and the author of '*The Discovery of India*' knew it quite well that unifying factors, in a highly diverse society, could never be imposed from above and any consensus-making on the accommodation of 'diversities' was Herculean task; especially for a country which had suffered wounds of partition. It would be wrong to say that the post-Independence Congress had abandoned its own pledge of linguistic reorganisation of India because the author of '*Unity in Diversity*' clearly understood the sensitivities of peoples and communities based on 'diverse identities' and the unfolding of events around the linguistic reorganisation of states proved that Nehru's 'caution' on the opening of Pandora's box was based on correct understanding of the politics of identity. India was Partitioned on the basis of politics of clash of religion-based identity and Nehru could not have been insulated from the tragic events of post-Partition India. Context determines the text and actions of the makers of history. Nehru was doubly troubled because his commitment to diverse pluralism of India seemed to be coming into conflict with his firm belief that democratic consensus is the prime mover of governance in a country of diversities and pluralities. Nehru's handling of the emotive issue of linguistic reorganisation of India, especially after the tragic events for separate Andhra from Madras Presidency Province. He piloted the issue of language politics without sacrificing the basic principle of consensus-based democracy.

The deft political handling of the States Reorganisation by Nehru and keeping democratic sensitivities intact can be understood only by narrating the main events around the exercise of reorganisation. The State Reorganisation Commission was set up on December 22, 1953 with Syed Fazal Ali as Chairman, and Sardar K.M. Panikkar and H.N. Kunzru as members. The Commission submitted its 250 page report to the Government of India on September 30, 1955 together with summary of recommendations which was the result of 21 months of hard work by the Commission. The present political map of India is completely different from the recommendations for the creation of 16 new states by the Fazal Ali Commission.

The process of decision-making by the Nehru government and the Congress party is illustrative of the fact that Nehru's government did not push the recommendations from 'above' and the Chief Ministers and various parties and groups were actively involved with the recommendations of the Commission. The Home Ministry acted as a 'nodal agency' beginning from October 19, 1955 for processing the report. The Congress Working Committee was immediately seized of the ticklish problems relating to the reorganisation and on November 9, 1955 it took important decisions. They were:

(a) greater Bombay, Maharashtra, including Vidarbha, and Gujarat should be formed into three separate states;
(b) subject to the wishes of the people concerned, the Telangana area to be merged with the Andhra state;
(c) accepted the proposal of the States Reorganisation Commission for the creation of a new state comprising Maha Koshal, Vindhya Pradesh, Madhya Bharat, and Bhopal.

A sub-committee was also constituted with U.N. Dhebar, Jawaharlal Nehru, Maulana Azad and Govindvallabh Pant to 'consider, in consultation with the people concerned, the question of Punjab, PEPSU and Himachal Pradesh and also regarding the proposed Karnataka State, including Mysore and various border issues arising out of Commission's report'. Further, Uttar Pradesh was to remain 'as at present.' Nehru, while speaking in the Lok Sabha on December 21, 1955, stated that "Whatever be the decision Parliament might take on the report, he would suggest the division of India into zones, north, south, east and west with the Centre including and each zone having a Zonal Council to function as an advisory body to tackle the economic problems......" Nehru further said that "these zones might have a common Governor or High Court but above all they must work for a common economy" and Nehru concluded that "these were his personal views on the recommendations."

Nehru was not only leading and guiding but encouraging full debate on contentious issues arising out of the recommendations of the States Reorganisation Commission's report. Nehru pursued his recommendation on Zonal Councils and stated on December 26, 1955: "If each state plans without reference to its neighbour-States, then it would not be a good plan….And in that way also help in lessening, in mitigating and controlling this narrow-minded state-consciousness, a tendency which goes against the unity of India." Nehru's concern for the unification of a highly diverse society is reflected repeatedly, but in achieving this goal, he never abandoned his commitment to the role of public opinion in a democracy. Many new Fronts were opened by political parties and groups which were making claims and counter-claims, regarding the new shape of reorganised India. B.C. Roy, the Chief Minister of West Bengal, proposed a 'reunion' of West Bengal and Bihar, and on February 22, 1956, while responding to the opposition parties' criticism of his 'reunion proposals' in the State Assembly, he not only stated that "You (the opposition) betrayed West Bengal", he also declared that "in the demarcation of States, though it was an important point, "linguism could not be the dominating factor". B.C. Roy was going against the mainstream of political thinking which believed that "language is the basis of territorial identity and plays the role of a link between rulers and ruled in a democracy". Every claim and counter-claim on issues raised by the recommendations of the States Reorganisation Commission was justified and opposed on the basis of the meaning and substance of democracy, in a multi-lingual country where the alien rulers had ruled with the help of foreign language namely the English.

This demand for the reunification of West Bengal and Bihar found a legitimacy on January 24, 1956 when it was endorsed in a 'joint statement' by the Chief Ministers of West Bengal and Bihar. This 'joint statement' by the two Chief Ministers led to resentment in both the States and the United Front of Bengal Leftist parties formed the West Bengal Linguistic State Reorganisation Committee and also decided to launch a civil disobedience movement from February 24, 1956 and it also called "for a general strike to protest against the Bengal-Bihar union move. " The United Front of all Leftist parties in West Bengal jumped into the fray and mobilised people against 're-union' move of two states. U.N. Dhebar chaired Congress Working Committee's sub-committee meeting on February 19, 1956, on the ticklish issue of merger of Andhra state and Telangana, and discussions were held with the "representatives of these two areas jointly to consider what safeguards, if any, should be provided to secure the development and the needs of the comparatively backward Telangana". In spite of the attempts by the leadership, separate Telangana demand refused to die. The 61st session of the Indian National Congress ended on February 12, 1956 by passing a resolution which favoured "the formation of bilingual states wherever possible and said unilinguialism should not be made a fetish." The Congress party was compelled to abandon its idea of 'bilingual states' in the face of stiff resistance from the majority of areas which were affected by such proposal. The government of India took decision on SRC on January 17, 1956 and decided to circulate a draft bill to the states and bring a law before Parliament after this.

Nehru had known that each and every proposal for the merger or unification of areas on the basis of Parliament's Legislation, in spite of popular participation of the concerned groups, will lead to controversies including violence because politics of language-based identity is both a uniting and a dividing social force in a multilingual society. The government decided on January 17, 1956 that Bombay city should be constituted as a centrally-administered area and two proposed states of Maharashtra and Gujarat were to create on the basis of law to be passed Parliament. A hell broke out on the issue of the status of Bombay city and the Congress Working Committee, in its meeting on January 23, 1956, admonished Maharashtra PCC which demanded Congress Ministers to resign and Bihar and Orissa PCCs were also warned against passing such resolutions because PCC "was not competent to ask for such re-organisation." It is not only that the Congress party was facing 'turmoil' in it own rank and file, every political party like the Praja Socialists, Communist, Akali Dal et al. were involved in struggle against one or the other proposal of the government on the implementation of the SRC recommendations. The only exception to this general rule was M.S. Golwalkar's RSS, Jan Sangh/BJP because the ideologues of religion-based identity of Hindutva had never accepted language-based pluralism of India. Not only this, Linguistic pluralism is considered a 'divisive force' by the believers of homogeneous and hegemonic Hindu Rashtra.

The reorganisation of the states in the 1990s leading to the creation of Chhattisgarh, Jharkhand and Uttaranchal has been possible because the BJP had emerged as a significant factor in Indian politics and the Congress party of the1990s had no historical memory of its own past. It is not only Nehru but Indira Gandhi also had resisted the demand for the creation of Punjabi Suba of the Akali Dal and she conceded it only when issue became very emotive because Sant Fateh Singh announced self-immolation and separate states of Punjab, Haryana and Himachal Pradesh were created by reorganising Punjab State.

The above narrative is helpful in the understanding of complex democratic process during the founding period of the Indian Republic from 1947-64. It also deserves to be stated that Nehru was imposing neither or was able to always impose his ideas and opinions on his own party or on the profile of India. The journey of State's Reorganisation is a testimony to the fact that pressure groups were always active in democratic India. Nehru's phase of democracy witnessed a lot of democratic dissent and recognised opposition parties and non-political groups which were very active in moulding public opinion against government's decisions and policies. The Samyukta Maharashtra Samiti, the Maha Gujarat Samiti, the United Front of Leftist parties and Morchas by Akali Dal were a common practice followed by political and non-political formations which agitated against government's decisions. Nehru altered his government's decisions under public pressure. The adventurism of Bombay-city, as centrally administered area, led to mass protests and the protestors compelled the government to abandon its plan. It also deserves to be stated that Nehru was aware about the pitfalls and dangers of 'linguistic chauvinism' and in his famous '*Letters to the Chief Ministers*' he continuously reminded them that 'reorganisation of states' should be handled with great care and sensitivity. Democracy-at-work was witnessed during Nehru's phase of politics while dealing with the emotions of people on public issues.

The ruling class of every country, including India, wish to use the state as an instrument and an agency for their own class interests, and Nehru established a system of balance of power between the state and the pressures of the ruling classes and in the process, states during Nehru's phase of power from 1947 to 1964 (May 27) maintained there relative autonomy from the attempts of the ruling classes to dominate over the state. The Industrial Policy Resolution provided a framework for the private corporate sector and this framework was decided and implemented by India. Such illustrations can be multiplied to substantiate the argument that Nehru recognised the power of the dominant and exploiting classes and he evolved strategies for checkmating the unlimited desires of the ruling classes to dominate over the state.

Nehru made every effort to maintain relative autonomy of the Indian state while dealing with powerful countries during the vicious period of the Cold War politics. Nehru's framework of non-alignment and peaceful co-existence, during the cold war era of international politics, provided an opportunity to "take decisions on difficult issues on merits of the case" and policy decisions on foreign policy were taken on its own by the Government of India. India decided about her friends and opponents (or not so friendly) in international politics. Nehru played an activist's role in international politics and friends and opponents were decided on the merits of the case.

Further, Nehru opposed and contested the forces represented by parties and groups which practiced religion-based politics. For Nehru secular state along with democracy was considered as the real protector of 'unity in diversity'. Nehru considered secularism as an integral part of democratic governance in India.

The multidimensionality of Nehru can be understood by keeping in mind a fact that India had embarked on a difficult journey of establishing a democratic state in an extremely hostile social milieu and the only redeeming feature was that modern India was a product of democratic struggles independence. The Indian leadership had learnt their lessons of democracy during struggle for Independence and such a lesson was learnt in a very hard way and immense sacrifices were made to achieve independence through democratic movements. Nehru nurtured and nourished the tender plant of democracy. An important lesson from Nehru Era is that democracy in India cannot be taken for granted and it has to be defended because it is our great national inheritance. If Nehru's socialism was attacked, both by the supporters of free enterprise and also the Communists, his foreign policy of non-alignment was attacked by the Western countries for its tilt toward the Communist bloc in the Cold War. Nehru stood in the middle and his domestic policies could be described as left-of-Centre and his foreign policy as an assertion of national independence vis-à-vis both the Communist and the capitalist blocs during the Cold War. How do we evaluate a leader who remained Prime Minister for fourteen years? What was Nehru's contribution to the building of modern, democratic Republic of India? This narrative will help us to understand his contribution by keeping in mind the historical period of 1947 to 1964.

NEHRU: A CRITICAL STUDY

In assessing Jawaharlal Nehru's contribution to modern India one should examine the various influences, both of ideas and persons, that shaped and moulded his thought and personality.

Nehru's education and early training brought him into contact with scientific and technological advancement in the West, and the working of democratic institutions in England. This impact of Western science and liberalism made Nehru a life-long believer in democracy, individual freedom and the power of science and technology for social transformation of backward societies. The most precious thing for Nehru was individual freedom, and he strove hard to establish a social order which would guarantee, preserve and maximise the area of freedom. The impact of western liberalism is writ large on his personality and way of thinking. He was convinced that technological advancement will liberate Indians from the 'shackles of medievalism and feudalism.' Nehru's rationalism, humanism, agnosticism, concern for individual freedom (he believed that the content of liberty is equality), belief in democracy and science were the result of his early training and education. While in England, he came under the influence of Fabian Socialists who believed in 'gradualism' and the importance of the State as an instrument for the establishment of socialism.

Soviet Impact

During his visit to Europe and Soviet Russia in 1926-27, he was greatly influenced by the achievements of the Soviet Union in the field of economic development. During the freedom movement, he developed socialist ideas and later tried to practise and implement these ideas through 'economic planning' in independent India. The influence of Marx is clearly seen in his *Glimpses of World History* where he employs Marxist terminology and tools of analysis to understand historical processes. While he did not accept all the fundamentals of Marxism, he did believe that there are class antagonisms and exploitation of workers and peasants by property-owners in a capitalist society. He also accepted that social organisation on socialist principles is better than the exploitative capitalist social order.

Method

But the question was how to transform an acquisitive society into a socialist one, and what should be the method of social revolution in India. Nehru was in quest of replies to these questions, and was dissatisfied with the violent methods advocated by the Communists. His attitude to Communists first found expression when he attended the Brussels Congress of Oppressed Nationalities in February 1927. At that Congress, as well as at subsequent committee meetings of the League, he came into contact with the Communists who were strong in the Congress.

He writes: 'So I turned inevitably with goodwill towards Communism, for, whatever its faults, it was at least not hypocritical and not imperialistic.... These attracted me, as also the tremendous changes taking place in Russia. But Communists often irritated me by their dictatorial ways, their aggressive and rather vulgar methods, their habit of denouncing everybody who did not agree with them. This reaction was no doubt due, as they would say, to my own bourgeois education and upbringing.'

He found the answer to the question of methods for social revolution in Gandhi's philosophy of 'Ends and Means'. One of the most important influences in the making of Nehru's thought and philosophy of action was Gandhi. Though fundamentally opposed to each other in their approaches to the problems of life and society, Gandhi and Nehru worked together with the true spirit of comradeship; and Gandhi exercised great *influence* over the value-pattern and thought-processes of Nehru. Nehru had great faith in Gandhi.

Gandhi's Influence and Congress Party

Gandhian leadership and the nature of the Indian national movement had its impact on the making of Nehru's philosophy. India did not achieve freedom through violent revolution. If a leader comes to power after a successful violent revolution, he can afford to have a complete break with the past and construct a society according to the ideology of the revolution. Nehru's position was different. He had grown within the Congress and had been making efforts to mould and change the Congress according to his beliefs. After independence the leadership of the party fell on him. The nature of the Congress Party, the character of its membership, the intra-party pulls and pressures—all these factors have to be examined to assess the personality of Nehru and his contribution.

The character of the Congress Party is best described by Nehru himself. Writing about the pre-1920 Congress, Nehru wrote:

> "My politics had been those of my class, bourgeoisie. Indeed all vocal politics then (and to a great extent even now) were those of the middle classes, and Moderate and Extremist alike represented them and, in different ways, sought their betterment...."

Nehru describes the post-1920 Congress as the 'New Congress'. About the Congress of the Gandhi era he writes: "The whole look of the Congress changed, European clothes vanished and soon only Khadi was to be seen; a new class of delegate, chiefly drawn from the lower middle classes became the type of Congressman...." But even this 'new Congress' had not been convinced of Socialism. Nehru complains repeatedly that Congress was not aware of social objectives to be achieved after freedom. "Yet I felt that, bourgeois as the outlook of the National Congress was, it did represent the only effective revolutionary force in the country."

Nehru was not the leader of a socialist or ideological nationalist movement. The Congress had all sorts of people in its fold. An active and articulate proletariat was not the vanguard of the nationalist movement. Thus Nehru's formative influences, the values that were dear to him, the method of social revolution that he developed, the character of the national movement, the nature of the Congress and above all the country in which he was working and living—all these aspects have to be considered.

'Practical'

A serious charge levelled against Nehru is that he failed to create an appropriate organisational and institutional structure for the proper implementation of ideas which he sincerely believed in and stood for. He talked of social and economic planning, but never cared to work out the detailed implications in the light of its conceptual bearings.

Two observations of Gandhi are worth noting regarding the personality traits of Nehru. Gandhi observed that he (Nehru) "is undoubtedly an extremist, thinking far ahead of his surroundings. But he is humble enough and practical enough not to force the peace to the breaking point." Gandhi's saying that Nehru was 'practical enough' not to create acute crises may help us in understanding the so-called 'grand failures' of Nehru. An idea may be excellent but the fact of its acceptance by the people has also to be taken into account by the leader. Moreover, Nehru, as Gandhi said, "does not feel happy if he is bogged down by the smallness of the task immediately on hand." Nehru needed a 'broader canvas to work upon'; he gave 'big ideas' to the nation and the world. When it came to execution, his performance perhaps could not be described as remarkable. There may be valid explanations for these deficiencies. Perhaps the social and cultural setting of the country was not congenial for a 'breakthrough', or the ideas were far in advance of his times. Perhaps the tools he employed, i.e., the state apparatus, the bureaucracy and the Congress Party were defective and inadequate for the gigantic tasks.

Educator

Keeping in mind this total background in which Nehru was functioning, let us study some specific aspects of Nehru's political and social ideas. According to Nehru the first step to awaken the exploited masses was the establishment of democracy. Universal adult franchise was a revolutionary step in the Indian context. The teeming millions living in the far-flung villages, with different stages of socio-economic development, were, for the first time, made partners in shaping the nation's destiny. These destiny makers participated in general elections and exercised their right to elect and reject leaders, and in the process the consciousness of the importance of the 'ballot' as an instrument of socio-economic transformation of the country gradually developed in the minds of the people.

Many had apprehensions about the success of democracy in India. They doubted whether democracy could succeed in a country of mass illiteracy, economic backwardness and social inequality. But Nehru was active in nurturing the plant of democracy in India. He not only provided political stability to India, but also showed the path to the 'emerging social forces' and taught them the manner of struggle against entrenched vested interests. Instead of taking any radical steps such as the confiscation of property, and creating an acute class crisis, he concentrated on educating and preparing the people for the struggle to divest the vested interests. In his whirlwind election tour, Nehru put across his ideas of secularism, socialism, economic planning and democracy before the masses, and thereby tried to wake up the sleeping giant that was India. In a country where the majority of the masses were illiterate, Nehru acted as a great. teacher. Through the spoken word, he made efforts to educate the masses in the problems of poverty, its causes and remedies, and also on the role that the common man should play in moulding the destiny of India. He made people realise the importance of their being sovereign, and urged them to exercise sovereignty against entrenched exploitative social forces and liberate themselves from the shackles of poverty and ignorance.

He also made the common man realise the value of Parliament as an instrument of social change. As leader of the majority party, he always tried to act on the basis of 'consensus'. During his Prime Ministership, he never allowed the army to meddle with civilian affairs. Nehru's refusal to nominate or even indicate his successors, and his supreme confidence that 17 years of his labour would not prove worthless, and that a successor would be found in a democratic manner, proves his faith in democratic values and in the democratic destiny of the country.

Step by Step

During the freedom movement, Nehru's socialist ideas influenced the youth and the intelligentsia. In 1929, at the Lahore session of the Congress, Nehru, as President, declared: "The philosophy of socialism has gradually permeated the entire structure of society the world over. And almost the only point in dispute is the pace and methods of advance to its full realisation. India will have to go that way too if she seeks to end her poverty and inequality, though she may evolve her own methods and may adopt the ideal to the genius of her race."

In 1931, at the Karachi session the Congress passed an important resolution of Swaraj, indicating fundamental rights, and its economic programme. Nehru writes: "In the Karachi resolution it (Congress) took a step, a very short step, in a socialist direction by advocating nationalisation of key industries and services, and various other measures to lessen the burden on the poor and increase it on the rich. This was not socialism at all, and a capitalist State could easily accept almost everything contained in that resolution."

At the Lucknow session in 1936 he said: "I am convinced that the only key to the solution of...India's problems lies in socialism....I see no way of ending the poverty, the vast unemployment, the degradation and the subjection of the Indian people except by changes in our political and social structure, ending vested interests in land and industry, as well as the feudal and autocratic Indian States system. That means the ending of private property except in a restricted sense, and the replacement of the present profit system by a higher ideal of cooperative service... the present order has reached the evening of its day, and it is up to us to try to mould the future as we would like it to be...." He reiterated his belief in socialism in his Presidential address to the Faizpur session in 1936.

In 1938, Subhas Chandra Bose, as President of the Congress, appointed Nehru as the Chairman of the National Planning Committee. Nehru said 'For me this has been fascinating work and I have learnt much from it.... It is also clear that any effective planning must involve a socialisation of the economic structure.'

Nehru's Approach

When this believer in Socialism and economic planning became Prime Minister, it was expected that there would be radical changes in existing property relationships. The question to be discussed is: What is Nehru's contribution to the establishment of Socialism in India?

The socialists outside the Congress Party were greatly disappointed and were very vocal in their criticism of Nehru who according to them, had betrayed the cause of socialism.

Before any assessment of the failures and the contribution of Nehru to the building of socialism is made, one fact should be stated clearly: Nehru was concerned with evolving a set of principles and ideas to achieve a socialist reconstruction of society with democratic means rather than with a violent revolution. His conviction was that socialism without democracy would mean tyranny in the Indian context. Further, his assessment of the existing Indian situation was that radical transformation was not possible because of the compulsions of the objective situation. The masses were deep-rooted in superstition, fatalism and ignorance. Class distinctions had not yet crystallised. A revolutionary working class movement, ready to fight me entrenched vested interests, did not exist.

In Nehru's opinion, in such a social context the journey to socialism should be slow. These thought processes influenced his activities as Prime Minister.

To achieve socialism, Nehru believed that public sector should occupy the commanding heights in the Indian economy. He believed that the major sectors of the Indian economy should be under public ownership. He believed in large-scale industrialisation which he considered essential for the eradication of poverty. As chairman of the Planning Commission; he piloted Five-Year Plans for economic growth. The pillars of this economic planning were industrialisation, agrarian reform, community development, education and social welfare. It has been estimated that the rate of economic growth achieved in India since 1950-51 is 2 to 3 times as high as the rate recorded under British administration. As a result, the percentage increase in national income in the 13 years till Nehru died was higher than the percentage increase realised in India over the preceding half century.

'Mixed Economy'

But is this Socialism? The abolition of landlordism and emphasis on the public sector were steps towards the building of a socialist society. But Nehru's concept of a 'mixed economy' encouraged and strengthened capitalism in spite of the 'public sector'. The monopoly power of the capitalists increased during the 17 years of Nehru's socialism. He did not bring any radical change in property relationships, and as such, the foundations of the 'acquisitive society' remained intact. He was so obsessed with increase in production that he could not realise that the benefits of economic development would go more to the already well-of sections. His rejection of a ceiling on wealth and nationalisation of banks as doctrinaire beliefs made him blind to the direction of development of capitalism in his scheme of 'mixed economy', and a socialist Prime Minister had to appoint the Mahalanobis Committee to report on concentration of wealth during the period of planning. Neither land reforms nor economic planning benefited the common man to an appreciable extent. Thus in the evolution of Nehru's socialist ideas from the mid-twenties to the time of his death, there are two stages. During the pre-independence period, he was vocal about and firm on the content of socialism and was dissatisfied with Gandhi and the Congress for not accepting the full goal of socialism. In the second stage he started decrying what he called a 'doctrinaire' approach to socialism and emphasised flexibility and pragmatism which led even to the dilution of the essentials of socialism.

Unsuited Tools

Who is responsible for the failure of Nehru's ideals of planning and socialism? The tools employed by Nehru for achieving the socialist goals were the bureaucracy and the Congress Party. Were these the right tools? Were they committed to Socialism or economic planning? For any radical socialist programme Nehru required the support of a well-organised political party. Without strong political support, he could not have achieved his objectives. What was the character of the party of which Nehru was the leader? The Congress is a 'coalition of interests', a united front of all kinds of social interests and classes. Big businessmen and big landlords control it by making huge contributions to its election funds. In a parliamentary democracy, with a strong capitalist class, the Congress had to depend on it for finances. With the present membership of the Congress, and with its dependence on capitalists for finances, and with powerful Congress bosses not convinced about socialism, it would have been a miracle for Nehru or any other leader to get effective political support for any radical programme.

The critics, however, say that if such support was not forthcoming, he should have resigned from the party and formed a new one. After all Nehru was most popular leader among the masses. Instead of becoming leader of a party which by and large had no faith in socialism, he should have mobilised the masses to form a new party. Why did he not do it?

There are two answers. First, it was too much to expect Nehru (or any other leader) to sever relations with an organisation with which he had life-long association and loyalty.

Second, instead of leaving the Party, he chose to make sincere and herculean efforts to convert the largest political organisation to the ideas of socialism. Even in pre-independence days, he had been making such efforts. He continued these efforts till the end of his life. Nehru's belief was that if the Congress Party could commit itself to socialism, it would be very difficult either for his successors or the party to give up socialism and economic planning. He was trying to make socialism a national goal, and for this he was educating the masses and converting party men. His faith was that progress towards the goal through his methods might be slow but it would be steady and firm. Perhaps the poor performance of the Opposition socialist parties in the elections made Nehru stick to the Congress and try to convert it. Nehru believed that revolution could not be made to order.

Nehru believed that if a revolutionary idea (socialism) could capture the imagination of the people, it would become a material force. People inspired by great ideas are capable of great deeds. He tried to imbue Indians with great ideas so that they could perform great deeds. It is alleged that the Congress Party is responsible for Nehru having been not able to lay the foundations of a socialist society in India. It is further alleged that so-called conversion of the Congress Party was doomed to failure, in view of its class character.

Bureaucracy

His failure is also ascribed to his reliance on the bureaucracy. Nehru believed that with the help of the state machinery he would be able to achieve his targets. But the administrative apparatus inherited by independent India was hardly suited for the tasks of social reconstruction and economic development. It is surprising that Nehru who had been so critical of the bureaucracy in the pre-independence period, should have accepted it as an instrument for the establishment of a socialist society.

The Nehru of post-independence India not only protected the rights and interests of the ICS but relied on them for achieving his social objectives. For the modernisation of the country, economic growth had to be accelerated, the backwardness of centuries had to be removed in decades. How could this be achieved by the slow-moving, procedure-bound bureaucracy? Further, modernisation did not mean only industrialisation but also transformation in the way of living of the people. Could the bureaucracy, with its snobbishness and exclusiveness, reach the masses and influence their way of living and thinking? A new system of economic production creates new relationships in society and changes the way of living of the people. But the new system of economic production—the use of machines and technology—has to be accepted by the people who were using antiquated methods of agricultural production. Who was to create this awareness among the masses? Did the bureaucracy have the social attitude necessary to perform the gigantic task of creating a social revolution simultaneously with the economic revolution? Were our civil servants so public-spirited? An absolutely different kind of bureaucracy was required to fulfil the tasks which Nehru wanted to perform. Career seekers, and mercenaries were hardly fit for the new tasks.

Basic Mistake

It may be argued that Nehru should have deployed Congress Party workers for creating a social awakening among the masses. But the faction-ridden Congressmen interested in capturing power for personal gain were neither competent nor to be trusted for this job. This job has been done in other countries by political parties organised on strong well-knit ideological foundations. Russia was a backward country. It had to be industrialised and modernised, and the pace of modernisation had to be accelerated.

Devoted and dedicated cadres of the Communist Party were given the task of conveying to the people the new message of educating them in socialism. Nehru admired Russia and its economic development. But one of the important things which could have been learnt by him from the Russian experience was that without a cadre of political workers devoted to socialist ideology the masses could not be awakened. Nehru failed to create 'soldiers of socialism'. It must be stated that he did his best to spread the ideology of socialism in India. It is also a fact that the establishment of democratic institutions and periodic general elections created awakening in the masses. These were no mean achievements. But talking to and trying to educate an unorganised and amorphous mass of people has limited utility. It should have been supplemented by creating a band of political activists who would have taken Nehru's message to the far-flung areas of the country. They would have obtained strength from Nehru and would have sustained Nehruism much better than the Congress Party or the bureaucracy.

Lack of Austerity

Much of the failure of Nehru's plans has been attributed to his reliance on the Congress Party and the bureaucracy. It may be worthwhile to examine some of his personal failings also.

Much should not be made of his petty bourgeois background but one effect of this background was obvious, i.e., Nehru did not set any standards of austerity or simplicity or Swadeshi before the people. The Gandhian tradition of 'simple living', instead of being strengthened, was abandoned. If a backward economy was to be transformed and a new social order was to be created, austere living was essential. When Nehru talked of 'sacrifices' for a better future, the common man did not respond. In India, the common man looks to the top leadership for setting social standards. When Nehru failed to set any social standards, people started copying the way of living of the richer classes. Nehru's India saw the erosion of social and moral values. His own living did not show that he was the leader of a poor country. Congressmen and capitalists were adding to their wealth. The common man had hot been given any values by the leader.

Poor Organiser

Nehru was not a great organiser. He gave excellent ideas, but could not give proper institutional and organisational expression to those ideas. Although he was the most important leader of the Party, he did not do anything to reorganise it for socialistic objectives. Except under the Kamaraj Plan, there was no weeding of undesirables. What kind of structural changes were required to make the Congress an effective instrument of modernisation and socialism? Nehru did not concern himself with these questions of party organisation. In the field of administration under Nehru's Prime Ministership, no radical reorganisation was affected. India inherited à system of administration suitable for a law-and-order state. After independence, the administration had to perform social welfare functions. A different kind of administrative set-up was needed to achieve socialistic objectives. But Nehru never gave enough thought to the reforms needed in the administrative structure.

The Nehru era will be known as that of 'revolution from the top'. The reverberations were not felt by the common people. Parties, leaders, movements all remained in the background as long as Nehru was alive. True, this was not his fault. But the fact that the Opposition parties and leaders could not play their role during the Nehru period resulted in a sense of complacency in the people. Many felt that Nehru would do the job; those who were not satisfied with Nehru's achievements became frustrated and cynical. India got both the best and the worst of the 'revolution from the top'.

Power Structure

The successful functioning of parliamentary democracy in India will depend, among many other things, on how far and how quickly a new social order based on industrialisation, economic planning and socialism is created. If India could achieve socialism and destroy the foundations of the acquisitive society through democratic means, and without violent class conflict, Nehru will go down in history as a path-finder. He would have been more successful if he had paid attention to required reforms in the traditional system of parliamentary democracy, and thought about devices for adapting and adjusting the form of democracy to the new tasks which it will have to perform in India. If parliamentary democracy becomes the defender of the status quo and the vested interests, it will be challenged by the exploited but emerging and conscious new working class. If parliamentary democracy becomes the vehicle of a new social order and an instrument for the devesting of vested interests, the latter may try to subvert it, resulting in clashes and conflicts. Nehru's belief that parliamentary democracy is suitable for Indian requirements remains open to question.

Stability and Peace

This critical analysis should lead us to the pinponting of his singular contributions. Nehru's greatest contribution is the importance that he attached to science and technology. He was convinced that India cannot make progress without industrialisation. This was why in the Five-Year Plans he gave great importance to the development of basic and key industries. He was convinced that planning would take the country to self-generating growth by the end of the Fifth Plan. For this political stability was essential. His very important contribution was the provision of political stability. Once the economy becomes self-generating, he thought, India would be able to face any storm.

For economic development of the country, peace was very essential. His clear understanding of international forces convinced him that India could progress only if she kept away from 'Cold War' and 'bloc' politics. Any involvement in bloc politics would endanger India's economic development. The policy of non-alignment, peace, and emphasis on negotiations for the settlement of international disputes were the essential conditions for socialism in India. Nehru strove hard to achieve this. He was emphatic that a strong industrial base was essential even for the defence of the country. The Chinese aggression of 1962 was a shattering blow to his dreams because the demands of defence would hamper the pace of economic development. The Chinese aggression in fact provided an excellent opportunity to the militarists and communalists in India to attack Nehru's policies of peace, non-alignment, co-existence and socialism. Nehru had a world perspective, and had a clear understanding of the relationship between the problems of the country in the context of world happenings and events. He brought before his countrymen the implications of the Nuclear Age.

Nehru was a fighter against the main currents of socio-cultural life in the country. He never concealed his opposition to moth-eaten traditions and superstition. He believed that industrialisation and economic development were prerequisites for the successful operation of secularism. He emphasised the importance of the 'scientific outlook' and, thus, was truly a Renaissance leader. He had a coherent picture of the tasks facing the country. Secularism, democracy, economic planning, modernisation and socialism were all an integrated approach to the problems of a communal, backward and agricultural society. If we are to live in the modem world as an independent country, with the power to take decisions independently, a modem way of life and modem techniques of economic development have to be employed. This was Nehru's vision of modem India: where science and not superstition, reason and not blind faith, humanism and not religious bigotry will reign supreme. This is the unfinished task left by Nehru to us. This is his message.

—*Mainstream*, 11 November, 1967.

NEHRU AND NATION-BUILDING

During the struggle for freedom, Nehru was spreading the message of his value-beliefs among the masses of India. After Independence he got an opportunity to translate his social and political ideas into practice with the help of state power. It is worthwhile to examine how far Nehru succeeded in achieving his goals and objectives.

Before attempting an evaluation of Nehru, it is appropriate to describe in brief the tasks that Nehru had set for himself. In pre-independence days, Nehru had repeatedly said that he was a republican and a socialist. In his presidential address at the Lahore Session of the Congress (December, 1929) he stated:

> "The philosophy of socialism has gradually permeated the entire structure of the society the world over. And almost the only point in dispute is the pace and methods of advance to its full realisation. India will have to go that way too if she seeks to end her poverty and inequality, though she may evolve her own methods and may adopt the ideal to the genius of her race."

Thus socialism, equality, freedom for the individual, and democracy were the cherished goals of Nehru. Further, he stood for secularism, a scientific attitude towards life and industrialisation of the country. He was clear in his mind that only industrialisation would liberate the Indian masses from the shackles of mediaevalism and poverty born out of colonial domination. Thus quintessence of Nehruism can be stated as:

> "It is based upon a secular rather than a sacred view of human relations, a rational outlook, an acceptance of the substance and spirit of the scientific approach, a vigorous application of an expanding technology, an industrialised organisation of production, and a generally humanistic and popularistic set of values for political life."

The institutional arrangement created by Nehru to achieve these values, was a Constitution, an elected Parliament, a Planning Commission, and an expanding Public Sector. Democratic Parliament and economic Planning (with its system of institutional arrangement) were the main pillars of Nehru's efforts at nation-building.

The question that arises is: Did this value structure and institutional arrangement become an accepted philosophy of a large number of people in the country? Is this legacy of Nehru safe in the post-Nehru India? The answer to these questions will determine the success or failure of Nehru in nation-building.

Nehru's values and institutional arrangements for the management of national affairs evoked different responses from different segments of the Indian elite. His philosophy of economic planning was attacked by the Rightists as encouraging statism, leading to a progressive diminution of individual freedom and private initiative. According to them planning stifled the spirit of individual enterprise. On the other hand, the Leftists appreciated the role of 'public enterprise' but criticised the Public Sector undertakings for being bureaucratically managed institutions, which in actual working went against the spirit of socialism. Further, economic Planning in the country helped the rich and the disparities between the classes in the country went on increasing during the period of Nehru's economic Planning. Economic Planning in India helped the growth of monopolies and the concentration of wealth in a few hands. Economic Planning instead of establishing a socialist society strengthened capitalism in India. Thus Nehru was criticised by both the Left and the Right though for different reasons.

His another pillar of nation-building was political democracy in the form of periodic elections, adult franchise etc. Nehru believed that in building modem India, people's active support and popular participation were essential. Not only this. Through the medium of these elections and adult franchise, Nehru wanted to create consciousness among the people regarding their role in the processes of nation-building. Again among the elite, there is a difference of opinion regarding the effectiveness of democracy as established by Nehru in India. The response of the elite to the functioning of democracy is mainly of three kinds.

First, opposition has come from a section of the elite who believe that Nehru imposed Western ideas and institutions on a society whose soil is quite unsuitable for the functioning of such institutions. It is argued that Western type of party democracy does not suit the genius of India. Hence we should have a communitarian type of democracy, with the place of pride given to the village panchayats. These critics of Nehru betray romantic clinging to the past, to an imaginary golden age which they would like to come back. It was suggested that the issue is the management of diversity and unity, more specially the need to relate the parochial and the universal, to fuse basic components of the indigenous culture with the standards and practices to the modem world. Nehru was criticised for ignoring the past, on whose basis only the present and the future could be built.

Second, opposition has come from the capitalists who say that democracy has created great social conflicts in the country and that sectional demands have assumed greater importance than the desire to add to the size of the national cake by producing more wealth. Democracy is being viewed as the anti-thesis to the economic development of the country. It is argued that the worst casualty of Indian democracy has been economic production.

The third and the last attack on Nehru has come from the socialists who allege that democracy in India is a tool in the hands of the capitalists. The entrenched classes are using it for their own benefit.

If both the Rightists and the Leftists are unhappy with Nehru, then the question arises: where exactly did Nehru fail? His failure lay at three different levels:

(a) He could not create any 'symbols' around which the masses of India could rally. He described the Bhakhra Dam and the Bhillai Steel Plant as 'New Temples' but they did not replace the old symbols which were ingrained in the minds of the Indians during the past thousands of years. He wanted to change the attitudes and ways of thinking of the masses, but he could not establish concrete alternatives to the images cherished by the people. Thus modernisation, scientific temper, secularism—all remained paper slogans.

(b) His values did not percolate down to the masses. What to say of the masses, even his partymen and cabinet colleagues remained unconvinced about the validity of many of Nehru's ideas. The almost unceremonious farewell to the policy of 'Independence and non-alignment', given by the successors of Nehru illustrates this point. Thus compeers and compatriots shed no tears on the demise of India's foreign policy.

(c) Nehru did not build any political movement or party for the preservation or perpetuation of his values. The Congress Party as it is constituted could hardly act as the defender of Nehru's ideology. Nehru was a keen student of world history. He knew it very well that ideas can shake the world if they become part of a movement. He admired Lenin, but did not learn anything from him. He acknowledged it in the *Discovery of India* that: "A study of Marx and Lenin produced a powerful effect on my mind and helped me to see history and current affairs in a new light." But Marx had also said that the time had come to change history. This could only be achieved by a strong political movement committed to the ideology of change.

Nehru's strategy of nation-building was defective. In the absence of a cadre of committed party workers, and a net work of media of communication the message of ideology cannot spread. Those leaders who live from hand to mouth, who simply concern themselves with the problems of today, and who have no vision of tomorrow can afford to ignore the importance of party workers. But Nehru was different. With all his faults, he had a clear vision of the future of India. He laid the foundations of modernisation and industrialisation. Perhaps it would be difficult to reverse this process. But there is a chance element in it. Democracy may be subverted if the entrenched classes fear the challenge of the emerging classes. Socialism and economic planning have already been devalued in the country. Nehru made no attempt to create soldiers of socialism and defenders of democracy. Here lies the greatest failure of Nehru.

On the ideological plane also, Nehru's attempt to follow a middle path between Western liberalism and Marxian socialism created a situation where his ideology is not a part of the inheritance of any party or movement. His attempt to adapt socialism to the Indian genius ended in a confused kind of pragmatism.

This ideological confusion in Nehru becomes clear when in his *The Basic Approach* a stand is taken that the distinction between Capitalism and Socialism is wearing thinner and thinner. He writes: "Socialism is basically a different approach from that of capitalism, though I think it is true that the wide gap between them tends to lessen because many of the ideas of Socialism are gradually incorporated even in the Capitalist structure."

It is not surprising that even in the Left Movement in the country Nehru's impact is insignificant, though his contribution to the making of modem India is generally admired and appreciated by the Left.

—*Mainstream*, 16 November, 1968.

PARLIAMENTARY DEMOCRACY: NEHRU'S PERSPECTIVE

The basic goal of India's struggle for freedom was to establish democracy in the country, and the Indian masses were mobilised against British imperialism by the national leadership for achieving the goals of free and democratic India. After the transfer of power on August 15, 1947, it fell on the shoulders of Nehru and his other colleagues of the national movement to nurture and nourish the experiment of democracy in India. After independence of the country from foreign rule, many negative and hostile forces were at work against the experiment of democracy in India, and the Indian leadership had to fight against communal and feudal elements in the country to safeguard democracy. Nehru was very conscious of anti-democracy forces in the country, and he struggled against them by making the masses conscious of the enemies of democracy.

Nehru's strategy to fight against the opponents of democracy had many essential components. First, Nehru recognised the role of leadership in struggle against feudalism and communalism, the twin threats to democracy, and he used his political and administrative power in his fight against enemies of democracy. While Nehru recognised the potentialities of leadership role in generating positive ideas in the country, he was fully aware of its limitations and inadequacies. To supplement his efforts of building democracy, he vigorously worked for mass mobilisation through adult franchise.

Nehru's second strategy of strengthening Indian democracy was directed towards the masses. Apathetic and inactive people cannot safeguard democracy. Masses should be made politically very conscious to confront challenges and threats to democracy. Three general elections of 1952, 1957 and 1962 were utilised by him to educate the people in the merits of democracy.

Third, Nehru was aware that a lip service would be paid to democracy if its institutions were not strong enough to check the ruler's arbitrariness. Democracy can be a formal thing if its institutions are incapable to exercise effective control, with proper checks and balances, on people in the government. History knows many instances of democratically legitimised authoritarianism, and no one was more aware of this fact than Nehru himself. Hence, he made every effort to strengthen Indian Parliament. Nehru wanted Parliament to become the focus of national power. Hence he attached great significance to Parliamentary debate and discussions. It is only democratically elected Parliament which can ventilate people's grievances and evolve appropriate programmes for people's uplift. If Parliament is strong, it can hold the cabinet accountable and project people's demands effectively.

But Parliament cannot be strong if party system is weak and if one leader is supreme in the nation. Parliament would be weak and ineffective in the face of an extremely powerful leader who would use it as a rubber stamp. Nehru strengthened the institutions of Parliamentary democracy in India by focusing attention on the central role of Parliament in the governance of the country.

Fourth, Nehru recognised the need of collective and coalitional leadership in the Congress Party to safeguard Parliamentary democracy against very powerful and authoritarian leader. Nehru had many conflicts with his comrades and party colleagues, and he involved himself in democratic struggles against his opponents in the party. This is a very important strategy to strengthen democracy in a country where serious challenges and threats to democracy exist. Nehru believed that if a leader cannot tolerate opposition and criticism of his own party, he would not tolerate and accept the criticism of opposition parties. Authoritarianism starts by purges within the party and then cleaning process is extended to all the parties. A leader who cannot stand criticism of party colleagues and political opponents cannot also manage parliamentary democracy. Nehru was competent to manage parliamentary democracy because he showed tolerance towards the opposition, and involved himself in debate and discussion with his critics.

Nehru's strategies of safeguarding Parliamentary democracy in India were based on a firm belief that as a tender plant it has to be consciously nurtured, and its institutions have to be strengthened, and challenges have to be faced by extending democracy and debate, and not by circumventing democratic debates in the country. Nehru recognised that Parliament is safe only in a country where free press exists because Parliamentary debate should be reported and commented upon. Parliament can perform its vital role of governance of the country if the masses know the inside story of Parliament. A free press is an essential component of Parliamentary democracy, and Nehru attached a great significance to it.

Nehru believed that Parliamentary democracy was a vehicle of gradual and peaceful social transition in India and through Parliament challenges of poverty and social inequality would be met. Parliament would represent the collective will of the nation, and its power would be used to eradicate poverty and establish social justice in India.

In Nehru's perspective, Parliamentary democracy was essential for bringing social transformation in India. Nehru never said that he failed because opposition was creating problems or Parliament was more powerful than the Prime Minister. Nehru would have felt amused if he were told that Parliamentary democracy is obstructing the programmes of gradual social transformation. On the contrary, Nehru's firm belief in Parliamentary democracy was based on the fact that gradual social change in India is possible on the basis of national consensus, and parliamentary debates help in arriving at national consensus.

—*Link,* 16 November, 1980.

NEHRU AND ADULT FRANCHISE

A few historians of modem India maintain that parliamentary democracy is a gift of the British to our country. Nothing can be farther from truth than this kind of interpretation of our history in the modern period. A fundamental pillar of democracy is universal adult franchise, because it is an institutional mechanism for the people's participation in the governance of a country. Universal adult franchise in India was resisted by the British rulers, and the national movement in India had struggled to achieve it. Thus democracy is not a gift of the British but it is the result of India's struggle in which millions of people participated and made sacrifices.

A relevant question is: What is the significance of adult franchise for nation-building in India? A related question is: What was Nehru's contribution to the functioning of adult franchise, with which democracy is intimately related, during the first decades of Independence?

The post-Independence phase was a formative period for strengthening the institutional arrangement for democratic governance and the functioning of adult franchise in India. Nehru played an active role in the first three general elections of India held in 1952, 1957 and 1962. All these three elections were significant for strengthening the base of Indian democracy.

A few aspects of the actual functioning of adult franchise in India during the Nehru phase may be highlighted to understand its proper significance in a critical manner.

The most significant implication of the introduction of adult franchise in India was felt in remote lakhs of villages in the country. The masses of rural India were politically apathetic, and the colonial rule and their local collaborators, i.e. the feudal landlords, had left the rural masses under their political control. Adult franchise demanded that political parties would mobilise voters to elect their representatives. Such a large-scale mobilisation of the rural voters during the elections helped in raising their political consciousness. While it is a fact that caste, community and linguistic loyalties influenced voters in their voting decision, and many a time 'vote banks' operated under the guidance of traditionally established rural leadership, the other aspect of electoral mobilisation and campaigning is that the voters ask questions and evaluate governmental performance. The introduction of adult franchise raised the level of awareness of people about their political environment, and farms, factories and families became centres of political debate.

Nehru's contribution in raising the level of political consciousness of the Indian masses was pre-eminent during his marathon election campaigning of 1952, 1957 and 1962. He acted as a great teacher, and educated the people in the meaning of democracy. His very well-attended election meetings were an occasion for the masses to pay their respect and regard for their beloved leader, and also slowly and gradually imbibe the message of the leader who asked them to shed their apathy and participate in governance.

Further, adult franchise helped in making politics a competitive activity. To begin with, competition among various political parties was marginal, and Nehru and the Congress party dominated the national political scene. But political competition increased with every new election. Voters were subjected to competitive political education. The process of political competition also helped in increasing the level of political consciousness among the voters of India. Intensification of political competition alters the quality of political debate in the country. When a voter is presented with different view points, he develops a sense of discrimination. It is a slow process, but all fundamental transformations in any society take their own time.

Adult franchise and the growing involvement of masses in the political process of India created a new situation in which the old socio-economic order started showing strains and stresses. It was a logical development, and Nehru had recognised this. Voters cannot be satisfied with an empty right of vote. With growing political consciousness, they demand new rights, and government has to respond to them. Nehru's election speeches always emphasised the new tasks of government, and he linked adult franchise with economic and social transformation of the country. Mobilisation of voters, slowly and gradually, created a new situation in the country where demands on government increased and the status quo was threatened.

While the elections are constituency-centred, the results of elections are relevant beyond the boundaries of a constituency. The dynamics of adult franchise helped in the creation of national image of government among the voters, and Nehru in his election campaigns emphasised on national goals, national priorities and national tasks. India has to be welded into a nation so that its diversities find their fulfilment in national unity. National integration of India is a continuing task, and those who are responsible for nation-building should consciously do it. Nehru was conscious of this great task of nation-building, and in this he recognised the significance of creating a sense of national identity among the Indians who were plagued with many primordial loyalties. Adult franchise is a mechanism which links local loyalties with regional and national centres of power. Localism has to be transcended, and new loyalty structures have to be created. Such a creation of new loyalties cannot be commanded. It has to be a slow process in historically old societies. Adult franchise generated a new awareness in India about the significance of Parliament, Cabinet, Prime Minister etc. Nehru's great attachment to Parliament was not a formality. He was really devoted to Parliament because of his faith in adult franchise.

How has the adult franchise operated in the post-Nehru phase? Has adult franchise taken deep roots in the country? What has been the record of the system established by Nehru?

In the post-Nehru phase, two serious challenges emerged on the scene by groups and individuals who were anti-adult franchise. The first opponent of the adult franchise was infantile Left in India which debunked elections as a bourgeois luxury. Elections were boycotted, and violence was adopted to achieve political goals. Infantile Left, which glorified violence did not succeed in this country because its theory and practice was wrong. The people of India have opted for adult franchise, and they are its defenders. Hence the Naxalite movement could not become a part of Indian mainstream. It is bound to be a fringe movement in Indian politics because its understanding of Indian history and political culture is faulty. Adult franchise and Parliament gets its support, strength and sustenance from the masses, and it is not just a superimposed superstructure.

The second attack on adult franchise and Parliament was launched by adventurists in polities who did not want to hold the elections. Political adventurists also did not understand the political evolution of India. Hence on the first opportunity in February-March 1977, the people of India reaffirmed and reasserted their faith in adult franchise, and proved that Nehru's efforts along with many others were not a waste. Political analysts are still debating the reasons for the holding of elections in March 1977. Whatever may be the reasons for such a decision, the result was astounding, and democracy was restored in this country.

What is the moral of the experience of adult franchise during the last 33 years? The moral is very clear and it may be summed up as follows:

(a) The people of India would not accept infringement of adult franchise and Parliament.

(b) Adult franchise has awakened the masses who are now struggling against the 'status quo'. Both these struggles are interconnected.

(c) The most important institutional safeguard for democracy in India is adult franchise. The leaders of India's national movement had recognised this; and those leaders who wanted to tinker with it were taught a lesson. The people of India defeated its Prime Minister because they identified her as an opponent of Parliament and adult franchise. The lessons of 1977 elections should be clear to all political leaders and groups. In a way, Nehru's success was experienced only after his death, i.e. in March 1977.

—*Link*, 15 August, 1980

LEFT IN INDIAN POLITICS

The word 'Socialism' enjoys so great a prestige in Indian political vocabulary that even the conservative and middle-of-the-road parties are at pains to disguise themselves with pseudonyms borrowed from the vocabulary of their enemies. Even anti-socialist parties sometimes have to affirm that they stand for 'Hindu Socialism' or 'Gandhian Socialism'. However, the popularity of the word 'Socialism' in India does not mean that the socialist parties have bright chances of capturing the 'levers of power's in the near future'. But it establishes one fact regarding Indian political scene very clearly—that the majority of people, who are actively involved in politics are guided in their approach towards the issues of the body-politic on the basis of ideology. Ideology gives them a coherent set of beliefs, values and opinions on the basis of which they are able to construct an image of the picture of future India, as also analyse and evaluate the existing social, economic and political institutions of the country. With growing political awakening in the country it is presumed that clashes and conflicts among the various sections and groups of society will be fought and resolved on an ideological plane. Ideology is a great factor in Indian political debates, and the issues are examined, evaluated and justified with the help of competing ideologies. European countries also underwent great ideological ferment in the mid-nineteenth and the early twentieth century, when the serious problems created by the Industrial Civilisation were tried to be resolved on an ideological plane. The elite in modem India, which was spearheading the movement for national independence, could not remain immune from the impact of the European ideological movements and the October Revolution in Russia.

In the Western countries, the intellectuals have started doubting the relevance of ideology in the modern age as a result of the stability that the 'developed' societies have achieved. It is stated that the important socio-economic problems created by the industrial revolution have been solved; now the guide for action should not be any ideology (which is well-thought out plan of action on the basis of scientific understanding of issues and also includes value beliefs) but cold realism. The reasoning made in this regard by Professor Lipset in *Political Man* (1960) is like this: "the ideological issues dividing left and right have been reduced to a little more or a little less government ownership and economic planning" and it makes little difference "which political party controls the domestic policies of individual nations". Upset has further observed "...the fundamental political problems of the industrial revolution have been solved, the workers have achieved industrial and political citizenship, the conservatives have accepted the welfare state, and the democratic left has recognised that an increase in overall state power carries with it more dangers to freedom than solutions for economic problems. This very triumph of the democratic social revolution in the West ends domestic politics for those intellectuals who must have ideologies or Utopias to motivate them to political action."[1]

It is difficult to accept the stand that the age of ideology has come to an end, because the Industrial Revolution was not an once-and-for-all affair, and the problem of social injustice and the glaring disparities of income and wealth have not yet been settled. The political dialogue on the question of property relationships, and distribution of income and wealth in society still continues. These socio-economic and ethical questions are very important in the 'developing societies'; the role and importance of ideology, therefore, is paramount. This is the reason why the ideological clash and dialogue between the defenders of the *status quo* and the believers of radical change is getting crystallised in the form of various political organisations in India. 'Radicals' and 'changers' also differ amongst themselves about the direction, nature, pace and methods of change; and the result is the emergence of many categories of Radicals in the country. If social forces are allowed to operate freely, without any authoritarian imposition from above, the divisions among the Radicals are inevitable under the present state of India's social development.

The theory and practice of socialism in India has been influenced by Marx, Gandhi and the West European democratic socialist movements. During the course of the freedom movement, the Communist and democratic socialist movements also originated in India. No doubt the socialist ideas started developing in the thirties, but their real import and significance came into focus only after India achieved independence. The Communist Party was established in 1924 under the leadership of M.N. Roy and important members of the Kanpur Conspiracy case like S.A. Dange, Muzzafar Ahmad, Shaukat Usmani and Nalini Gupta. R. Paime Dutt, an important member of the British Communist Party, continued to play an influential role in the growth and activities of the Party. The British Government was not sympathetic to the Communist Party, and its important leaders were arrested and tried on the charge of conspiracy in the famous Meerut Conspiracy case of 1929. The Party was declared illegal, and banned in 1934. The Communists were active in the Trade Union movement and were actively working in co-operation with the Left wing of the Congress, but World War II found the Communist movement bewildered, confused and disarrayed, and this state continued to exist down to the first few years after independence.[2]

Within the Indian National Congress (which was the main forum of the freedom struggle), in nineteen thirties, the socialist ideology started taking roots. In Nasik Jail (1932-33), Jayaprakash Narayan, Achyut Patwardhan, Asoka Mehta and others discussed the problems of Indian society, and projected the idea of creating a national 'Congress Socialist Party'. On May 17, 1934, the first All-India Conference of Socialists was held in Patna under the chairmanship of Acharya Narendra Dev. Another conference was held on October 21-22, 1934 at Ready Money Terrace in Bombay and the Congress Socialist Party (CSP) was formally established with the declared objective of "the achievement of complete independence, in the sense of separation from the British Empire, and the establishment of a Socialist society".[3] These Congress Socialists were opposed to the willingness of the Congress to participate in legislative activities in pre-independent India, and wanted the Congress to pursue a more revolutionary socialist policy in the economic field. An important section of the CSP leadership was under Marxian influence. At the second conference of the CSP held at Meerut on 20 January 1936, a statement was issued by the party declaring that "Marxism alone can guide the anti-imperialist forces to their ultimate destiny. Party members must, therefore, fully understand the technique of revolution, the theory and practice of class-struggle, the nature of the state and the processes leading to the socialist society".[4] During the War and the Quit India movement, the Socialist members of the Congress party played a very active role in the struggle for independence. But the differences started developing between the Congress leaders and the CSP on the issue of association with the All-India Trade Union Congress which had come under the influence of the Communists. The Congress wanted to set up its own labour organisation to be known as 'Indian National Trade Union Congress'. The Socialist members, led by Asoka Mehta, were opposed to it. While the differences between Socialists and the Congress leadership were developing, Gandhi, who was sympathetic to the Socialists, was assassinated in 1948. The Patel group in the Congress, never sympathetic to the Socialists, got a resolution passed by the AICC outlawing political parties within the Congress ranks. Owing to these manoeuvrings of the Rightists within the Congress, at the Nasik Congress in 1948, the Socialists decided to leave the Congress and form a separate Socialist Party with democratic socialism as the goal. Ever since their birth as a separate party, the Socialists have been making efforts to have a programme and an ideology distinct from those of both the Congress and the Communists. Indianisation of Socialism has been another crucial issue with the Socialists. The democratic socialist movement in India did not have a smooth sailing. Ideological indecision and the clash of personalities leading to divisions and mergers have been the bane of socialist movement in India. The socialist movement has always been a divided house, and it has never been able to exercise any appreciable impact on the Indian political scene. In 1952, after the first general elections, the Praja Socialist Party was formed as a result of the merger of the KMPP (formed in 1951) and the Socialist Party. Before the Party could settle down, a controversy on the question of their attitude towards the Congress party arose among the PSP leaders. At the Betuil Conference of 1953, Asoka Mehta, the General Secretary of the PSP, in his report put forth the idea of 'political compulsions of the backward economy' and suggested that the Socialists should cooperate with the Congress (which was committed to nationalism, democracy and socialism) by delimiting areas of agreement and disagreement. The Party was divided on this issue. Dr. Ram Manohar Lohia put forward the alternative idea that the Socialists were 'equidistant' from both the Congress and the Communists, and the Socialists should be equally ready to enter into electoral adjustment with Congress or Communists, but that "in all areas where Socialists are strong and are becoming the alternative to the party of capitalism or mixed economy, there is no need for an electoral adjustment". The growing dissensions within the Party were further aggravated by the issue of the 'police firing' in Cochin. The General Secretary of the PSP, Dr. Ram Manohar Lohia, demanded that the PSP Ministry of Travancore-Cochin should resign on the question of 'police firing'. The PSP Ministry, however, thought otherwise. These differences among the PSP members culminated in the formation of a separate Socialist Party in 1955 under Dr. Lohia's leadership.[5] Lohia Socialists were very critical of the moral lapses of the PSP leadership, and the democratic socialist movement was involved in ugly bickerings and character assassination. In the meantime, Jayaprakash Narayan started moving away from Socialism to Vinoba's Sarvodaya movement. The electoral failures of the PSP and the SP in the elections of 1957 and 1962 created further frustration among the leadership and the rank and file of the two parties. After the Third General Elections in 1962, the Socialists started re-thinking about their prospects as a separate movement. Asoka Mehta accepted the Deputy Chairmanship of the Planning Commission, and advised his followers to join the Congress. His argument was that the cause of Socialism could be served better by being within the Congress. He was of the view that the Congress was in a state of ferment and desired to rally together Socialist forces around an articulated programme of democratic socialism. On the basis of this reading of the situation, Asoka Mehta and many of his followers joined the Congress party.

The PSP and the SP leadership and rank and file realised the weaknesses of the divided Socialist movement, and decided to merge together, and in June 1964, the Samyukta Socialist Party (SSP) was born only to be split after seven months of uneasy compromise and personal rivalries. After the merger. Dr. Lohia, came with the thesis of 'radical politics', which would include a 'no war' agreement between the SSP, the CPI, the Jana Sangh and the Swatantra Party. He had moved far away from his theory of 'equal irrelevance' (not equidistance), of the Congress and the Communist Party. He was now prepared to enter into agreements with parties committed to nationalisation, free enterprise and Hindu chauvinism—all with the sole aim of destroying the 'coiled cobra' that is, the Congress party. The followers of Dr. Lohia in the SSP agreed with his thesis that somehow or the other through political alliances of all the opposition parties, the Congress party should be dislodged from the seat of power. But the former PSP members of the SSP did not agree with this line of argument. These bickerings continued and the Party could not evolve any political programme, and a Foundation Conference, to lay down the foundations of the Party's policies and programmes, was called at Varanasi in January 1965. At this Conference, the PSP members withdrew from the SSP and stated that it could not agree with the idea of 'united front politics' and it could not compromise with the Communists and the Communalists. The PSP group also felt that the SP members were developing a personality cult around Dr. Lohia. The PSP leaders announced that the Party was being revived and would function as a separate organisation. At this Conference, the SSP adopted the resolution that the Party will "work out arrangements with other opposition parties to minimise the splitting of the opposition vote and ensure the defeat of the Congress at the polls", and the SSP will contest elections only in constituencies 'where it has sizable support'. Thus clash of personalities and differences on political programme split the Democratic Socialist movement.

This story of mergers and splits is responsible for the sad plight of the Democratic Socialist movement in the country. The result has been that the movement has failed to evolve a political programme and ideology which could be an effective rejoinder to the Socialism of the Congress. The Indian Socialists, who are divided on ideological and personality basis, find it difficult to convince the common man as to who amongst them is a genuine socialist. The net result is that the Congress party with its socialist slogans, vast organisational net work, strong rural base, huge finance and political patronage, is able to secure an easy walk over these Socialist parties. One very important problem facing the Indian Socialists is the question of 'differentiation'. With everyone talking of Socialism, the masses get confused. In the context of the prevailing illiteracy in India, 'differentiation' is a herculean task, and the divided Socialist parties, with little organisational contact with the masses will not be able to achieve it without presenting a united front of the Socialist forces.[6] The Socialist movement is in a dilemma. Without mass support it has no future; and the existing leadership, which mainly comes from urban educated middle class sections of society, has failed, to establish a proper rapport with the masses and involve them in the political mainstream of the country. The Socialist movement has not been able to train and groom a cadre of leaders and workers who could mobilise the underprivileged sections of society for the cause of Socialism. On this state of affairs, a Socialist leader has himself commented: ...the chief enemy of the socialist movement is within its own ranks. The Socialist movement in India is built up largely and overwhelmingly out of the lower middle class, and the working class and the peasantry have little place in the echelons of its leadership, top or bottom.... More than three-fourths of the Indian people are outside the main currents of politics; those who are expected to make history are out of it. To bring them into the great halls of collective life, as creators and not as objects, should be the supreme aim of a socialist party in India'.[7] To gain mass support for Socialism, the present leadership has to give up its academic approach to politics.

The other Left force, besides the democratic socialist movement, is the Communist Party of India. After independence, the Communist Party of India indulged in adventurism and a militant policy of class struggle leading to the fiasco of Telangana type of peasant struggles. Owing to the change in policy, the Communists actively participated in parliamentary elections, and affirmed their faith in parliamentary institutions. In the three General Elections, the Party has polled a large number of votes, won seats in Parliament and legislatures of many states, formed government in Kerala, and acted as the main opposition Party in Parliament. But happenings in the international sphere and on India's borders brought a great rift in the Party and at the Tenali Convention (July 7 to 11, 1962) the Left Communists formed a separate party, and thus we have the Communist Party of India (Right) and the Left Communist Party.[8] Thus, factions and splits are not the characteristic of the democratic socialist movement alone; even the well-organised and disciplined Communist movement stands divided due to national (Chinese aggression over India) and international (Sino-Soviet ideological rift) factors. The split being ideological, sets aside any possibility of a merger in the near future. The Sino-Soviet ideological rift, among many other things, revolves round the questions of the character of thermo-nuclear war, the efficacy of peaceful co-existence, the character of the struggle between the two world systems, the nature of socialist revolution in the colonial countries, the relative strength of the Socialist and the Imperialist Power Blocs and the importance of the pursuit of the international class struggle through the forms of peaceful coexistence and peaceful competition. On these important questions there exists a fundamental difference between the Soviet and the Chinese stand points, and this rift has affected the whole international Communist movement. This rift was bound to have its impact on the Communist movement in India but the situation was aggravated by the Chinese aggression over India, because the Communist Party was called upon to take a stand against a fraternal Communist Party or be alienated from the mass of the people in the country.

Apart from the above mentioned happenings, the Communists were involved in their assessment of the role of 'national bourgeoisie' in the politics of the country. The attitude adopted by the members of the Communist Party of India towards the 'national bourgeoisie' divide them between the Right and the Left.

The Right Communists, following Lenin, believe that the national bourgeoisie in India (a former colonial country) is an anti-imperialist and anti-feudal revolutionary force. Politically, the Congress Party, which is an organisation of the national bourgeoisie, and which is involved in anti-imperialist and anti-feudal struggle, cannot be just condemned as a totally reactionary organisation. The Right Communists believe in a National Democratic Front consisting of all patriotic forces, i.e., working class, peasantry, agricultural labourers, intellectuals and the non-monopolist bourgeoisie. The Party says that this National Democratic Front cannot be real unless the vast mass following of the Congress at various levels take their place in it and emphasises that "it is the task of the Communist Party to make ceaseless efforts to forge unity with the progressive forces within the Congress directly and through common mass movements for the realisation of the demands of the National Democratic Front. It will be the constant endeavour of the Communist Party to win the SSP for the National Democratic Front. The Jan Sangh and Swatantra are reactionary parties and the national democratic front cannot grow without firmly combating the reactionary communal, chauvinistic leadership of these organisations and weaning the masses away from their influence."

The Left Communists argue that power is held by the bigger and 'monopoly' sections of the bourgeoisie which "is developing strong links with foreign monopolists and sharing power with landlords". The government, which is controlled by the monopolists, is following 'anti-people' policies; so the Communists should pledge themselves to an anti-capitalist strategy and have a more militant programme which may attract a greater following to the People's Democratic Front.[10]

The polemics and other personal feuds have divided the Communist Party of India into two separate organisations.

What are the prospects of the Left in India? After seventeen years of independence in India, the pious resolutions of the Congress, from 'Avadi' to 'Bhuvaneshwar' have only strengthened capitalism. The Mahalanobis Committee has arrived at the conclusion that the first Two Five-Year Plans have resulted into an increase in the 'concentration of economic power'. Scarcely more than 14 business houses control two-thirds of the total share-capital in the private sector. Half of the total private investment belongs to only a half per cent of the country's shareholders. Five banks control a third of the total paid-up capital, and more than half of the total deposits with private banks. Every industrial house exercises close influence over an important Bank of the country, e.g., the Central Bank of India Ltd., is controlled by the Tatas; the Bank of India Ltd., the Khatau-Mafatlal Group; the Punjab National Bank Ltd., the Dalmia-Jain Group; the United Commercial Bank Ltd., by the Birla Group; and the Hindustan Bank Ltd. by the J.K. Group. This great concentration of economic power does not only lead to exploitation and inequality, but also becomes a threat to democracy and develops into the formation of a 'parallel government'. How are the Socialist forces going to challenge the capitalist system of economic production and social relationships effectively?

Coupled with this economic situation is the domination of one political party in the country, the real character of which is an enigma for many students of Indian politics. The Congress, before independence, spearheaded the bourgeois national movement in the country, converging into a 'coalition of interests'. From the pre-independence era, the Rightists had been thoroughly entrenched in the Congress organisation, and they continue to exercise control and influence. The Left in the Congress is trying to exercise some influence and pressure on party policies, but it is a weak force in the Congress organisation. It is too much to expect the Congress to pursue a radical programme of changing the property relationships and the structure of society. By its very character, the Congress has to be a party of 'compromise' with the tilting of the balance in favour of the property owners. At the same time by its 'socialistic slogans', the Congress has been successful in confusing the masses and creating an impression that a radical socialist policy and movement in India is 'irrelevant in the present situation'. To the Congress the urgent need is production rather than equitable distribution, which in turn requires incentives for the capitalists, and hence a mixed economy. So the Socialists have to face a formidable challenge from the Congress which is a well-organised, well-financed and very broad-based political organisation in the country, but which is most unsuited to achieve any socialistic ideals.[11]

Socialists in India have to face the challenge from other Rightist and communal forces also, such as the Swatantra Party and the Jan Sangh.

The Swatantra Party was founded in 1959 to oppose the Congress programme of cooperative farming and economic planning, which according to the Swatantra Party leaders is leading to the establishment of statism and totalitarianism in the country. The Swatantra Party believes in the sanctity of private property and rejects the 'methodology of totalitarian planning'. Criticising the Congress policies, the Party's statement of policy states: "In its efforts at pursuing psuedo-socialist policies, the government has had to expand controls and increase non-productive expenditure. It has gone on an orgy of borrowing, *mortgaging* the country's future. It has taken over business concerns in spite of its inability to manage them efficiently and economically in order to exploit them for revenue purposes regardless of the consequent rise in the cost of living." After narrating the many other evils of planning and statism the Party declares that "it is a party that the country needs in order to fulfil its destiny—party of ordered progress in and through freedom." This Party of free enterprise with its proclaimed opposition to Socialism, was politically successful in those states where the former ruling princes had great influence, i.e., Rajasthan, Bihar, Gujarat, etc. It is the party of Big Business and feudal lords (former ruling princes).

The Jan Sangh was founded in 1951 with the objective to protect 'Bharatiya culture and tradition'. The Jan Sangh, with its communal base, is a threat to secularism, democracy and socialism. With a pronounced communal bias, the Jan Sangh is influential in the Northern part of the country and gets full support from a well-organised and well-disciplined para-military Fascist organisation, i.e., the RSS. The Jan Sangh is making great efforts to spread its area of influence towards South India (where it has no moorings at the present) and rural areas of the country. In its struggle against the socialist and secularist forces in the country, the Jan Sangh exploits Hindu-Muslim tensions and is able to mobilise sections of Hindu society by its aggressively chauvinistic and revivalist appeals. Rightists in India are well-entrenched in the ruling party, and have also organised the Swatantra and the Jan Sangh to fight against the Left in the country. The Right in India is nurturing the Swatantra party to fight against the Socialists on the democratic plane. But the Right is very well prepared to fight out socialism by violence as well. This is the reason why the property owners extend great support and patronage to a militant organisation like the RSS, the political platform of which is the Jan Sangh.

Will the divided Socialists be able to face the challenge? The capitalists will not surrender willingly. They have never done so. To the capitalists, democracy is good till it defends the property interests. When the capitalists cease to receive protection of property interests under political democracy, they labour to subvert it into Fascism. The history of the origin, rise and growth of fascism in Italy bears a testimony to this. The fascists set the Socialist Party offices on fire, burnt newspapers, and murdered Socialist workers, while the bourgeois state stood indifferent to the whole scene of barbarism and savagery, and the Fascists came to power on the basis of the support of the capitalists.[12]

In the light of the prevailing political and economic situation in the country, there are many 'ifs' for the success of Socialism in India. Unity, ideological clarity, concreteness of programme and a 'mass base' are the pre-requisites for its success. Socialism is a peasant's and worker's movement. How can the Socialists face the challenge of Rightist movements without the political support of the masses? One of the great drawbacks of the Indian Socialist movement has been its primary and exclusive concern with the 'politics of election'. The Socialists have to be throughout (more than on the occasion of General Elections) active in mobilising public opinion on every specific issue of injustice and inequality. The Socialists may do well to strengthen the method of non-violent Civil Disobedience, and take an active interest in the Trade Union movement, peasant organisation, cooperatives and the student's forums. They will only make their future dim, if the Socialists bank exclusively upon the parliamentary elections. In fighting elections against the well-financed Rightist parties, the Socialists are always at a disadvantage. They can compensate it by contacting the masses and fighting for them on specific issues. Only in this way can Socialism be a broad-based movement, and hope to have any prospects of success. This important fact has been clearly stated by a writer thus: "And if any one thing is certain about Socialism, it is that such changes—if they are to be conscious and controlled—require the dedication and active participation of vast numbers of people. They cannot be brought about by a few dozen party leaders, or a few hundred men in Parliament, whatever the laws they make. But what is a party's way to such mass energy, to a harnessing of the popular will which alone can really bring a new social order into being? Its way is the people in it, its socialist militants, those now commonly referred to even on the Left by the odious label of 'the rank and file'. From a socialist point of view, they are the party and the movement; it is they who can turn ideas into a material force and become the guiding nucleus of otherwise indeterminate energies".[13]

The fact has to be brought home to the Socialists that to fight against the old order and to create a new social system requires great, persistent and taxing efforts, more so when the opposite forces are deep-rooted and formidable. Parliamentary elections are only one plank of the Socialist movement. The tragedy is that it has been equated with the whole programme of the movement. The real plank of the movement is to awaken the masses and involve them in the struggle against inequality, injustice and exploitation.

In sum, the prospects of Socialist movement are linked with its approach to politics, which has to be non-bourgeois. A dynamic Socialist movement, capable of mobilising public opinion against the forces of reaction, can never be created by an arm-chair approach to politics.

—*Political Science Review*, Vol. 4, No. 1, April 1965

NEW DIMENSIONS OF INDIAN FEDERALISM

The Constitution of India establishes a federation, with powers divided between the Centre and the States. The Constitution divides and fixes the areas of jurisdiction of both the Centre and the State governments, and makes them 'autonomous' in their respective spheres of activity.[14] In spite of this division of power, the Centre has been given more authority than the States. The Constitution assigns to the Centre a larger field for the operation of its legislative and executive authority than is to be found in any other federal constitution, so much so that Rt. Hon'ble Patrick Gordon Walker is inclined to include it in the category of 'hybrid constitutions, partly unitary, partly federal.'[15]

The Constitution gives Central Government the power to 'issue directions' to the State governments. It also lays down that the executive power of the States shall be so exercised as to ensure compliance with the laws made by Parliament and not to impede or prejudice the exercise of executive power of the Union. The Union can give necessary directions to the States for these purposes.[16]

If a State fails to carry out the directions of the Union Government, the President can proclaim a breakdown of constitutional government in the State under Article 356 and proceed to take into his own hands all the powers of the Governor or any other State Officer.[17] Many times Central Parliament can legislate on State matters as under Articles. 249, 252, 253, 256, 256 (I)(b), 357 (1) and (2). According to Articles 3 and 4 State territories can be changed by the Union law. All these provisions show that the Union Government is more powerful than the States.

Moreover, in India two of the most important services, the Indian Administrative Service and the Indian Police Service, though common both to the Union and the States, are recruited and controlled by the Union Government. They provide an important instrument of control by the Centre over the States. The Comptroller and Auditor General of India supervises and controls the accounts and audit both of the Union and the State governments. The superintendence, direction and control of all elections (Federal and State) is vested in an Election Commission appointed by the Union President.[18]

Thus, these provisions of the Constitution make the Central Government very dominating. The dominance of the Centre over the States has increased owing to the programme of large-scale economic planning during the last twelve years.

The study of socio-economic structure of society, the aspirations of the people, and their ideological moorings is necessary to give the right perspective to the understanding of any constitution. The working of a constitution is as important as its theory, and practice is conditioned by the demands and pressures of society. The Indian federation should thus be studied in the context of the 'Welfare State' and 'economic and social Planning'. The State in India is dedicated to secure to all its citizens *Justice—social, economic and political and assure the dignity of the individual and the unity of the nation.* The Indian Government through the instrument of 'political democracy' has to establish a socio-economic system in which the living standards of the people improve so that *equality before law* and *equality of opportunity* which the Constitution guarantees to every individual may be achieved. The method adopted for achieving 'economic and social progress' in the country is economic and social planning. A planned development has been preferred to unplanned growth.

Poverty, illiteracy, ignorance, disease, unemployment, etc., are problems facing the whole country, and they are not limited to a few States alone. Food shortages or epidemics do not recognise the State boundaries, neither do they care for State autonomy. When the problem is national, it is through national efforts that the problem can be solved. This is the reason why *the Centre has become the centre of all planning for India,* though the constitution-makers had kept economic and social planning as a concurrent subject. Moreover, planning involves making the best use of the available resources of the country. It involves the problem of fixing priorities for achieving maximum economic benefits. This objective of planning (allocation of scarce resources, and consequently fixation of priorities) can be achieved if the Central Government (or a central agency) performs this function. Moreover, planned economy creates the problem of 'coordination' of the economic activities of the whole country. From all these reasons it is clear that economic planning in order to be effective has to be the responsibility of the Central Government. The very logic of planning involves centralisation.[19]

The Cabinet Resolution of March 15, 1950 emphasised that the need for comprehensive planning based on a careful appraisal of resources and on an objective analysis of all the relevant economic factors has become imperative and the Government set up a Planning Commission to formulate and secure the execution of plans for the "most effective and balanced utilisation of the country's resources." Even at the risk of repetition it may be pointed out that in spite of India being a federation a central organisation like the Planning Commission was 'inevitable' for several reasons. First, a very important aim of planning is to strike a balance between different regions and different sectors of the economy. A central agency can perform this task of 'striking a balance' better. Second, planning is a continuous process. In it not only efficient execution but also constant evaluation and perspective thinking is required. The economic problems of coming twenty to twenty-five years are to be considered and solved through planning. The problem of 'perspective' planning and 'coordination' on a nationwide scale requires a centralised body like the Planning Commission. Third, in a planned economy, the economic development has to be 'accelerated' and this can be done when one body is solely devoted to this task. This is the reason why Neogy Committee had recommended that the very nature of the task warranted that a "single, compact, authoritative organisation directly responsible to the cabinet should be set up at the Centre to devote itself continuously to the entire field of economic reconstruction of India."

The formulation of Plans for the whole country is the main responsibility of the Planning Commission. The implementation of the Plan is the main responsibility of the administrative Ministries of the Central Government and of the State governments. The advent of planning and assumption of development tasks by the government has led to the creation of planning cells within executive departments and Ministries, full-fledged planning departments and planning advisory bodies at the State level, and a National Planning Commission with a network of advisory panels and groups at the Centre, and the establishment of special offices and agencies to execute particular Plan Programmes and of evaluation units to assess the progress achieved in selected fields.[20]

The Centre-State coordination and cooperation in the Plan formulation and implementation, in actual working and process, gives more authority to the Centre and the Planning Commission vis-a-vis the States. The 'Centre-State' cooperation is going to increase in the future because the State governments have been called upon to do 'perspective planning' for their States. In this 'perspective planning' there shall be greater collaboration between the State government and the Planning Commission.[21]

Some observations may be made here on certain facts and aspects of planning in the context of federalism:

(1) Due to the system of matching grants, *vertical federalism*[22] is developing in India. In this system of matching grants the Centre may agree to bear half of the cost of a project if the other half is

paid by the States. These grants are issued through the respective Central Ministries on the recommendation of the Planning Commission. The result is, all the Central Ministries have come to occupy position in which they can dictate to the corresponding State Ministries.

(2) The Planning Commission plays an important part in the annual and periodical allotment of finances. The proposals of the States for schemes are discussed by the Planning Commission with the State governments a few months in advance of the presentation of their budgets. The ceiling of outlay, overall and under particular heads, are indicated. Annual plan discussions take place with the States for the assessment of the current year's performance and the formulation in broad terms of the following year's programmes. Annual plans of the States are drawn up in consultation with the Planning Commission.

(3) The difficulties of foreign exchange have made it compulsory for the Planning Commission to be associated with the formulation of these annual plans by the State governments.

(4) The Estimates Committee in its 21st Report (1959) reported that the 'generally prevalent feeling' of the State governments is that the Planning Commission was not just an advisory body but an additional authority to be reckoned with at the Centre. State governments had occasions to complain that they had not received their due share of the Plan allocation, and that the system of referring their proposals to the Commission often resulted in avoidable delay.[23]

(5) A State government has not only to satisfy the Planning Commission for allocation of funds but also the administrative Ministries at the Centre.[24]

(6) Moreover, the State sources of revenue being inelastic, it is dependent on the Planning Commission for resources.

A feeling is growing in some quarters that federalism in India is becoming weak. Land policies, concerning land holdings, ceilings, etc., are being initiated by the Centre and followed by the States. Another aspect of this new development is that the States are developing the habit of accusing the Centre for any failure in policy. There is a feeling that comprehensive direction of economic policies by the Planning Commission and the Central Ministries is 'tending' to reduce State autonomy to a mere formality.[25]

Are States bound to accept what the Planning Commission says or what the Central cabinet says in matters of planning? Theoretically the States can refuse to accept the advice of the Planning Commission or the

Central Government in matters relating to economic and social planning. It will not be unconstitutional. But the States can refuse it only if they are prepared to sacrifice the finances which the Central Government will give them for development purposes. About 70 per cent of the total expenditure on planning in the First Plan and about 65 per cent in the Second Plan relates to matters which have been exclusively assigned to the States like education, health, forests, agriculture, irrigation, electricity etc. Central control over States is with the 'consent' of the States and is due to the inevitability of the economic Planning.[26]

Another important field in the context of which Centre-State relations can be studied is the Community Development Programme. No doubt all the subjects in the programme namely, agriculture, animal husbandry, health, education, etc., are State subjects, but the main policies, The pattern and direction of development of this programme came from the Centre.

In the wake of Community Development an administrative structure was created which may be said to be opposed to the principle of federalism. The Community Projects Administration was established on the 31 March, 1952 to implement the Community Development Projects. It functioned as an independent administrative unit under an 'Administrator' who was responsible for planning, directing and coordinating the Community Development Projects throughout India under the general supervision .of the Central Committee of the Planning Commission. This 'Administration' was incorporated into the Ministry of Community Development with effect from 28 September, 1956. The 'Administrator' exercised detailed control over the programmes in the States. BDOs and their selection was to be approved by the Community Projects Administration. Block Programmes, budgets and detailed periodical reports concerning every Block were sent to it. Further, Administrator and the Community Project Administration officials toured the Blocks intensely. Thus at the end of 1957, the Balwant Rai Mehta team had to advise that 'the Centre should lay down the policy and prescribe the broad outlines of a scheme and then leave it to the State governments to work it out in accordance with their own practices and in consonance with local circumstances, the Centre only satisfying itself that the general objectives of the scheme are carried out.[27] The only proper role which Balwant Rai Mehta Committee gives to the Ministry is that of coordination.

Should there at all be a Ministry of Community Development at the Central level? Community development is a State subject. Why should there be a Ministry at the Central level? If there is a Ministry what shall be its role? B. Mukerjee wants to give this Ministry the role "to propagate and work for the ideology of Community Development" and to focus "attention on the problem of rural development and rural areas".[28]

Community Development Programme has to be integrated and 'coordinated' at the national level with national planning. The Ministry of Community Development is required to lay down policy at the national level and coordinate planning and policy making at all levels. For the purpose of 'guidance at the national level' Ministry of Community Development is required.

By the following methods the Centre influences community development programme which is a purely State concern.

(i) The first method by which the Centre controls the Community Development Projects is through 'policy formulation'. The main policy is formulated and initiated by the Centre. The Central Government offers policy guidance to the States. The broad structure of policy is laid down by the Centre to which the States try to conform.

(ii) The second method by which the Centre has influenced Community Development Programme is by establishing training institutions and imparting training facilities to the State personnel. The Ministry of Community Development has established a Central Institute of Study and Research with a view to imparting 'basic' training or orientation courses. But it is already beginning to acquire "the position of leader among the training institutions giving training in Community Development."[29] The Principal of the Central Institute aided by experts in different fields 'visits' other training centres and 'guides' them in their work. A 'clearing house' of information of Community Development Programme is proposed to be established in conjunction with the Central Institute.

(iii) Advised by the Central Ministry, the States have formed training committees to look after the whole field of training. "The effort from the side of the Ministry of Community Development has been to draw the State Governments fully into a *partnership* with itself in the work of training."[30] Orientation Courses to the *Instructors* are provided by the Ministry of Community Development at several centres all over the country. The pattern and content of training has been influenced by the Central Government.

(iv) The Central Government substantially participates in the 'Package Programme' in which the States have obligation to match the federal aid.

(v) The Central Government exercises great influence by conducting periodical conferences, meetings and seminars.

(vi) The Central Government influences the States by producing literature which is sent to the workers.

(vii) Evaluation of Community Development Blocks in all the States is done by the programme evaluation organisation under the Planning Commission whose annual reports exercise great influence over the State administration of the Community Development Programme.

(viii) Loans, Grants-in-aid, and 75 per cent of the non-recurring expenditure is borne by the Central Government.

The Central influence over the State in the field of Community Development Administration has taken many forms. The Community Development Administration has been designated as a '*Coalition Administration*'. Still the increasing reliance by the State government on the Union Government for grants-in-aid (and many times 'aid with strings') has increased "Central control over States in regard to this programme". The advantage of this 'Centre-State partnership' has been the development of a "uniformity of pattern and nomenclature from the village level up to the top". The Central Government has better talent and it has given the lead. The pooling of resources, knowledge, and personnel has added to the vigour and strength of the scheme. But the inherent evil in such a programme is uniformity and rigidity. Whenever any plan comes from above, the natural desire is to apply it uniformly. The scheme may be applied to a place where the situation is different. Diversities are not given proper importance. But the extension of the Central influence is with the consent and acquiescence of the State governments. It is also due to the financial dependence of the States over the Centre.

From the above facts the 'purist' of federal theory may conclude that Indian Federalism is in danger. Before such a conclusion is arrived at, prevailing conditions in the country which have created an 'inevitable situation' for the Central Government to take lead and initiative should not be forgotten. The compulsion of circumstances, the need for economic and social planning, the logic of welfare State, the desire on the part of the Constitution-makers to create a 'social milieu' in which justice, social, economic and political could be guaranteed to all, the availability of better talent at the Centre, the need for uplifting the 'whole' country, and the financial dependence of the States over the Centre has created a situation where the Centre is taking the lead in the fields which the Constitution denied to it. The Constitution itself visualised a strong Centre and the challenge of times has only made it doubly important. This centralisation has many positive advantages and should result in the balanced development of the country and great regional diversities in backwardness should not ultimately exist. The development shall cover the whole country, and people of no State shall suffer if by nature they are placed in 'unfavourable circumstances' as far as resources etc., are concerned. If policy, initiative, and leadership come from the Centre this may not result in evil, but if *policy implementation* is done with uniformity and rigidity, this may have evil effects. Excessive centralisation in implementation should not be insisted on. This evil can be checked by foresight in administration, by vigilant leadership, by creating some institutional apparatus to look to it. The State governments in discussions, conferences and meetings with the Central Government, Planning Commission and in National Development Council can put forward their view points and indicate the alternatives, thus checking excessive centralisation in implementation. It is heartening to note that the State governments are following the policy of land ceilings but they have not accepted the rigid limit of 30 acres as laid down by the Planning Commission. The regional variations have thus been respected.

Indian federalism under the impact of circumstances is thus entering a new phase of development. They are the *new dimensions of Indian Federalism* according to which Centre-State cooperation or partnership in important matters is increasing. No doubt the States are the weaker partners but there is no way out. This is true of other Federations also. The federations of the United States of America, Australia or Canada have become 'Quasi-federal'[31] according to many writers. The American Federal system before the economic depression of the 'Thirties' and thereafter and especially under the New Deal of President Franklin Roosevelt, underwent great change. In America the New Deal created more obligations of the Federal Government towards the people. The nation was called upon to determine 'fair wages', 'reasonable hours of work', preparation of plans for the improvement of the farmers and removal of unemployment. It was called upon to supervise industry, transport and other public utility services. The New Deal strengthened the idea of Welfare State making dual Federalism "apparently dead and beyond revival".[32] The American Supreme Court in *United States vs. Durby* (1941) established the doctrine of 'national supremacy' in place of 'autonomy' and "in so doing it imprinted more clearly the stamp of the New Deal on the development of American constitutional law".[33]

If this centralisation is inevitable why not establish a unitary State? Why have a farce of Federalism? There are people who think that unitary system is suited to the country's needs.[34] Whatever degree of federalism is there in India is essential for the democratic growth of the country. In democracy there should be different centres of authority where people can exercise their powers and where regional diversities are given due consideration. In a country with different customs, traditions and way of living, all development cannot be on uniform lines. The divergent needs and requirements of the people and their different value-pattern have to be taken into consideration. These are factors which stand for federalism. There are also forces, as indicated above, which tend towards centralisation. The necessity is to create proper balance and adjustment. No doubt, economic and social planning has made Indian Central Government very strong, but it is exactly due to the federal character of the Constitution that centralisation which is in the logic of economic planning has not been able to reach its logical conclusion. Federalism is a check, a moderating influence over the tendency of centralisation involved in economic planning. Federalism is working as a half-way house between excessive centralisation and decentralisation. The very existence of sixteen States with some powers of their own acts as a restraining influence over excessive centralisation,[35] and often gives scope to variation in Plan implementation.

There are some who say that from the point of view of administration, the Central Government is very weak and dependent on the States for the implementation of 'important national programmes'. Plan implementation is the primary responsibility of the administrative Ministries at the Centre and of the State Governments.[36]

For the proper coordination of the planned programmes and their implementation more 'all-India services' should be created. They will become the 'back-bone' of development administration in the Centre and the States. A number of arguments can be advanced in support of this proposal. First, there should be a minimum standard of efficiency to which personnel involved in economic services should conform. But no such personnel for such functions are recruited by the States. The standard of the candidates varies from region to region and there are great differences in their capabilities and efficiency. Second, the All-India services bring a new vision to the States whereas persons recruited from these States may be parochial in outlook. Third, the All-India services serve as a link between different parts of the whole country. Lastly, as the control over these services is not vested solely in the State governments, the officers will discharge their responsibilities without 'local pressures' or local influences. By organising all-India services for the administration of welfare State, minimum uniformity of standard in the administration and the development of the country can be attained.

But the States have opposed the creation of more all-India services for reasons of: (i) autonomy, (ii) more burden on the State exchequer, (iii) divided control of the services, (iv) 'unrepresentative' character of the services and (v) sons of the soil not getting opportunity.

In spite of this opposition all-India services are to be increased and the quality of the State's services has to be given due importance. Their training programmes, education and recruitment should be paid the greatest possible attention.

The new dimensions of Indian Federalism, as discussed above, are the product of centralised economic planning, the dependence of the States on the Centre for finance, and the dominance of one political party at the Centre and in almost all the States. What about the future? What kind of relations will exist between them when different parties have come in power at the Centre and the States after the 1967 election?[37] One possibility is that every State Government (irrespective of party considerations) will have to accept the policy decisions of the Central Government in the field of economic planning due to the financial sanctions of the Centre. If a particular party which is in power in a State does not want to allow the 'informal trespass' of the Central Government, it will have to forego the financial doles coming from the Centre. Will the State Government be able to afford it? It is not only the financial dependence of States on the Centre which will determine the future trend of relationships between the two, but the competitive spirit of the States with one another may necessitate the States conforming to Central dictations. The bargaining capacity of the States will determine the pattern of future relationship between the Centre and the States. Students of Federal Theory will have to watch the future developments with great interest.[38]

—S.A.H. Haqqi (Ed.), *Union-State Relations in India*,
Meenakshi Prakashan, Meerut, 1967.

THE GOVERNOR AND THE EMERGENCY

A proper appraisal of the role and position of the Governor[39] in India is possible if he is studied in the context of federalism and Parliamentary democracy. The executive power of the State is vested in a Governor. He acts as an 'agent' of a State Government.

In the Indian federal set-up, the Central Government is very strong and it has many over-riding powers over the State Governments. The Constitution of India gives the Central Government the power to 'issue directions' to the State Governments. It lays down that the executive power of every State shall be so exercised as to ensure compliance with the laws made by Parliament and not to impede or prejudice the exercise of executive power of the Union. The Union Government can give necessary directions to the States for these purposes.[40] The Constitution further lays down that if a State Government fails to carry out any direction given in the lawful exercise of the executive power of the Union, the President can hold that a situation has arisen in which the Government of the State cannot be carried on in accordance with the provisions of this Constitution. (Art. 365). He can proclaim a state of emergency under Article 356 and proceed to take into his own hands all the powers of the Governor or any other State Officer.[41]

A strong Centre is a characteristic feature of the Indian Federal system. Further, the constitution establishes a Parliamentary system of Governments in the constituent States. The constitutional head of the State Government is the Governor. He is aided and advised by a Council of Ministers and in normal circumstances acts on its advice. The tenor and trend of discussions in the Constituent Assembly was that the Governor is only the Constitutional head of the State, and the real power lies in the hands of the cabinet.[42]

The question that arises is: Is Governor a mere figure-head? Is he a stamping machine for the decisions of the Cabinet? This is not the case. Two things must be kept in mind. First, he has some discrctionary powers, e.g., selection of a Chief Minister when no party has a clear majority, or inviting various parties to form a coalition in the absence of any single party getting a clear majority. The possibility is that the Governors in future may have to exercise this discretion more frequently. In India the multi-party system is developing and there may be occasions when no single party may secure an absolute majority. If in future coalition cabinets are formed in the States, the Governor may have to play a very vital role in selecting the leader of the coalition.

Second, the Governor has to play a *dual role.* He is the constitutional head of the State Government, and in this capacity he is to act as 'a sagacious counsellor and adviser to the Ministry, one who can throw oil on the troubled waters of the State Politics'. He is also an 'agent' of the Central Government. He is the President's representative on the spot to see to it that the Centre's constitutional responsibilities for the proper governance of the whole country are properly discharged.[43] Thus, on the one hand the Governor has to advise the State Cabinet on various important political and administrative issues; on the other hand he has to keep the Central Government informed about the working of the constitutional machinery of the State. He is appointed by the President and holds office during his pleasure. The President depends on the Governor for the discharge of his constitutional responsibilities with regard to the administration of the State. This dual role of the Governor at many times creates a conflict of loyalties, and is a challenge to the holder of the Governor's office how to steer clear from conflicts, if any.

This conflict of loyalties and the problems of dual role of the Governor gain prominence in abnormal times of constitutional and political crises. Clause (i) of Article 356 of the Constitution lays down that if the President of India on receipt of a report from the Governor of a State or otherwise, is satisfied that a situation has arisen in which the Government of the State cannot be carried on in accordance with the provisions of the Constitution, may proclaim emergency and take over the administration of the State in his own hands. No doubt the President can proclaim emergency in a State if he is 'otherwise' satisfied, but the report and advice of the Governor plays a decisive role under this situation.[44]

As the President's representative on the spot, and as a nominee of the Central Government, the Governor's evaluation of the situation has a great significance. In reporting to the President regarding the necessity for the Proclamation of Emergency, the Governor acts in his discretion. It is possible that the State Cabinet may be against Presidential intervention whereas the Governor himself may be in its favour. The Constitution makers expected that the Governor will act as a custodian of the constitutional Government in the State and will not act merely as a "rubber-stamp of his cabinet or a post office between his cabinet and the President or between his cabinet and the official gazette". In times of emergency his supreme loyalty is to the Constitution.

The role of the Governor in Indian States is very difficult because he is the head of a Parliamentary system of Government which has to function under a very strong Central Government. His role assumes further difficulty when the State Government is of a party which is different from the party that is in power in the Centre. He may be sandwiched between party tug-of-war. These difficulties can be best illustrated from the study of Kerala affairs of 1957-59. In Kerala after the second General Elections of 1957 for the first time in the country a party, different from the one that held power at the Centre, formed a Government. Its rule came to an end on 31 July, 1959 by a Proclamation of Emergency by the President.[45]

Under Article 356 of the Indian Constitution the Administration of the State was taken over by the Centre. The Ministry was dismissed and the Legislative Assembly was dissolved. When the proclamation came for approval before Parliament, the Home Minister said that the action was taken on the report of the Kerala Governor.[46]

The following were the charges levelled against the Communist Ministry:

(a) Release of prisoners who were Communists or fellow-travellers.
(b) Insecurity of persons and property.
(c) Political murders.
(d) Attempts at indoctrination of students.
(e) Party interference in administration resulting in the demoralisation of the services.
(f) Discrimination in administration.

(g) Use of cooperative societies for the consolidation of the party.
(h) Deterioration of the financial position of the State.

The situation in Kerala became very stormy and the opposition parties formed a joint front against the Communist Ministry and the Governor reported "that the administration of the State (could) not be carried on in accordance with the Constitution any longer."

The Governor's report stated: "The crux of the legal and constitutional question is whether the Kerala Government has lost the support of the overwhelming majority of the people and whether the allegations made of mal-administration and subversion of democracy are substantially true. I have already expressed my view on both these points. The allegations made against the Government are substantially true and I am convinced also that the Government has lost the support of the majority of the people. While the securing of a majority of seats in the legislature, however meagre, is very relevant at the time of forming a government, *it cannot be pleaded as conferring a continuing right to claim the confidence of the majority.*[47] There is no doubt that there has been a tremendous shift in the minds and in the feelings of the people. I do not think that this public opinion can be ignored without serious consequences for the future. The only solution which is available to us, therefore, is the exercise of power under Article 356 of the Constitution."

The Communist Ministry was against the President's rule. The Communist Chief Minister denied that the Governor had consulted him regarding the report. Here the Governor acted in his discretion.

This proclamation of emergency in Kerala brought to the forefront the role of the Governor and the "problems of how to work parliamentary democracy in the concrete conditions of today, when the problem of different parties forming governments in different States has been posed in a realistic manner." This central intervention in Kerala has been viewed as a case of political prejudice. It is alleged that the Congress Party at the Centre had on political grounds dismissed the Communist Ministry in Kerala, and the Governor acted as a political puppet in the hands of political party in power at the Centre.[48]

Coming to the report of the Governor, let us examine his charge that "the allegations made against the (Communist) Government are substantially true". It raises the question of the constitutional responsibility of the Governor with regard to the administration of the State. What was the Governor doing when the Communist Ministry was committing these actions? Was he a helpless spectator of this so called 'mal-administration' for over a period of two years? Was he waiting for the people and the parties to level these charges to 'put his seal of approval' on these charges later on? He had taken the oath to 'preserve, protect and defend the

Constitution'. But here the defenders of the Constitution were the people and the opposition parties. They took the initiative and protested against the so called 'mal-administration.' The conclusion that emerges is that if these allegations were true, the Governor was a party to it. If these mal-practices could happen over a period of two years, the Governor was guilty of not acting according to the oath of his office.

His further observation "that the Government has lost the support of the majority of the people" was not borne out by the voting percentage of the mid-term elections in Kerala. The percentage of voting in favour of the Communist Party increased in the mid-term elections.

The following observation of the Governor requires examination. He observes: "While the securing of a majority of seats in the legislature, however meagre, is very relevant at the time of forming a Government, it cannot be pleaded as conferring a continuing right to claim the confidence of the majority. There is no doubt that there has been a tremendous shift in the minds and in the feelings of the people."

In a Parliamentary system a party which secures a majority of seats in the legislature has a right to form the Government. It continues to hold the office till it enjoys the confidence of the House. The Communist Party had the majority behind it, and it enjoyed its confidence. The Communist Ministry was not defeated on the floor of the House. Thus the Communist Ministry could not be made to resign because it never lost the majority in the House, but because "there has been a tremendous shift in the minds and in the feeling of the people". First, the charge is very vague. Second, is the Governor entitled to 'Study the Shifts' and recommend the dismissal of the Government which has a majority behind it? The theory and practice of Parliamentary democracy does not confer this right on the 'nominated Governor'. Certainly the Constitution of India does not give such a right to the Governor because such a right will be fatal to the working of democracy in the States. If the Governors can get the majority supported cabinets dismissed because of the 'shifts in public opinion' the Parliamentary system cannot work properly. In the context of party politics, it will encourage indiscipline and lawlessness. The opposition parties in the States will 'manufacture' disobedience movements and create lawlessness if the Governor or the Central Government start dismissing duly elected State Governments on the plea of 'shifts in public opinion'. If political movements are the basis of judging the 'shift in public opinion' and dismissing the Ministry, then the Punjab Ministry should have been dismissed because there were mass movements against its language policy (Akali and Hindi Agitation). Why was the Punjab Ministry not dismissed? When these movements were going on in Punjab, it seemed that the majority of the people were against the Government. There was great communal tension in the State. Hindus and Sikhs were becoming very hostile to one another. The State of Punjab was facing great linguistic and communal tension, and peaceful life was always threatened. Why was the President's rule not proclaimed in Punjab? There is a feeling that Congress Party in the Centre could not tolerate Communist rule in Kerala, so it dismissed the Ministry and used the Governor as a party tool. It is alleged that situations have arisen during recent years in many States, similar to the situation in Kerala, but different standards were applied to different States because of party considerations.[49]

This had led many people to believe that the so called 'mass upsurge' was manufactured by the Congress Party; and the Congress Party at the Centre made use of the Kerala Governor to cover up the constitutional niceties. The report of the Governor was used as an excuse to dislodge the Government of a party that happened to be different from the party in power at the Centre.

The problems of Kerala are not over. After the mid-term elections in 1960, Pattam Thanu Pillai's flirtation with the office of the Chief Ministership ended, and the Congress Party formed its own cabinet under the leadership of R. Shanker. In September, 1964, some Congressmen rebelled against the leadership of Shanker, and on 10 September, the Constitution was suspended and the President's rule was established for the third time in Kerala. The mid-term elections were held on 4 March, 1965 in the background of utter political confusion. The Congress Party was a divided House. The CPI. did not want to give the privilege of factionalism to the Congress Party. Two CPIs were formed—Left and Right. About two months before the new elections, all the known Left CPI, members were arrested under the DIR In spite of all this, the Left CPI. emerged as the largest single party with 40 seats to its credit. The Party would have formed a coalition Government, but out of its 40 elected MLAs 29 were in the Jail under the DIR, and the Government of India refused to release them. It was alleged that these arrests were due to party considerations. After the elections, the Governor talked to the Party leaders regarding the formation of the Ministry (a coalition), and he reported to the President that no stable Ministry can be formed under the existing circumstances, hence a fresh proclamation of emergency should be issued under Article 356 of the Constitution. The newly elected Assembly was dissolved without the members taking any oath etc. The opposition parties were for the convening of the newly elected Assembly, and providing it an opportunity to express its confidence on some leaders on the floor of the House. If no one gets the vote of confidence on the floor of the House, the Assembly should be dissolved. This procedure was not accepted, and the Emergency was proclaimed.

The period of six months of the proclamation was to end on 11 November, 1965. The Governor of Kerala sent a report to the President on 17 October, 1965, and recommended that the President's rule in Kerala should be extended for a further period of six months. A summary of the report of the Governor was placed before Parliament. The Governor reported (there were inaccuracies of names of party members in the Report) that "there has been no shift in the alliances of the political parties in the State and no party or group of parties will be able to form a stable government even if elections are held again". He further wrote that the leaders of all the parties, except E.M.S. Namboodiripad of the Left Communists, have said with varying degrees of emphasis that it would not be advisable to hold elections during the present emergency. E.M.S. Namboodiripad had told the Governor that he would be able to form a coalition Ministry with the support of the Right Communists and the SSP But the Governor reported that both the other parties had refused to join any coalition with the Left CPI

How did the Governor try to forecast the outcome of an election that was not held? It is a queer logic: as no party will be able to secure majority, why hold the elections in Kerala. Why hold elections in the other States of India, since no party except the Congress party will definitely manage and manipulate to secure the majority and form the Government. Further, Hiren Mukerjee, the leader of the Right CPI, in the Lok Sabha, said the Right Communists in the State were ready to support the Left Communists in forming a Government. Thus the Governor's contention that the Right CPI was not ready to enter the coalition with the Left CPI was challenged on the floor of the House. The opposition parties charged the Governor being partisan in his report. As the Congress party is in a very bad shape in Kerala, it will not be possible for it to win the election. The Congress rulers in Delhi knew about it. A non-Congress Government is not a happy spectacle for the Congress party bosses. They wanted time to set right the Congress party affairs in Kerala. The Governor, who is Congress party man, recommended for the extension of the emergency period, on the advice of the Congress leaders at the Centre. As far as the Centre is concerned, it is continuing its policy of not allowing the opposition parties to form the Government to Kerala. The Centre dislodged the legally elected government in the State in 1959, and latter on prevented a duly elected Assembly from discharging its functions. In all these events the feeling gets confirmed that the Governor is a tool in the hands of the ruling party at the Centre. Was it for the Governor or the people of the State to say whether they would return a political party with sufficient majority in the Assembly to form a Government? Was it justified on the part of the Governor to make predictions on the basis of the previous election results? How far the Governor could be trusted in acting as 'a mirror' reflecting the wishes and aspirations of the people of Kerala?

To sum up, all this has been discussed to show the difficult role that the Governor has to play in time of constitutional crisis. He is to reconcile his loyalty to the Constitution and the Central Government with his loyalty to the State Government. His role assumes great importance in the case of a conflict between the State Cabinet and the Central Government. In the future when a different party is in power in the Centre and different parties are in power in the States, the role of the Governor will assume great importance. If the State Governments feel that the Governor is becoming an instrument of Central intervention (or party intervention) in the State administration, serious constitutional deadlocks will occur. Under such circumstances the success of the Governor will depend on his acting above party politics. Only then will he be able to inspire confidence in the people, and perform his constitutional responsibilities in rclation to State administration. A careful thought should be given to the qualifications and selections of the Governors. He is an essential part of the Constitution. He performs many essential constitutional functions. He is a connecting link between the Centre and the State and he is to act as an umpire between party conflicts. In times of emergency and political crisis, his role assumes great importance. So defeated politicians and political invalids should not be appointed to the Governor's office. The office of the Governor should not be treated with contempt by dumping useless persons in it.

To conclude, "A Governor can do a great deal of good if he is a good Governor and he can do a great deal of mischief, if he is a bad Governor, in spite of the very little power given to him under the Constitution we are framing."[50] Writing about her experiences as the Governor of Maharashtra, Vijaya Lakshmi Pandit describes the office of the Governor as a "redundant office on which a great deal of money is spent to no purpose very early in the day discovered files containing notes by my predecessors complaining of being swept out in the cold—of not being consulted or not being permitted to see files, and of a feeling of uselessness."[51]

If the Governor allows himself to become a pawn in the State party politics or surrenders himself to the big party bosses in New Delhi (as is alleged in the case of Kerala Governor) he loses all dignity and importance. Impartiality and independence in politics is essential if the Governor is to perform his constitutional responsibilities with decorum and dignity.[52]

—SA.H. Haqqi (Ed.), *Union-State Relations in India*,
Meenakshi Prakashan, Meerut, 1967.

NOTES AND REFERENCES

1. Lipset, *Political Man,* pp. 404-06. Also refer to Bell D., *The End of Ideology: On the Exhaustion of Political Ideas in the Fifties* (Rev. Ed., 1961), Charles C. Zimmerman: 'Ideological Movement and Social Change' in *Contemporary Political Ideological,* (ed.) Joseph S. Roucek, Vision Press Ltd., London, 1961.
2. For details refer to: M.R. Masani: *The Communist Party of India: A Short History*, Derek Veschoyle, London, 1954, John H. Kautsky, *Moscow and the Communist Party of India: A Study in Post-War Evolution of Communist Strategy*, Cambridge, Mass., and N.Y., 1956. Gene D. Overstreet and Marshall Windmiller, *Communism in India*, Berkeley, California, 1958.
3. Refer to: Acharya Narendra Dev, *Socialism and the National Revolution*, edited by Yusuf Meherally, Bombay, Padma Publications, 1946; Jayaprakash Narayan, *Towards Struggle*, edited by Yusuf Meherally, Bombay, Padma Publications, 1964; P.L. Lakhan Pal, *History of the Congress Socialist Party*, Lahore, 1946.
4. P.L. Lakhan Pal, *History of the Congress Socialist Party* (op. cit.), p. 144 M.R. Masani also says: "There were from the start two clear tendencies discernible among the participants,....One tendency, then represented by Jayaprakash Narayan, was Marxist....The other tendency, that of Democratic Socialism, was represented by M.R. Masani..." M.R. Masani *op. cit.,* p. 53. This position continued even up to 1946.
5. On the issues of conflict see Dr. Ram Manohar Lohia: *Marx, Gandhi and Socialism*: Navhind, Hyderabad, 1963.
6. It is rightly said the "...the fact, that in India 'Socialism' is widely accepted and 'Socialist' as an adjective of approval has paradoxically been a liability, not an asset, to the Indian Socialist Party." Saul Rose: *Socialism in Southern Asia*: Issued under the auspices of the Royal Institute of International Affairs, Oxford University Press, London, 1956, p. 58.
7. Ram Manohar Lohia, *op. cit.,* pp. 444-45.
8. Currently they are known as the CPI and the CPI (M).
9. Also refer to: Mohit Sen, "Great Divide in Communist Ideology", *India Quarterly*, Vol. XX, No. 4, October-December, 1964, New Delhi, pp. 351-71.
10. Also refer to J.M. Kaul, The Split in the C.P.I., *India Quarterly*, op. cit. pp. 372-90.
11. In a recent article about the Congress Party, Tom Kemp writes: "Of those who could do something about the situation the businessmen played an indispensable but behind-the-scenes role as the purveyors of funds. The Congress apparatus, which became complex and comprehensive enough to be considered a shadow administration by the 1930's could not have been built up and maintained by the few pennies demanded from the ordinary member. It became dependent upon contributions to party funds both from idealistic participants and also from rich men who took little or no active part in the formal activities of the movement. Congress developed its apparatus men and its vested interests and these were clearly welded to the

source from which a large part of its funds came. If the outside world saw Gandhi and Nehru, behind their activities lay planning, organisation and financial backing arranged by Vallabhbhai Patel. It was Patel's close links with wealthy businessmen, especially in Gujarat, which provided the funds for Congress activities." Tom Kemp: Leaders and Classes in the Indian National Congress, 1911-39: *Science and Society*, Winter 1964. Vol. XXVIII, No, I., N.Y., p. 11.

12. G.D.H. Cole, A History of Socialist Thought, Volume IV, Part I; *Communism and Social Democracy 1914-31*, London, Macmillan and Co., Ltd., 1958.
13. Tom Nairn, The Nature of the Labour Party I, *New Left Review*, No. 27, September-October 1964, International Socialist Journal, London, p. 55.
14. In the words of Dr. Ambedkar: 'It (constitution) establishes a dual polity with the Union at the Centre and the States at the periphery, each endowed with sovereign powers to be exercised in the field assigned to them respectively by the Constitution. The Union is not a League of States, united in a loose relationship; nor are the States the agencies of the Union, deriving powers from it. Both the Union and the States are created by the Constitution; both derive their respective authority from the Constitution. The one is not subordinate to the other in its own field; the authority of one is coordinate with that of the other.'—C.A.D., VII., p. 33.
15. Walker: 'Federalism in the Commonwealth' published in the *Journal of the Parliaments of the Commonwealth,* London, Vol. II, No. 4, Oct. 1961.
16. Articles 265, 257, (1), (2), (3) and (4).
17. Articles 258 (1), (2) and (3); 260, 261, 262, 263 give wide powers to the Centre over the States.
18. Also refer to Articles 355, 324, 150, 151, 317, 359, 217 etc. which clearly make Centre administratively stronger than the States.
19. "The master plan of economic development must be countrywide" In particular respects, the federating units might be left free to control the pace or direction of development and the plan itself would pay proper attention to all-sided development of all regions. At the same time, all federating units must accept overall direction imposed by the master-plan. The federal government must have adequate powers to evolve the general plan of economic development for the whole country and must have powers to carry out its essential features and to supervise and enforce its implementation by the federating units. This is only inherent in economic planning.'—D.R. Gadgil: *Federating India,* Poona, Gokhale Institute of Politics and Economics, 1945, p. 44.
20. In this connection the Third Five-Year Plan clearly mentions: "The Plan has to be implemented at many levels—national, State, district, block and village. At each level, in relation to the tasks assigned, there has to be cooperation between different agencies and an understanding, of the purposes of the Plan and the means through which they are to be secured. In a vast and varied structure organised on a federal basis, a great deal depends on being able to communicate effectively between different levels, and at the same level between different agencies."—*Third Five-Year Plan*, Government of India, Planning Commission, 1961, p. 267.

21. In this connection Third Five-Year Plan mentions: "During the next three years States will also participate in the drawing up of a long-term plan of development for the country.... This plan is intended to present the general design of development for the country as a whole over the next 15 years or so. It will be based on a study of the resources and possibilities of different parts of the country and will seek to bring them together into a common frame. This is a task of great complexity, as it is of great promise, and there will be need for close and continuous collaboration between various agencies at the Centre and in the States, especially those responsible for Planning...."—vide: *Third Five-Year Plan,* Government of India, Planning Commission, 1961, p. 289.
22. 'In other words, a sort of vertical Federation has been set up under the Planning Commission. The Constitution set up a territorial Federation; it is a horizontal Federation that was set up by the Constituent Assembly. The matching grants have set up a vertical Federation by which the Central Departments and the State Departments on the same subject as 'education' etc. form a unit for the purposes of programmes, projects, and most important of all, for expenditure—vide: K. Santhanam: *Centre-State Relations in India,* Asia Publishing House, p. 54.
23. The Committee appreciate that Planning involves allocation of scarce resources, and consequently fixation of priorities. They also realise that in a federal constitution, it has special difficulties. Also when it happens that the financial resources of the States are inelastic and they have to depend upon the Centre for financing a very large portion of their development programmes, very great importance is attached to the approval of the Planning Body as a pre-requisite to the release of funds by the Centre. The Committee would, however, suggest that the entire procedure now adopted should be reviewed so that if any practice has grown which lends support to this feeling, it could be rectified, vide: *Estimates Committee Report,* 1957-58, p. 5.
24. The same opinion was expressed by the Estimates Committee of the Second Lok Sabha in its Twenty-First Report on Planning Commission. The Committee suggested that for the purpose of schemes approved for Central assistance, the procedure should be so devised that the State governments should approach directly the Central Ministries concerned. The Ministries should take decisions on all such matters in consultation with the Planning Commission and the State Government concerned. In case there is any difference of opinion between the Planning Commission and a Central ministry the difference should be resolved by the Cabinet, and in case there is any difference between the Planning Commission and a State government, it should be resolved by the National Development Council, vide: *Estimates Committee Report* 1957-58, p. 5-6.
25. Cf. K. Santhanam, *Planning and Plain Thinking,* Higginbothams (Private) Ltd., 1958, p. 138-39.
26. "What I want to suggest is that Planning for purpose of economic development practically superseded the federal constitution so far as States were concerned but this supersession was not legal or constitutional but was by agreement and consent. Planning has been comprehensive. It has

covered all the spheres of activities of both Centre and the States." K. Santhanam, op. cit., p. 17.

27. "The Ministry of Community Development can justly claim that it has kept with itself less control over details of the programme, having passed on much of it to the State Governments, than what most other Ministries of the Central Government have in respect of schemes sponsored and financed by them wholly or partly though executed by the State Governments. It should also be stated that the Ministry of Community Development has used its control over the programme to the best advantage of the programme, has provided to the State Government dynamic leadership and much guidance, based on the Ministry's intimate touch with the field operation of the programme all over the country. The Ministry has also been able to establish genuine partnership with the States, holding itself jointly responsible with the latter for the successful operation of the Programme."—B. Mukerjee: *Community Development in India,* p. 169.
28. *Ibid*., p. 170.
29. *Ibid*.
30. *Ibid*., p. 272.
31. "The qualifying prefix 'quasi' indicates mere appearance or something that is seemingly so and is in fact different from what it appears to be...we must limit the term 'quasi-federal' to a constitution that maintains the constitutional autonomy only in name... . However religiously the federal principle is embodied in the constitution, it is possible that in course of time social and economic conditions become so complicated that the powers of the federal Government increase. It has to assume spheres of authority which did not originally belong to it."—S.P. Ayer: *Federalism and Social Change,* p. 91.
32. Kelly and Harbinson, *The American Constitution, Its Origin and Development,* p. 718.
33. Swisher, C.B., *American Constitutional Development,* p. 967.
34. "It is becoming more and more evident that if India is to realise fully her declared objectives to secure to all its citizens, justice, social, economic and political; fraternity, assuring the dignity of the individual and the unity of the nation, the structure of her administration should be reorganised to conform more to the unitary pattern with a well developed system of local government."—Ashoka Chanda, *Indian Administration,* p. 30.
35. "A local executive fully responsible to a local legislature ensures a good deal of local internal sovereignty and sovereignty means a State-hood, limited as it may be by the distribution of powers. Local States pursue local policies, sometimes in accordance with the policy of the Centre, sometimes not. This distinguishes them precisely from the position which prevails in administrative federations in which local units must toe the line and always follow the policy of the Centre. India is undoubtedly a federation in which the attributes of statehood are shared between the Centre and local States." Alexandrowicz, *Constitutional Development in India,* pp. 168-69.
36. "The power that is exercised organically in New Delhi is the uncertain and discontinuous power of prestige. It is influence rather than power. Its method is making plans, issuing pronouncements, holding conferences. Dependence

for achievement therefore, is in some crucial ways, apart from the formal organs of governance, in forces which in the future may take quite different forms."—Paul H. Appleby, *Public Administration in India: Report of a Survey,* Government of India, 1953.

37. Also refer to A.H. Birch, "Approaches to the Study of Federalism", *Political Studies* (Oxford), Volume 14, No. 1, February, 1966, pp. 15-33.
38. Mrs. Indira Gandhi after becoming Prime Minister said that she considered the Centre-State relationship as one of the major problems facing her Government especially because some non-Congress Governments have come into power in some States.—*Statesman,* March 13, 1967.
39. He is a creation of the Constitution. Articles 153-162 lay down the manner of his appointment, tenure, qualifications, oath, powers etc. Articles 163 and 167 lay down his relationship with the Chief Ministers and the Council of Ministers; and Article 213 lays down the power of the Governor to promulgate ordinances etc.
40. Refer to Articles 256, 257 (1), (2), (3) and (4).
41. Dr. B.R. Ambedkar, Chairman of the Drafting Committee of the Constituent Assembly observed: "It is quite clear in the judgement of the Drafting Committee that this is not only necessary but consequential, for the simple reason that, once there is power given to the Union Government to issue directions to the States that in certain matters they must act in a certain way, it seems to me that not to give the Centre the power to take action. When there is failure to carry out those directions is practically negative the directions which the Constitution proposes to give to the Centre. Every right must be followed by a remedy. Article 356 does not introduce any new principle at all. It merely gathers together or assembles the different sections in which the power to issue directions is given and states in general terms that wherever power is given to issue directions and there is a failure, it would be open to the President (of India) to deem that a situation has arisen in which there has been a failure to carry out the provisions of this Constitution... .The object of Article 356 is to make the thing complete (See the Constituent Assembly Debates of 15th, 16th and 17th Nov., 1949)." For the 'Nature of the Indian Union' refer to D.N. Banerjee: *Some Aspects of the Indian Constitution,* Calcutta, The World Press P. Ltd., Chapter IV, 1962. The Nature of the Indian Union: Relations between the Centre and the Constituent States, pp. 73-135.
42. Dr. B.R. Ambedkar observed that the Governor would have no functions which he is required (to perform) either in his discretion or in his individual judgement. According to the principles of the Constitution, he is required to follow the advice of the Ministry in all matters. C.A.D., VIII, p. 47; Similarly a Special Bench of the Calcutta High Court in the case of Sunil Kumar Bose and others vs. The Chief Secretary to the Government of West Bengal (1950) made the following observations regarding the power of the Governor: "The Governor under the present Constitution cannot act except in accordance with advice of his ministers...under the present Constitution, the power to act in his discretion or in his individual capacity has been taken away and the Governor, therefore, must act on the advice of his ministers. This is the

constitutional position as explained to us by the Advocate-General and we accept his view.

43. This is the sum and substance of Articles 356, 365, 256, 257 etc. Shri Mahavir Tyagi expressed the same opinion in the Constituent Assembly. He observed: "These Governors are not to be there for nothing. After all we have to see that the policy of the Centre is carried out. We have to help the States linked together and the Governor is the agent or rather he is the agency which will press for and guard the central policy. The Governor being the agency of the Centre is the only guarantee to integrate the various provinces or States. The Governor must remain as the guardian of the central policy on the one side, and the Constitution on the other." C.A.D. VIII, pp. 494-95.

44. This expression 'otherwise' is significant. It did not originally occur in the corresponding provision in the Draft Constitution of India i.e., Article 278 in it. The expression was later on inserted in the Article. On justification of this insertion, Dr. Ambedkar, Chairman of the Drafting Committee, stated in the Constituent Assembly on 3rd August, 1949: "With regard to Article 278, the first change that is to be noted is that the President (of India) is to act on a report from the Governor or otherwise. The original Article 188 provided that the President should act on the report made by the Governor. The word 'otherwise' was not there. Now it is felt that in view of the fact that Article 277-A (see pp. 97-99 ante) which precedes Article 278, imposes a duty and an obligation upon the Centre, it would be improper to restrict and confine the action of the President, which precedes Article 278, imposes a duty and an obligation upon the centre, it would be improper to restrict and confine the action of the President, which undoubtedly will be taken in fulfilment of the duty, to the report made by the Governor of the Province. It may be that the Governor does not make a report. None the less, the facts are such that the President feels that his intervention is necessary and imminent. I think as a necessary consequence to the introduction of Article 277-A, we must also give liberty to the President to act even when there is no report by the Governor and when the President has got certain facts within his knowledge on which he thinks he ought to act in the fulfilment of his duty.

45. The Communist rule in Kerala lasted for two years, three months and twenty-six days. For further details concerning Kerala Communist rule refer to: 1. Dr. Jitendra Singh, *Communist Rule in Kerala;* Diwan Chand, Indian Information Centre, New Delhi, 1959. 2. K.P. Bhagat, The Kerala Mid-term Election of 1960; the Communist Party's conquest of new positions, Bombay, Popular Book Depot, 1962. 3. Ellen Roy, 'Indian Party Politics', the Radical Humanist, July 24, 1955. 4. Marshall Windmiller, Indian Communism and the 'New Soviet Line'. Pacific Affairs, XXIX (December, 1956). 5. Marshall Windmiller, 'Constitutional Communism in India', Pacific Affairs, XXXI (March, 1958) 22-35. 6. Benjamin, N. Schoenfield, 'Kerala in Crisis', Pacific Affairs, XXXII (Sept. 1959), 7. Gene D. Overstreet, 'The Communists and India', Foreign Policy Bulletin, No. 1. 1959, pp. 29-31. 8. Selig S. Harrison, *India: The Most Dangerous Decades* (Princeton, N.J., 1960), pp. 193-99. 9. 'Kerala: A Tale of Lost Opportunities' by S.G. Managekar, *The Modern*

Review, Calcutta, for September, 1959, pp. 207-21. 10. Communist Party 'New Age' 1956-60, contains many articles on Kerala from the point of view of the Communist Party.

46. A fifteen page summary of the report of the Kerala Governor was placed before Parliament on 17 August, 1959, when the Lok Sabha debated the proclamation for approval. At the same time, it was maintained by the Central Government that the Governor's report was a confidential document. Only a summary of the Report compiled by the Governor himself was placed before the House.
47. Italics mine.
48. Political misuse of Emergency powers was even feared by the Constitution-makers and Dr. B.R. Ambedkar gave a very lame reply by observing "I do not altogether deny that there is a possibility of these articles being abused or employed for political purposes. But that objection applies to every part of the Constitution which gives power to the Centre to override the provinces....(The) proper thing we ought to expect is that such articles will never be called into operation and that they remain a dead letter." C.A.D. IX, p. 177.
49. There are many people who believe that all the charges levelled against Communist rule in Kerala can be levelled against the Congress rule in most of the States. Why not proclaim emergency in those States also? Writing about the Proclamation of Emergency in Kerala, The *Modern Review* writes: "There are many charges, in this memorandum, which some of the Congress Governments of many States may have to face. For the Congress is by no means free of the Party virus. Indeed today we have a government by the officials, for the benefit of the party in power and their minions to the complete denial of the Rights of the Common citizen. Nemesis will follow, may be soon, may be late, unless there is rectification." (The *Modern Review*, Calcutta, August, 1959, Vol. CVI, No. 2, p. 86.)
50. B.G. Kher, C.A.D., VIII, p. 434.
51. Bhavan: Governors in '*Cold War*'. *The Times of India*, November, 22, 1965. The Governor felt useless because Maharashtra had Congress Party Government. What about Governor in Kerala? He has great powers to thwart democracy and sabotage people's wishes.
52. For a very interesting discussion see Sri Prakasa, *State Governors in India*, Meenakshi Prakashan, Meerut, 1966.

3

Indira Gandhi: The Consolidational Phase

Nehru was under attack from 1962 to 1964 because his powerful opponents, within the Congress party, had viciously targeted him on his China policy especially when China launched a border war in 1962. A section of Indian and foreign commentators also began a speculation on After Nehru: Who? Because Nehru's legacy was considered as weak and his successors were not considered to be worthy of defending the challenges faced by democratic India. The speculation of After Nehru: Who? was laid to rest when Lal Bahadur Shastri, a Minister in the Nehru cabinet, was elected as successor, on June 9, 1964 and he continued as Prime Minister till his death on January 11, 1966. Gulzari Lal Nanda became a stop gap Prime Minister from May 27 to June 9, 1966, the Congress party elected Shastri as the leader of the government in place of Nehru. Nehru had also been accused of establishing a 'dynastic rule' in India and this propaganda got its legitimacy when Indira Gandhi became President of the Congress party during Nehru's life time. This propaganda died down only when Shastri succeeded Nehru and Indira Gandhi was nowhere in the reckoning for the office of the Prime Ministership of India. Lal Bahadur Shastri's untimely death re-opened the issue of finding a successor and the Congress party elected Indira Gandhi as its leader, in preference to Morarji Desai who believed himself to be a successor of Shastri. Indira Gandhi occupied the office of Prime Minister from January 24, 1966 to March 24, 1977 and after a break of about two and a half years, she came back to power from January 14, 1980 to October 31, 1984. Indira Gandhi's years-in-power as Prime Minister were not only historic but also most controversial and her term of office ended with her assassination on October 31, 1984. Unlike Nehru, Indira Gandhi's years of power brought glory as well as infamy to India and this is the reason that all evaluations of Indira are based either on admiration or hatred for her. Indira showed immense personal courage while leading the country and also while facing great personal difficulties during her years of power. A catalogue of her achievements in as prepared by commentators on her years of power, deserves to be stated here. Indira was elected by the Congress party with a view that she could lead the party during the Lok Sabha and State Assembly elections of 1967. The election results proved disastrous for the Congress party and it was for the first time, in post-Independence India, that one party dominance of the Congress party had been challenged by conglomerate of parties. The Congress organisational leadership lost their faith in Indira's capacity to win an election and factional conflicts between Indira and a powerful section of party organisational leadership became public and this factionalism within the Congress got intensified on the nomination of party's candidate for the office of President of India. Zakir Hussein's untimely death in 1969 created a situation for group and factional leaders to promote the candidature of their factional loyalists for the Office of the President of India. The factional leaders like S. Nijalingappa, the Congress party President, K. Kamaraj *et al.* succeeded in nominating their loyalist N. Sanjeeva Reddy as a party candidate for the Presidency of India. Indira Gandhi reacted by sponsoring V.V. Giri, as her own nominee and in a highly contested election V.V. Giri defeated Sanjeeva Reddy and the Congress 'split' in 1969 between Congress (Indira) and Congress (Organisation). Indira Gandhi as Prime Minister took steps like Nationalisation of Banks, abolition of Privy Purses of the erstwhile princely rulers and these actions were opposed by her critics within the Congress. The Congress 'split' of 1969 reduced Indira Gandhi's support in the Lok Sabha and she gradually started moving towards the direction of a fresh Lok Sabha elections. Indira contested the Lok Sabha elections of 1971 on the slogan of '*Garibi Hatao*' (Eradicate Poverty) and she secured two-third majority in the Lok Sabha. The Lok Sabha elections of 1971 made Indira politically secure and extremely assertive. Another occasion which made Indira an undisputed leader was provided by the Bangladesh war of 1971 because she could stand against American imperialism. Indira also showed statesmanship at the Shimla Conference and refused to humiliate the defeated Pakistani army in Bangladesh. The famous Shimla Agreement, between Indira and Zulfiqar Ali Bhutto of Pakistan, brought peace to both the countries. Indira's nationalist assertion also showed her militarist aggressive attitude which was revealed in 1974 when India exploded nuclear bomb at Pokharan. Social discontent in India was increasing during 1973 and 1974 and instead of tackling the causes of growing social discontent, she ruthlessly suppressed the Railway Employees strike of 1974. This restlessness gave birth to anti-Indira movement led by Jayaprakash Narayan and during 1974-75 people were mobilised against Indira and her discomfiture increased when Justice

Sinha of Allahabad High Court declared her own election to the Lok Sabha as 'illegal'. The events moved very fast and Indira decided to impose the Emergency on June 25-26, 1975 and the country was put under an authoritarian regime. The Emergency Rule ended in March 1977 when Indira Gandhi was decisively defeated in the Lok Sabha elections and a Janata Party government was formed with Morarji as Prime Minister. The Janata Party ruled from 1977 to 1979 and in this brief period, the party was 'split' by Charan Singh who became Prime Minister for six months. Indira 'split' the Congress party again in 1978. The Lok Sabha elections were held at the end of 1979 and Indira Gandhi came back to power as Prime Minister in 1980 and her second term in office began on January 14, 1980 and came to a tragic end by her assassination on October 31, 1984.

How does one evaluate Indira Gandhi's acts of omission and commission as Prime Minister for fourteen years, beginning from 1966 to 1977 and from 1980 to 1984? Indira's imposition of the Emergency Rule in 1975 had completely alienated middle class intellectuals who accused her of destroying democracy in India. The Sikh community was completely alienated when she decided to launch military action against the Golden Temple on June 6, 1984. The Blue Star Operation hurt the Sikh community who held her responsible for inflicting the great humiliation on the community by violating the sanctity of the Golden Temple at Amristar. The Assam Movement, which was launched by all Assam Student Union for the 'detection, deletion and deportation' of 'outsiders' who had illegally occupied Assam also brought brickbats and Indira was at her tenterhooks while dealing with the Assam Movement in 1979-80. The Communist parties which had supported Indira for her actions in 1969 to 1971 also turned against her during the Emergency and they also opposed her decision to ask for a mega loan of more than 5 billion US dollars from the International Monetary Fund. Indira Gandhi continued to pursue the foreign policy of Non-alignment and India and the Soviet Union concluded a Treaty of Friendship and Cooperation with one another. Indira's positive initiatives on foreign policy paled into insignificance because of her image of a ruthless and authoritarian leader who suppressed movements like the JP Movement, the AASU movement and her democratic credentials were always doubted by her critics and political opponents. Indira left a 'mixed legacy' of achievements and Himalayan blunders and she was a suspect 'democrat'. Every biography which has been written about Indira conveys the message about her complex personality. Her many contradictory political legacies have been mentioned by her biographers.

RELEVANCE OF THE INDO-SOVIET SUMMIT INDIRA GANDHI PHASE—1982

The bonds of friendship and cooperation between India and the Soviet Union have been further strengthened by extremely friendly and cordial meetings between Indira Gandhi and the Soviet leaders. Indira Gandhi has characterised her Soviet visit as a "decisive step forward in enlarging the area of friendship and understanding with the Soviet Union". The Soviet leadership has reaffirmed that India occupies a very special position in world affairs because of her commitment to world peace and disarmament. During her discussions with the Soviet leaders, Indira Gandhi was assured that the Soviet Union was committed to the self-reliant economic development of India and that India could rely upon the Soviet Union in strengthening her industrial base. Yet the real significance of discussions between Indira Gandhi and the Soviet leaders goes much beyond the strengthening of bilateral relationship between these two countries.

International peace and security is threatened by the imperialist countries whose leaders are indulging in military adventurism. The leaders of imperialist countries are talking of limited nuclear war and are trying to condition the minds of innocent people that such a war is winnable. During the Indo-Soviet Summit talks, the leaders reacted very sharply against the so-called limited nuclear war and the Soviet leaders expressed their firm commitment to negotiate the reduction and limitation of nuclear weapons. The Soviet leadership also assured the world community that their country would not be the first to use nuclear weapons. In spite of the fact that the Soviet Union has full capability to defend itself from the East and the West; its commitment to world peace is paramount, and during the Indo-Soviet discussion the world community was informed that the struggle for peace was more important than any preparation for war. To secure world peace and lessen the areas of global tensions, the Soviet Union offered that the NATO and Warsaw countries should seriously discuss the limitation of arms and the powerful countries should commit themselves to non-interference in Latin America, Asia and Africa. India and the Soviet Union have a fundamental convergence and identity of views on world peace and this led Indira Gandhi to remark that India and the Soviet Union have a similarity of approaches to world problems of peace and disarmament.

Further, during their discussions with Indira Gandhi, the Soviet leaders offered to sincerely work for the Indian Ocean as a zone of peace. A concrete Soviet suggestion is that no country should accelerate militarisation of the Indian Ocean and serious negotiations should take place during the UN General Assembly session on the Indian Ocean in 1983. The Soviet Union called for a moratorium on the deployment of sophisticated weapons in the Indian Ocean and demanded that various countries should confine themselves only to shipping facility in the Indian Ocean. As a littoral state, India is seriously concerned about the competition of powerful countries in the Indian Ocean. The Soviet Union has assured India repeatedly and it was reaffirmed during the Indo-Soviet discussion that the Indian Ocean should be a zone of peace and security of the littoral states. Hence, the Soviet Union called for a freezing of arms race in the Indian Ocean till the UN discussions of 1983. Thus peace, security and world disarmament occupied great attention of leaders and the Soviet Union's opposition to the theory of winnability of limited nuclear war was highly welcomed and appreciated by Indira Gandhi. Such other problems as the collapse of detente, the aggressiveness of imperialism, the threat of possible nuclear war, the brutal and unprovoked killings of Palestinians by the Israeli invading forces etc., also figured during the Summit. The leaders very sharply and concretely responded to the challenges posed by imperialism to world peace and security, and because of harmony of attitudes between India and the USSR on problems of world peace a very meaningful exchange of ideas took place. The support of the Soviet Union to the non-aligned movement, about which the imperialists have serious reservations, has reassured the peace-loving masses in the Third World that a powerful socialist country means serious business for the preservation of world peace. As leader of the non-aligned movement Indira Gandhi emphasised bilateral negotiations and political solutions for resolving world tensions and the Soviet leadership reciprocated it by suggesting that Pakistan and Afghanistan should resolve their issues through negotiations.

The Indo-Soviet summit was a warning to the imperialists that the forces of peace would exercise their full weight in international meetings and regional forums against militarism. The renewed cold war started by President Reagan would have to reckon with the forces of peace and this message was clearly conveyed at the Indo-Soviet Summit in an unambiguous manner by the leaders of the two countries. Specifically, the Soviet Union assured that the security of Vietnam, Mongolia and India would be fully guaranteed against imperialist adventurism. The Summit was a landmark in the quest for world peace and concrete steps suggested by the two countries would be welcomed by all peace-loving masses of the Third World. The Summit had a world focus and its deliberations have attracted global attention and the voices of peace have been heard all around the world.

The Indo-Soviet Summit addressed itself to the global problems of peace and specific issues of areas of conflict and proposed solutions and strategies for the strengthening of world peace. The meeting of minds between the Indian and the Soviet leadership on world peace is a historic gain of this Summit at a time in world history when mad people are talking about the possibility of a nuclear war. The discussions at the Summit registered their open opposition to warmongers and asserted their faith in world peace. This was the most positive content of the Summit because economic development can take place only in an atmosphere of peace and security. The collapse of detente was regretted and hope was expressed that world conflicts would be resolved through dialogue and discussion in the spirit of peaceful coexistence.

Besides expressing their firm faith to achieve world peace, the Indo-Soviet Summit talks concentrated on bilateral issues of economic cooperation. The material foundations of world peace depend on economic development of poor countries. The poor countries are always vulnerable to the pressures of imperialist countries, and economic strength is an essential safeguard of freedom. The Indo-Soviet economic relations are based on reciprocity and mutuality. India is in a specific stage of economic development, and cooperation with the USSR has brought many positive results for our country and the Summit talks and discussions at the joint Indo-Soviet Commission have brought many concrete results for Indian economic development.

During the last three decades Indo-Soviet economic cooperation has resulted in a phenomenal growth of bilateral trade and establishment of industries in the core sector of Indian economy. Indo-Soviet trade began in the early 1950s and by the middle of 1980s the Soviet Union would emerge as the largest trade partner of India. In 1953, the Indo-Soviet trade was marginal, i.e. Rs. 1.7 crore, and by 1985, as the result of the Seventh Indo-Soviet Joint Commission meeting the trade turnover would go up to Rs. 12,000 crore. Further, during the three decades of trade relations, a sea change has taken place in the items of exports and imports between these two countries.

The share of manufactured items in India's exports to the USSR amount to 60 per cent. For economic development India has received long-term credits and commercial credits from the Soviet Union amounting to Rs. 18,144 crore and Rs. 650 crore respectively. Credits and projects established in India with the Soviet help are in the field of steel, aluminium, iron ore, oil, coal, etc. Under the new agreements, emphasis is on the expansion of establishment of new projects in the area of aluminium and energy. The Soviet Union has expressed its desire to buy back arrangements of goods for which India cannot find market elsewhere. In the area of development of energy resources, i.e., oil, coal, and nuclear energy the Soviet Union has offered all facilities to India including an offer to set up a 1000 MW nuclear power station. If the Government of India accepts to establish a big Soviet aided nuclear power station, its significance for the Indian economy would be comparable to the role of Bhillai Steel Plant established in the 1950s. The Summit has advanced the frontiers of Indo-Soviet economic, scientific and technological cooperation by entering long-term agreements and active role of the Joint Commission.

During the discussions, leaders of both countries emphasised that their friendship and cooperation is not directed against any third country. Such an assurance was essential so that efforts for enlarging the area of peace by the Soviet Union and India are not misunderstood and misrepresented by the imperialist countries.

In the contemporary world, all bilateral relations are determined by the basic global issues of peace and security. When world peace is threatened and local wars are fought by proxy and innocent people are butchered in Lebanon and El Salvador, conscious world leaders should grapple with them, and the Indo-Soviet Summit attached great importance to the basic problems of detente, disarmament and nuclear freeze. The exchange of views among the leaders of these two countries is significant for strengthening the forces of world peace.

To conclude the Indo-Soviet Summit of 1982 should be characterised as a Summit for world peace and against madness of nuclear war. During the Summit, the leaders showed great determination to extend the areas of world peace and the Soviet leadership made concrete offers to the NATO powers for the reduction of world tensions. In the field of economic cooperation, the 1980s would witness a great expansion in Indo-Soviet economic cooperation, and if 1000 MW nuclear power station is established in India, its role for the Indian economy would be compared to the historic role of Bhillai Steel Plant, and the Summit of 1982 would be characterised as a historic landmark for extending the areas of self-reliant economic development of India.—*Patriot,* 3 October, 1982.

INDIRA GANDHI: 1982

Two Summits: An Assessment

Mrs. Indira Gandhi's visit to Washington and Moscow and her deliberations and discussions with President Ronald Reagan and President Leonid Brezhnev have attracted worldwide attention and comments. India like many other non-aligned countries is seriously concerned with deteriorating international security environment and the collapse of detente. The renewed cold war and the real possibility of a nuclear war poses a serious threat to the existence of humanity and this situation demands aggressive peace initiatives by the world leaders. Mrs. Gandhi's visits to the various world capitals are based on a belief that India can and should play an active role in strengthening the forces of world peace. Mrs. Gandhi's discussions with leaders in Washington and Moscow provided an opportunity for serious exchange of ideas on detente, disarmament and many regional conflicts. In Washington Mrs. Gandhi was hard pressed to explain that a non-aligned India was a significant positive factor for world peace and she had to repeatedly assure the US Administration that India's friendship with one country was not at the cost of another country. *Mrs. Gandhi's primary task in Washington was to explain India's foreign policy and to remove many misconceptions about India among the US foreign policy-makers.*

It would not be an exaggeration to maintain that Mrs. Gandhi achieved a very limited purpose in Washington because she could not persuade the US Administration either against supplying arms to Pakistan or heed to India's concern about military competition and use of Indian Ocean for military operations. Mrs. Gandhi clearly stated in Washington that India's security is threatened by US arms supply to Pakistan. On the supply of enriched uranium for Tarapur the US Government had persuaded the French to help India, and this irritant was removed before Mrs. Gandhi reached Washington. Perhaps Mrs. Gandhi had a limited purpose in visiting the US, i.e. to persuade the US Government not to see things in black and white, but to appreciate that a non-aligned country maintains independence of judgement on world affairs and India attaches great significance to friendship with all countries including the US. In Washington Mrs. Gandhi repeated many a time that India's friendship was not exclusively meant for a few countries. On the contrary, India's hand of friendship was extended to every country to achieve the goals of world peace and security. Mrs. Gandhi made efforts to persuade President Reagan to support programmes of economic aid to the developing countries through international institutions and agencies.

On the issue of economic aid. President Reagan told Mrs. Gandhi that India should search for commercial loans in the US capital markets. Mrs. Gandhi's plea that the Indian economy was at a stage that development aid was crucial did not find a positive response from the US policy-makers. Mrs. Gandhi's visit to the US did not bring any basket of aid for India and the conservative US Administration was not moved by India's plea for liberal aid for development. Mrs. Gandhi did not surrender any national interest in the US and she also achieved nothing except clearing the doubts about India's policy of non-alignment. The major achievement of Mrs. Gandhi in Washington was to break the ice of doubts and suspicions and clearly project India's achievements and policies. Perhaps this was her objective of visit to the US after a gap of eleven years and in this objective she was a success.

President Reagan's conservative economic and military solutions to world affairs is not open to influence by the Third World leaders. President Reagan is strengthening US military bases in the Indian Ocean and he is not ready to make any changes in his strategic concept of a limited nuclear war. On Israeli aggression over PLO in Lebanon, Mrs. Gandhi was unequivocal in Washington. To sum up, the Indian and the US perspectives were exchanged at the summit meeting in Washington, and Mrs. Gandhi had the satisfaction of explaining her view points to the US leadership both on global as well as bilateral issues. The summit meeting opened a dialogue between India and the US on crucial bilateral issues like the Indian Ocean, US arms supply to Pakistan and aid for development to India. In such a dialogue, a few misunderstandings were cleared which would pave the way for future deliberations and discussions. The US and Indian perspectives on world affairs have great divergence and this was reflected at the summit meetings. But it was essential to break the ice between the two countries and this limited goal was achieved during Mrs. Gandhi's visit to Washington. Her visit was the first meaningful step to convince the US policy-makers that India and the US could evolve some areas of reciprocity and mutuality to achieve world peace and economic cooperation.

Mrs. Gandhi's visit to Moscow was qualitatively different from her visit to Washington and the results of Moscow visit are naturally much more significant than the results of her visit to Washington. On global issues, the most crucial item on the agenda of discussion between the Indian and the Soviet leadership was the emerging threat of nuclear war. Two concrete and significant results of the Indo-Soviet discussions on nuclear weapons were the Soviet Union's declaration 'not to be the first to use nuclear weapons' and the comprehensive negotiations on the non-use and production and development of nuclear weapons. The Indo-Soviet discussions grappled with the total issue of disarmament, detente and world peace, but special attention was paid to the threat of nuclear war and the Soviet Union as a nuclear power assured the world that they would not be the first to use nuclear weapons while showing its earnest willingness to negotiate the freezing of deployment and production of nuclear weapons with other nuclear powers.

Similarly, on the Indian Ocean, the Indo-Soviet talks were much more significant and meaningful than Mrs. Gandhi's talks in Washington. Both India and the Soviet Union called for dismantling of foreign bases in the

Indian Ocean and make it a zone of peace. As a littoral state, India is concerned with its security which is threatened by the militarisation of the Indian Ocean. The Soviet Union shares the concern of India and other littoral states on the rapid militarisation of the Indian Ocean and the use of bases like Diego Garcia by the US for military operations. India and the Soviet Union have asked for a meeting of the UN General Assembly in 1983 to discuss the whole issue of military bases of the Indian Ocean. The earnestness of India about the demilitarisation of the Indian Ocean is confirmed by its support to the Government of Mauritius for the return of Diego Garcia from US control. The Soviet Union shares the feelings and fears of the littoral states and a comprehensive discussion took place between the Indian and the Soviet leadership on the Indian Ocean.

Mrs. Indira Gandhi's visits to Washington and Moscow were undertaken at a time when naked aggression was undertaken by the Israelis on the PLO in Lebanon. In Washington Mrs. Gandhi expressed her anguish against Israeli aggressive action, but in Moscow the whole Arab situation was reviewed very comprehensively. The Moscow review was based on a conviction shared by India and the Soviet Union that the PLO cause is just and genuine and the Israeli action is imperialism in its naked form.

Since the basic concern of Moscow summit was world peace, an appraisal on the situation in South-West Asia, South-East Asia and other regions led to the reiteration of a principle of non-intervention of outside powers in the internal affairs of other countries. In the Moscow discussions it was recognised that the restructuring of international economic relations and the abolition of traditional imperialist and neo-colonial discriminations was essential for world peace. The Third World is involved in an international class struggle against world monopoly capitalism which threatens world peace and indulges in open economic exploitation of the developing countries. World peace cannot be achieved if the capitalist countries continue to exploit the Third World. The establishment of new international economic order is an integral part of strategies for world peace. A close linkage between world peace and non-exploitative world economic order was appreciated at the Moscow discussions, and the leaders of India and the Soviet Union expressed that neo-colonial exploitations undertaken by the traditional colonial powers should come to an end.

It must be emphasised that bilateral relations cannot be delinked from perspectives on global issues like security and economic relations. When President Reagan advised Mrs. Gandhi to borrow money from the US capital market for India's economic development, the US leadership was selling a perspective on global affairs where security and economic relations are governed by 'strategic consensus and considerations'. Since

Pakistan agrees with the US perspective, it receives military and economic aid from the US with enthusiasm.

The Washington summit revealed a divergence of perspectives and the Moscow summit revealed a convergence and the results of discussions flow from this basic fact. Mrs. Gandhi's journey to the US was to remove misunderstandings and irritants in bilateral relations; her journey to Moscow was to a friendly country which had stood by us and extended support by insisting on equality, reciprocity and mutuality. The Indo-Soviet relationships are 'special' and the recent summit meeting proves it beyond any shadow of doubt. The Soviet Union has extended full support to Indian economy to achieve the goals of self-reliant economic development. Soviet support to India in industry, trade, sources of energy and development of science and technology has a firm base which is institutionalised by the establishment of Indo-Soviet Joint Commission. India has established many joint commissions with a number of other countries, but the policy of protectionism followed by the capitalist countries has made trade relations between India and the West a one-way traffic where India imports more than it exports. Mrs. Gandhi's visit to the US could not achieve any breakthrough in trade relationship between the two countries. In Moscow, it was resolved that the volume of trade between the two countries would register a two-fold increase by 1986.

Mrs. Indira Gandhi has explained India's perspective on global affairs in Washington and Moscow. Mrs. Gandhi's exposition of India's foreign policy in the capitals of two major world powers clearly revealed India's concern about world peace and threats to security of the developing countries. Bilateralism was built into the basic perspective as expounded by Mrs. Gandhi. In Washington she neither gave anything away on policy matters nor achieved any significant result from her meeting with President Reagan either on the Indian Ocean or supply of US arms to Pakistan. In Moscow, Mrs. Gandhi received assurances and concrete results in terms of economic development and national security. The explanation of dissimilarity of results from the two summits is not because of any marginal or peripheral differences or similarities between India and the two world powers. India has an identity of perspectives with the Soviet Union on world affairs; it has basic contradiction with the US militarism and the concept of strategic consensus. And this explains the turns and twists in Indo-United States relationships, and the solid friendship of three decades between India and the Soviet Union.

—*Patriot,* 5 October, 1982.

POLITICAL ECONOMY OF FOREIGN AID: 1980

India's foreign policy of non-alignment and self-reliant economic development would be subjected to serious stresses and strains during the eighties because of grave domestic crisis in the country, and a qualitative deterioration of relations between the United States of America and the Soviet Union. The collapse of detente and the emerging policy of global military confrontations between the two most powerful countries of the world will have a direct impact on the security and strategic policies of India which would be under compulsion to spend more on defence preparation precisely at a time when maximum public investment is needed for economic development.

Further India's economic development depends on favourable openings towards the United States of America and the Soviet Union especially for aid, trade and transfer of technology. India has to make foreign policy options so that it can maintain the best of relations with both the United States and the Soviet Union, and it has to follow a policy of 'double track' to maximise advantages in an adverse international situation. A few options in foreign policy are not available to a dependent and developing country, and the various implications of alternative choices should be seriously examined by public policy-makers.

India's goal of industrialisation and modernisation of agriculture depends on a proper balance between domestic mobilisation of resources and international cooperation, and any disturbance of such a balance would make India either a dependency of powerful countries or obstruct seriously the modernisation of Indian economy. To achieve a proper balance between internal and external aspects of economic development, India diversified its relationships and has tried to establish proper linkages with the Western industrialised countries and the Socialist countries for aid, trade and technology. Such a strategy of linkages with different centres of world powers and diversification of sources of aid and trade has been criticised and it has been alleged that India's foreign policy has a tilt and it is not a policy of genuine non-alignment.

During the last three decades India defended its strategy of foreign economic policy by pursuing bilateralism and established close liaison with multilateral institutions like the World Bank and the International Monetary Fund. India secured the highest aid from the World Bank, and its affiliate, i.e., International Agency for Development. India joined the Commonwealth of Nations and secured preferential treatment for trade in the British market and in the process it strengthened its relations with Britain. In dealings with the Western industrialised countries, India allowed private foreign investment and entered into joint collaboration agreements with the American and British investors, and the largest number of subsidiaries and branches of foreign companies operating in India are British, American, West German and French.

In 1980 alone the Government of India had approved 526 foreign collaboration agreements which was the highest since independence, and the Western industrialised countries had a major share in this. Nearly 70 per cent of these agreements involved foreign investment. Private foreign investment in India has been estimated at twenty-five billion rupees, and about one thousand foreign companies of UK, USA, West Germany, France, Switzerland and Japan have made investments in India or they have entered into licence arrangements for the transfer of technology.

India did not put its eggs only in the basket of Western industrialised countries. It entered into arrangements with the Soviet Union for public sector projects like steel and quota-based trade on the basis of rouble-rupee exchange, and relationship between India and the USSR has been institutionalised by setting up an Inter-Government Indo-Soviet Commission on Economic, Scientific and Technical Cooperation which negotiates long-term economic agreements between the two countries. In this manner, diversification and bargaining have been the pillars of India's foreign economic policy. The model of bargaining in international affairs is confronted with serious challenges in the eighties because of developments in India and in the international climate.

During the middle of the seventies, the United States of America was confronted with a serious challenge to its economic national interests when the Arab petroleum producing countries raised the price of oil and used its essential resource in international diplomacy. While the United States had not recovered from the shock of OPEC new strategy of oil prices, the Shah of Iran, a reliable regional ally of the Western powers collapsed in 1978, and Ayatolla Khomeini adopted an aggressive anti-American foreign policy. The Carter Administration immediately responded by delinking Egypt from other Arab countries by arriving at a Camp David Agreement and replaced the Shah of Iran by winning over President Sadat of Egypt as a regional ally.

Following President Carter's policy of winning 'regional influential' leaders, President Reagan evolved a global policy based on the concept of 'strategic consensus' to safeguard American national military and economic interests. In operationalising new American policy, President Reagan linked economic aid with strategic interests, and identified Egypt, Sudan, Somalia and Pakistan as major recipients of military and economic aid from the United States. The implication of Reagan's policies is that countries outside the American strategic consensus would not get the privilege of massive foreign aid from his country. Further, countries which did not become part of American strategic consensus would have to depend on private commercial borrowing from the American capital market if they needed resources for economic development.

India's strategic and national interests are at variance with American perceptions, and its result is that the flow of foreign aid from the United States to India may be reduced in future, while at present there is no indication of such change of policy in the US. India's trade with the United States is also restricted because of protectionist policies pursued by the Reagan Administration. It must be stated here that new emphasis of American foreign policy precedes involvement of the Soviet Union in Afghanistan. The pressure of American foreign policy on India is severe because Pakistan has opted to be part of the 'strategic consensus' and is recipient of more than three billion dollars of military and economic aid by the United States.

India needs trade relationships with the United States for its exports and import of important industrial technology and industrial raw materials from that country. The United States of America is the biggest market in the world and a developing country like India cannot afford hostile political and economic relations with such a big country. At the same time, India cannot involve itself in a severe arms race by accepting American global perceptions. The United States is shifting its global economic policies, and she is not enthusiastic to support multilateral institutions like the World Bank, of which India has been the largest beneficiary as recipient of aid.

Danger of Borrowing Becoming a Habit

While India is facing serious crisis in its relationships with the US, her relationships with the Soviet Union are expanding. The Soviet Union is expanding its aid to India in industry and energy development. Trade relations between the two countries are also increasing. In 1980, Soviet-Indian trade was worth 1,700 million roubles—a nearly two-fold increase compared with 1975. The Soviet Union has attached great importance to its relationship with India and a decade of treaty of friendship between these two countries has shown great mutual material benefits.

For India, the Soviet Union is not a substitute for the United States market. Hence India has to explore other options to resolve its economic and strategic problems.

A discussion of a few steps taken by India in foreign economic policy deserve a little elaboration to understand the potentiality of new policy directions. The first significant step taken by India in recent years is exploration of the European countries for economic relations. Traditionally India's economic and trade relationships in Western Europe were confined to the UK only, and the two-way trade between India and Britain totalled 1,337 million pounds sterlings for 1978-79 only. The Davy McKee of UK has got the consultancy contract for the construction of a Rs. 3,000 crore steel plant to be constructed at Paradip. British private investments in India around the seventies were about 500 million pounds sterlings. For many years Britain has extended 100 million pounds sterlings per year as aid and technical assistance to India. In spite of different perspectives between India and England on many foreign policy issues, bilateral relations between the two have been expanding.

With the Federal Republic of Germany, India has established close relationships, and besides Rourkela Steel Plant, the FRG has extended aid for many Indian projects. It is not without reason that India did not recognise the German Democratic Republic till 1972. India valued its relationship with FRG, and did not want to precipitate issues with her by recognising the GDR till these two partitioned countries had not settled their inter-relationships. Many important private investors from the FRG are involved in Indian market, the most important of them is Siemens.

During the eighties India looks towards FRG investments and aid with great hope because on political levels these two countries have no tensions or conflicts of perspectives on world affairs. Similarly India is cementing its relationships with France, and the new socialist government in France wants to establish close relationships with three developing countries like Algeria, Mexico and India. Further, India is trying to attract European Economic Community for aid, trade and investments. India has posted an ambassador at EEC headquarters at Brussels, and the EEC is planning to open an office in India in 1982. Thus India is trying its best to establish strong relationships with Western Europe with which it does not have serious political and diplomatic conflicts.

The pursuit of foreign economic policy is facilitated if political interests converge or political conflicts are of a marginal nature. India's foreign economic policy with the USSR and Western Europe is not encountering any serious difficulties because their political perspectives on global affairs either converge or they have marginal differences.

Another option exercised by India to overcome its present economic difficulties in the phase of conflicts with the US foreign policy approach is to borrow money from international institutions and Euro-currency and petro-dollar countries. India has taken the largest loan of five billion SDRs from the International Monetary Fund. India proposes to borrow three billion dollars from the Asian Development Bank. India has joined in 1981, the African Development Fund and African Development Bank. The Government of India has encouraged the State governments of Maharashtra and Gujarat to borrow money from petrodollar countries.

When the flow of foreign aid is shrinking, and the country is facing an adverse balance of payments situation, the Government has adopted the policy of borrowing from abroad.

The strategy of large-scale borrowing from abroad is full of risks, and they should be seriously considered. The growing rate of borrowing demands payment of interest. The total interest paid on foreign loans in 1978-79 was Rs. 245.65 crore, in 1979-80 it was Rs. 255.33 crore and in 1980-81 Rs. 252.24 crore.

If borrowing in international markets becomes the mainstay of foreign economic policy, its consequences can be disastrous. Not only the lenders start dictating terms of loans, they also impose conditions of performance, and many domestic policies have to be pursued or altered in response to the priorities and philosophy of the lenders. The experience of every borrower in the international market has been quite bitter, and India may not prove an exception. Hence in difficult international situations, India can defend its policy of non-alignment and self-reliance by exploring other options than large-scale borrowing or permitting private investors from abroad to capture the country's market.

It is true that India's options have been limited by the increase of prices of oil and oil products and it has created adverse balance of payments situation for the country. But it is not correct to say that we are making serious efforts to overcome this crisis. The Government has opted for a soft solution by incurring heavy loans in international market. Many things can be done within the country to minimise the crisis created by the rising oil bill. First, Indian economic performance can be streamlined. Bharat Ram of the DCM has stated that the country can save about Rs. 2,000 crore by cutting at the import bill of many non-priority items. Second, India's present economic crisis is partly the result of inefficient management which is reflected through deterioration in the capital-output ratio and incapacity of the public sector industries to generate adequate surpluses.

The Sixth Five-Year Plan document has clearly stated that growth performance has been generally less than the targeted. Costs of every project have been pushed up because of delay in completion and execution. Inefficient management of economy, and lower quality of products has made Indian goods non-competitive in the world market. Thus India is losing in export earning because its products are proving non-competitive, and within the country we are losing because inefficiency has turned actual capital-output ratios higher. A mismanaged economy makes a nation surrender many options in world market, and this is happening to India.

Third, every borrowing in international market, and every invitation to foreign investor has to be rigorously examined on the basis of national priorities. Openings to foreign investors in Hotels, or Wilkinson blades or electric type-writers reveal that discipline of a nation in distress is not visible quality of the Indian elite and decision-makers. When borrowing becomes a habit, it degenerates national leadership.

If maximum discipline is not exercised in economic management, the present crisis would compel India to make many compromises in foreign policy.

Fourth, the goal of economic self-reliance can be achieved by vigorous Research and Development policies in science and technology. Import liberalisation is in contradiction with import substitution. The foreign investors would insist on import liberalisation because it assures them quick return on their investments. But the national interest of self-reliant economic development demands a tilt in favour of import substitution and against import liberalisation. If 1966-67, devaluation of the rupee was the policy recipe of aid-givers, in this decade import liberalisation is the remedy prescribed by foreign investors in India. Import liberalisation by India generates jobs in the Western industrialised countries, and it resolves their economic crisis.

To sum up, India's foreign economic policy based on bargaining and diversification is still valid if internal management of economy is made efficient. Political relationships among nations either facilitate or obstruct foreign economic relations. Since foreign policies of some countries are at variance with India's national interests, efforts should be made to streamline domestic economy and on the basis of internal strength, bargaining with other nations should be undertaken.

—*Patriot,* 2 and 3 March, 1981.

DEBT TRAP: POLITICAL CONTROL THROUGH AID

The Indian policy-makers are placing great reliance on foreign aid, private foreign investment, and foreign trade for resolving the crisis of capitalist development in India. This new emphasis on the role of foreign aid and foreign private capital is a fundamental shift from Jawaharlal Nehru's perspective who was quite cautious in his approach towards foreign aid-givers and investors. It is well-known that Nehru did not agree to the setting up of a steel plant in the private sector as suggested by the World Bank and the US Government. In the Mahalanobis model of economic development which was fully reflected in the Second Five-Year Plan, the role of foreign aid was marginal.

In spite of Nehru's reluctance to rely on foreign aid, the institutional foundations for the flow of aid were laid down during the formative period of India's economic development. The Aid India Consortium was formed in August 1959 to coordinate the flow of official aid to India, and the World Bank acted as a catalyst for the establishment of the Club of the capitalist countries to oversee India's economic performance. While in the fifties and the early sixties, the World Bank and its affiliate, the International Development Association, extended limited aid to India for the development of infrastructure in transport and power, the middle of the sixties witnessed serious penetration of the Bank in India's agricultural development around the philosophy of the Green Revolution.

The middle of the sixties were years of serious political and economic crisis in India. The critical droughts in the country, war with Pakistan, the death of Lal Bahadur Shastri and the election of Mrs. Indira Gandhi, was followed by the devaluation of the Indian rupee in 1966. Further, the poor performance of the Congress Party in the elections of 1967 provided a fertile ground for foreign aid-givers to push their policies into India. The World Bank and the IMF forced devaluation of the Indian rupee in 1966, and it showed their strength vis-à-vis the Indian policy-makers. During the sixties and the seventies India was the largest recipient of 'soft' loans from the IDA for agricultural sector. Everything was going smooth for India and the policy-makers were enjoying a period of honeymoon with the World Bank-Aid India Consortium till the oil shock of 1973.

The dreams of the policy-makers of an uninterrupted capitalist development built on testimonials given by the aid-givers were shattered and when they failed to find any viable solutions, they ended up borrowing from the International Monetary Fund. The loan of five billion US dollars from the IMF exposed the serious nature of the Indian crisis. India entered the eighties by knocking at the doors of the IMF and the World Bank to resolve its balance of payments crisis. It is well known that the balance of exchange reflects the basic crisis of the economy and its resolution or lack of resolution can push a country further into a 'debt trap'.

Some major developments in the international environment have taken place in the eighties which have an adverse effect on India as they pose a serious threat to India's sovereignty. First, the United States has killed detente and it has accelerated arms race in the world, including our neighbour Pakistan. India's security environment in the eighties is such that it compels the country to spend more on defence preparations. Second, the capitalist countries are facing a serious recession which has made them protectionist. In spite of India's great efforts to raise its exports, adverse balance of trade would be a feature of the eighties. Third, economic recession and inflation in the capitalist countries has worsened the terms of trade for India, which would have to pay more for imports from the industrialised countries and earn less on its exports. Fourth, the crisis of debt repayment of a large number of Third World countries has brought the World Bank and IMF quite close to exercising surveillance over the economies of the developing countries. India's policies would now be dictated by international agencies, and Mrs. Indira Gandhi admitted this fact in her Raul Prebish Lecture delivered at UNCTAD-IV at Belgrade.

Besides this crisis, a few specific hostile actions of the United States would have to be taken note of by the India policy-makers. First, India was the largest recipient of soft loans from the IDA during the sixties and the seventies but the United States is exercising great pressure over the World Bank and its affiliates not to extend such a concession to India.

Second, the US is consistently opposing aid to India, compelling the latter to borrow from the commercial markets on high interest rates.

During the last three years, India's commercial borrowing in the international market has been a million dollars per year. Third, the US is making every effort to pressurise the Asian Development Bank against giving any aid to India. Thus the hostility of US and the crisis of world monopoly capitalism is pushing India deeper into a debt trap.

A few other aspects of India's linkages with the world monopoly capitalism deserve to be mentioned to understand the nature of relationship. India's balance of payments crisis has made the policies of the country vulnerable to foreign pressures. Concretely, import liberalisation was the direct outcome of India seeking a loan from the IMF. Further, the multinational corporations are asking for more and more concessions for their operations. India is an attractive market for the multinationals which have no qualms in using the World Bank, IMF, and the Aid India Consortium to wrest attractive terms for foreign investment in this country. The World Bank team extended a loan of 500 million US dollars for the modernisation of the Indian Railways in 1983, and they also suggested that technical members of the Railway Board should continue in the job to implement schemes for the modernisation of the Indian Railways. The very fact that the aid-givers could suggest the names of Indians for the implementation of a policy shows the extent to which they play a role in the country.

It should not be forgotten that the World Bank and the IMF were the institutional response of imperialism to the post-World War II situation. The political interventions of the World Bank and IMF in Chile, Jamaica, Tanzania and the humiliating devaluation of the Indian rupee in 1966, imposition and of import liberalisation as a conditionality clause of the IMF loan to India are well known illustrations of interventions through international institutions. With the deepening of world capitalist crisis, India should seriously practise self-reliance to safeguard freedom.

—*Patriot,* 27 June, 1983.

FEDERALISM: LIMITS OF RESTRUCTURING

The Government of India has appointed the Sarkaria Commission to examine the actual functioning of the Centre-State relations because many political parties in the country have expressed serious dissatisfaction with the existing constitutional division of powers between the Central and the State Governments. Since 1967, many non-Congress political parties have come to power in different States and have expressed a feeling of helplessness to undertake developmental activities because of lack of fiscal resources and inadequacy of powers. The DMK and the Communist parties were the first to raise the issue of an excessive concentration of powers with the Central Government. They had also alleged that the State governments were like glorified municipalities in the existing constitutional framework.

The non-Congress opposition parties agreed that the Central Government had misused constitutional provisions and to check such a misuse of powers, Centre-State relations needed a revision. Specifically, the role of Governors appointed by the Central Government and unjustified dismissal of duly elected State governments irritated many non-Congress opposition parties which came to power in States like Kerala, West Bengal etc. Thus the theory and practice of Centre-State relations has created a cleavage between the Central Government and some State governments which persistently demanded a re-examination of the constitutional provisions regarding the distribution of powers between the Centre and the States. In the light of this background, the appointment of a one-man Commission has raised many hopes, fears and apprehensions in the country about the appropriate role of the Central and the State governments.

Many people fear that any weakening of the Central Government would encourage regional chauvinism and a breakdown of the Indian nation. Such apprehensions are not theoretical. Many people are really concerned about the growing assertions of regionalism in Punjab, Assam and other States and Union Territories in eastern India. The Akali agitation in Punjab and the movement against foreigners in Assam led by the AASU and the AAGSP are viewed as negative developments which could be contained only if the Central Government has adequate strength to intervene effectively and put down communal and caste-based movements such as in Assam and Punjab.

Not only regionalism is viewed as a threat to national unity. In the international context too it poses a serious challenge to the integrity of the nation. Only a strong Central Government can ward off external pressures. India is confronted with internal and external threats and this is hardly the time to weaken the Central Government. However, while keeping the constitutional framework intact, healthy conventions could be developed to resolve Centre-State irritations and conflicts. If the rules of the game have not been followed, healthy conventions can be set up for the functioning of cooperative federalism. The Akali Dal and AASU and AAGSP have raised many issues which concern many States and it is only a strong Central Government which can resolve these problems.

A weak Central Government cannot bring Haryana, Punjab and Rajasthan together to settle their mutual conflicts. The Centre needs powers to act as an umpire and arbiter in north-eastern India. Many inter-State conflicts regarding boundaries or sharing of river waters or pooling of common resources for resolving common regional problems depend on an umbrella role by the Central Government—a role of effective leadership. To sum-up, a section of political mainstream is convinced that distortions in the existing Centre-State relations can be resolved by a change in the style of the functioning of the Central Government and by developing healthy conventions. The need of the hour is restoration of confidence among the various political parties which are committed to national unity. They need to be told that regionalism and imperialism are a serious threat and any weakening of the Central authority would be a dangerous activity.

The votaries of restructuring of Centre-State relations argue that the Central Government cannot be strong if the State governments are weak and reduced to the status of glorified municipalities. The federalists want powers for the State governments to meet the growing demands of the people for economic development and social transformation. India is a country of regional imbalances and diversities and such imbalances can be corrected only if the State governments have adequate financial and legislative powers to respond to the specific challenges of development. If the Left Front government wants to implement radical land reforms, it is obstructed by the Central Government. If the AIADMK wants to provide mid-day meal to poor school-going children, it has to seek the Central Government's approval.

The State governments are elected by their people who expect services and solution of problems. The masses look up to the State governments for programmes of development and the latter approach the Central Government for resources and clearance of developmental projects. But a vast country with a variety of languages and cultures cannot be ruled with weak State governments. The Communist parties believe that economic development cannot take place if they have to operate in the present policy framework of the Centre. The constitutional balance of power does not give Communist parties room to follow any alternative policy of economic development in West Bengal or Tripura. The DMK and AIADMK feel that under the constitutional arrangements they cannot implement a cultural policy which is at variance with the all-India policy. The Federalists are convinced that a restructuring of the Centre-State relations is imperative in the context of special and specific requirements of economic development of regions and that the Centre should share more fiscal resources with the State governments.

In the light of the above two views, the Sarkaria Commission would have to examine seriously the apprehensions of the centralist and arguments of the federalist and try to balance the two viewpoints and evolve a new consensus on federal structure.

It may be mentioned here that all the ills of Indian politics do not flow from constitutional provisions alone. Many of the distortions in the Centre-State relations have emerged because of the misuse of constitutional provisions for narrow political ends. The Constitution has no solutions for manipulative partisan politics. If someone is looking in the Sarkaria Commission for a solution of all the ills of Indian politics, he would be sadly mistaken. The regional chauvinism of Akalis and Assam student leaders is a problem which has nothing to do with the Constitution of India. Regionalism in India is based on a manipulation of religion, caste and language for gaining political legitimacy. Regionalism of the Akalis and Assamese is a challenge to the secular Indian identity of citizenship and nation, and it can be contained only by exposing and opposing regionalism and not by redefining the provisions of the Constitution.

A sea-change has taken place in Indian politics and during the last thirty-five years powerful lobbies of industrial capitalists, rich farmers, foreign investors and multinational corporations have emerged. These lobbies are very active in influencing the course of Central and State government policies. A large number of concessions have been extracted by powerful lobbies from the Central and State governments. Would the influence of powerful lobbies on decision-makers end with the restructuring of Centre-State relations? The answer is in the negative. A large number of State governments are as inefficient and corrupt as the Central Government. Both the Central and a large number of State governments have mismanaged public institutions, and this would not end with the redistribution of powers between the Centre and the States. Like the Central Government many State governments have revealed great incapacity to face the problems of poverty, under nourishment, disease and illiteracy. Many State governments, again like the Central Government, have become captives in the hands of vested interests. Thus the Sarkaria Commission does not provide an Aladdin Lamp for the solution of numerous political ills of the country. If the national political parties are collapsing, the Sarkaria Commission cannot rejuvenate them. It needs to be emphasised that a constitutional change may not be an adequate response to the fast changing political scenario of this country, and many solutions to problems lie in politics and not in formal constitutional framework.

To sum up, opinion in the country is sharply divided on the appropriateness of the existing pattern of Centre-State relations but the debate on federalism cannot ignore the international milieu in which India has to exist. It is poverty of thinking if the challenge of imperialism is not linked with Centre-State relations. India needs a strong Central Government to face effectively imperialism and regionalism, but the State governments should be actively associated with this national task and irritations between the Centre and the States should be resolved. Many developmental tasks can be undertaken only by the States because of regional specificities and they should be encouraged and strengthened to do so. Federalism is based on balance of powers and this is possible to achieve if empirical reality is kept in mind.—*Patriot,* 6 April, 1983.

ANTI-CENTRE MOVEMENTS:
Dangers of Regionalism

A recent seminar held at a South Indian university revealed an alarming trend because a large number of intellectuals took an anti-Centre stand and referred to the role of Central Government in India in a derisive manner. The argument based on facts that the strong State Governments would not be able to deliver the goals without a strong Central Government evoked negative responses.

During the fifties and sixties, movements for State autonomy or in favour of the sons of the soil were considered aberrations in a vast country, like India and even positions were taken against the DMK and Shiv Sena. The late K. Kamaraj continued his struggle against the DMK till his death.

The picture in the eighties is qualitatively different. The defence of the legitimate role of the Central and State Governments is becoming weak because strong anti-Centre movements have emerged in different parts of the country and regionalism is being acclaimed even by those who know that serious attempts are being made to balkanise India. In no modern country of the world decentralisation is an ideology without achieving a high level of centralisation, and modern India cannot be an exception to this general rule.

It must be stated very clearly that the movements for an absolute regional autonomy are being spearheaded by political parties which are communal, or representatives of dominant castes in the region. It is not without reason that the Akali Dal and the BJP leader Atal Bihari Vajpayee are talking the same language of so-called decentralisation of powers to the State Governments. The real motive and interests of anti-Centre movements in India require an exposure.

The Akali Dal is a communal organisation which exploits the sentiments of the Sikh masses to promote the interests of capitalist farmers of Punjab. The Akali Dal has challenged the secular state in India by openly involving religion in politics. It has challenged the democratic state in India by encouraging the rule of gun to achieve its demands. It has challenged the federal character of the Indian state by its Anandpur resolution of 1973 which reduces the Central Government to the position of a mere spectator in the affairs of the country. Many leaders in the Akali Dal have mobilised the Sikh youth on communal and secessionist slogans.

Sikhism is an organised religion with its clearly identifiable religious scriptures and official interpreters of such scriptures. The great spirit of tolerance and brotherhood of the Sikh religion has been perverted by the Akali leadership to establish their political hegemony over a Sikh state and to achieve this goal they have come out openly against a Central Government which should have powers and authority to deal with all-India socio-economic programmes of eradication of poverty.

The capitalist farmers in the Akali Dal have openly questioned the role of the Central Government to regulate an all-India economy for the development of the whole country. The Akali Dal has used religion to play on the sentiments of the patriotic Sikh masses to achieve its real goals of a State Government in Punjab which should be an instrument in the hands of capitalist farmers who feel constrained in achieving their goals of exploitation by a Central Government which is committed to the regulation of national economy on the basis of planning.

For the Akalis, religion is an instrument for political goals and their anti-centralism ideology is to subserve the interests of Sikh property-owners in Punjab. This is the reality of Akali movement whose separatist tendencies were legitimised by a motley crowd of regionalists who have been talking in different languages for the redefinition of powers between the Central and the State Governments.

It is not maintained here that the last thirty-six years have not experienced distortions in the actual functioning of the Indian federal system. It is also not maintained that a few distortions should not be corrected for the healthy functioning of strong Centre and strong States in India. But the Akali Dal has a different perspective and the political parties which help in the legitimisation of the Akali Dal, are encouraging separatism in the name of redrawing of Centre-State relations.

The events of 4 to 6 June 1984 clearly show that a week Central Government could not have saved Punjab from communal holocaust and bloodshed of the innocent people. The moral of the Akali Dal challenge is very clear that an effective Central Government is essential to fight communalism and separatist forces in the country.

India is witnessing a competition among various ideologies and movements with the sole aim to reduce the Central Government to the level of a rubber stamp, even a cipher. The nature of such movements should be clearly understood so that the bandwagon of anti-centrism is demolished. The crux of the Akali Dal challenge is to weaken the Central Government and communalism is its strategy and rich peasants are its backbone.

Outside Punjab, the rich peasants and the political parties belonging to dominant castes are spearheading anti-Centre movements. The ideology of rich peasants is divisive and the basic slogan of rich peasant movements is rural versus urban, agriculture versus industry and Centre versus the State governments. The rich peasant movements are mystifying rural reality by raising the issue of rural versus urban and decentralisation versus centralisation.

The rural society in India is highly stratified and the distribution of land is extremely shrewd. The absolute majority of the rural people who depend on agriculture for their livelihood and survival, are landless agricultural workers and marginal farmers. The absolute majority of people living in the rural areas are victims of exploitation by the landlords and the rich peasants.

In the rural areas the landless agricultural workers are involved in a serious struggle with landlord and rich peasants for the payment of minimum wages to the landless agricultural workers. In order to deal with the growing resistance of the exploited strata of rural society, the landlords and rich peasants would prefer State Governments which have more financial resources to benefit the rich peasants.

The rich peasant political leaders and parties have a vested interest in the transfer of huge financial resources from the Central Government so that they can be invested in projects and programmes which are directly beneficial to the rich peasant. Landlords and rich peasants have floated either regional parties or have joined some existing parties with a goal to scuttle the national planning process by making the Central Government either weak or ineffective to intervene in the national economy.

The rich peasants in India cannot have a national party because caste divisions among the peasantry fragments them around regions. The Lok Dal of Charan Singh cannot enthuse any voter in western or eastern or north-eastern India.

The rich peasant political leadership knows its political limitations because caste loyalties on which rich peasant politics is based are coterminous with regions and sub-regions in the country. The political logic of caste-based politics of rich peasant is around a region and rich peasant parties are regionalists. The rich peasants want to be masters of the region in which they exercise political and caste control and thus regionalism and more powers for the State Governments by weakening the Central Government is a natural ideology of the rich peasant political parties.

The decentralisation of political power in India is viewed by the rich peasants as transfer of power to their class. The current debate and movements for the redistribution of powers between the Central and the State Governments has a class and caste component. The Lok Dal, the Telugu Desam and the Janata Party in Karnataka fully represent this reality.

The anti-Centre Governments are also getting support from some members of the big bourgeoisie who do not like planned economic development of India. They think it is relatively easy to control and influence the State regional parties.

It is not without reason that N.T. Rama Rao of the Telugu Desam has attacked the Industrial Policy Resolution of India. He has demanded powers to license industries and to invite foreign capital without restrictions and regulation by the Central Government. What kind of industrialisation can take place in India if the 22 State governments are allowed to go their own way?

The main objective of above discussion is to show that caste, religion and class are the basis of ideology of anti-Centre movements in India. The anti-Centre movements have emerged in the eighties because communalists, votaries of caste politics, rich peasants and regional bourgeoisie sce the State governments as their instruments of power.

In such a situation, a correct perspective on federalism in India should be clearly spelt out. First, the colonial India was exploited and underdeveloped, and the tasks of development require economic planning based on an all-India perspective. The eradication of poverty in India is a national task and it cannot be achieved without national planning which is possible if the Central Government plays a leading role in national affairs.

Second, within underdeveloped India, some regions are more underdeveloped than others and removal of regional underdevelopment can be undertaken on the basis of an active cooperation between the Central Government and the State Governments. During the sixth Five-Year Plans, the State governments have accumulated enough experience to deal with specific regional problems of development and they should be given enough authority and encouragement to deal with regional demands in the overall context of the national plan.

Third, many existing institutions which are lying dormant should be revived and strengthened to achieve cooperation and harmony between the Central and the State governments to accelerate the processes of economic development.

To sum up, the real character of anti-Centre movements should be exposed and no effort should be made to legitimise separatist ideologies in the garb of decentralisation of power. The legitimate role of the State Governments in this vast country is recognised and it should be strengthened without harming the unifying role of the Central Government.—*Patriot,* 11 June, 1984.

POLITICAL ECONOMY OF INDIA

The Indian society is undergoing basic transformation and politics is the initiator of societal restructuring. While performing the tasks of social transformation, politics enters in a network of relationships with economy, culture and history of society. The essence of politics lies in its dual character, that is, it *reflects* social forces and it *intervenes* to transform social structure. Thus politics is a passive and an active force in society and this dual character of politics is reflected in all its activities.[1]

Politics in India is conditioned by its colonial past. The British colonial rule in India disrupted indigenous social arrangements and left a legacy of an underdeveloped economy. On the eve of independence, India inherited an underdeveloped agrarian economy based on feudal, semi-feudal and landlord dominated socio-economic structures. During the colonial period, a few modern industries emerged in India without modern industrialisation. The British colonial rule disrupted the natural economic linkages between agriculture and industry, and as a consequence India inherited a primitive and underdeveloped economy. Underdevelopment was our inheritance on the eve of independence in 1947 and the last four decades have been spent in breaking the inherited structures of economic underdevelopment and stagnation. The essence of post-independence politics is its developmental role.

The central goal of the political economy of development was to transform the material foundations of society with the help of new productive forces in the country. Industrialisation of India was the kingpin of the political economy of development. Industrialisation could not succeed without changing the archaic inherited agrarian structure and land reforms became an integral part of the developmental goals of the post-independence Indian state.

Development goals require concrete strategies and they were worked out in the various Five-Year Plans of India. A two-front strategy was evolved to bring about modernisation and industrialisation of India. First, the absentee landlords were abolished and landownership was given to the peasant proprietors and a landholding peasantry, which actually worked on the land, was created through legislation in India. Land reforms in India had many components but the basic goal of the abolition of absentee landlordism was top in the hierarchy of the agrarian restructuring of society. Jawaharlal Nehru, in his letter to the Chief Ministers, observed:

> I think I have previously written to you that in spite of the more obvious problems that confront us, the basic problems still continue to be economic. We dare not delay in tackling it, however, occupied we might be. I trust that your government will push ahead with development schemes for our ultimate future depends upon them. Provinces which have been thinking of liquidating the zamindari system or of other measures of social reform, should finish these tasks as soon as possible.[2]

The package of land reforms was based on the abolition of absentee landlordism, ownership rights to the peasant, security to tenants, ceiling over ownership and distribution of the surplus land to the landless. The goal of the package of land reforms was to regenerate the agrarian sector of economy which had become stagnant and underdeveloped due to the policies of the British rulers in India.

Second, the strategy of industrialisation was based on a dominant role by the public sector, a legitimate role for the private corporate sector and relative self-reliance while dealing with advanced industrial countries of the world. Industrialisation of India required development of science and technology and the post-independence phase of India has devoted a lot of attention and energy to expand the scientific and technological base of India.

The central feature of the political economy of development of the last four decades is that many tasks have been performed with the active leadership of the Indian state which has acted as an engine of development.

Politics has been a central factor in the social and economic development of India and the basis of Indian politics is universal adult franchise and regular elections. Economic development with people's participation has been a peculiar feature of the Indian political economy. A large majority of newly liberated countries of Asia, Africa and Latin America followed the path of authoritarianism in achieving their goals of economic development. The Indian political tradition of democracy distinguishes us from other Third World countries. During the last four decades India has reconciled democracy, economic development and social transformation, and in evolving the yardstick for evaluation of the last four decades all these interconnections have to be kept in mind.

Further, political economy has to take cognisance of the power relations in a society because the socially powerful groups play a leading role in the management of polity and economy. Political economy does not have neutral social goals. Political economy is influenced and even controlled by the power groups in society. The political economy of India has operated in the context of the power relations in society and an understanding of the linkages between the power groups and goals of political economy deserve an analysis.

Politics in India has dealt with socially powerful groups through legislation and regulation. The socially powerful groups in India have dealt with political power by influencing and controlling the political decision-makers.

Land reforms in India have been partially implemented because the rural oligarchy scuttled their implementation, because legislators, Ministers and Chief Ministers represented interests of land owners. In the agrarian political economy, the share of the labour force in agriculture has not declined while the assets and economic surplus of the landholding peasantry has increased, especially in the Green Revolution regions of the country. During the fifties and the sixties land reforms were on the agenda, during the seventies and the eighties, remunerative prices and subsidies to the landholding peasantry are the crucial political issues.

During the last four decades, the political debate in rural India has changed from land reforms to support prices for such peasants who have a marketable surplus. Political power in rural India is wielded by the rich peasant who denies minimum wages to the landless agricultural workers. And the rich peasant is on the march to control public resources. While the foodgrains production in India has increased, and a resource surplus rich peasant has emerged, rural poverty persists. What is the explanation for such contradictions in the political economy of rural India? The socially powerful landholding peasantry has effectively scuttled land reforms and this class has been successful in capturing the levers of political power to its advantage.

The political economy of rural India is in the grip of a crisis. First, the landless agricultural workers are poor and without employment for most part of the year. The landless agricultural workers are either without a job or they are not paid legal minimum wages for their work. Second, the rich landholding peasantry is fighting political battles to promote their interests. The agrarian political economy is structured on the basis of development without social justice and equity and this has intensified social conflicts and violence in the rural society in India. Many economists are writing in favour of institutional reforms in rural India but the rural oligarchy will not allow such reforms.[3]

Social contradictions are not confined to the rural areas alone, they are observable in urban India too.

The political economy of industrialisation in India was based on commanding heights for the public sector, and a role for the private corporate sector without allowing it to become monopolistic. The public sector in India plays a crucial role in many critical sectors of the national economy like steel, heavy machine tools, basic metal industries, petroleum crude, etc. and its role has expanded during the last four decades as is shown in Table 3.1.

Table 3.1: As a Percentage of National Production

	1968-69	*1986-87*
Fuel		
Coal	17.66	97.71
Lignite	100.00	100.00
Petroleum Crude	51.07	100.00
Industries		
Basic Metal		
Steel Ingot	57.14	75.23
Saleable Steel	55.74	76.80
Non-Ferrous Metals		
Aluminium	Nil	37.52
Copper	—	100.00
Primary Lead	100.00	100.00
Zinc	80.59	86.93
Fertilisers		
Nitrogenous	73.85	46.47
Phosphate	25.24	33.61
Communication Equipment		
Teleprinters	100.00	100.00

Table 3.1 clearly shows the expanding and critical role of the public sector in crucial areas of the national economy of India. The public sector in India has also played a significant role in the development of 'in-house' Research and Development activities. The Department of Scientific and Industrial Research observes that the number of registered units performing R&D work has increased from 600 in 1980-81 to 1069 in 1988 and during this period their expenditure increased to Rs. 200 crores. This DSIR informs that, of this expenditure, 40 per cent is accounted for by more than 100 public sector units and 60 per cent by private and joint sector units.[4]

While the public sector has played an important role in the industrial development of India, the growth in the power of the big industrial private corporate sector is clearly visible as revealed by Table 3.2.

Table 3.2: Statement showing assets, turnover, and assets: turnover ratio in 1986-87 (accounting year ending April, 1986 to March, 1987) of companies registered under section 26 of the MRTP Act and belonging to the top ten business houses ranked according to their assets in 1986-87

(Rs. in crores)

Sl. No.	*Name of the House*	*Assets*	*Turnover*	*Assets: Turnover ratio*
1.	Tata	4940	4940	1: 1.0
2.	Birla	4771	4360	1: 0.9
3.	Reliance	2022	951	1: 0.5
4.	J.K. Singhania	1427	1143	1: 0.8
5.	Thapar	1151	1060	1: 0.9
6.	Mafatlal	1050	1231	1: 1.2
7.	Modi	860	1104-	1: 1.3
8.	Larsen & Toubro	831	560	1: 0.7
9.	M.A. Chidambaram	808	432	1: 0.5
10.	Bajaj	778	847	1: 1.1

Note: Assets and turnover are in Rupees crores.

Table 3.2 clearly shows that concentration of industrial power of the private corporate sector has expanded during the last four decades in spite of the MRTP Act powerful strata of society in rural and urban India have benefited from the developmental process of India and such powerful sections play a crucial role in determining the directions of Indian politics. The rural oligarchy and industrial power groups have managed public affairs with the support of political leaders and its consequence is that India has achieved the political economy of growth without social justice and equity.

The domestic political economy of India is integrally linked with the economies of the advanced industrialised countries for international trade, import of technology and foreign aid. An interaction between the economy of a developing country and the economies of the advanced industrialised countries has many pitfalls and it cannot be a smooth interaction. The political and economic concerns of a developing country may be at variance with the political and economic interests of the developed industrial countries. Many pressures are exercised by the foreign aid-givers and exporters of technology on the developing countries and India cannot be an exception in such a global structure. India has tried to manage its international environment very prudently but the logic of political economy is quite complex and some danger signals are emerging for India from the international political economy.

Of late, India has been facing a serious balance of the payments crisis. The Government of India has admitted the following facts:

(a) The interest paid during 1988-89 was Rs. 2700 crores and it includes the NRI deposits.
(b) The outstanding external debt of India (including the deposits by non-resident Indians) is estimated at Rs. 64,779 crores at the end of 1987-88.
(c) The debt service payments, that is, the repayment of principal and interest payment on external debt (excluding the NRI deposits) as a percentage to exports, plus the gross invisible earnings in 1988-89 were estimated at 23-24 per cent.
(d) The ratio of debt as a percentage of the Gross National Product was 11.8 per cent for India.[5]

During the 1980s, concessional aid to India had been declining, and the country was compelled to borrow commercially in the international market, as for example, in 1987, India's commercial borrowings abroad amounted to $2.358 billion and in 1988 to $2.47 billion. It has been observed that "while the domestic economy has posted a remarkable recovery in the current year after the severe drought of 1987-88, the strains of the balance of payments position have continued and, to some extent, intensified."[6]

India has to import some industrial equipment, some industrial raw materials and technologies in thrust areas, and in spite of national efforts exports have not matched the import requirements of India. India is involved in a continuous adverse balance of trade as is revealed by Tables 3.3 and 3.4.

Table 3.3: India's Foreign Trade: A Profile

Year	*Exports*	*% change*	*Imports*	*% change*	*Balance*
1980-81	6711	+4.6	12549	+37.3	–5838
1981-82	7806	+16.3	13608	+8.4	–5802
1982-83	8803	+12.8	1293	+5.4	–5490
1983-84	9771	+11.0	15831	+10.8	–6060
1984-85	11744	+20.2	17134	+2.2	–7632
1985-86	11012	–6.2	19766	+15.4	–8754
1986-87	12569	+14.1	20201	+2.2	–7632
1987-88	15742	+25.2	22400	+10.9	–6658
April-Oct. 87	8708	—	12192	—	–3984
April-Oct. 88	10625	+22.0	15561	+27.6	–4936

Tables 3.3 and 3.4 clearly show that in spite of diversification of the export basket, India has registered a continuous adverse balance of trade

and even precious raw materials like iron ore have to be exported to earn foreign exchange.

Table 3.4: Export Performance in Thrust Areas

(Rs. in crores)

Item	*1986-87*	*1987-88*
Tea	549.7	591.7
Processed Foods, Fruits and Juice and Meat	146.5	150.8
Marine Products	477.4	525.1
Iron Ore	679.6	710.0
Leather and Leather Manufacturers	787.1	1148.2
Handicrafts	14.9	248.3
Basic Chemicals	473.8	822.9
Fabrics, Piece Goods and Made-ups	569.7	1063.8
Readymade Garments	1037.9	1790.8

Three inter-related critical areas of the political economy of India have emerged. They are:

(a) The rising costs of agricultural inputs have made Indian agriculture a 'high cost economy' and this has generated serious pressures by the rural oligarchy for higher remunerative prices for agricultural products. The rural oligarchy has become very active in Indian politics to safeguard and promote its economic interests. C.T. Kurien observes:

> If in the fifties the institutional aspect was related to absentee landlordism and large ownership in the nineties it will be kept alive through the proliferation of tiny holdings on the one hand and the question of remunerative prices on the other. Dealing with them will be much more difficult than the 'land reform' measures attempted in the fifties and the sixties.[7]

The development of the agrarian political economy during the last four decades has scuttled land reforms, social justice for the poor landless agricultural workers and it has brought into power the rural oligarchy which is using the levers of political power for promoting its class interests.

(b) India experienced deceleration of industrial growth during the sixties and the seventies and to overcome it, the Government of India has launched a massive liberalisation and modernisation scheme for industrialisation.[8]

Many steps were taken during the eighties to accelerate industrial growth by delicensing, broad-banding, capacity re-endorsement, raising the minimum asset limits of the MRTP companies, and a Long Term Fiscal Policy was evolved. In spite of these efforts of the Government of

India, accelerated industrial growth has not achieved the critical social goal of new employment generation in the country.

(c) The political economy of India has come under great pressures from the advanced industrialised countries which are demanding reversal of many national policies like intellectual property rights and a greater inflow of foreign capital into India. The present policy package of the Government of India to deal with the global pressures has brought a warning from Nirmal Chandra. He observes:

> The 'liberal' alternative which calls for greater freedom for foreign investors or for removal of all restrictions on foreign collaboration agreements as an essential means of earning foreign exchange, is just irrelevant in the present context. Foreign exchange shortage is just one, not even the main, problem facing the Indian economy. Even if exports could be pushed up appreciably beyond the present levels by pursuing 'liberal' policies, it would leave unaffected the vast majority of the population.[9]

The central issue of deceleration of industrial growth is the structural demand constraint because the absolute majority of Indians live on a subsistence level and below the poverty line and they have no purchasing power of industrial products in the country. The economic liberalisers have failed to grapple with this fundamental constraint over economic development in India.

It is not without reason that economic liberalisation of the eighties has been supported by sections of the prosperous society in India. Atul Kohli observes:

> The reforms have been pushed by a technocratic leadership that appears to firmly believe in the economic merits of liberalisation. Major support, at least for domestic, as distinct from international liberalisation has come from industrial and commercial groups. The mostly urban middle classes have also appreciated the tax reforms and the availability of consumer goods in the market.[10]

During the last four decades, India has broken the back of the inherited stagnant economy, and industry and agriculture have developed in an interconnected manner. Indian industry has been diversified and structural transformation has emerged in India. While economic growth has been achieved, social justice and equity have not been established because political power has been exercised by the rural oligarchy and the industrial and commercial classes for their own benefits and advancement.

Poverty in India persists because powerful social groups are managing the levers of political power for their own advancement. Rural and Urban unemployment and poverty have brought social violence in society and powerful social groups are responding to social violence by using state power. Para-military forces are being deployed as a substitute for social justice for the poor. —*Mainstream*, 21 July, 1990.

FOREIGN ECONOMIC POLICY OF INDIA

The policy of non-alignment has emerged as a broad and general framework on the basis of which a large number of post-colonial societies have attempted to establish their relationship with the international political and economic system. The genesis of the Non-aligned Movement lies in the colonial history of a large number of Third World countries, and it is realised by the majority of developing countries that the struggle against colonial exploitation does not come to an end with the formal withdrawal of the colonial powers. Thus the policy of non-alignment is a continuation of the struggle of the colonial world against imperialism.

But imperialism is not a weak force. Imperialism had structurally integrated the colonies with the world capitalist system, and the real struggle of the post-colonial societies lies in breaking and destroying their structural linkages with the dominant and exploitative world capitalist system. The erstwhile colonial world has seen many ups and downs in dealing with the extremely powerful capitalist world system, and many post-colonial societies have failed to liberate themselves from the control of the colonisers and in spite of their commitment to the policy of non-alignment, many developing countries have established 'neo-colonial relationship' with the imperialist countries. As Ulyanovsky rightly observes:

> However, imperialism not only continues, but it seeks to extend its exploitation of these liberated lands by using the economic elements of the colonial structures, still under its control. It is impeding the break up of these structures, at the same time trying to devise new levers for maintaining these countries under its economic and political control, it is preventing them from leaving the capitalist path of development. Such is the strategic aim of capitalism of our day.[11]

If a large number of Third World countries have failed to break their linkages with the imperialist countries, the study of India would throw up many lessons for the Third World.

Policy-Making

The public policy-makers in India have offered many explanations in support of their argument that they have been able to establish relative autonomy in international affairs. It is maintained by India's public policy-makers that by following a package of complex policies and strategies of economic development, India has established a relationship of reciprocity and relative equality with the world capitalist system. A few major arguments of the policy-makers may be summed up here:

(a) During the colonial period, especially during the twentieth century, an indigenous entrepreneurial class had developed in India and in spite of discriminatory and obstructive policies of the colonial rulers, indigenous industries had developed in the country. After independence from British rule, an important impediment in the way of industrial development of the country was removed.

(b) In the post-Independence period governmental initiative was essential to develop an infrastructure for industrial development of India. The Indian state became the motive force for industrial development and the state in India mobilised domestic resources for industrial growth. During the last thirty-five years, the Indian state has shown a great capacity to mobilise domestic savings to the extent of 23 per cent, and domestic savings have played a crucial and critical role in the industrial development of India. Further, the Indian state has played a central role in the development of science and technology for industrial development. During the colonial period, industrial development of India was obstructed because of the absence of a scientific and technological base for industry. After Independence, the Indian state laid great emphasis on the establishment of scientific laboratories for R&D. Thus domestic resources, development of science and technology and the modernisation of agriculture have played an essential role in Indian industrialisation and this has been achieved by following conscious policies based on the framework of economic planning. Since modern industrialisation cannot take place in isolation from developments in the industrialised world, the Indian state diversified its linkages with the industrially advanced societies for foreign aid and import of technology. By following a conscious policy of diversification, India has established relationships with advanced capitalist countries and the socialist societies. India is not dependent on any one source for foreign aid and import of technology. Such bargaining has helped India to develop appropriate linkages with different centres of world power without becoming dependent on or the satellite of any one centre of power.

It has been suggested by the public policy makers that India has been able to pursue an economic foreign policy of relative autonomy in international affairs because we have been able to bargain with the capitalist and the socialist countries without surrendering freedom of choice before any one centre of world power.

Many Marxist scholars have argued that India has been able to develop non-satellite relations with global powers because India has a conscious capitalist class which emerged in the struggle against the colonisers. The Indian capitalist class was an essential component of the struggle for freedom and they had objectively experienced that colonialism was a great obstacle in the way of their development. The Indian capitalist class consciously fought for control of the Indian market, and they would not surrender the domestic market to neo-colonial exploitation by the erstwhile colonisers. Such an anti-imperialist leading class provided a social base for a foreign economic policy of relative autonomy from various centres of global dominance.[12]

To sum up, the defenders of India's foreign economic policy have argued their case on the basis of the social character of the capitalist class, and essential socio-economic policies of the post-colonial phase in India, and it has been suggested by the policy-makers that India is a unique and specific case in the Third World which has not become an appendage of the imperialists. On the contrary, the foreign economic policy of India is based on diversification and bargaining with major centres of global power.

The claim of public policy-makers will be examined at two levels. The first level of argument will be based on the nature of relationship between India and the capitalist countries, and India and the socialist countries. The second level of analysis will be based on a periodisation of foreign economic policy which would be divided into two phases, that is, 1950-80 and 1980-83. After examining these two levels, some major trends in India's foreign economic policy in the Eighties would be identified to show the directions of future development.

India and the Capitalist World

Since India is building capitalism, its linkages with the world capitalist system have been strengthened during the last thirty-five years. India has received foreign aid, has negotiated a large number of technological collaboration agreements and has allowed private investment from the capitalist countries. Out of a total foreign debt of Rs. 20,533 crores, the largest amount has been extended by the capitalist countries. Table 3.1 clearly reveals this.

As Table 3.5 shows, FRG, UK and USA are the largest donor countries for India. Because of India's linkages with the capitalist world, multilateral institutions like the World Bank and IMF, which are controlled by the

Table 3.5: Country-wise break up of Foreign Loans received by India

Sl. No.	*Name of the Country/Institution*	*Utilisation of Credit, i.e. External Borrowings up to 31.12 1982 (Provisional)*		*Rate of Interest (Per cent)*
		Govt.	*Non-Govt.*	
1.	Austria	39.82		2 to 5.5
2.	Abu Dhabi	14.27	—	4
3.	Belgium	74.37	—	Nil to 3
4.	Canada	520.98	4.76	Nil to 6
5.	Czechoslovakia	98.04	—	2.5
6.	Denmark	39.19	—	4 to 5 (presently interest-free)
7.	France	554.81	—	Treasury portion: 3 to 3.5, Bank portion: 6.85 to 10.65
8.	FRG	1642.89	116.17	0.75 to 6.75
9.	Iraq	157.15	—	2.5 (Interest-free service charges @ 0.5% for the current loan)
10.	Hungary	12.27	—	2.5 to 4.5
11.	Italy	35.82	—	2.5 to 5.00
12.	Japan	907.54	1.70	2.5 to 6.25
13.	Kuwait Fund	88.00		—
14.	Netherlands	554.63	—	0.75 to 5.5
15.	OPEC Fund	74.70	—	0.5 to 0.75 (service charges)
16.	Poland	29.96	—	2.5
17.	Saudi Fund	75.41	—	4
18.	Switzerland	38.17	—	1 to 3
19.	United Kingdom	1211.00	—	Interest-free since 1965
20.	USA	4436.30	370.00	0.75 to 8
21.	USSR	967.11	—	2.5
22.	UAE	61.44	—	2.5
23.	Yugoslavia	18.18	—	3
24.	IBRD	1087.39	745.94	4.875 to 11.6
25.	IDA	5218.84	—	0.75 (service charges)
26.	EEC (Special Action Credit)	41.68	—	0.75 (service charges)
27.	IFAD	30.04	—	1.00 (service charges)
28.	IMF Trust Fund	537.51	—	0.5
29.	Iran	882.11	—	2.5 to 5
	Total: (Rs. in crores)	**19,440.68**	**1238.99**	

Source: *The Lok Sabha*, March 18, 1983.

leading capitalists countries, have been quite generous in extending loans to India.

Similarly, private foreign investment also increased from Rs. 1,163 crores in 1965-66 to Rs. 2,232 crores in 1975-76. If a country is recipient of a large amount of foreign aid, it has to permit foreign private investment and transnationals of the donor countries to operate in the domestic market. The capitalist countries are committed to market economy, and the individual capitalists and transnational corporations of aid-givers have to be provided facilities and entry by the recipient of aid, and India is not an exception to this general rule. The Government of India spokesmen and agencies like the India Investment Centres make conscious efforts to attract private foreign investment by assuring the foreign investors that no discrimination would be practised against them regarding remittances of profits. The Government of India has assured the foreign investors that unnecessary nationalisation of foreign firms will not be undertaken. It is not only a verbal assurance; concrete evidence is demanded by the foreign investors. The Government of India nationalised domestic private banks, but foreign banks were not touched. One hundred and thirty-one branches of foreign banks like the Bank of America, Bank of Tokyo, and Grindlays Bank are operating in India. Table 3.6 helps in understanding the reality.

Table 3.6: Branches of Foreign Banks in India

Sl. No.	*Name of Foreign Banks*	*No. of Branches in India*
1.	Algemene Bank Nederiand NV	3
2.	American Express International Banking Corporation	3
3.	Bank of America National Trust & Savings Association	4
4.	Bank of Tokyo Ltd.	3
5	Banque National De Paris	5
6.	British Bank of the Middle East	1
7.	Chartered Bank	24
8.	City Bank NA	6
9.	Grindlays Bank	56
10.	Hong Kong & Shanghai Banking Corporation	20
11.	Mitsui Bank Ltd.	1
12.	Sonali Bank	1
13.	European Asian Bank	1
14.	Emirates Commercial Bank	1
15.	Bank of Oman Ltd.	1
16.	Banque De L'Indochine Et De Suez (INDOSUEZ) France	1
	Total	**131**

Source: The Lok Sabha, March 25, 1983.

The smooth functioning of the foreign banks in India is an assurance to foreign investors that their investments arc safe. International banks play a catalyst role in attracting clients from their parent countries and act as informants to induce prospective investors. Similarly in the field of technological collaboration, out of 7,000 such collaborations, the largest number are with the capitalist countries. The above general profile of India and the capitalist world would help in appreciating India's foreign economic relations with the United States which is the most important leader of the capitalist world.

It must be stated very clearly that India's political and economic international relations with the capitalist world have seen many ups and downs and the journey has not been smooth. The basic point is that India has made conscious efforts to establish linkages with the capitalist world and efforts have been made by the Government of India to receive generous foreign aid and private foreign investments. This central argument of the paper would be proved by a brief reference to the Government of India's relationship with the United States. Politics facilitates international economic relations and convergence of international perspectives helps in the flow of aid and facilities of trade. In spite of India's difficulties and differences with US foreign policy, India could establish economic relations with the US Government and US private investors. The US investors' trust in India is clear from the fact that from 1957 to 1982 the Government of India approved 7,056 collaborations, of which US share was 1,332 or 19 per cent, which represents US investment of $500 million. Over the last years, the trend of US-India collaboration has been increasing, and its basis has been laid by the institutional arrangement of the Indo-US Joint Commission set up in October 1974. A large number of US transnationals like the Ford Motor Company, International Harvester, etc., operate in India. Not only this. Many important public sector enterprises in India like Bharat Heavy Electricals Ltd., and the Heavy Engineering Corporation at Ranchi have collaboration with US firms.

While in the 50s and 60s US aid to India under PL-480 was quite considerable, in the 70s it has stabilised at less than $100 million per year. In spite of difficulties in trade between India and the USA the picture is not dismal. India's imports from the USA mainly consist of fertilisers, industrial equipment and industrial raw materials, and India's export trade with the USA consists of traditional as well as non-traditional items like diamonds, readymade garments, etc. The US exports to India have increased from $1,290 million in 1975 to 1,599 million in 1982; and India's exports to the USA during the same period rose nearly three-fold from $548 million to $1,404 million. The two billion dollar turnover of trade between India and the USA during the latter part of the 70s is significant because it excludes the earlier large-scale import of food by India from the USA.

If economic relations between India and the USA are taken in totality, the facts are quite revealing in the fields of trade, aid and technological collaboration. India's economic relations with the USA are not only at bilateral level; the US Government and industrialists exercise significant direct and indirect influence over multilateral global institutions like the World Bank and IMF. India's success story in the World Bank for the last two and a half decades has been with the open as well as hidden approval of the US policy-makers. India and the USA had many open-confrontations in foreign policy on global and regional matters, and in spite of many contradictions between these two countries on foreign policy perspectives, their economic foreign policy has many success stories beginning with PL-480 Food Aid. The explanation for the multiple level of relations between India and the USA is that India has consciously built bridges with the most important capitalist country in the world, and the leader of world imperialism has adjusted its policies towards India at many levels of hostility and friendship. A global imperialist power may not follow a strait-jacket policy, it may adopt many contradictory and conflicting approaches in bilateral relationships. Even in the worst phase of the 'First Cold War', India and the USA kept many reciprocal openings and operated their foreign economic relations which were considered beneficial, to both countries.[13]

India and the Soviet Union

The cornerstone of 'diversification model' of India's foreign economic policy is friendship and close relationship between India and the Soviet Union. Beginning with the Trade Agreement of December 1953, the climax of relationship was achieved on August 9, 1971, in the form of the Indo-Soviet Treaty of Peace, Friendship and Cooperation. The solid basis of the Soviet-Indian Treaty had already been established by significant economic cooperation between the two countries during the 50s and 60s. During the 70s, economic relationship between India and the Soviet Union deepened and diversified in many critical areas of development for India. The material foundation of the relationship between India and the Soviet Union was laid by economic, scientific and technical cooperation covering a large and diversified field of heavy industry, bilateral trade on the basis of barter and long-term development projects in the field of scientific research.

The Soviet Union has assisted India in the construction and building of over 70 projects like steel, oil, coal mining and nuclear energy. In the face of protectionism followed by the Western countries, the Soviet Union is an important alternative market for India's foreign trade. The trade turnover between India and the Soviet Union in 1981-82 was Rs. 3,174 crores, the exports from India amounted to Rs. 1,921 crores, the Soviet Union imported goods worth Rs. 1,253 crores. Similarly in 1983 the expected trade turnover between the two countries is Rs. 3,625 crores. A serious problem between the two countries has emerged because the Soviet Union is facing a large deficit in trade with India, but efforts are being made to resolve it and achieve a proper balance.

Indo-Soviet relationship proves that political understanding facilitates the development of smooth foreign economic relations. Sometimes the opposite of this may not be true because many contradictory things happen in complex international relations and it is proved in the case of relationship between India and the USA that in spite of political difficulties, significant foreign economic relationships have developed. It must be emphasised here that the quality, content and depth of Indo-Soviet relationship depends on their common perspectives and appreciation of mutuality in international politics.[14]

Perspectives for the Eighties

Since the foreign policy-makers of a country have to make many adjustments with the dynamic international situation, premises underlying one phase of foreign policy of a country may not prove relevant and valid in the light of new developments. The decades of the Eighties would reveal growing militarism and international economic crisis, and the processes which are at work would create many difficulties and new challenges for Indian foreign policy-makers. Serious recession, unemployment, protectionism, closer links between the interests of the big economic power groups and capitalist state, and the role of international finance, banking institutions and transnationals reveal deepening of the crisis in capitalist countries and this crisis has a direct impact on the developing countries. President Fidel Castro correctly captures this picture when he states that:

> ...a new form of dependence is being imposed upon our countries, thus turning them into exporters of simple manufactured goods, trapped in the network of transnational production-marketing systems, while continuing to import capital and capital goods which determine the course of development.[15]

Further, India has to grapple with domestic economic crisis in the context of international crisis and India's strategy to deal with the emerging crisis situation was revealed by approaching the IMF for a loan of US$5 billion. This large-scale IMF loan would not help India to overcome its domestic crisis. T.P. Bhat rightly observes:

> The growing deficit in the balance of payments did deplete foreign exchange currency reserves. The deficit was financed by net aid flows, drawings from IMF Trust Fund, compensatory financing facility and drawing down in foreign currency assets. In order to meet the structural problems emerging from deteriorating balance of payments, India contracted a huge amount of loan from IMF....This, in effect, provided only a breathing time to the economy to get out of the current difficulties.[16]

The IMF loan and the conditionality clauses are not the only issues, the basic issue is growing dependence and linkage of Indian foreign economic policy with the capitalist world and the IMF loan to India has assured a significant role to international banks, transnationals and foreign exports to the Indian market. In spite of special efforts by the Government, India has an adverse balance of trade amounting to Rs. 4,000 crores to 5,000 crores per year. Hence the payment of interest on international loans and repayment of debts would create a serious crisis for foreign economic policy-makers at the end of the Eighties.

The IMF loan is only a signal for the difficulties of India; many new developments are taking place which would have a direct impact on the country's foreign economic policy. The international banks have surplus Eurodollars and the governments of capitalist countries have clearly asked India to borrow Eurodollars from banks on commercial terms and adjust with the slashing down of the concessional aid given by IDA, an affiliate of the World Bank. Many Indian capitalists and public sector undertakings are busy borrowing from the international banks. All public financing institutions like IDBI, ICICI, the Import-Export Bank, and all modern sectors of industry, public or private sector, are involved in financial and technological collaboration with the international banks and transnationals. The World Bank is also encouraging programmes of co-financing with the participation of commercial banks to the aid receivers. The Government of India has clearly stated that our burden of repayment of foreign loans and interest will be about Rs. 900 crores to Rs. 1,100 crores annually for the next ten years. The political motives and pressures of donor countries on vulnerable recipients of aid are well known and India has direct experience of pressure, dictation and arm-twisting by the aid-givers.[17]

The foreign economic relations of India during the 80s have posed qualitatively different issues than in the previous decades of the 50s, 60s and 70s. The IMF loan has successfully imposed import liberalisation on India which would perpetuate adverse balance of trade for years to come, and with the failure of the developing countries to achieve any breakthrough either at UNCTAD or GATT, situation for India is pretty difficult.

Crisis of Model of Diversification

The foundations of foreign economic relations of India were based on bargaining and diversification of the sources of foreign aid and trade, and this model was based on the premise that India would be able to build a relatively self-reliant economy to pursue the policy of non-alignment. This basic model of bargaining and diversification is in the process of erosion and India is getting effectively linked with the world capitalist system. The explanation for such an erosion lies in the crisis of the capitalist path of development followed by India. The domestic market base of Indian capitalism is quite narrow because more than 350 million people are out of the market system as they are living below the poverty line.

The leading classes of India and their political representatives have not exercised the difficult option of restructuring of agrarian relations and deepening and extension of the domestic national market. Politically, foreign aid and international borrowing has been considered a soft option and political representatives and leading classes are extending full support to the opening of the Indian market to international capital. When the soft and concessional aid by IDA, an affiliate of the World Bank, is shrinking, the Indian leadership has gone for commercial borrowing in the international market. It is not without reason that the International Finance Corporation, an affiliate of the World Bank, which has played a marginal role in India, has now opened an office in Delhi to attract foreign private investments to this country. IFC has been welcomed in India. In an editorial, the *Economic Times* commented:

> The major thrust of IFC operations will of course be directed at large-scale private and joint sector projects. In view of the overall shortage of investible resources for the private sector, especially for financing foreign exchange requirements, IFC is bound to play a crucial role in India's growth. Apart from its own funds, IFC has the additional advantage that it can raise syndicated finance through the international banking system. (August 11, 1983).

Thus IFC would act as a bridge and a link between India and the Consortium of international banks. The implication is quite clear, that India would be a junior partner under the umbrella of international finance.

The public policy-makers who still support the diversification and bargaining model of India's foreign economic relations advance two major arguments to defend their position. First, the world capitalist countries should not be viewed as a monolith. They have many contradictions amongst themselves and India can bargain with USA, EEC and Japan, which are three centres of global power. India is making efforts to get advantages from Japan, the EEC countries and USA on a competitive basis. After all India's exports to EEC in 1982 increased by 37 per cent, and Japan is taking new interest in India as is revealed by many Indo-Japanese collaborations like the Suzuki-Maruti project.

In response to this argument, it must be stated here that the capitalist countries deal with India as a solid bloc when it is convenient to them, and they also open themselves to India on a bilateral basis when it is profitable to them. The annual meetings of the Aid India Consortium are the best illustration of the united capitalist countries versus India. In the climate of recession, inter-capitalist competition increases and the industrialists of capitalist countries compete in the Indian market. But it is doubtful if India can manipulate inter-capitalist competition.

India is a leading advocate of South-South relationships, and the Government and industrialists are making active attempts to develop economic relationships with the developing countries. To attract rich oil-producing countries, India has opened the India Investment Centre at Abu Dhabi and has established many joint commissions with Third World countries.

In spite of sustained efforts by India, the rich oil-producing countries in the Third World have limited economic relations with our country. After all a large number of Third World countries are structurally linked with the capitalist world, and transnationals of the capitalist countries have definite advantages over the Indian firms. The oil-producing rich countries are investing in advanced capitalist countries and reaping a lot of profits out of it. The development of South-South linkages has many structural weaknesses and no firm policy can be built on it. South-South relationships have not provided an alternative market to India, and this explains our attempts to go again and again to the capitalist countries and their financial institutions. Indo-Soviet relationship is quite firm and deep, but it has serious limitations in acting as a catalyst for the resolution of India's crisis. The IMF loan proves this point beyond any shadow of doubt.

To sum up, the foreign policy of a country is part of a process of national and international development, and an effort should be made to identify trends in the process. The basic trend in India's foreign economic relations for the coming decade is penetration by the capitalist world and to quote President Castro the danger of India, like other Third World countries, becoming a production and trading subsidiary of transnational corporations. This would definitely bring about a subtle and sophisticated tilt in India's foreign policy towards the capitalist countries. The explanation for this disastrous development lies in the domestic politics of India and changes in the perceptions of the Indian leading classes which want a soft option of international tie-ups.

—*Mainstream*, Annual, 1983

NOTES AND REFERENCES

1. Peter Lassman (Ed.), *Politics and Social Theory,* London, Routledge, 1989.
2. Jawaharlal Nehru, *Letters to Chief Ministers 1947-64,* Volume I, 1947-49, Delhi, Oxford University Press, 1985, p. 23.
3. P.C. Joshi, *Institutional Aspects of Agricultural Development,* New Delhi, Allied Publications, 1987.
4. "Marked Rise in R&D Activities", *The Economic Times,* Delhi, May 22, 1989, p. 1.
5. *The Economic Times,* Delhi, April 29, 1989.
6. *Economic Survey: 1988-89,* Government of India, New Delhi, 1989, p. 103.
7. C.T. Kurien, "Indian Economy in the 1980s and in the 1990s", *Economic & Political Weekly,* Bombay, Vol. XXIV, No. 15, April 15, 1989, p. 797.
8. R.M. Sunderam, *Growth and Income Distribution in India: Policy and Performance since Independence,* New Delhi, Sage Publication, 1987.
9. For failure to relate social structural constraint with industrial deceleration see: I.J. Ahluwalia, *Industrial Growth in India: Stagnation since the Mid-Sixties,* New Delhi, Oxford University Press, 1985.
10. Atul Kohli, "Politics of Economic Liberalisation in India", *World Development,* Vol. 17, No. 3, 1989, p. 323.
11. Rostislav Ulyanovsky. "Neocolonialism: Forms and Methods", *Social Sciences* (Moscow), Vol. XIII, No. 4, 1982, p. 133.
12. For the struggles and politics of Indian capitalist class, see Rajat K. Ray, *Industrialisation in India: Growth and Conflict in the Private Corporate Sector, 1914-47,* Delhi, Oxford, 1979.
13. For details see R.K. Jain, *US-South Asian Relations, 1947-82,* New Delhi, Radiant Publishers, 1983, Vols. 1-3.
14. Bimal Prasad (ed.), *Indo-Soviet Relations, 1947-72: A Documentary Study,* Delhi, Allied, 1973.
15. Fidel Castro, *The World Economy and Social Crisis,* New Delhi, People's Publishing House, 1983.
16. T.P. Bhat, "Trends in International Trade Reflections on India", *Economic Trends,* Vol. XII, No. 1, April 1, 1983, New Delhi, FICCI (Supplement), p. 19.
17. For an opposite view, see Werner Handke, "Foreign Aid in Indian Domestic Politics", in *Aussen Politik* (Hamburg), Vol. 33, 4/82, pp. 408-15.

4

Congress: Rajiv to Sonia

The story of Indian politics beginning from October 31, 1984 to 2004-06 can be narrated by focusing attention on the ups and downs faced by the Congress during these twenty years. The rationale behind this approach is that the Congress, except for a brief period of 1977 to 1979, had dictated the agenda of Indian politics by occupying a dominant position in post-Independence India. Today the Congress is a pale shadow of its former self and Rajiv Gandhi was the last Prime Minister of the party with a majority support in Lok Sabha who completed his term beginning from October 31, 1984 to December 2, 1989. It has been suggested that Rajiv Gandhi won the Lok Sabha elections of 1984 only because of 'sympathy wave' which was created by the assassination of Indira Gandhi. Hence it was an 'abnormal' election and every other Lok Sabha election of 1989, 1991, 1996, 1998 and 2004 were normal elections and the voters of India did not give any clear verdict in favour of any party or group during the elections. The Congress could not get a clear majority in the Lok Sabha election of 1991 in spite of the fact that an attempt was made by the party to win over the sympathy of voters because of the assassination of Rajiv Gandhi in 1991. Further, the Congress party vacated its pre-eminent space which it had occupied from 1947 to 1989, its replacements were also not able to win over a clear majority in the Lok Sabha elections. The 'decline' of the Congress party led to the phenomenon of the formation of 'coalition governments' at the Centre beginning with V.P. Singh in 1989 to Manmohan Singh in 2004. V.P. Singh was Prime Minister from December 9, 1989 to November 10, 1990, Chandra Shekhar from November 10, 1990 to June 21, 1991, H.D. Deve Gowda from June 1, 1996 to April 21, 1997, Inder Kumar Gujral from April 21, 1997 to March 19, 1998 and Atal Bihari Vajpayee from March 19, 1998 to May 22, 2004. The only exception was P.V. Narasimha Rao who could manipulate to remain in office from June 21, 1991 to May 16, 1996. India entered a new phase of coalitional politics at the centre and consequently coalition governments have been either unstable or stable and it is very difficult to make any generalisation about the longevity of coalition governments in India. Why is it that the story of twenty years of Indian politics from 1989 to 2004-2006 is built around the Congress? The Congress has been an important player even when it has been in power or in opposition from 1989 to 2004-2006. The V.P. Singh government followed by Chandra Shekhar or H.D. Deve Gowda or Inder Kumar Gujral could form their short-lived coalition governments at the centre with the 'outside' support of the Congress, which was the major opposition party when not in power. The Congress party played the role of 'opposition' and did not extend any support to the BJP-led government of Atal Bihari Vajpayee from 1998-2004. Congress has remained a critical factor in Indian politics from 1989-2006 and this was the reason that politics of these years revolved around the Congress. V.P. Singh or Chandra Shekhar or H.D. Deve Gowda or Inder Kumar Gujral were stop gap and purely temporary Prime Ministers and the only notable achievement of V.P. Singh, for which he is remembered, is the announcement in August 1990 of the forgotten report of Mandal Commission for reservations of the backward castes. V.P. Singh felt politically threatened from his own supporters and he played a trick and announced the implementation of Mandal Commission but in spite of this, he could not save his position as Prime Minister of India. V.P. Singh survived in office from December 9, 1989 to November 10, 1990 on the basis of a full-fledged support of the BJP when the Sangh Parivar withdrew its support to V.P. Singh. L.K. Advani was the only beneficiary of political tricks played by V.P. Singh on Mandal Commission, and he launched the most infamous Yatra from Somnath to Ayodhya for the construction of Ram Temple by destroying the Babri Mosque.

The decade of the 1990s can be described as the phase of Divide and Rule in Indian politics. V.P. Singh laid the foundations of caste driven politics and the BJP succeeded in dividing Hindus and Muslims and elections were won or lost on the basis of targeting of caste versus caste and religion versus religion. A full-fledged caste-based and religion-based politics emerged in the1990s and the socially cohesive agenda of the Congress party completely failed to checkmate the casteist and communalist politics which dominated the political scene of India. The post Nehru-Indira and Rajiv Congress became just one of the player among multiple contenders of caste-based and religion-based competitions in electoral politics. Not only this. Even with P.V. Narasimha Rao's projection of "liberalisation, privatisation, globalisation and structural adjustment" could not become an alternative package for the voters in village India. It has been suggested that during 1991 Lok Sabha elections the Congress could emerge as the single largest party with 232 seats only because of 'sympathy factor' as a fallant of Rajiv Gandhi's assassination.

The Table 4.1 is helpful in understanding the growing erosion of the strength of the Congress and emergence of the party of Hindutva.

Table 4.1: Vote Share and Seats: Congress and BJP (1952-2004)

Sl. No.	*Year of Election*	*Total Seats*	*INC*		*BJS/BJP*	
			Seats	*% of Vote*	*Seats*	*% of Vote*
1.	1952	489	364	45.0	3	3.1
2.	1957	494	371	47.8	4	5.9
3.	1962	494	361	44.7	14	6.4
4.	1967	520	283	40.8	35	9.4
5.	1971	518	352	43.7	22	7.4
6.	1977	542	154	34.5	—	—
7.	1980	542	353	42.7	—	—
8.	1984	542	415	48.1	2	7.4
9.	1989	543	197	39.5	86	11.5
10.	1991	543	232	36.5	120	20.1
11.	1996	543	140	28.8	161	20.3
12.	1998	543	141	25.8	182	25.6
13.	1999	543	111	28.3	182	23.8
14.	2004	543	145	26.69	138	22.16

The Table 4.2 clearly shows that the dominance of Congress over national politics came to an end and the vacuum created by the decline of Congress has been filled by the BJP and other regional parties.

Table 4.2: Electoral Performance of Pan-Indian, Hindu Revivalist and Other Ethnic Parties: Share of Valid Vote (percentage wise) Election Year-wise

Party	*1952*	*1957*	*1962*	*1967*	*1971*	*1977*	*1980*	*1984*	*1989*	*1991*	*1996*
Congress	45.0	47.8	44.7	40.8	43.7	34.5	42.7	48.1	39.5	36.4	28.5
Others All	22.1	23.0	29.7	28.2	32.0	—	—	26.3	30.8	26.5	25.9
Pan Indian Parties	67.1	70.7	74.5	69.0	75.7	—	—	74.4	70.3	62.9	54.4
Hindu Revivalist Parties	5.9	7.2	7.7	9.4	7.4	—	—	7.5	11.6	21.0	21.4
Other Ethnic	5.6	4.2	6.6	7.8	7.0	8.1	6.5	10.0	12.9	12.6	13.5
Ethnic Parties	11.5	11.3	14.3	17.1.	14.4	—	—	17.5	24.5	33.6	34.9

Notes:

(1) The Congress denotes the Indian National Congress for 1952-69, Congress in 1971 and 1977, and Congress (I) thereafter.

(2) The main Hindu revivalist party, the Bharatiya Jan Sangh, merged with some Congress offshoots to form the Janata party in 1977 and remained part of it until after the 1980 elections. The Bharatiya Jan Sangh poll as many votes as all other ethnic parties combined from 1957 to 1971, the Janata party won in 1977 and was the second strongest party in 1980. So, it is difficult to distinguish the share of the pan-Indian parties from that of the Hindu revivalists for 1977 and 1980.

Table 4.3: National, State and Registered Parties Since 1989
(Cumulative seats and vote percentage)

Year of Election	*No. of National Parties*	*No. of State Parties*	*Registered Parties*	*Total*
9th Lok Sabha 1989	6 (471) (78.13)	8 (27) (6.24)	10 (19) (4.16)	24
10th Lok Sabha 1991	7 (470) (80.67)	13 (52) (9.93)	4 (4) (0.73)	24
11th Lok Sabha 1996	7 (403) (68.98)	19 (127) (18.97)	4 (4) (0.73)	30
12th Lok Sabha 1998	7 (387) (67.10)	20 (101) (17.76)	12 (49) (8.33)	39
13th Lok Sabha 1999	7 (369) (67.10)	23 (158) (23.34	8 (10) 1.50	38
14th Lok Sabha 2004	6 (364) 62.89%	22 (159) 28.90%	9 (15) 3.96%	37

Indian party system continued its fragmentation and the Table 4.3 clearly shows that the number of political competitors were proliferating and its impact was felt on the process of government formation at the Centre.

What has been the 'agenda of political mobilisation' in post-1989 India? V.P. Singh in 1990 took recourse to Mandal Commission recommendations it led to the emergence of full-fledged phenomenon of caste-based politics and following in the footsteps of V.P. Singh, Sonia Gandhi too Congress led has taken refuge behind caste-based politics by announcing the policy of reservations in educational institutions for the other Backward Castes in 2006. Caste-based politics is the order of the day and everyone from V.P. Singh to Sonia Gandhi is seen as following the path of mobilisation of caste against caste to establish a specific caste-based vote bank. The BJP, a party of Hindutva, launched a movement which led to the demolition of Babri Mosque at Ayodhya on December 6, 1992 and in this way caste versus caste politics was replaced by religion versus religion politics.

The Congress party from Rajiv Gandhi to Sonia Gandhi has been politically 'reactive' to the challenges posed by religion-based and caste-based political formations. Rajiv Gandhi had announced some new policies for the modernisation of India and his government announced literacy Mission and Missions for the spread of science and technology to rural areas. However, all his new ideas were overshadowed by political events of 1984 to 1989. Rajiv Gandhi had inherited contentious issues like Punjab problem and Assam problem and he tried to resolve these issues by signing peace accord on Punjab and Assam. Rajiv got involved in political controversies with Zail Singh, the President of India, and the other famous controversies were on the purchase of Bofors gun from Sweden. Zail Singh, had almost decided to 'dismiss' Rajiv Gandhi and V.P. Singh's campaign against Rajiv on Bofors gun issue had completely paralysed Rajiv's government. Rajiv Gandhi blundered badly on his dealing with the challenges posed by the forces of Hindutva on the issue of Ram Janmabhoomi-Babri Mosque controversy. Not only this. Rajiv had shown great confusion in his responses to the issue of Muslim Personal Law and the result of all this was that Rajiv-led Congress was defeated in 1989 Lok Sabha elections. The Indian Peace Keeping Force sent to Sri Lanka also brought brickbats to his style of foreign policy decision-making. Rajiv became leader of the opposition in the Lok Sabha in 1989 and his own erstwhile colleague V.P. Singh, who had walked out of the Congress, became Prime Minister though for a very short period from December 9, 1989 to November 10, 1990. After the split among the supporters of V.P. Singh, Chandra Shekhar assumed the office for a very short period from November 10, 1990 to June 21, 1991. The Congress returned to power and P.V. Narasimha Rao remained in power from June 21, 1991 to May 1996. Sonia Gandhi became the President of the Congress party in 1998 and under her leadership, the Congress could form a coalition government at the Centre in 2004.

What is the explanation for the decline of this Grand Old Party of India? Has India bid good-bye to the phenomenon of an all-India national party system? Has 'regional politics' replaced all-India party system? What are the prospects of a party of, by, and for the Hindus to emerge as an all-India alternative to secular all India Congress party?

India in the Twenty-First Century is faced with many open-ended questions in the sphere of politics. The core issue of India for the Twenty First Century is: How would the centripetal and centrifugal tendencies be managed politically?

RAJIV: HOPES RAISED AND RAZED

The assassination of Rajiv Gandhi on May 21, 1991 is an act of the section of society which does not believe in the power of ballot. The believers of the politics of bullet have again assaulted Indian democracy at a time when the electoral process was in full swing in the country. The timing of assassination of Rajiv Gandhi is quite significant because the assassins are determined to derail the electoral process in India. A peculiar feature of the centrist parties in India is their dependence on a single leader. If the leader is removed, the party is paralysed. Hence the assassins have to target the leader to achieve their goal of destroying a party and spreading political confusion in the country.

Rajiv Gandhi entered politics after the death of Sanjay Gandhi. Unlike his brother, Rajiv was quite reluctant to enter politics. When Rajiv Gandhi came to politics, he became the general secretary of the Congress-I and also an MP in 1980. He began his political journey from the Centre and he had no understanding of the complexities of grassroot politics of the country and also of the Congress party system. Since Mrs. Indira Gandhi presided over the Congress, Rajiv was inducted to learn the internal dynamics of the party and politics of the country.

After the assassination of Mrs. Indira Gandhi in 1984, the then President of India, Gyani Zail Singh, appointed Rajiv as the Prime Minister of India. Rajiv Gandhi and the Congress won the Lok Sabha elections of 1984 on the basis of "sympathy" factor and he was launched as the elected Prime Minister.

Rajiv started with many assets in 1984. First, he was different from his brother and mother. Both Sanjay and Indira Gandhi were linked with the Emergency regime of 1975-77 and a large section of political class was against the authoritarian politics of Mrs. Gandhi. Rajiv had nothing to do with the Emergency regime and the new Prime Minister in 1984 started with goodwill by the people who viewed him differently than his dominating mother.

Second, he applied a healing touch in the Punjab and Assam. The Rajiv-Longowal Accord of 1985 and the Assam Accord of 1985 were welcomed as a breakthrough in these two troubled States of India.

Mr. Clean

Third, the Indira Gandhi regime was suspected to be very corrupt by a section of the political class, and Rajiv was viewed as 'Clean'.

Fourth, Rajiv's performance as the Congress President was quite refreshing because the Congress under Mrs. Gandhi was a private property of the leader. Rajiv in his address at the Congress session in Bombay attacked 'power brokers' within the Congress, and promised to hold elections within the party.

The critics of Mrs. Gandhi and the Congress were quite happy with Rajiv because democratic Congress would safeguard Indian Democracy. If the Congress party does not practise internal democracy, such a party cannot be trusted to defend democracy in the country.

Fifth, Rajiv was young and modern and his outlook on economic development was welcomed by a section of the elite in India. Rajiv's attempts to liberalise and modernise Indian economy created a social constituency for Rajiv's economic policies.

Asset

Thus Rajiv's democratic credentials, a clean image and a moderniser became his great assets for the first two years of his becoming the Prime Minister. The Bofors bomb exploded and from 1987 to 1989, the Rajiv regime was on the defensive on the issue of corruption. From Clean to Corrupt was Rajiv's downhill journey. in India.

While Rajiv Gandhi's personal integrity was in question, many serious political questions also emerged on the scene. Rajiv and the President of India came to a head-long clash. Rajiv[1] as Prime Minister did not perform his constitutional responsibility of meeting the President. The President wanted to dismiss Rajiv. It would have been a constitutional blunder on the part of President Gyani Zail Singh. Rajiv was vehemently criticised for his childish behaviour vis-à-vis the President.

Rajiv's much promised election within the Congress remained on paper. Neither the elections were held nor the Congress leaders were trusted. A coterie of advisers and friends of Rajiv emerged as managers of politics. Rajiv also showed centralist tendencies of his mother when he dismissed Surjit Singh Barnala in 1987. A section of the political class disapproved Rajiv's action of dismissal of the Akali Dal government in Punjab in 1987. It was also alleged that the Barnala Ministry was dismissed with a view to influencing Haryana elections of 1987. The Congress was badly defeated in the Haryana Assembly elections.

Rajiv was also criticised for compromises with the Muslim fundamentalists on Muslim Personal Law. While Rajiv was welcomed as modern and forward looking leader, his compromise on the Shah Bano case revealed that his commitments to modernity were not deep.

Fragility

Rajiv's assassination has shown the fragility of the largest party of India. The killers have to kill the leader, and the party gets paralysed. The Congress politics is around personality, and the removal of the person can prove disastrous for a party. After Nehru's death, many tall leaders within the Congress were available to lead the party, K. Kamaraj, Morarji Desai, Lal Bahadur Shastri and many others were available to collectively lead the party. Mrs. Gandhi destroyed the collective leadership structure of the Congress. Rajiv promised to restore it, but failed to do it. Other parties should learn a lesson. The building of personality-cult in a party destroys the party in the long run. The democratic process in India cannot be entrusted to tall individuals without strong party organisations and collective leadership structures at all levels within the country.

—*The Financial Express*, 26 June, 1991.

•

THE CONGRESS PARTY: A CRISIS THAT'S AN INDIVIDUAL'S DOING

The brutal assassination of Rajiv Gandhi on May 21 has paralysed the Congress at a time when the election process for the Lok Sabha is on. While the National Front, the Left parties and the BJP are actively campaigning for the elections, the Congress organisation is in a shambles.

All efforts of the Congress are concentrated on finding a transitory arrangement to meet the current vacuum within the party. Such a deep crisis of the Congress was not witnessed when Pt. Jawaharlal Nehru died on May 27, 1964. Pt. Nehru was a tall personality whose impact was felt on the national affairs and also on the working of the Congress. After Pt. Nehru's death, the then Congress president K. Kamaraj evolved a consensus in favour of Lal Bahadur Shastri. The untimely death of Lal Bahadur Shastri in 1966 again brought the Congress organisational leadership to elect a successor to Shastri. The central and State leadership of the Congress performed this job by electing Mrs. Indira Gandhi whose candidature was contested by Morarji Desai. Thus neither Nehru's death nor Shastri's death immobilised the Congress in electing successors either through consensus or through properly contested elections.

Nomination

Mrs. Indira Gandhi's tragic assassination in October 1984, again brought the issue of succession and it was resolved by installing Rajiv Gandhi as Prime Minister of India. The procedure of nominating a successor to Mrs. Gandhi was fundamentally different from the procedures followed by the Congress in the post-Nehru phase. The fundamental characteristic of the post-Nehru Congress was its democratic functioning and procedures for electing the leaders. Mrs. Indira Gandhi slowly and gradually destroyed the Congress democracy and evolved a 'nomination culture' for running the Congress organisation. The result of Mrs. Indira Gandhi and Rajiv Gandhi's 'nomination culture' is pathetic situation within the Congress to find even a temporary successor to Rajiv. The present crisis is quite deep and the processes generated by Mrs. Indira Gandhi and Rajiv Gandhi are solely responsible for paralysis of the party.

The Congress party had a very strong all-India presence because its organisation was visible in all parts of the country. The party organisation was effective because it had built its structure on the basis of democratic elections within the party. The Congress had an army of leaders at the local, state and national levels. Leaders and personalities are very important in politics but the legitimacy of leaders depends on their democratic foundations. The Congress party organisation was based on the city Congress committees, the taluka Congress committees, the district Congress committees, the provincial Congress committees and the All-India Congress Committee. The Presidents of all these committees at various levels were elected persons and they carried enormous weight within the party.

The party was always involved in factional and personality politics, but the ultimate resolution of conflicts within the party was resolved democratically. Party democracy nourished the Congress. The Congress evolved a system of High Command whose essence was a collective leadership in the hands of tall Congress party leaders. Differences of opinion and dissent were the hallmark of Congress democracy and personality clashes where not unknown to the Congress. But democracy within the party was not scuttled. After Independence of India, the tall Congress leaders like Pt. Nehru, Sardar Patel, Abul Kalam Azad, Rajendra Prasad and others managed the Congress with the support of state level leaders who were equally important in their states and regions.

Mrs. Indira Gandhi inherited this kind of Congress party and it was a rich inheritance. Instead of building the Congress, she destroyed its essentials. Mrs. Gandhi inherited the tradition of factionalism and the culture of dissent within the Congress. She fought against factionalism and destroyed the democratic culture of dissent within the Congress. Instead of recognising that factional competition in the Congress reveals the co-existence of plural tendencies, she suppressed it.

Rich Heritage

The consequence of Mrs. Gandhi's approach to the Congress was the replacement of the collective leadership by the personality cult. Loyalty to leader replaced the spirit of tolerance of multiple leadership. The renewal of the Congress party came to an end because elections within the Congress were not held by Mrs. Gandhi. Instead of elected PCCs and elected PCC Presidents, Mrs. Gandhi started nominating party functionaries.

Cut to Size

The so-called chief ministers ceased to be effective spokesmen of their States because they were nominees of Mrs. Gandhi and not elected by the party at the State levels. Mrs. Gandhi removed popular leaders who had deep roots in their states and replaced them by rootless leaders by nominating them to the office of the chief minister.

A.R. Antulay in Maharashtra or Abdul Ghafoor in Bihar were nominated as Chief Ministers not because they represented the wishes of the Congress parties of Maharashtra or Bihar. The chief ministers and PCC presidents were not elected democratically but nominated by the leader. Even this practice of Mrs. Gandhi did not succeed in eliminating factionalism in the Congress. Instead of learning lessons in favour of democratic practices for the Congress, Mrs. Gandhi persisted in imposing leaders of her own choice.

Two inter-related issues demand a little probing and analysis. What were the political and personal reasons for Mrs. Gandhi to destroy democracy and collective leadership of the Congress? What were the reasons and explanations for the capitulation of tall leaders before Mrs. Gandhi? The Congress had split in 1969 and 1978. It reveals that many congressmen stood up against Mrs. Gandhi but the current was in her favour and a large number of Congress functionaries always succumbed before Mrs. Gandhi.

Dynasty

Mrs. Gandhi was personally bitter with many Congress leaders whom she thought as obstructionists. Mrs. Gandhi had a concept of prime ministership based on pre-eminence of the leader. Such a pre-eminent role of Mrs. Gandhi was contested by some tall leaders of the Congress from 1966 to 1969. Instead of resolving the issue of the role of Prime Minister, Mrs. Gandhi resolved to eliminate the critics within the Congress. And once some of these leaders of the Congress were marginalised, Mrs. Gandhi emerged as the tallest leader in the country.

Having established her unquestioned authority on the Congress. Mrs. Gandhi could have revived democracy in the party. It should have been clear to Mrs. Gandhi that an all-India party needs capable and acceptable leaders. Since Mrs. Gandhi did not revive party democracy even after establishing her supreme position, the explanation of her dynastic ambitions assumes credibility. Mrs. Gandhi weakened Congress leadership to pave the way for her children to assume power. Mrs. Gandhi had disposed of all challenges within the party against her family rule.

Further, Mrs. Gandhi became the fountain source of money for the Congress. The congressmen looked towards Mrs. Gandhi for money and electoral victories. The tinpot Congress leaders emerged on the scene who looked towards Mrs. Gandhi for patronage, protection and promotion in politics. Naturally, the vacuum of leadership within the Congress was beneficial for dynastic rule. Hence, the tragic end of dynasty has revealed the tragedy of the party which has no capacity to stand on its own.

If the Congress has not to disintegrate, it will have to reject the Indira-Rajiv Congress traditions. The Congress survival depends on the revival of the democratic traditions of the Congress. It is a big challenge to tinpot leaders of the Congress but they have no options. The Congress stands at the crossroads. The Party can either disintegrate or slowly renew itself by following democratic procedures. The Congressmen have to blame themselves for their pathetic situation where they find themselves as leaderless and rudderless. —*The Financial Express*, 9 September, 1991.

PUNJAB AS WE SEE IT: POLITICS AND ECONOMICS DON'T MIX

The politics of guns has destroyed secular and democratic politics in Punjab. Thc ongoing orgy of killings in Punjab has seriously fractured inter-community relations and mutual suspicion has taken over inter-community normal relations. A few explanations have been offered to understand the tragedy of Punjab. It has been suggested that the Green Revolution in Punjab has exhausted its potential for future development. Such a development should have been anticipated by the public policy-makers and industrialisation of Punjab should have been taken up in right earnest as a logical step after the Green Revolution.

Can the politics of guns industrialize Punjab? Can the destruction of secular and democratic politics help in the economic development of Punjab? The political economy approach to the understanding of terrorism in Punjab ends up as a rationalisation of the cult of violence. The central issue is that the terrorist option was exercised to achieve genuine and imaginary grievances of a section of the Sikh community during the 1980s in Punjab. During the 1950s, 1960s and 1970s, Punjab's economic and political developments were linked with the progress of democracy in the state. Many political parties competed in Punjab politics and many tall Sikh leaders gained political power through democratic participation. Sardar Pratap Singh Kairon, Parkash Singh Badal and Gyani Zail Singh were Chief Ministers and they contributed to the building of a modem Punjab by operating democratic political institutions. The Sikh community enjoyed full religious freedom on the basis of which the Shiromani Gurudwara Prabandhak Committee operated the gurudwaras. Jagdev Singh Talwandi, G.S. Tohra, Harchand Singh Longowal and Parkash Singh Badal operated freely as religious and political leaders of the Sikh community in the democratic Punjab.

The political economy explanation is therefore, inadequate to grapple with the rising tide of terrorism in Punjab. It has been suggested that Sant Jarnail Singh Bhindranwale was created by Mrs. Indira Gandhi to manipulate Akali politics. It is maintained that manipulative politics of Mrs. Gandhi is responsible for the tragedy of Punjab. This explanation is also partially correct. Even before Mrs. Gandhi's discovery of Bhindranwale, the Congress Party and the Akali Dal had competed in democratic politics and many Akali leaders notably Sardar Swaran Singh, left the Akali Dal to join the Congress. What Mrs. Gandhi did in 1980 was not new in the party politics of Punjab. Mrs. Gandhi's creation grew into a monster in collusion with the All-India Sikh Student Federation. Gun politics emerged in Punjab in 1983 which culminated in the assassination of Mrs. Indira Gandhi. Even as the community was recovering from the shock of operation Blue Star, the November 1984 riots against the Sikhs in Delhi, Kanpur and Bokaro set the clock back. This led to the legitimisation of terrorism in Punjab. The Sikhs were hurt and hence terrorism in Punjab became respectable.

The justification of terrorism in Punjab on the basis of the Sikh psyche is partially correct. The Blue Star Operation of June 1984 was not fatalistically inevitable. What was the role of the Sikh leadership in the building of Bhindranwale cult during 1983-84? Talwandi, Tohra, Badal and Longowal failed to confront Bhindranwale taking over the Akal Takht and the conversion of the Golden Temple as the headquarters of terrorist activity. The Blue Star Operation was Mrs. Gandhi's failure but all tall Sikh leaders and the Sikh institutions were equally responsible for the tragedy. Similarly, the November 1984 riots against innocent Sikhs drew condemnation from democratic forces within India. The assaulted Sikh community was not isolated from the democratic mainstream of India during November 1984 riots. The failure of Sikh leadership was to permit the terrorists to appropriate the feelings of hurt of the Sikh community. Every event weakened the democratic forces and every acceleration of terrorism brought tragedy to Punjab.

A new chapter was added to Punjab on the basis of the Rajiv-Longowal Accord of July 24, 1985. Within a few days of the Accord, the terrorists assassinated Sant Longowal. The architect of Punjab Accord died and with him the basis of an accord also collapsed. By this action the terrorists and their supporters gave a clear message that they want secession of Punjab. The goal of Khalistan was unambiguously stated by the symbolic killing of Sant Longowal. Even after this, many Akali leaders like G.S. Tohra, and Jagjivan Singh Ummranangal have been targets of the killers in Punjab. Within three years, i.e. from 1984 to 1987, terrorists regrouped themselves and again captured the Golden Temple for terrorist activities. The High Priests of the Akal Takht were not spared by terrorists and Darshan Singh Ragi had to run away from the Golden Temple. In 1987, the Black Thunder Operation had to be launched to remove the terrorists from the Golden Temple. The Black Thunder was a grand success and terrorists emerged as very small people and their image as heroes was completely demolished.

It has been suggested that if Chandigarh is transferred to Punjab, the detained Sikhs at Jodhpur are released and if the guilty of November 1984 riots are punished, a new chapter in Punjab could be opened. It was further argued that the Black Thunder Operation of 1987 had completely exposed the terrorists and it was a good opportunity to start a new chapter in Punjab. The Lok Sabha elections of 1989 brought new hopes to Punjab because V.P. Singh made tall promises of a healing touch. He was supported in this approach by Inder Kumar Gujral but new star had emerged in Punjab by the name of Sardar Simranjit Singh Mann. The euphoria built up by the V.P. Singh government failed to resolve the Punjab issue. Chandra Shekhar succeeded V.P. Singh as Prime Minister in November 1990 and wild hopes were raised that negotiations can take place with Sardar Simranjit Singh Mann who had united all the factions of the Akali Dal. Mann's leadership has been vetoed by terrorist groups and the Chandra Shekhar Government is also dead-locked in Punjab.

The above developments have solidified terrorism in Punjab. The terrorists define their agenda and implement it. They have a so-called reform movement which they implement with the help of the gun. They have a code for the print media and they implement it by killing the innocents connected with the print media.

It has been maintained that the political process should be started in Punjab and solutions will emerge if the State Assembly elections are held. This is based on another argument that the bureaucracy and police in Punjab are responsible for the alienation of the Sikhs. Unless alienation of the Sikhs is redressed, terrorism cannot end in Punjab. The masses of Punjab are suffering from the tyranny of the police and the tyranny of the terrorists. Both must end. It is also maintained that many innocents have been killed by the police in fake encounters. Police repression has increased the ranks of terrorists. Such a logic leads to equating of the Indian State with the terrorists. Both are an evil. This way of reasoning is completely flawed. The police, with all its imperfections, is performing the job of protecting the citizens against terrorist attacks. It is well known that the terrorists are well armed and they are protected with in and outside India. Within India, the judiciary in Punjab has collapsed. Hence trials against suspected terrorists cannot be held because of fear in the judiciary. Outside India, the terrorists have a sanctuary in Pakistan. All efforts of the Indian police to deal with terrorism in Punjab come to grief because of these two reasons. It must be clearly understood that the Indian State is handicapped in its dealings with terrorists because neither the leaders of the Sikh community are available to stand against terrorism nor is the crippled judiciary able to facilitate justice.

It must be stated that explanations for the growth of terrorism in Punjab around the political economy, or the hurt Sikh psyche, or brutality of the police or the role of Pakistan are partial and like all partial explanations they are flawed.

Terrorism in Punjab has grown in strength because the political response of the Indian State has been based on manipulations, vacillations and opportunistic compromises. Political consensus in India is a pre-requisite for the solution of Punjab problem—the starting point for which has to be a consensus that terrorism is an illegitimate activity and a challenge to democracy and secularism. Further, it has to be clearly understood that the Sikh community's real or imaginary grievances can be tackled and accommodated only within the Indian democracy.

In its fight against terrorism in Punjab, the Indian State is fighting the cause of the Sikh community which is not able to participate in the democratic process because of terrorism. It has to be a part of the political vocabulary in India that Sant Longowal was assassinated not by the Indian state but by the terrorists.

The Indian State has to be on an ideological offensive against terrorism. The terrorists want Khalistan, the Indian state should unambiguously champion the cause of Indian unity because the Sikh masses do not want secession. It must be stated that the political process in Punjab has been derailed by the gun-wielding killers. Elections in Punjab were held in difficult situations in 1985 and 1989. Elections will be held in future also if political parties are free to campaign during the elections and newspapers are free to publish news and views. The democratic process has been assaulted by terrorists because a democratic verdict is against secession. Terrorism in Punjab can be combated if all the national political parties agree that democratic process in Punjab can not be restored without taming the terrorists. During the 1980s, terrorism in Punjab emerged as a marginal activity and in due course it took over the whole State. The advocates of a quick solution are responsible for the lease of life to the terrorists.

A lesson from the Naga insurgency of the 1950s and 1960s may be mentioned here. Unlike Punjab, the Naga leadership was not part of the mainstream democratic politics of India. Hence the fight against Naga insurgency was to bring the people into the democratic process of India. The Indian Army fought against the Naga insurgency and the political process accommodated the Nagas within the Indian democratic arrangement. In Punjab, the terrorists have been trying to take the Sikh community out of the mainstream of the Indian democratic process. Punjab was and continues to be an integral part of mainstream India. Hence the Indian State has a great responsibility to fight against terrorism and to restore to Punjab its place of honour in India.—*The Financial Express*, 3 March, 1991.

PUNJAB, ASSAM: TURMOIL ALL THE WAY!

The announcement of the Government of India to hold the Lok Sabha and the State Assembly elections in the troubled states of Punjab and Assam has evoked sharp and mixed responses within the country. The Chandra Shekhar government, the President of India and the Election Commission had serious differences of opinion on the issue of elections in Punjab and Assam. The President of India sent back to the Central Cabinet the ordinance for the holding of elections and the Council of Ministers reiterated its recommendation. The President of India agreed to issue the notification for the holding of elections in the two troubled states only after the Council of Ministers reconsidered and reiterated its recommendation to the President.

T.N. Seshan, the Chief Election Commissioner (CEC) announced that elections in Punjab will be held on May 20 and in Assam on May 23 along with the other states in India. The only exception is J & K where elections will not be held now. Within a few hours of the announcements of the dates, the CEC received a letter from the Home Secretary to the Government of India that May 20 and May 23 for Punjab and Assam are not suitable for the holding of elections and they may be held after elections are over in the other states of India. The Government of India has suggested June 10, and June 20 for elections in Assam and Punjab. The Government of India, the President and the Election Commission could resolve their differences on elections after hectic consultations, the national political parties are in the process of formulating their strategies to meet the challenge of elections in Punjab and Assam.

On Assam, various political parties may decide in favour of elections. On Punjab, the first reaction of the Congress-I and the CPI-M was extremely sharp and they announced the boycott of elections. The CPI and the BJP have announced an extreme action of the boycott of elections. A few details about the political situation in Punjab and Assam may be mentioned to provide a perspective on elections in these two states.

The 1980s has witnessed the growth of terrorism in Punjab. The first victim of terrorism in Punjab was the Congress government headed by the late Darbara Singh. The terrorists had killed innocent passengers travelling in a bus, and the President rule was imposed in Punjab in 1983 and the Darbara Singh Ministry was dismissed. The situation in Punjab deteriorated and June 1984 witnessed the Operation Blue Star, the assassination of Mrs. Indira Gandhi and the November 1984 riots against the innocent Sikh community in some major cities of India.

The Accord

The Rajiv-Longowal Accord of 1985 led to the holding of elections in Punjab and the Akali Dal formed a government under Surjit Singh Barnala. The Barnala government was dismissed in 1987 and the Central Government undertook the Black Thunder Operation to clear the Golden Temple from the occupation of the terrorists.

Terrorism persisted in spite of the Blue Star and Black Thunder operations and despite the dismissal of the Darbara Singh and Surjit Singh Barnala governments. Neither democratic governments nor the President's rule could contain terrorism in Punjab. Another democratic opportunity was provided to Punjab during the Lok Sabha elections of 1989. The leaders supported by the terrorists like Attinder Pal Singh, Bimal Khalsa and Simranjit Singh Mann were elected to the Lok Sabha. It was assured that the participation of these leaders in the democratic process will open new opportunities for negotiated settlement of the problem of Punjab. This hope was not fulfilled. After the Lok Sabha elections of 1989, and the success of the terrorist supported candidates in 1989 elections, the situation in Punjab deteriorated.

During 1990-91, the Central Government had to change the Governors to control the situation. O.P. Malhotra, the present Governor is a former Military General.

These developments have convinced an important section of the political class that administrative actions have proved inadequate. Punjab needs democratic openings so that political representatives of the people of Punjab play a role to resolve Punjab crisis. Bureaucratic and police responses to terrorism have complicated the issues because a simple law and order approach is inadequate to meet the genuine aspirations of the people. Further, if bureaucracy is not accountable, it behaves in an authoritarian manner. The innocent citizens become a victim of double oppression, i.e., terrorist oppression and bureaucratic highhandedness and arbitrariness. This vicious circle should be broken in Punjab by holding the Lok Sabha and the State Assembly elections.

The opponents of elections in Punjab are major democratic parties who contend that 'fair and free elections in Punjab cannot be held because 'peaceful' conditions for elections in Punjab do not exist. The targets of terrorist's killings are political activists of major parties and newspapers in Punjab. Elections depend on free campaigning and holding of meetings. In Punjab, the democratic parties have to campaign against the terrorists, the secessionists and the political culture of the gun. Elections in Punjab will polarise the democratic nationalist forces against the foreign inspired terrorists and religio-fundamentalists.

Gun-Toting

The campaigning by the terrorists will be done on the basis of AK 47 rifles to terrorise the voters into submission. How would the democratic parties spread their message to the voters? It has been very firmly suggested that during the 1989 Lok Sabha elections, the results of a sizable Lok Sabha constituencies was determined by the gun. How could Attinder Pal Singh or Bimal Khalsa or Simranjit Singh Mann win the elections? Did they have any political or democratic background to contest the elections? The only qualification of these candidates was that they were acceptable to the terrorists.

The history of the 1989 Lok Sabha elections will be repeated on a much larger scale in 1991 especially in the State Assembly elections. The State Assembly elections can be managed effectively by the terrorists and the candidates supported by them can win a majority of seats in the assembly.

The democratic parties with a nationalist cause in Punjab are at a disadvantage in facing the terrorists because free campaigning during the elections will not be possible. The United Akali Dal leader, Simranjit Singh Mann, is propagating the goal of 'Azadi' or Khalistan. The traditional Akali leaders' like G.S. Tohra or P.S. Badal are quite irrelevant in the Sikh politics. The All-India Sikh Student's Federation will provide men and muscles to various militant candidates who are committed to Khalistan. Peace is a pre-condition for elections in Punjab.

The supporters and opponents of elections in Punjab have different perspective on the reality of democratic electoral process in Punjab. The supporters are the Janata Dal, the Janata Dal (S) and the United Akali Dal (Mann) and the opponents are all major national parties like the Congress (I), the CPI (M), the CPI and the BJP. The major national parties are not against the elections per se but on the issue of appropriate dates for elections and the capacity of the Government to hold 'peaceful' elections which will be free and fair.

Thus the holding of elections in Punjab is a gamble. It may open the democratic process for negotiated settlement. The situation can worsen. If the terrorists supported candidates capture the State Assembly, they are surely determined to internationalise Punjab issue. The common man in Punjab is caught between the gun of the terrorist and the authoritarianism of the bureaucracy. This is the dilemma of a common citizen of Punjab.

Big Gamble

Similarly, the political class is also divided on the issue of solutions to Punjab problem. Administrative approach has not brought any solution to Punjab problem. Why not try a democratic solution?

Two approaches may be suggested to deal with Punjab problem. The reasoning of democratic nationalist parties should be taken very seriously. The State Assembly controlled by terrorists supported MLAs is bound to play havoc with the Indian nation. First, all democratic nationalist parties in Punjab should contest a United electoral battle. The issue of nationalism versus secessionism should be the rallying point of elections. Second, during the 1980s, Punjab problem has been complicated because of politics of manipulations by the national parties in India. A common policy framework based on genuine consensus can be evolved to respond to Punjab. The national parties should evolve a genuine national consensus on Punjab to meet the electoral and post-electoral situations in Punjab.

Assam Story

The Assam story is as complicated as that of Punjab. During the 1980s, Assam has witnessed an agitation against the Central Government. While the AASU-AGP agitation was in full swing, the late Indira Gandhi ordered elections in Assam in 1983. The AASU-AGP boycotted the elections and it was a very successful boycott. Thousands of innocent people were massacred after the elections in Nellie.

During 1985, Rajiv Gandhi signed an accord with the AASU-AGP. The elections to the State Assembly were held in 1985 and the AGP formed the Government. The AGP Government during 1985-1990 was involved in intra-party factionalism.

The United Liberation Front of Assam (ULFA) took to arms for the secession of Assam and the State Government of Assam failed to check the growing terrorism indulged by the ULFA. Many activists of the ULFA were erstwhile colleagues and members of the AASU-AGP movement. This was a handicap for the Assam Government in its dealing with the ULFA challenge. While the AASU-AGP state government launched many anti-Centre agitations during 1985-90, its response to the ULFA challenge was weak and even compromising. The Central Government dismissed the Prafulla Mohantta Government of Assam, and deployed the Indian Army to deal with the ULFA insurgents. A question arose: How do we deal with the Assam problem? Like Punjab, an extended and longdrawn law and order approach to Assam may worsen the situation. Why not hold the elections in Assam?

The ULFA made the Congress party activists as their targets of attack and it also asked other parties not to participate in the elections. The elections in Assam have been announced and the ULFA has declared a ceasefire. An apprehension exists in Assam that the ULFA will break this ceasefire after the elections and troubled Assam will become an area of ULFA insurgency. The major national parties and the regional parties in Assam are reconciled to elections in June 1991.

A fundamental fact of Punjab and Assam problem is foreign support to the terrorist movements for secession and elections cannot resolve this issue. The 'low cost war' through insurgency is fought by foreign powers by supporting terrorist and secessionist movements in Punjab, Assam and J & K and the secessionist movements have strong international linkages and the foreign intervention can take place during the elections.

How can Pakistan ignore Punjab elections? Pakistan is fully involved in terrorist movement in Punjab. The Government of India will have to show a lot of vigilance during Punjab elections regarding the flow of money and arms to Punjab terrorists from Pakistan. Similarly, in Assam, the ULFA has a network of linkages with other insurgent groups in North-East India who have foreign patrons.

Elections in Punjab and Assam are a big gamble and a lot of vigilance will have to be maintained by the Government of India to ensure free and fair elections. The foreign intervention during the elections is a reality which cannot be ignored. Restoration of democracy in Punjab and Assam is a laudable goal but it puts immense responsibilities on the shoulders of the Government. —*The Financial Express*, 28 April, 1991.

THE CACOPHONY OF RESERVATION POLITICS

The politics of V.P. Singh, Lalu Prasad Yadav and Mulayam Singh Yadav, has accelerated and intensified caste confrontations in North India. During the last 47 years, multiple social constituencies have been mobilised on the basis of primordial loyalties. However, the new phase of caste politics is fundamentally different from the early post-Independence political process in India.

First, the Congress evolved a coalition of high caste Hindus, Scheduled Castes and Scheduled Tribes to win elections. The Congress system of a 'patron and client' caste coalition did not target castes outside its coalitional politics.

V.P. Singh, and the Yadavs, Lalu Prasad, Mulayam Singh, have mobilised the upwardly mobile backward peasant castes by targeting the upper caste domination which is presented as a historical fact of Indian society. The 'new caste politics' is confrontational because it is situated in the philosophy of 'undoing the cruelties of history' whose present representatives and custodians are upper caste Hindus, irrespective of their economic status.

Such a mobilisation of caste in politics has been built around 'hatred' and the manageable levels of social violence. This has been happening during the last four years of caste politics and is a definite break from the earlier phase of Indian politics.

Second, the Congress system, while winning the elections on the basis of a 'caste coalition', did not govern the country on the basis of mere caste factors. A political party mediates and harmonises conflicting and competing social interests after winning elections because the government stands for the whole society.

It is true that such neutral governance is a 'pure model' but a ruling party by definition is 'relatively autonomous' of its specific social support structure.

The Janata Dals or the Samajwadi party on the other hand, are not political formations of an autonomous character. They are mere instruments in the hands of the elite of their castes.

This is a casteisation of politics where the upwardly mobile backward peasant castes and the elite of the other dalit castes are not mere voters; they are the rulers. The only yardstick of governmental performance in Uttar Pradesh and Bihar is the successful promotion and protection of specific caste interests.

Lalu Prasad and Mulayam Singh have to show to their caste supporters that their governments are openly practising policies of discrimination against the so-called upper castes.

The current phase of caste politics is a negation of the modernisation and secularisation of Indian society and polity. How can such a reversal of history go unchallenged by the secular and modern intelligentsia of the country? How can maverick caste operators receive intellectual support?

Democratic politics is based on multiple sources of legitimacy. The ongoing casteisation of society and erosion of the secularisation process has great intellectual support in India.

Ram Manohar Lohia in the fifties made a powerful intellectual case against Western capitalism and Soviet-type Communism. He evolved a complex model of an Asian path for peasant societies and specifically for India. He pleaded for mobilising the backward castes for social change and a peasant model of socialism.

Those who believe in the progressive potential of backward castes in democratic politics in India can be traced to Lohia's 'Asian model'. Many caste reform movements have been in existence in India and they have exercised great influence over social change in various regions of the country. But caste mobilisation for elections to change peasant India for egalitarianism was Lohia's contribution.

It is not without reason that Mulayam Singh Yadav claims legitimacy from Lohia in spite of the fact that so-called socialists like Sharad Yadav, Ram Vilas Paswan, Lalu Prasad or Mulayam Singh have caricatured Lohia by ignoring his complex social philosophy that too without answering some important questions about the serious limitations of the Lohia model.

First Lohia was extremely marginal in Indian politics because the Congress' caste coalition was more successful in gradually changing Indian society. Second, many progressive socialist contemporaries of Lohia, did not accept Lohia's diagnosis or analysis as relevant for India.

Lohia's claim that the backward peasant castes have the potential of causing progressive change in India was a non-starter even when he was alive. Charan Singh, the most conscious caste and class leader of the upwardly mobile peasants, never practised caste exclusivism. The current caste leaders cannot appropriate even the politics of Charan Singh because he imbibed some values of the national movement and dissociated himself from Lohia.

A section of academics led by Rajni Kothari has projected the role of caste in politics as a secularisation of society. Kothari, in his numerous writings on caste in Indian politics, has maintained that, "in reality, the consequences of caste-politics interactions are just the reverse of what is usually stated. It is not politics that gets caste-ridden, it is caste that gets politicised" and in the process India will move towards modernity on the basis of traditionalisation process.

It is not without reason that Kothari was excited by V.P. Singh's acceptance of the Mandal Commission report. If intellectuals like him have any commitment to modernisation in India, a visit to the villages and towns of Uttar Pradesh and Bihar will suffice to find out that not only is modernisation in a mess but its very element has been eroded by casteism.

Caste relations have always been oppositional and conflictual. The caste system is based on an ideology which determines the world view, beliefs and value structures of every *jati* and sub-*jati* in India. Caste is a system of social organisation with a view to hierarchically organise society on the basis of '*do's* and *dont's*' for every *jati*.

Rajni Kothari escapes by taking an easy way and saying Indian modernisation will proceed by involving traditional social categories in the new democratic process. The real issue is to weaken caste loyalties by making people transcend the local and attain the cosmopolitan.

Politics has to play a crucial and critical role in the process of modernisation. Caste loyalties have to be weakened before they are replaced by new reference points which are secular. Jawaharlal Nehru had this vision because he linked his modernisation enterprise with nation-building.

Politics of goals was the tool of mobilisation. Gradually, socially weaker sections were changing their social status and politics consciously followed policies of social accommodation.

Caste politics minus that of nation-building is the current reality and caste competition has been deliberately accentuated so that V.P. Singh or Lalu Prasad or Mulayam Singh do not have to answer questions regarding their governmental performance.

It will be helpful to intellectuals like Rajni Kothari to listen to the warning of Paul Brass in his *Ethnicity and Nationalism* (1991): "Political and economic elites who make use of ethnic group attributes are constrained by the beliefs and values which exist within the group and which limit the kinds of appeals which can be made".

Ethnic politics in India has the same dangers as caste politics. Leaders strengthen ethnicism and casteism because their universe is limited and only confrontations can bring political dividends. In the process, neither is caste weakened nor can it be used for social harmony and governance.

—*The Hindustan Times*, 12 September, 1994.

MANDAL HAS DEVOURED ITS MARXIST MESSIAHS

A powerful intellectual support to the practitioners of low caste politics has come from the radical secular intelligentsia because the former leaders have talked of the same social goals of egalitarianism as the latter have claimed to believe in V.P. Singh, Mulayam Singh Yadav and Lalu Prasad Yadav are the new messiahs of social justice and the radical intelligentsia has actively supported their caste politics.

In politics, excellent slogans have been coined by dictators and even power-seekers in a democracy. Rural India cannot have growth with equity without land reforms and appropriate institutional answers for land and wage contradictions.

What is the track record of the current practitioners of caste politics in rural restructuring?

The nature of contradiction in the most backward states of Uttar Pradesh and Bihar is on the 'land question' and the 'wage question'. The social class which is led by V.P. Singh, Mulayam Singh and Lalu Prasad in the real villain along with other dominant groups.

The radical intelligentsia should see the record of these two State Governments and seek the so-called qualitative differences between the earlier regimes in U.P. and Bihar and the present political formations.

If political rhetoric makes leaders radical and acceptable to the progressive intelligentsia, these new legitimisers are fully responsible for the atmosphere of caste hatred in the villages and towns of U.P. and Bihar.

Marxist analysis of caste in India was linked with the overall materialistic interpretation of history and its concrete application to the social reality of India. D.D. Kosambi, an important Marxist historian, analysed caste as an arrangement where India achieved social stability without large-scale violence. This, which European societies were formed on the basis of violence.

Caste's negative consequence was that Indian forces of production and relation of production remained backward and the crisis in feudalism did not lead to the resolution of contradiction since caste, as a stabilisation factor, operated in full strength. Thus caste in India played a highly negative and regressive role.

E.M.S. Namboodiripad and many other Marxist intellectuals maintain that caste in India played a class role because it was a social arrangement for the appropriation of surplus value by determining the social status of the Scheduled Castes as labouring classes. Thus the 'twice-born' and the *shudra* were related in such a manner that the *shudra* was an Indian variant of the slave.

Contemporary India beginning, with the late 19th century has been involved in a new economics, where, with all its weakness, distortion and fault, the capitalist system of production has come to stay.

In spite of the fact that caste may have played a class role, in contemporary India, caste is a relic of the backward, feudal past. India is burdened by history and the new India has to struggle against many inherited categories and loyalty structures.

Caste belongs to the past social arrangements and it has to be opposed. Only then can class consciousness emerge in India. Caste limits and divides; class consciousness is based on a larger solidarity where members of a class transcend every local loyalty including their status in their own factory or farm.

It must be a great surprise to even V.P. Singh, Mulayam Singh and Lalu Prasad that a rich reservoir of Marxist intellectuals see them as revolutionaries and liberators of the downtrodden. The Marxists are not worried that caste politics in U.P. and Bihar has completely pushed them away even from their traditional areas of strength. Trade unionists in Bihar and *kisan* leaders in U.P. have become ciphers in the face of assertive backward casteism.

Marxists are committed to an 'alternative politics' which requires strengthening of the ongoing democratic revolution in India. India is a society of many contradictions but it is the democratic process which has made people assertive.

Mass struggles have to be launched to deepen the forces of democratic revolution. Will intensification of caste divisions strengthen the forces of united mass struggles?

Casteisation of trade unions and *kisan sabhas* cannot be stopped if the caste discourse becomes the dominant ideology of politics. The caste ideology is a historical specificity of India. It is involved in an antagonistic contradiction with the class ideology. Class mobilisation is fundamentally different from caste mobilisation. Mobilisation of textile or steel or workers is different from the mobilisation of Yadavs, Kurmis and Koeris.

—*The Hindustan Times*, 17 October, 1994.

RELIGIOUS QUOTA WILL DERAIL SECULARISM

Since the public announcements of important political leaders have to be taken seriously, their arguments in favour of reservations for a religious community deserve close attention. One argument is that specific policies are required to help the Muslim community emerge from its current backwardness. Two reasons are advanced in favour of reservations to so liberate the community. First, public policy in a democratic country has to aim at special community interests and Muslims in India require affirmative action to achieve at least a measure of equality with other religious communities. Secondly, if the policy of reservations for the Scheduled Castes and Scheduled Tribes is legitimate, so are reservations for the Muslims.

Fallacious Reasons

These seemingly weighty arguments are fallacious because the social status of the Scheduled Castes and Tribes is not comparable with that of any other group in India. The oppressed *shudras* in India are the victims of long years of social, religious and cultural prejudices against them. The *shudras* were oppressed by the twice-born castes and the land owning classes who saw them as a means to enhance their personal wealth. Indeed, the Indian variant of slavery is represented by the *shudras*. The Muslim community cannot claim the same rights because it has never been exploited as a religious community.

The institutional arrangements in India, whether social, economic or political, have created prosperity and deprivations in a secular manner and these processes cut across religious boundaries. The agenda for the eradication of poverty and social backwardness is a secular agenda and to link it with religiously-determined social backwardness will destroy the country's secular foundations. The history of the wretched in India is fundamentally different from the history of Indian Muslims and hence the latter cannot advance the argument of injustices of history to claim reservations. The only and real victims of Indian history are the *shudras* and the redressal of their historical grievances through reservations is a legitimate democratic agenda. Reservations for Muslims is a sectarian political agenda.

It is often claimed that the bureaucracy discriminates against the Muslim community and that, therefore, an increase in its representation in the public service, will safeguard its legitimate interests. It is similarly also suggested that the police is often biased while dealing with the Muslims. These are serious allegations against the essentially secular nature of the Indian administration and they must be rebutted. If the police and the bureaucracy are sometimes moved by communal considerations, the remedy does not lie in reserving a quota for a religious community but in purging the secular institutions of such communal elements.

The struggle in India is to strengthen the secular forces and this calls for a clear stand against militant communalism of all kind. Any quota based communal representation in the public services will not just communalise the country as a whole but also turn it into a confederation of religious communities. The Indian state apparatus cannot remain secular if religion becomes the basis of entry into the public services. If this is done, there can always be an argument for extending reservations to Muslims in the state assemblies too. Will India be better governed by a religious-quota based elected Parliament? The answer is an emphatic no.

Total Negation

If an individual enters a public institution on the basis of a religious quota, he will always remain partial to his religious community. The 'us and them' syndrome which governs religious identities in India will only be strengthened by religion-based reservations. Democracy will be derailed if public policies encourage the institution of a permanent minority and a permanent majority. The self-appointed guardians of social justice seem determined to destroy the interdependence involved in social relations. This is a total negation of our struggle for freedom and the cherished goals of democratic and secular India. It is not without reason that the CPM has alerted the nation against the policy of reservations for Muslims as advocated by Kesri, Mulayam Singh Yadav and Lalu Prasad Yadav. It deserves to be mentioned here that the BJP wants this kind of policy which is consistent with its religion-based politics.—*The Times of India*, 3 December, 1994.

FOLLY OF RESERVATIONS

The Constitution (Amendment) Bill which provides for 33 per cent of reserved seats for women in the Legislatures has not been openly opposed by any political party or group because everyone wants to be branded as progressive by empowering the effectively disenfranchised women of India. The only opposition to the Bill has come from caste and community leaders who by joining the bandwagon of reservations want that such reservations should be on the basis of caste and religion of the women. Thus, these leaders want the casteisation and communalisation of the Legislatures.

If one follows the yardsticks of the political class of the 1990s, the makers of the Indian Constitution would be dubbed as social reactionaries because they showed great caution in dealing with the whole social project of affirmative action for safeguarding the rights and interests of sections who were inheritors of historically determined social discriminations. It is essential to mention that the Constitution tried to reconcile many irreconcilables by adopting a balanced middle path while dealing with the complex and contradictory social realities.

If, on one hand, a bold experiment was launched by adopting the principle of universal adult franchise, on the other, reservation of seats in Legislatures was provided for the Scheduled Castes and Scheduled Tribes. It was a powerful intervention by the Constitution to empower the most underprivileged and discriminated sections of Indian society. The authors of the Constitution did not go berserk on the policy of reservation of seats in Legislatures because they clearly rejected the demand for communal representation. Not only this. The reservation of seats for the Scheduled Castes, Tribes and for Anglo-Indians was only for a temporary period and it was to be reviewed after ten years of the commencement of the Constitution.

By various amendments of the Constitution, especially the Constitution (Forty-fifth Amendment) Act of 1980 and the Constitution (Sixty-second Amendment) Act of 1989, it is proposed to extend it up to 2000 AD only. This cautious attitude of the Founders of the Indian Republic is also clearly reflected in adopting a policy of reservation of seats in public services for the deprived strata of society. If, on one hand, every citizen was guaranteed equality of opportunity, on the other, reservation of seats for the Scheduled Castes and Scheduled Tribes was provided to take care of the inherited social disabilities of sections of society who were to be protected against the unregulated principle of abstract equality.

Further, even these reservations in public services were to be consistent with "the maintenance of efficiency of administration." Many a time, the Supreme Court has applied correctives in reminding the policy makers about the limits of the policy of reservations in public services. The Supreme Court in 1951 in the *Venkataramana vs. State of Madras* case held that a person could not be kept out of public services because he was a Brahmin or again in the *Balaji vs. State of Mysore* case in 1963, observed that reservations made "under Article 16(4) beyond the permissible and legitimate limits would be liable to be challenged as a fraud on the Constitution."

When V.P. Singh, a self-appointed messiah of social justice, found the recommendations made by Mandal Commission on reservations as a profitable political commodity, he created a stir by suddenly announcing the acceptance of the Mandal report on August 7, 1990. This raw politics of reservations was played by V.P. Singh and others without any holds barred and the Supreme Court again intervened to tell the adventurist political class that reservations in services cannot go beyond 50 per cent and that the policy of reservations in public services shall exclude the 'creamy layers' of the reserved social categories.

By abandoning the note of caution administered by the Constitution, the new messiahs of reservations in Legislatures and public services have completely fragmented and factionalised the already divided society. Politics is not just a mirror reflection of social reality. It is equally concerned with changing the inherited social categories and identities. The political class by following a reckless policy of reservations has encouraged social antagonisms based on caste versus caste, sub-caste versus sub-caste and now it is wanting to bring this division among the women in India.

India has inherited a very complex caste system, but the policy of reservations has solidified and institutionalised caste divisions and caste identities. Politics of reservations generates and stimulates caste, community and gender consciousness and every group in India is involved in targeting the other group as villain of the piece. Social deprivations are not attributed to the Himalayan failures of the economic path of development followed by the country. The political class does not want to become a target of the deprived people and by following a policy of reservations, politicians have successfully created a situation where different social groups are targeting each other for their deprivations.

The journey of casteism began with Forward Castes versus Backward Castes and it has reached a stage where every sub-caste is against every other sub-caste. Tamil Nadu has witnessed violence by backward castes against the Scheduled Castes and the rural population of Uttar Pradesh and Bihar is actually involved in a violent caste war. Has the policy of reservations brought social justice for the really deprived groups in society? The answer to this question is a Big No.

If the unending system of reservations has promoted serious social cleavages, it has also displaced from public controversy the serious agenda of economic growth with justice. While Mulayam Singh Yadav, Lalu Prasad Yadav, Kanshi Ram, Miss Mayawati and future women representatives in the State Legislatures have created assured social and sectarian constituencies for winning an election, they have completely failed to evolve socio-economic programmes for the real empowerment of the Dalits. Lalu Prasad Yadav is electorally invincible because of the electoral support of Muslims and Yadavs of Bihar, but the landless agricultural workers of Bihar have to migrate in distress to search for their livelihood to Haryana and Punjab. All political factions which are masquerading as champions of the Dalits have not undertaken a single real step which can empower people living below the poverty line.

The Constitution favoured limited reservations because it was believed that gradually the need for reservations will not be felt because the successful implementation of the programmes of socio-economic development will create new opportunities for the development of the whole of India. Not only has India badly messed up its developmental agenda, the self-appointed guardians of caste, community and gender reservations do not have any agenda for the social and economic development of the country. Lalu Prasad Yadav, Mulayam Singh Yadav, Kanshi Ram, Miss Mayawati, who are the product of casteisation of Indian politics, have failed to pull out their states from the existing stage of poverty and underdevelopment.

The politics of Forward Caste versus Backward Caste, or Hindu versus Muslim or Male versus Female had succeeded not only in dividing the society, it has legitimised the idea of politics for the sake of power alone. The believers in the policy of reservations have reduced social justice to a meaningless slogan. The unfinished task of land reforms has not been implemented by the practitioners of social justice and the landless agricultural workers have not escaped from the continuing tyrannies of the landowning castes.

Every political party has become a victim of the aimless politics of reservations. The Communist Parties resisted and very reluctantly fell in line with V.P. Singh's politics of Mandal. The BJP's Hindutva has no answer to the politics of caste versus caste among the so-called Hindus whom the BJP claims to represent. The growing decline and decay of the Congress can be attributed to its failure to respond to sectarian politics of the votaries of reservations. Fragmented society has also fragmented politics. Since the 1990s the Central Government has become weak, unstable and vulnerable to domestic and foreign pressures because the electoral verdict is fragmented.

The upshot is that the policies of reservations are mere rhetoric because the real flesh and blood of empowerment and social justice is conspicuous by its absence in the agenda of the champions of reservations. This policy is socially disastrous because it has generated the feelings of social distancing. The political parties which emerged as champions of reservations have failed to provide stable governments because the electoral verdict has been fragmented as a result of sectional reservations. There is no evidence that political empowerment of Dalits has brought any change in the life of the Dalits. Similarly, political empowerment of women will not bring any benefit to the landless agricultural women of India.—*The Hindustan Times*, 23 May, 1997.

THE TWO WHITE PAPERS

The demolition of the Babri Mosque at Ayodhya on December 6, 1992 has brought into sharp focus the powers and the role of the Central and State Governments in upholding the fundamental values of the Constitution. The events of Ayodhya compelled the Centre and the BJP to publish their White Papers in February and April 1993. These two White Papers are an attempt to explain to the public the roles played by the Centre and the BJP Government of Uttar Pradesh regarding the events of Ayodhya. The two have made an effort to shift responsibility on each other and the two White Papers conceal the truth and reveal falsehood. The BJP White Paper alleges that the 'mosque-like' structure at Ayodhya was demolished by the kar sevaks but the manipulative Prime Minister P.V. Narasimha Rao, disrupted all negotiations and wilfully prevented reference of the dispute to the Supreme Court. How could the BJP Government in U.P. deal with the sentiments of the devoted kar sevaks who had felt cheated by the acts of omission and commission of the Prime Minister?

While the BJP White Paper is a testimonial in self-defence, the White Paper of the Centre is a self-admission of the political leadership which failed to provide any direction to the country during its hour of crisis on Ayodhya. The White Paper of the Centre correctly mentions that "a constitutionally elected Government (of Uttar Pradesh) could not discharge its duties..., therein lay the failure, therein the betrayal."

Is the Constitution silent on the crucial issue of the legal and Constitutional responsibilities of the elected Central and State Governments? Does it permit an elected Government to go berserk and violate the law with impunity? The answer is a definite 'No'. The Constitution has established a federal system with a very strong Central Government. During the last 45 years, the theory and practice of Indian federation has clearly established the pre-eminent position of the Central Government in relation to the State Governments. It is precisely because of the overriding powers of the Centre that many political parties and regional movements have demanded restructuring of Indian federalism. In spite of many movements for the reorganisation of the power system, the Centre continues to be in the driver's seat in managing the affairs of the country.

Article 355 of the Constitution clearly States that it is the responsibility of the Centre to ensure that "the Government of a State is carried on with the provisions of the Constitution". The Centre has the power, to issue 'directions' to the States. And if a State fails to comply with, or to give effect to, any directions given by the Centre, the President can issue a proclamation under Article 356 and dismiss the State Government concerned because "the Government of the State cannot be carried on in accordance with the provisions of the Constitution". Thus Articles 355 and 356 of the Constitution are devoted to the defence of the constitutional legality against the illegalities of the elected Governments.

The White Paper of the Centre alleges that the U.P. Government 'betrayed' the Constitution on December 6, 1992 at Ayodhya, but the interpretation of the Constitution clearly shows that the Narasimha Rao Government 'betrayed' India by not upholding the values of the Constitution on December 6. The Narasimha Rao Government had legal and Constitutional powers to pre-empt the kar seva on December 6, to dismiss the Kalyan Singh Government on a specific charge of failure to defend the constitutional legality linked with temple-mosque controversy.

It is essential to analyse the possible reasons for the failure of the Narasimha Rao Government in dealing firmly with the defiant State Government. It cannot be accepted that Narasimha Rao was concerned with any high moral values in not exercising powers given to the Central Government under Article 356. During the last 45 years, the Congress controlled Central Government has misused and abused Article 356 many a time. The Sarkaria Commission report on Centre-State relations has highlighted the distrust created between the Central and the State Governments by the misuse of Article 356, and has clearly stated that it should be used only under exceptional circumstances. The Congress under Jawaharlal Nehru and Indira Gandhi, the Janata Party under Morarji Desai in 1977, and Janata Dal under V.P. Singh in 1989 have made their own contributions in the distortion of Centre-State relations. While a clause was inserted in Article 356 by the 42nd Amendment, 1978—"the satisfaction of the President... shall be final and conclusive and shall not be questioned on any ground"—it opened the possibility of a judicial review of a Presidential proclamation. The Madhya Pradesh High Court held the Presidential proclamation on the dismissal of the Sunder Lal Patwa Government as not legally valid and the Supreme Court has constituted a full nine-Judge Bench to review the legality and validity of Article 356 in the case of the dismissed State Governments of Madhya Pradesh, Himachal Pradesh and Rajasthan. The upshot of the above discussion is that Article 356 has always been in controversy and Narasimha Rao was not unaware of his constitutional powers in dealing with the breakdown of law and order in U.P. in the first week of December 1992.

All major parties except the BJP had extended full support to Narasimha Rao to uphold the Constitution in U.P. and many of these parties had never supported Article 356. The Centre was at the strongest wicket because it had the full backing of the major parties in the exercise of its responsibility to defend secular democracy in the country. The federal system works smoothly if there is a consensus on an issue of national significance. The temple-mosque issue concerns the whole nation because the growing communal divide has weakened the fabric of Indian democracy.

The Narasimha Rao Government should have pre-empted the kar seva at Ayodhya and a clear lesson should have been learnt from the experience of the Mulayam Singh Government of U.P. The firing on the kar sevaks at Ayodhya on October 30, 1990 made Mulayam Singh the villain of the piece and the so-called defenders of *Hindutva* emerged as martyrs. The Narasimha Rao Government should not have allowed the kar sevaks to assemble at Ayodhya on December 6, 1992. On the basis of open support of the parties, the Centre should have issued a 'direction' to the Kalyan Singh Government to disallow the assembly of kar sevaks at Ayodhya. The failure of the Kalyan Singh Government in implementing this direction should have been followed by the proclamation of emergency in U.P. This way the Rao Government would have followed the letter and spirit of the Constitution.

The Rao Government failed to defend the federal principles of the Constitution because it had clear obligation to issue 'directions' and ask the President to dismiss a delinquent State Government. It failed at a time when every condition was fulfilled for dealing with a berserk State Government. First, the national political consensus existed in favour of defending secular democracy by intervention by the Centre. Second the judiciary considers harsh action by the Indian State as legitimate if it is in defence of public order. Third, the exercise of Article 356 by the Narasimha Rao Government in pre-empting kar seva at Ayodhya would have been the first and foremost legitimate intervention in dealing with a recalcitrant State Government. It is not that the BJP betrayed the Rao Government, it is the Rao Government which betrayed the Indian nation by its failure to uphold the essentials of Indian federalism at the most critical time.

Every country has the Constitutional arrangement for emergency situations and the Indian Constitution had taken advantage of the "experience of other federations in providing for emergency provisions". The Centre's White Paper reveals the total failure of the Rao Government. The Centre showed a lack of awareness about international repercussions of the demolition of the Babri mosque. It is the Central Government which has to defend India in international forums and this responsibility cannot be performed if the Centre is unable to deal with the illegalities of its own State Government. The Constitution recognises the exceptionally significant role of the Centre in dealing with foreign countries and it cannot offer an alibi that a so-called State Government failed to defend the Babri mosque. India is facing criticism by foreign countries because the Rao Government failed to perform its Constitutional responsibilities in relation to Ayodhya. —*The Hindu*, 13 May, 1993.

NEED FOR IMPARTIAL JUDICIARY

Political decision-makers have a tendency to bend legality to achieve partisan and personal advantages. The tendency should be curbed to ensure fair governance. Every democratic political system has evolved an elaborate institutional arrangement to enforce the principles of legality in governance. An independent judiciary is important to safeguard the rule of law in a democracy. Judicial intervention curbs the arbitrariness of the executive and legislature. Since our Constitution has established a federal system, the Indian judiciary has to mediate between the Central and the State governments.

Conflicts between the various levels of government are to be resolved by judicial interpretation and intervention. Of late, the judicial intervention in resolving Central-State disputes has increased. Thus the Central Government is guided by political and partisan considerations in dealing with the state governments especially when the ruling parties at the state are different. This fact has again been highlighted by the judgement of the Madhya Pradesh High Court which has invalidated the Presidential Order of December 15, 1992.

A duly elected government of Madhya Pradesh was dismissed on the basis of Presidential Proclamation under Article 356 of the Constitution of India. The High Court has exercised its right to interpret the Proclamation of Emergency under Article 356 and it has invalidated the Proclamation because the Central Government failed to make out "any case or bring forward any material which would justify invoking the extraordinary powers under the Article".

Partisan Verdict

This judgement of the Madhya Pradesh High Court has brought into sharp focus all the complex issues of the role of judiciary in a democracy. The clear implication of this judgement is that the Central Government has misused and abused the Constitution of India for partisan goals and this action of the Central Government has deprived the people of Madhya Pradesh to be governed by their own elected government.

A question has arisen about powers of the High Court in relation to the power of the President of India under Article 356 of the Constitution. The system of checks and balances in a democracy always gives rise to the problems of jurisdiction of Parliament, Executive and Judiciary. Since judiciary inspires more confidence among the people, the Judges tend to extend their jurisdiction in the grey areas of politics and this judicial activism is a recognised fact in all democracies. Since India has a written Constitution, roles and limitations of every institution are well defined.

Since the provisions for the Proclamation of Emergency under the Constitution have attracted a lot of criticism and opposition, the 42nd Amendment of 1976 and the 44th Amendment of 1978 are important reference points to resolve the jurisdictional issue of the High Court of Madhya Pradesh. The 42nd Amendment had made a Presidential Proclamation under Article-356 'immune from Judicial review' but the 44th Amendment specifically mentioned that "Courts may interfere if the proclamation is mala fide". On the basis of 1978 Amendment of the Constitution, the Proclamation of Emergency has been contested by political parties which feel that the action of the Central Government is 'mala fide' and on this basis Sunder Lal Patwa and other BJP leaders of Madhya Pradesh challenged the Presidential Proclamation in the High Court. Hence it is wrong to maintain that the aggrieved parties do not have a legal power to seek judicial intervention in the redressal of grievances under Article 356 of the Constitution. D.D. Basu, a Constitutional jurist, is clear that on the basis of the 44th Amendment Act, 1978, the Supreme Court has no fetter on judicial review and the Court can revise its earlier opinion on this issue.

The Precedents

It is not the first time that judicial pronouncement has raised a political storm in the country and all major political parties are involved in evolving political strategies in dealing with the political fall out of the judgment of the Madhya Pradesh High Court. Mrs. Indira Gandhi imposed the Emergency on June 26,1975 to escape from judicial pronouncement on allegation of corruption in elections. Mrs. Indira Gandhi dissolved the Lok Sabha in 1970 to seek voter's verdict on the platform of radicalism which was obstructed by a section of politicians, and judiciary. Mrs. Gandhi raised the issue of 'committed judiciary' and her argument was that the thinking of the judges should be in tune with the changing political process in the country. Many a time, the judges have been described as a conservative force by political leaders who want to hasten the process of political and social change. Thus the Judiciary has been always part of political storm in India and events of the 1990s are a repeat story Indian politics of the 1970s.

Party and Law

How can a political party be allowed to participate in elections if it does not uphold the Constitution and does not respect the Judiciary of India? The BJP State Government was put on the defensive on the events of Ayodhya because it had given clear undertaking before the Supreme Court of India. It is a serious political liability for a political party if it is projected as a violator of law and pronouncements of the judiciary. If the citizens have respect for the Judiciary, political parties cannot be disrespectful and still win the elections.

Another important trend has emerged in India where the politicians are involving the Judiciary in purely political disputes whether on Reservation of Jobs or on Temple-Mosque controversy. Political parties are shifting their political responsibilities and they are seeking refuge of the Judiciary in resolving contentious political issues. The BJP, the RSS, the VHP and the Bajrang Dal have launched an immense mobilisation that Ram Temple at Ayodhya is a matter of faith with the Hindus. The contending political groups and parties in this controversy have involved the Judiciary to decide the dispute at Ayodhya. The major political parties of India have failed to evolve any consensus on Temple-Mosque dispute and Judiciary has been considered a convenient mechanism to escape political responsibilities.

When the V.P. Singh Government announced the policy of Reservations on August 7, 1990 the anti-reservationists and the pro-reservationists approached the Courts to resolve this political issue. The Reservations were a main political plank of the V.P. Singh Government and Temple-Mosque dispute is a major political plank of the forces of *Hindutva* and the secularists. The contentious vote-bank politics has sharpened social cleavages on the basis of caste versus caste and community versus community. In this situation of growing social discord and politics of polarisation, the Judiciary has been activised to resolve contentious political issues. A new dimension has been added to the role of judiciary in the political process of India during the 1990s because political parties are only competing for power and some level of co-operation among the parties has not emerged.

The elections to the State Assemblies of Uttar Pradesh, Madhya Pradesh, Rajasthan and Himachal Pradesh will be held in 1993 and judicial pronouncements will be the basis of election campaigns. Every major political party in these states will campaign on the basis of accusations against each other on the basis of pronouncements of the High Court and the Supreme Court. Political parties will be painted as defenders of the Judiciary or as offenders of the Judiciary.

It is a moot question for the Judiciary to ponder and reflect because judicial activism in a politically divided society is not helpful for the ultimate moral authority of the Courts. Judgements of the Courts will be challenged during the election meetings and judicial credibility may erode along with the decline of credibility of the politicians. Judiciary plays significant role in political process of India but it should also impose some limitations over its role. It has become clear that the politicians want the judiciary to rescue them from the burden of contentious issues but the Judiciary should not oblige such politicians. Political issues should be decided politically and Constitutional norms should be protected by the Judiciary. A proper balance of power between Judges and politicians is essential to strengthen the system of checks and balances of the Indian Constitution. —*Financial Express*, 1 May, 1993.

NARASIMHA RAO'S FOREIGN POLICY

The Narasimha Rao Government inherited a serious balance of payments crisis and foreign policy which was in a shambles because of neglect and incompetence of the Chandra Shekhar and the V.P. Singh Governments. After assuming office in June 1991, the Rao Government had to meet the challenges of economic crisis and it had to evolve an appropriate foreign policy for the pursuit of India's national interests.

Atal Bihari Vajpayee, the BJP leader in the Lok Sabha, has accused the Rao Government for not properly defending India's national interests. Vajpayee has alleged that the Rao Government's foreign policy has led to the *'marginalisation'* of India in the Third World and also in the Non-Aligned Movement. Further, Vajpayee has accused the Rao Government for not taking aggressive stand against Pakistan's interventions in the domestic problems of India especially in Kashmir.

According to Vajpayee, the Rao Government does not have any Kashmir policy and the Government has not condemned the new stand of the United State's Government on Kashmir. Vajpayee's own vision of Indian foreign policy is based on an image of *India as a world power.* In reality, Vajpayee and the BJP want an aggressive foreign policy for India especially to dominate the neighbours like Pakistan and Bangladesh. The BJP foreign policy is based on an extension of its *Hindutva* ideology, in which the Hindu State of India through its military might and nuclear teeth deal effectively with Muslim neighbouring countries like Pakistan and Bangladesh. The BJP will communalise Indian society and will pursue a foreign policy based on religious considerations. It is pertinent to refer that Atal Bihari Vajpayee was foreign minister in the Janata Party Government during 1977 and 1979, and he encouraged Moshe Dayan of Israel to visit India in great secrecy. The pro-Israeli and anti-Arab foreign policy of Atal Bihari Vajpayee is based on religious considerations towards Muslim countries of West Asia. The BJP foreign policy is conditioned by its *Hindutva* philosophy and it is directed against all Muslim countries and it has a very narrow perspective of the national interests of India.

It will not be out of place to mention here that the BJP critique of Narasimha Rao's foreign policy is a continuation of the Jan Sangh/BJP opposition to the foreign policies pursued by Pt. Nehru, Indira Gandhi and Rajiv Gandhi. The Jan Sangh/BJP leadership had never accepted the pillars of Indian foreign policy of Non-Alignment, world peace, disarmament, Anti-Racialism and Anti-Zionism and independent stand of India during the period of Cold War politics of Power Blocs. Pt. Nehru laid down the foundations of a very activist foreign policy for India because he was aware that the future of India is integrally linked with world developments. An aggressive and militarised India was not the goal of Nehru's foreign policy. Indian foreign policy during Nehru, Indira Gandhi, Rajiv Gandhi and Narasimha Rao has been built on the basis of extension of the areas of peace and reduction or minimisation of armed solutions in international disputes. This is not the perspective of the BJP leadership. Thus Vajpayee's critique of Rao's foreign policy is based on a fundamental clash of perspectives on world affairs.

Further, the Rao Government is dealing with a very different world which has emerged after the end of Second Cold War and the collapse of all erstwhile communist countries of Eastern Europe. An important pillar of the foreign policy of India was friendship with Soviet Union. The Iraq-Kuwait dispute in which the western countries militarily intervened against Saddam Hussain of Iraq and its impact on world affairs has not been properly appreciated by the critics of Narasimha Rao's foreign policy.

India has to adapt and adjust itself with a really *new world* and the salient features of present day international relations have to be recognised. First, the Power Bloc Cold War has come to an end and India has to redefine some of the contents of its foreign policy of Non-Alignment. Second, the United States has emerged militarily a very powerful country because of the collapse and disintegration of the erstwhile Soviet Union. Third, along with security and defence components of foreign policy has emerged the significance of economic factors in foreign policy of every country. Economic interests and considerations will determine the agenda of foreign policies of advanced industrialised countries of the West and developing countries of the South. The Rao Government has rightly recognised that economic goals of India have become central factor in deciding on foreign policy issues during the 1990s. The IMF, the World Bank, the GATT, the United Nations and multilateral and bilateral economic relations of India with developed and developing countries and global institutions become the priority areas of the foreign policy of India. While militarily, the United States may be talking of *uni-polar* world, in terms of economic power, the US, the EEC, the Germans and the Japanese are multiple centres of power and India has to deal with militarily *uni-polar* world on the one hand, and multiple economic giants on the other. The Rao Government has formulated its policy while keeping in mind the qualitative and fundamental changes in post-Cold War global situation.

The end of Cold War and the collapse of erstwhile Warsaw Pact countries has made the global situation extremely complicated for the foreign policy-makers of India because the western countries have asserted that the old concept of *national sovereignty* is not acceptable to them in this new stage of international politics. The Rao Government has to renegotiate and continuously bargain with the western countries because they want India to defend its 'human rights' record especially in Punjab and the Kashmir Valley.

The Rao Government has stood against the Western pressures in important contentious areas like the Nuclear Non-Proliferation Treaty and transfer of missile technology. A very important achievement of Narasimha Rao's foreign policy has been a definite improvement in India-China relations. It may be mentioned that the Jan Sangh was very critical of Pt. Nehru's policy towards China. While China betrayed India in 1962 border war, Rajiv Gandhi and Narasimha Rao have opened new vistas of negotiations and confidence-building with China. Atal Bihari Vajpayee has not extended his full support to the Rao Government on its positive steps towards improving relationships between India and China.

India-Pakistan relationships have deteriorated because Pakistan is involved in low intensity war against India by supporting terrorism in

Punjab and Kashmir. While the BJP wants a direct confrontation between India and Pakistan, the Rao Government has followed a sophisticated foreign policy by keeping in mind the changing world situation. Rao has asserted that India and Pakistan should involve themselves in bilateral discussions on Kashmir under the provisions of Shimla Agreement. At every international forum, the Government of India has exposed Pakistan's direct involvement in promoting terrorism in India and it has also asserted that Shimla Agreement is the framework for bilateral disputes between India and Pakistan. The Rao Government has alerted powerful western countries against Pakistan and it has suggested to the United States to declare Pakistan as a *terrorist State.* Thus on Kashmir, the Rao Government is neither silent nor aggressive and this is the best strategy to defend and promote national interests of India under the new global situation during the 1990s.

While the BJP wants India to emerge as a military power, the Rao Government has followed a foreign policy of winning over our neighbours. It should not be forgotten that small countries always suspect a large neighbouring country. Except Pakistan, the Rao Government has established friendly relations with all neighbouring countries.

Narasimha Rao has followed an 'activist' foreign policy for promoting national interests of India and this is the continuation of Nehru, Indira Gandhi and Rajiv Gandhi tradition. Vajpayee is wrong in asserting that India has been marginalised in world affairs because of failure of Rao's foreign policy. The fact is that Rao has adjusted and adapted India's foreign policy with fast changing global situation and the emerging challenges of 1990s. It is a fact that India is under great pressure from the United States but the Rao Government has correctly followed the policy of bargaining without surrendering essential national goals on nuclear issues or Kashmir.

—*Financial Express*, 22 October, 1993.

5

Bharatiya Janata Party

It is a truism to suggest that a meaningful explanation for the growth of any powerful social-ideological tendency at a particular stage in the development of any human society has to be located within the total dynamics of that particular society. A powerful social-political ideological movement emerges from the social soil of a particular society and it gains momentum when the social support for such an idea and movement exists in society and new ideas, ideologies and movements emerge when important social groups feel a need for such an alternative ideology at a given movement in their historical development. Further, erstwhile colonies of Asia, Africa and Latin America were structurally integrated with capitalist-imperialist countries, even after their decolonisation, politics of such erstwhile colonies cannot be explained by focussing attention on endogenous factors only because exogenous factors like New Global Capitalism exercise deep influence on the ongoing social development of peripheral capitalist states and societies of the Third World. Politics of peripheral capitalist countries which are still in the early process of capitalist development cannot be explained by focussing attention on only the so-called 'domestic' without logically linking the 'domestic' with global capitalism which is not an 'external' factor in the politics of peripheral developing capitalist societies. This methodological approach which logically and structurally links the so-called 'internal social processes' with Global Capitalism is valid for identifying the reasons for the phenomenal development of any powerful social tendency including the ongoing Hindu right-wing shift in Indian society, economy and polity. A minimum consensus exists among social scientists that a Rightist "political party or group consists of members who support social traditional values and the institution of private property and free market economy". The forces of Hindutva represented by every group of the Sangh Parivar (i.e., Hindu Joint Family) fulfill the criterion of Indian Hindu Right-Wing social tendency as defined minimally by social scientists. At the same time, Hindutva in India is much more than a mere right-wing movement because it has a world-view which is similar to the racist right-wing movements in capitalist countries and Islamic movements like the Taliban of Afghanistan.

Modernity-Anti-Modernity Theoretical Perspective

Many western scholars have devoted great attention to the growth of right-wing extremism in western capitalist countries and the challenges posed by the phenomenon of so-called Islamic Fundamentalism which inspired Samuel Hunington to write a book on "the Clash of Civilisations". The western bourgeois social scientists have been analysing politics and society of Third World countries on the basis of a theoretical framework of Tradition-Modernity continuum and they have no difficulty in studying right-wing religious movements in the Third World on the basis of Modernity versus anti-Modernity problematic. While this theoretical approach only grapples with the 'appearances' and 'observable' features of right-wing religious movements, it is worth examining this approach to understand the growth of forces of Hindutva because the absolute majority of Indian social scientists operate under the umbrella of theoretical apparatus provided by the western scholars. Michael Minkenberg while on "the Renewal of the Radical Right" observes: "….right-wing radicalism is defined as a political ideology, the core element of which is a myth of a homogenous nation, a romantic and populist ultranationalism which is directed against the concept of liberal and pluralistic democracy and its underlying principles of individualism and universalism. The contemporary radical right…wants government by the people, but in terms of ethnocracy instead of democracy. This definition focuses explicitly on the idea of the nation which is situated somewhere between the poles of *demos* and *ethnos*. The nationalistic myth, as the core of radical right-wing thinking, is characterised by the effort to construct an idea of nation and national belonging by radicalizing ethnic, religious, cultural and political criteria of exclusion and to condense the idea of nation into an image of extreme collective homogeneity."[1]

The salient features of right-wing extremism in Europe have been identified as 'extreme nationalism', 'anti-communism', 'a law-and-order mentality' and 'anti-Americanism' and on the basis of Nationalism and Modernisation Theory, right-wing extremism in Europe has been explained in terms of 'normal psychological condition of anxiety faced by the people under the stress of modern-technological societies and right-wing extremism thrives on insecurities and psychological anxieties of the common man or woman. The western scholars have dichotomised the phenomenon of right-wing nationalism or Islamic Fundamentalism as a contest between 'politics of recognizing differences' versus 'politics of inclusion' or consociational Nationalism versus Islamic Fundamentalism and suggested prescription is 'multiculturalism' or as Charle Taylor puts it on 'Politics of recognition'.[2]

A very complex issue of the right-wing religious extremism which is epiphenomenal because deep association of religions with politics of Hindutva as defined and practiced by V.D. Savarkar to Atal Bihari Vajpayee can not be explained on the basis of psychological anxieties experienced by Hindu majority community in India and this argument also is valid for the growth of Islamic Fundamentalist movements in some socially backward Muslim societies. Religious-based politics may have all the feature associated with European right-wing extremism but in societies where religion plays the role of deciding the meanings of politics and the essential content of state power, modernity versus anti-modernity theoretical approach is unhelpful in identifying explanations for the growth of Hindutva. At a symbolic level, Atal Bihari Vajpayee, as Prime Minister of India, fits in with the main elements of right-wing European extremism as defined by the western scholars. On 15 August, 2000, in his speech on the Independence Day of India, Atal Bihari Vajpayee observed :

> "Kargil has earned us international respect. India's international standing has been enhanced. Our voice is being heard attentively in the capitals of the world".[3]

The themes concerning Hindu national glory, or dignity for Hindus, and the recognition of great importance of India by the United States of America and other related issues linked with the pride and glory of Hindus have emerged as the main political and cultural discourse in India during the BJP-led central government. Not only this. The concept of the 'Other' which is the mainstay of the forces of Hindutva is now practiced by the Sangh Parivar (Hindu Joint Family) with great missionary zeal because of the protective umbrella provided by the BJP-led central government.

The American Academy of Arts and Sciences alongwith the University of Chicago Press, Chicago, has brought out multiple volumes in the 1990s on *Major Religious Fundamentalisms* and in the first volume on *Fundamentalisms Observed*, Martin E. Marty and R. Scott Appleby as editors have claimed that religious fundamentalism is preferred over 'traditionalism', 'Conservatism' or 'Orthodoxy' and 'Orthopraxis' because they are not appropriate to understand this new phenomenon and hence 'fundamentalism' is here to stay. The essence of 'fundamentalism' as described by the editors of *Fundamentalisms Observed* is found in the ideology and praxis of the Sangh Parivar (Hindu Joint Family) Martin and Appleby observe :

> "These essays make clear a feature which in our inquiries to date have struck us with surprising force and have appeared with astonishing frequency : fundamentalists begin as traditionalists who perceive some challenge or threat to their core identity, both social and personal. They are not frivolous, nor do they deal with peripheral assaults. If they lose on the central issues, they believe they lose everything. They react, they fight back with great innovative power."[4]

The above mentioned description of 'Fundamentalism' provides a comprehensive picture of Hindutva in India. The Rashtriya Swayamsevak Sangh (RSS) the parent organisation of the Sangh Parivar was established in 1925 by Dr. Hedgewar to 'unite Hindus' and make 'Hindus' strong enough to stand against three enemies identified by the Sangh Parivar i.e. Muslims, Christians and communists. Hindu Youth is trained in Shakhas (branches) for the defence of Hindu motherland. Daniel Gold observes:

> "Members of the RSS would realise their vision of a Hindu Nation by servicing as an active nucleus for it."[5]

For members of the RSS and other members of Hindu Joint Family, the 'Other' has been identified quite unambiguously by M.S. Golwalkar, the Sanghchalak of the RSS: a Muslim "has a choice in a person of his individual life. For the rest he must be one with the national current."[6]

It is not without reason that the 'Muslim Others' were targeted by the Sangh Parivar on the issue of so-called Ram Temple at Ayodhya on the basis of a specious argument that Mughal King Babar destroyed the Temple and constructed a Mosque which came to be known as the Babri Mosque. The essence of Hindu mobilisation against the Muslims and for the last few years militant Hindu targeting of Christians lies in projecting the image of a threatened Hindu by religious believers whose religions were not born in India. Hence Muslims and Christians are a threat to Hindus and according to Savarkar "a Hindu means a person who regards this land of Bharatvarsha from the Indus to the Seas, as his Fatherland as well as his Holyland."[7]

In a very competent study on '*Organised Hinduisms: From Vedic Truth to Hindu Nation*' in *Fundamentalisms Observed*, Daniel Gold does not answer the question : How have the forces of Hindutva become powerful during the decades of 1980 and 1990 while they were always marginal during the 1950s and 1960s and even in the 1970s?

Marxist Perspective and the Phenomena of Hindutva

Karl Marx in his '*On the Jewish Question*' had alerted scholars that Judaism was not a theological issue in countries where a state has been politically formed and he had suggested that the United States of America was a fully politically formed state. Similarly, a close association between Hindu religion and politics during the last two decades should be explained by looking very closely at the level of political process of India. Politics is a conscious activity of social groups who were involved either in the defence of the existing social order or who are struggling to create a new social order. Politics is the site of struggle among contending and competing social groups and the role of politician has been aptly defined by Antonio Granisci Gramsci observes that :

> "The active politician is a creator, an initiator (who) basis himself on effective reality…on a relation of forces in continuous motion and shift in equilibrium. If one applies one's will to the creation of a new equilibrium among the forces which really exist and are operative-basing one-self on the particular force which one believes to bc progressive and strengthening it to help it to victory-one still moves on the terrain of reality, but does so in order to dominate and transcend it."[8]
>
> Similarly Karl Marx in *Communist Manifesto* observed that class struggle in history has "ended in a revolutionary construction of society at large or in common ruin of the contending classes".

Thus Marxists believe that politics is an active intervention in society at a given time to create a new society and politics is a contest among the contending social classes. A few distinctive features of politics of India may be stated for the purpose of finding an appropriate relationship between the emerging forces of Hindutva and the social soil on which Hindutva is currently thriving. The most significant feature of the current phase of politics of India is that the major contesting classes belong to the different fractions of the dominant-exploiting classes and this contest among the fragments and fractions of the ruling classes is taking place at a time when the exploited classes are not in a position to effectively challenge the agrarian and the industrial exploiting classes. Since the fractions of the ruling classes are competing against one another for a share in the surpluses of economy, they need to capture the state power to achieve their goal of ensuring a lion's share in the economic surplus. This political competition is quite severe and fierce because without capturing the state apparatus no segment of the ruling classes is able to corner a greater share of economic surpluses than other fractions of the exploiting classes. The explanation for competition among the fractions of the bourgeoisie lies in a fact that while Indian bourgeoisie was not a hegemonic class even during the struggle against colonial rule, the

Congress party effective hegemonised the society during Indian national struggle for independence. Indian historiography has been engaged in the evaluation of the Indian bourgeoisie in the colonial setting of India and evaluations of historians have fundamental differences because an important School of Indian National History writing maintains that because of the colonial setting, the Indian bourgeoisie alongwith very powerful Indian National Congress was ideologically quite advanced in their critique of colonialism and in their picture of future independent India. The 'subaltern school' of historiography as launched by Ranjit Guha maintain that the Indian bourgeoisie claimed to speak for the nation, but in reality the Indian bourgeoisie failed to speak for the nation because according to Guha "There were vast areas in the life and consciousness of the people which were never integrated into their hegemony."[9]

Irrespective of the interpretation of the Subaltern historians led by Ranjit Guha, sufficient historical evidence is available to maintain that the Indian National Congress had emerged as 'Sole Spokesman of India' during the crucial negotiations for the Transfer of Power in 1947, and the Indian bourgeoisie had established a very strong position through the Indian National Congress. The essence of Indian National Congress was while its social positions were bourgeois and class interests of the Indian bourgeoisie converged with the ideological positions of the Congress, it had a 'relative autonomy' of its own from the dominant exploiting classes. Hence Nehru phase of Indian politics from 1947 to 1964 witnessed the development of Indian capitalism with agrarian reforms which were led by a relatively autonomous capitalist state of India. Congress as a party of dominant exploiting classes maintained its political dominance by winning the elections which helped it to manage the State in a relatively 'autonomous' position vis-à-vis the ruling-dominant classes. The fractions of the bourgeoisie and the landlord-peasant classes competed for their share of economic surplus within the Congress and gradual decline of the Congress political Umbrella began with the withdrawal of some fractions of the exploiting classes from the Congress. The fractions of classes and formations of separate fraction-specific political parties and groups begins in India after the fourth general elections of 1967. It must be stated at the outset that the disintegration/decline of the Congress as a 'grand coalition of classes' from 1967 to 2000 is not a process of realignment of politics as maintained by the bourgeois social scientists and this process should not be confused with the phenomena of an 'alternative politics' because contest and competition is among the fractions of the dominant classes and different political groups representing fraction-class interests have not abandoned the 'capitalist path of development' which remains the goal of every political group represented in power at the central government. Not only this. The left-of-centre politics of the Congress, in the process of splits of class-fractions, has matured into a full-fledged right wing politics. The consolidation of rightist political forces begins with the crisis periods of 1967-75, when peasantry started walking out of the Congress-led coalition of classes on the issue of the 'Terms of Trade' which were accentuated during the years of drought and oil price shock and this crisis situation was very fertile for contest among the fractions of ruling classes because every class-fraction was suffering because of the crisis of capital accumulation. While some fractions of the exploiting classes supported the Jayaprakash Narayan Movement, a few others accepted the leadership of Indira Gandhi's Congress. The middle of 1970s is the beginning of polarisation between full-fledged 'right wing' coalition led by *Jayaprakash Narayan* confronting the 'authoritarian' political coalition led by Indira Gandhi. This polarisation in politics as represented by social forces represented by 'JP' and 'Ms. Gandhi', has become the reality because Congress has been pushed out of the leadership and social fractions have shifted to the Bharatiya Janata Party which is supported by backward caste middle peasant caste-based political formations, and Hindu communalism is the ideological framework of right-wing politics which is supported by caste-communal parties.

Further, the right-ward shift in politics has taken place alongwith the New Economic Policy of the 1990s, and both politics and economics of the decade of 1990s is a definite break with the four decades of post-independence politics of India. Instead of building a national productive economic system (capitalist) on the basis of self-reliance and relative autonomy of the state from global capitalism, the politics and economics of the 1990s has made a decisive right-wing shift by accepting that without global capitalist investments Indian economy cannot grow to the extent that a reasonable share of surpluses gets generated to satisfy the multiple fractions of the ruling classes. Politics of liberalisation, privatisation and globalisation of the 1990s is a product of the crisis of accumulation of capital which is commonly talked as fiscal deficit or fiscal crisis of the State. The ideology of Hindutva has grown in the 1990s in the context of serious social discontent in the country because of crisis of capital accumulation and in this socially turbulent situation, right-wing Hindutva has emerged as an answer to the problems facings the people of the country.

The growth of the BJP and other members of the Joint Hindu family can be explained by the of the social base of Hindutva which has expanded beyond its original 'Bania-Brahman' social constituency. The post-independence capitalist development of India, with all its infirmities, distortions and weaknesses, has expanded the strata of owners of private property throughout the country and the social base for globalisation and Hindutva has emerged from these beneficiary classes and strata of Indian society. While the Indian State and Capital (all fractions of industrial and agrarian capitalist classes) have been fully integrated with one another and the so-called 'Partnership' between the state apparatus, its functionaries and the capitalist groups has been fully cemented, this phenomenon has created a situation where big bourgeoisie, upwardly mobile entrepreneurial and professional large middle classes and agrarian capitalist farmer and upwardly mobile agrarian backward castes and Dalits along with political and bureaucratic groups have come to occupy a large space in society and this is 'quasi hegemonic power-bloc' of India. This ruling-bloc has its internal conflicts but it has successfully ejected from every centre of social and political power 350 million people who are living 'below-poverty line' and about 400 million people who are involved in daily struggle for survival. Such a social situation is a logical consequence of peripheral capitalism of a backward-developing country where bourgeoisie has limited capacities to undertake the task of leading democratic revolution for the transformation of the whole society in capitalist directions. The failure of capitalist classes of peripheral capitalist society to transform the whole society has resulted in the creation of *many Indias* in which people are living with social relations and cultural attitudes beginning with the most backward pre-capitalist social relations and productive system alongwith a large middle class which is linked directly with capitalism and the State which is building capitalism in India. A society where many modes of production are existing in an uneasy stage of social equilibrium and the capitalist mode of production is the dominant one, heterogeneities of multi-structural society are significant social realities. Further, the ongoing process of globalisation has not only accentuated the domestic social disparities, the relative autonomy of the nation-state and national bourgeois productive system is getting gradually eroded. This is the setting in which on the one hand, Hindutva has flourished because it is creating a dream world of strong Hindu India, and on the other economically prosperous India by opening Indian economy to the foreign investors which will usher the era of economic prosperity for the country. Since every fraction of the ruling classes and every political formation of the fractions of classes is a supporter of free market economy and global penetration of capital into the country, political mobilisation of the masses cannot take place on the basis of the ideology of free market economy or globalisation of Indian capitalism. Political formations have to invest ideological slogans for political mobilisation because masses cannot be enthused by the slogans of free market economy. Hence identity politics has come to play a big role to fill up the vacuum created by the ideological collapse of liberalisers. India is witnessing a competition on the basis of identity politics because political groups can make 'identity' as an emotive issue to gain political support from the masses. Hindutva has emerged as a natural candidate in the stage where political struggles are being launched around identities. Identity politics appeals to the 'false consciousness' of the people because they get attracted towards social and cultural categories on the basis of which their social existence has been defined. The growth of Hindutva is linked with the crisis situation created by the distorted path of capitalist development followed by India and because of its incompleteness and inadequacies old identities determining social relationships continue to holed their sway over the consciousness of the mass of people because either new capitalist social relationships create new levels of social consciousness or the old reference points continue to persist. This is the concrete social situation of India where a riot of identities is taking place and Hindutva is one of the important candidates in this competition of identity politics. Since India is a multi-religious, multi-cultural, multi-lingual and multi-identity country, Hindu construction of identity by the Sangh Parivar is divisive and based on violence and coercion because its ideology is fundamentally opposite to the reality of India which is a country where a 'unity' exists 'among diversities'.

To sum up Hindutva is an instrument in the hands of Sangh Parivar (Hindu Joint Family) to capture political power and gain political legitimacy in a democratic political system. The BJP without Hindutva is a hollow and rotten shell. Political ideology of Hindutva can not become the foundational principle of the modern Indian nation-state because its inherent logic will lead to divisions, social violence and mini civil wars.

BJP: ALTERNATIVE DREAMS DURING THE EIGHTIES

The Bharatiya Janata Party is making a serious attempt to come to terms with the compulsions of a democratic electoral system and it is involved in a struggle to make itself a broad-based political party. It is making a serious effort to project itself as a national political alternative to the Congress (I) and for this reason, its leadership has given a call for the formation of a National Democratic Front. In the pursuit of its new strategy, it is approaching non-Congress bourgeois parties for an electoral understanding with a view to provide an alternative to the Congress (I). The BJP is also trying to expand its base in the southern States of India, besides being seriously engaged in attracting Muslims, Scheduled Castes and Scheduled Tribes and many other strata of society who were keeping themselves away from the BJP. For the first time the BJP leadership has seriously undertaken to extend its influence in the rural areas so that it can penetrate various electoral constituencies.

The BJP is an exclusivist, and high caste Hindu-dominated political party based on a cadre of workers provided by the RSS. During the last thirty-five years, Hindu communalists have been striving to make a dent in Indian politics, but the successes of the Bharatiya Jana Sangh were confined to a few northern States, limited as they were to some towns of Rajasthan, Madhya Pradesh, Punjab, Haryana, Uttar Pradesh and Bihar. The electoral appeal of the Hindu communalists did not go beyond the trading communities and the lower levels of the bureaucracy, and the concept of hegemonic Hindu Brahmanical culture put off the minority communities, and the Scheduled Castes and Scheduled Tribes which always voted for secular political parties during the elections. In spite of great fanfare, the Jana Sangh, or the BJP later failed to influence the large majority of voters in the countryside. The greatest shock to the BJP came from the Delhi electorate in March 1983 when the party was rejected in its traditional strongholds.

The secular political parties in India do not seem to clearly comprehend the menace of the BJP and the challenge it poses. Some sections have been trying to suggest that the RSS and the BJP leadership have developed serious differences and the BJP is a political party and the RSS is a cultural organisation and both have different goals, organisational structure and leadership. Such differences, if there are any, between the RSS and the BJP are a myth and need to be exposed. The BJP is a political extension of the RSS and all important MLAs, MPs and organisational leaders of the BJP are either RSS activists or products of the RSS hierarchy. The BJP leadership has no separate existence from the RSS and anyone in the BJP is reduced to the position of insignificance if he or she does not show complete loyalty to the RSS culture. Sikandar Bakht, the current vice-president of the BJP, has been reduced to the position of a showpiece. The total organisation is controlled by the RSS activists. It is quite clear that any analysis or evaluation of the role of the BJP in Indian politics cannot be divorced from an assessment of the RSS. The RSS and the BJP are committed to Brahmanical Hindu cultural mythology and to use political power to impose communal ideology on India's multi-religious and multi-cultural society. It is not surprising that the RSS is always active in Hindu-Muslim riots, and the BJPs newfound love for secularism, therefore, is an attempt to conceal the face of Hindu communalism. While the BJP is busy making claims that the Scheduled Castes have supported its candidates in Delhi and Karnataka State Assembly elections, it has taken care to hide the ugly face of its involvement in the Assam agitation. The Muslim activists of the AASU and AAGSP have openly alleged that the Hindu leadership of the AASU and AAGSP have links with the RSS and the BJP and the Assam movement has degenerated into a Hindu versus Muslim conflict under the inspiration of the BJP leadership. There is no evidence to suggest that the BJP has ceased to be a communal party. On the contrary, whether it is Assam or Meerut, the BJP was actively involved in promoting communal hatred and division. The explanation for its basic communal role lies in its internal organisation, its ideology, and its perspective of Hindu society and its history. In Jammu and Kashmir, the BJP plays an openly communal role both against the National Conference and the Congress (I).

This background of the BJP is a warning to everyone that the threat it poses has to be tackled by all secular political parties and its call for a National Democratic Front has to be rejected.

In India, communalism of one community legitimises communalism of the other community. The Akali agitation in Punjab bears testimony to this truth. The Akali communalism has inspired Hindu communalism represented by the BJP. Communal politics is divisive and leads to hatred, to violence and bloodshed. Communalism in politics is a challenge to all secular parties. Have the secularists accepted the challenge posed by the BJP? It is doubtful because secular parties have shown unique ambivalence and vacillation towards the BJP. The Janata Party experiment in 1977-79 legitimised Hindu communalism by making the Jana Sangh a partner in the administration of the country. On the bandwagon of the Janata Party and Jayaprakash Narayan, the Jana Sangh also captured power in the northern States.

The socialists and the secularists in the Janata Party could not understand the dangers posed by the Jana Sangh and in their desire to remain in power surrendered themselves to Hindu communalists. In calling for a National Democratic Front, the BJP in reality wants to revive the old Janata experiment, and it has already established contacts with the Lok Dal and the Congress (J). History has shown that democratic parties made peace with the fascists and in the process were overtaken and ultimately crushed by the enemies of democracy. The secularists would repeat history if they make peace with the BJP.

While the Janata and other fragmented democratic parties like the Lok Dal or the Congress (J) or the Congress (S) may not be relied upon to confront the BJP, the Congress (I) also is showing serious weaknesses in dealing with the growth of communalism in politics. As a secular force, it has become weak. The tall leaders of the Congress (I) are going out of the way to pay respects to gods of various religions and they are not tired of advertising their visits to mandirs, mosques and gurudwaras. The ruling party can face the challenge of communalism only if its leaders do not identify themselves with religion in public and if it implements programmes of socio-economic transformation with sincerity and commitment. Communalism is linked to backward socio-economic relations in society, and the ruling party has a responsibility to strengthen secularism by bringing about a change in productive relations in society. A backward culture is the product of backward economy which becomes the backbone of communalism and stronghold of parties like the BJP.

In the ultimate analysis, the task of confronting the BJP falls on the shoulders of the Left political parties. In Kerala the BJP is a challenge to the Left. All opponents of the Left parties in Kerala have come to terms with the BJP by clandestinely patronising it. The BJP is very active in Kerala. During the elections, the BJP is bound to divide the votes and indirectly help the non-Left parties. Thus the existence of the BJP in Kerala is a boon to non-Left parties which tolerate it. In Assam, before the AASU and AGSP movements of 1979, BJP was a minor factor in State politics and the Left parties had a standing of their own. However, in the last four years of the movement, the BJP and the AASU and AGSP have made the Left parties the real targets of attack and successfully eroded their base.

The BJP is a natural adversary of the Left parties. It is a party of the petty-bourgeoisie, communal, anti-communists and pro-imperialist in outlook. It is a threat to the Left parties because its perspective on national unity is based on the elimination of cultural diversities of India and its ideology is a leveller of all minorities, i.e., cultural, linguistic and religious. On the other hand, the Left parties believe that the unity of India depends on the preservation of linguistic and cultural identities of multiple groups in society. The clash between the Left parties and the BJP on the international front too is basic. Left politics in India is based on support for non-alignment and the struggle against imperialism. The BJP support to non-alignment movement is formal. Its basic opposition is directed against socialist countries. It does not condemn imperialist conspiracies in Afghanistan, Kampuchea and West Asia.

Its open support to Israel and its hostility to the PLO are quite well known. In objective terms, the BJP is pro-American and militarist. The National Democratic Front of the BJP in India would thus be a prop for imperialistic interventions and a bastion against socialist countries and movement for world peace. The BJP is anti-communist at home and abroad; it is communalist in domestic politics. It would like to move the country away from non-alignment, and make India an appendage of world monopoly capitalism.

The Left parties alone cannot fight communal and pro-imperialist policies of the BJP. In their struggle against the BJP they should mobilise democratic elements in the country. It is becoming quite clear that bourgeois democratic parties are becoming weak in their struggle to preserve secularism. This weakness will be the strength of the BJP.

To sum up, the BJP's strategy of National Democratic Front and its attempts to spread its network in the countryside are a serious bid to capture power in India and take the country backwards. The BJP has therefore to be exposed and opposed. It is deliberate mischief to suggest that the BJP and the RSS are involved in factional fights. They have great capacity to confuse public opinion and the RSS cadre is well known for spreading rumours and half-truths. Since the secular parties are revealing serious weaknesses in fight against communalism and social reaction, the parties have to take up seriously the challenge posed by the BJP. The National Democratic Front would be a platform of all pro-imperialists in the country, and its exposure is essential for the healthy development of Indian politics.—*Patriot,* 28 April, 1982

BJP AGENDA: HIDDEN OR REAL?

The Atal Bihari Vajpayee Government defended itself on the floor of the Lok Sabha by maintaining that its 'real' agenda was contained in its National Agenda which was a product of a consensus of the BJP and its alliance partners. Opposition parties alleged that the BJP as the major partner of the Vajpayee Government has a 'hidden' agenda for achieving its socio-political goals of Hindutva because none of its regional partners have ever contested the Gandhi-Nehru framework of secularism by dubbing it as pseudo-secularism or pro-minorityism. The BJP, on the other hand, has always maintained that it believes in 'genuine secularism' which finds a place in the National Agenda as defined by the BJP.

This is the genesis of a serious debate on the 'real' or 'hidden' agenda of the Vajpayee Government. It is alleged that though *Sarva pantha sarvadara,* that is, the Indian tradition of equal respect for all faiths, finds a mention in the National Agenda of the alliance, in reality this is the real Hindutva agenda of the BJP masquerading as promotion of 'genuine secularism'. The crux of the issue is that the Vajpayee Government as an alliance of assorted regional groups and assorted independent individuals, currently supported by the TDP and NC from outside, has two faces. The present reality of governance of India under the BJP dispensation can be further demystified by recognising that all its regional partners like BJP or Trinamool Congress or Lok Shakti, etc., are confined to specific regions. Moreover, they are out of the present state governments in their respective states. The BJP occupies a large space in the governance of the country because Gujarat, Rajasthan,

Himachal Pradesh and Uttar Pradesh are managed by the BJP and along with Shiv Sena, Akalis and HVP, the party participates in the governance of Maharashtra, Punjab and Haryana.

The real agenda and purpose of the Vajpayee Government is quite clear to the Sangh Parivar, which, alongwith the BJP, has a full-fledged agenda for pursuing the politics of Hindutva. The cat was out of the bag when three national dailies on April 8, 1998, carried the new programme of the RSS, the Bajrang Dal and the VHP. A few special features of the programme announced by the Sangh Parivar deserve to be mentioned in order to understand its real meanings and implications for the future of Indian society, polity and culture. Another mobilisation for Hindutva may not be undertaken on the Ram Janmabhoomi issue but similar kind of Hindutva forces are bound to be unleashed for the "liberation of Government-controlled temples in non-BJP ruled states". Three such temples identified for liberation are the Shivagarhi Mutt in Trivandrum, the Tirupati Balaji Temple and Vaishno Devi. It is not accidental that Hindu mobilisation will be anti-Communist in Kerala, anti-Muslim National Conference in J & K and anti-TDP in Andhra Pradesh.

A pure Hindu agenda with political militancy around sacred temples in these three religiously sensitive states may lead to a Hindu-Muslim-Christian divide but that will only help to strengthen the base of the Sangh Parivar.

This is because temple issues can play upon irrational Hindu emotions. The politics of emotions is the hallmark of the Sangh Parivar. Its programme announced on April 8, 1998, is a comprehensive programme of the mobilisation of Hindus by setting Bajrang Dal units in all 750 districts and 7,531 blocks in the country. These units of the Bajrang Dal *bal upasana kendras* (centres to pay obeisance to strength) are where Hindu youth is trained in 'judo-karate and other martial arts' to give a fitting reply to the Pakistan Inter-Service Intelligence Agents, Christians and carriers of cultural invasion. The BJP-led alliance's National Agenda for Governance mentions the need for harnessing youth power by establishing National Reconstruction Corps. The National Agenda mentions that, "Our youth is the strength of the family, village, locality and the community, they are also the future of our nation...For them, we will create a National Reconstruction Corps". This programme for the youth as envisaged in the National Agenda and as concretised by the Hindu Parivar deserves an analysis to properly appreciate its real implications.

The BJP is the only cadre-based party in the real sense of the term. While the Communist parties and the Congress have their front organisations, these parties have their own clear identity. Such is not the case with the BJP, which is only a political arm of the RSS meant to implement its programme. Thus, the Hindu youth of India has always been the target of the Hindu parivar and it is not without reason that the RSS was established in 1920s to instil Hindu philosophy in the Hindu youth.

The Sangh Parivar has always targeted Christian missionaries by alleging that they convert poor Hindus to their religion by providing allurements. The VHP was established in the 1970s to launch anti-Christian Missionary Campaigns in the North-East. The new programme is an aggressive continuation of the Sangh Parivar's confrontationist attitude towards Christian missionaries. The BJP umbrella is now available to the Sangh Parivar to launch movements in the North-East, which is a sensitive and troubled region.

A particular kind of Hindu ethos is being promoted by the BJP Government where temples, rituals, priests, *tilak* on the forehead of ministers and MPs are on public display. The PM inaugurated Lord Krishna Temple with fanfare in Delhi, the Education Minister enters office with *tilak* on his forehead, and Shankaracharyas and saints are new role models for Indians who have always cherished a quiet and private relationship with their gods and goddesses. Professor Morris-Jones in his perceptive book on Indian politics in the 1960s had talked of modern and saintly 'idioms of politics of India'. But his identification of the saintly idiom was with Gandhi or Vinoba Bhave. Leaders who distance themselves from the politics of power are respected in India and they act as "moral conscience keepers of the Indian politics". JP's movement in the 1970s proved Morris-Jones' analysis of the 'idioms of Indian politics' right.

India has turned full circle and the Hindu saints in politics in the 1980s and 1990s are legitimising a politics of militant Hindutva directed against every minority community in the country. Gandhi, Vinoba, and JP were political saints who believed in the cleansing of ugly power politics, but *sant sammelans* are being used today for targeting Muslims by raising the issue of 'liberation of temples' from 'Government control' or for using violence to halt the so-called invasion of foreign culture, Muslim, Christian or a vaguely defined Western.

The National Agenda and the Sangh Parivar's elaboration of that Agenda on April 8 herald a new era in Indian politics where official interpreters of Hinduism or Indian history will be fighting unlicensed street battles and a sympathetic Government will not intervene, as it happened in Gujarat when the Christian missionaries were under siege by VHP and Bajrang Dal activists. The central issue is that regional partners of the BJP Government do not have any national concerns. Only the BJP has a national agenda and its real agenda is the promotion of Hindutva through the Sangh Parivar. It does not have any hidden agenda of its own. This is the crux of the matter.—*The Pioneer*, April 15, 1998.

HINDUTVA: IDEOLOGY AND ORGANISATIONAL STRUCTURE

A very critical and crucial question is : How has a political party during its fifty years of existence come to occupy a central place in Indian politics? How has the BJP broken the monopoly of political power of the Congress? How has the BJP emerged as the most important political alternative to the Congress? The Jana Sangh had a very disastrous beginning because in the first Lok Sabha elections of 1952 it obtained only 3.06 percent of the votes and only three candidates of the party could get elected. A political party which was completely ignored by Indian voters during the first Lok Sabha elections has been able to win the support of about 25 percent of the voters at the end of Twentieth Century. A party which opened its account with 3 members only has a strength of 183 members in the present Lok Sabha. Not only this. The President of India requested the BJP leader, Atal Bihari Vajpayee, to accept the office of the Prime Minister after the Lok Sabha elections of 1996, 1998 and 1999. Atal Bihari Vajpayee was the leader of the single largest party in the Lok Sabha and remained a Prime Minister for thirteen days in 1996. Vajpayee became Prime Minister in 1998 and 1999 because he was the leader of the coalition which had a majority of seats in the Lok Sabha. An important question worth examining is : How has the BJP been able to break its complete political isolation and become the leader of coalition governments at the Centre? The party of Hindutva was considered 'untouchable' by every national and regional political formation because multiple regional and all-India political groups proclaimed their firm belief in secular politics and they considered the party of Hindutva as their principal opponent. The political 'untouchables' of the previous years have become acceptable to many political groups who have very enthusiastically joined the coalition government at the centre which is led by the BJP. Such a rapid growth of the forces of Hindutva in Indian politics deserves serious analysis and explanations. Political parties are a mirror reflection of social reality. Political parties are formed because they satisfy socially felt needs of various sections of society. Political parties gain in strength because many groups and segments of society are able to identify themselves with their ideology and programmes. Political parties wither away if their supporters have shifted their support to some other party. Thus parties are formed, they grow or decline and new parties are formed to satisfy new social needs and aspirations of the voters. A few scholarly works on the party of Hindutva have provided us with an inside story of the party and efforts have been made to offer explanations for the emergence and growth of this party. The earliest work of Craig Baxter provided a description of the party and its relationship with the RSS. While Craig Baxter tells us about the early history of the BJP during the 1950s and 1960s, Bruce D. Grahman completes this story up to late 1980s. Baxter and Graham were grappling with the problems of leadership, organisation, electoral support and political performance of the BJP during the phase of Indian politics when Congress party dominated the political scene and BJP was one of the opposition political groups. BJP made a gradual and an unsteady growth during the 1950s, 1960s, 1970s and 1980s; it is during the 1990s that it has emerged as an important pillar of Indian politics. A few significant scholarly studies of the 1990s help us in finding explanations for the dynamic growth of the forces of Hindutva.

An important explanation for the growth of Hindutva at the close of Twentieth Century has been offered by scholars who have interpreted Indian society essentially in terms of Hindu culture. It has been argued that the social soil of India is fertile for the growth of Hindutva because in a country of believers of Hindu religion, a religion-based party has natural advantage over other secular parties because Hindu cultural symbols can be politically manipulated and appropriated by the party of Hindus. This line of argument has been extended to the National Movement of India and it has been maintained that "religion was central to most forms of Indian nationalism".[10] Peter van der Veer observes :

> "I would argue that to understand the growth of religious nationalism we cannot reduce the context and the formation of religious identities to the maximising behaviour of elites, essentialised value systems, or the hegemonic project of the colonial state."
>
> "......If we want to take religious discourse and practice as relevant to the project of religious nationalism, we have to attempt to understand religious identities as historically produced in religious institutions that are in a constant process of transformation."
>
> "This social reformist effort can, in my opinion, be seen as part of a long-term process of 'Hinduisation' of India".[11]

In his argument, he can not see the absurdity of equating Gandhians and the Hindu 'joint family', popularly known as Sangh Parivar. He observes :

> "In this connection it is important to see that 'Gandhians', as well as members of the RSS and the VHP, do not take the Hindu identity of untouchables and tribals for granted but are actively engaged in the so-called uplift of those sections of the Indian population.
>
> "This social reformist effort can, in my opinion, be seen as part of a long-term process of 'Hinduisation' of India."[12]

If this argument is extended, the secular, welfare, and democratic State of India is promoting the agenda of 'Hinduisation' by undertaking special programmes for the uplift of the Dalits. The central issue is that Peter van deer Veer cannot distinguish between the so-called Hindu Nationalism and secular plural Indian National Movement.

This 'essentialist' argument which equates majority religion with nationalist movement's strategy of mobilisation deserves to be closely scrutinised and examined. While it is not denied that the Indian National Movement appropriated a few important Hindu cultural symbols, it will be wrong to maintain that Hinduism provided the main source of strength for the national movement of India. Indian National Movement maintained an equidistance from the Hindu Mahasabha which was established in 1905 and the Muslim League which came to into existence in 1906 and the reason for maintaining distance from these two parties of the Hindus and Muslims was that the Indian National Movement made every effort to 'unite' every 'social and cultural' diversity of India. V.D. Savarkar was the ideologue of Hindutva in pre-Independence India of the Twentieth Century and his definition of Hindutva and all his formulations regarding Hindu Nation were completely rejected by Gandhi-Nehru leadership of Indian National Movement. Congress had leaders like Bal Ganga Dhar Tilak or Lala Lajpat Rai or Madan Mohan Malaviya who took inspiration from Hinduism and who tried to combine their Hindu perspective with all-India national movement but they were not the only leaders of national movement of India. Many other tall leaders of the Congress, the socialists and the communists not only rejected their Hindu perspective, on the contrary, they provided a very powerful secular and pluralist perspective to national movement.

Hindutva of the BJP and the Hindu 'joint family' is best expressed by V.D. Savarkar. In his *Hindutva*, Savarkar defined that "Hindutva is not a religion but a history. Not only the spiritual or religious history of our people as at times it is mistaken to be by being confounded with the other cognate term, Hinduism. Hinduism is only a derivative, a fraction, a part of Hindutva....Hindutva embraces all the departments of thought and activity of the whole being of our Hindu race".[13] Territoriality and

Hindu culture are co-terminus and this is the meaning of Hindustan which is a 'holy land' (*pitrabhoomi*) of the Hindus. 'Hindu' is one whose religion has grown 'out of the soil of India.' Savarkar and the Sangh joint family appropriates indigenous religions like Buddhists, Jains, Sikhs and the multiple Hindu sects because they belong to their 'holy land' (*pitrabhoomi*) and by this definition of Hindutva, Muslims and Christians are completely excluded because their 'holy lands' are beyond the territories of India. Pope of the Christians and their places of worship and Prophet Mohammad of Islam are 'outsiders' and Hindus are 'insiders' because they live on their 'holy land'. Hindutva is constructed on the ideology of 'we' and the 'others' and Hindu cultural symbols are appropriated for mobilisation and in this logic the liberation of temples of Ayodhya, Varanasi or Kashi, and Mathura is a sacred task of the Hindus. This self-definition of Hindutva was further elaborated by M.S. Golwalkar who was nominated Sar Sanghchalak, the RSS chief, after the death of Dr. Keshav Baliram Hedgewar on June 21, 1940. Golwalkar in his '*We, our Nationhood defined*' (1938-39) and in his collections '*Bunch of Thoughts*' (1966) advances further the Hindu racist argument of Savarkar. RSS represents and reflects the militancy of Golwalkar who asserted that Indians who do not maintain the purity of Hindu culture "fall out of the pale of National Life" and they "deserve no privileges, far less any preferential treatment—not even citizen rights"[14]. While Savarkar emphasised the idea of 'Holy Land' of the Hindus, Golwalkar propagated the idea of Motherland (*matrabhoomi*) of the Hindus and that this Motherland belongs to the great Hindu race.

The idea of 'holy land and motherland' propagated by the ideologues of Hindutva deserves to be contested and rejected because they are manipulating history of India to establish a false claim that Hindus are the real indigenous inhabitants of the territory known as Hindustan. Migrations from other countries to India have been part of our history and India was never insulated from Indo-European, Indo-Egyptian, Indo-Iranian and Central Asian migrations and cultural interpenetrations from neighbouring lands. Further, the myth of Aryans of India as original inhabitants of the country has been completely falsified by archaeological and other evidence. In his scholarly work Prof. Sharma observes[15]:

> "The view that the Indo-Aryans came to India from outside is not acceptable to Hindu fundamentalists and the western champions of the continuity of the local cultural tradition. The implications of the theory of the continuity of the cultural tradition need consideration…..

> "A purely localistic continuity approach neither advances archaeological understanding nor helps historical reconstruction. It is necessary to assess the relative importance of change and continuity in the context of time and place."[6]

The changeless India is a myth and cultural changes have taken place in the country as a result of exogenous and endogenous factors. India has received from and has also contributed to the world civilisation.

Prof. Romilla Thapar has contested V.D. Savarkar's view that "an Indian/Hindu is one for whom India is *pitrabhoomi* and his *punya bhumi*, the land of his ancestors and the land of his religion" by highlighting the existence of Indus civilisation because it helps us in questioning, "The Aryan beginnings of Indian history", Prof. Thapar observes[16]:

> "The question of Aryanism and the beginnings of Indian history ... in fact is not so central....It's real function....is political in that it is used to separate the supposedly indigenous Hindu Aryans from the alien, the Muslim and the Christian....:"

While not denying that the mobilisation of Hindu majority has some 'built-in' advantage for the forces of Hindutva, it is wrong to maintain that Hindutva can be equated with 'religion based concept of Nationalism'. The concept of Indian Nationalism was fundamentally different from the meanings of religious-cultural Hindu Nationalism of the forces of Hindutva and the western scholars who are describing Hindutva as Hindu Nationalism have not answered a basic question : If Hindu religion could be a fundamental reference point for building Indian National Movement, the secular and pluralist Indian Nationalism could not have got any public space in India. On the contrary, it is the pluralist secular nationalism succeeded in its opposition to Hindu and Muslim religion-based mobilisations during the first half of the Twentieth Century. The explanation that 'religious nationalism' was always central to 'most forms of Indian nationalism' and the Hindutva could easily build itself on the given 'reserves' of Hindu religion (Peter van dar Veer 1994) is not very satisfactory because the ideology of Hindutvas as defined by Savarkar and Golwalkar was not at all acceptable to the mainstream leaders of Indian Nationalism who successfully mobilised Indians in an anti-colonial struggle on the basis of secular-pluralist platform. Further, if Hinduism as interpreted by the Jana Sangh had a mass appeal, it would not have obtained a miserable 3.06 percent of the votes during the Lok Sabha elections of 1952. The so-called Hinduism of the Sangh joint family was a marginal factor in our struggle for freedom and this was further confirmed in the very first Lok Sabha elections of 1952. A further probe is required to understand the rise and growth of the forces of Hindutva at the close of Twentieth Century.

The Bharatiya Janata Party celebrated its 20 years in April 2000 and the *Organiser* under the caption 'BJP—then and now' observed "The progress of BJP in 20 years is a fascinating study in the political acumen of its leadership. In earlier coalitions BJP used to play second fiddle. Now it is the pivot of the coalition. In fact in the context of fractured mandates, BJP has become the pivot of Indian politics.[17]

In the same enthusiastic manner L.K. Advani observed that :

> ".....the ten years between 1989 and 1999 had been a watershed decade in the party's history as the party saw miraculous rise... It was only because of the BJP's association with the RSS that it had been able to imbibe the feeling of cultural nationalism."[18]

What is the explanation for the growth of the BJP remains a central issue and a French scholar Jafferlot (1996) attempts an answer in his detailed study *The Hindu Nationalist Movement in Indian Politics.* Jafferlot devotes a lot of attention on the organisational structure of the forces of Hindutva and he links it with political strategies followed by the Sangh Brotherhood for extending and expanding its area of influence. The Hindutva has come to occupy a significant public space in India because its organisations have worked very hard for decades to spread its ideology. Jafferlot attempts an explanation for the success of Hindutva in overcoming 'its geographical and social limitations' and observes :

> "By the early 1980s the failure of the Hindu nationalist leaders to integrate their movement in a larger structure had left it isolated. However, the wider political context was then more favourable and enabled them to return to their original combination of strategies. The militancy-proselytising and targeting of certain minorities evolved a new feeling of vulnerability within Hinduism, and many religious leaders responded to it by joining the Hindu nationalist movement."[19]

While mobilisation strategies seem neutral term but Jafferlot links it with "a strategy of identity-building through the stigmatisation and emulation of the other", which was effectively propagated by "ethno-religious network of activists". Jafferlot concludes that :

> "The strategy of stigmatisation and emulation of 'threatening others' is based on a feeling born of a largely imaginary threat posed by 'aliens', principally Muslims and Christians. This strategy is the cornerstone of the Hindu nationalist movement; it was the first to be formulated, and sustains its ideology".[20]

The crux of the argument is that BJP cannot be understood without its ideology of Hindutva and an ideology which is religio-cultural is carried forward by the activists of multiple organisations of the joint family of Hindus. The activist organisations are an integral part of the politics of Hindutva and for understanding the inside story of the BJP, it is essential to refer briefly to RSS, VHP, BMS, ABVP and Bajrang Dal. Dr. S.P. Mookerjee, the founder of Jana Sangh in the early 1950s, was completely depended on Guru Golwalkar of the RSS and his trusted lieutenants who worked within the Jana Sangh. The Jana Sangh was a political face of the RSS. While Rashtriya Swayamsevak Sangh precedes the birth of the Jana Sangh (BJP), many other organisations of the Sangh Parivar or Hindu 'joint family' were established in post-independence India. It is essential to elaborate on the essential character of the RSS, and a few facts may be mentioned about other organisations of the Hindutva:

(a) *Akhil Bharatiya Vidyarthi Parishad (ABVP)* : was formed in 1948 to counter communist influence on the campuses but it became very active alongwith the RSS during 1974-75. The Nav Nirman Samiti of Gujarat in 1974 and Jayaprakash Narayan's Movement in Bihar in 1975 was provided strong shoulders by the ABVP and RSS. ABVP is very active in campus politics and it is a recruitment place for future leaders for the politics of Hindutva.

(b) *Bharatiya Mazdoor Sangh (BMS)*: The RSS set up a trade union wing in 1955 and its membership has increased during the last two decades.

(c) *Vishwa Hindu Parishad (VHP)* : A few religious leaders were mobilised by the newly created Vishwa Hindu Parishad in 1964 to help in the creation of a 'Unified Hindu Society'. The VHP has been very active in mobilising Hindu saints and priests in its programmes which are anti-Muslim and anti-Christian. The VHP spearheaded the movement for Ram Temple at Ayodhya and the targeting of Christian missionaries for their alleged activities on the conversion of Hindus into Christian religion. This has been a staple diet of the VHP.

(d) *Bajrang Dal* : It operates as a youth wing of the VHP and aggressive and destructive activities of various Hindu organisations are performed by the Bajrang Dal.

(e) *Bharitiya Vanavasi Kalyan Bhram (BVKB)* was established in 1977 and the VHP assigned it the task of exclusively working with the tribals.

The key to the understanding of the essence of Hindutva including the BJP lies in unravelling the essential reality of the Rashtriya

Swayamsevak Sangh (RSS). Atal Bihari Vajpayee, L.K. Advani, Murli Manohar Joshi, Keshubhai Patel and every luminary of the BJP is trained by the RSS and once the RSS certifies about their strong Hindu credentials leaders can rise in the hierarchy of Hindu organisations. RSS certificate is essential for the survival of any leader in the Sangh Parivar. The Kalyan Singh of Uttar Pradesh and Shankar Singh Vaghela of Gujarat came to grief because the Sangh leadership expelled them from its ranks. Every minister or Chief Minister or Prime Minister has to be given a testimonial of legitimacy by the RSS by certifying that they are our '*social-cultural torchbearers*' and only then they are inducted in the Council of Ministers.

What is Rashtriya Swayamsevak Sangh (RSS)?

Every action and activity of the forces of Hindutva is an extension of the preachings of the Rashtriya Swayamsevak Sangh (RSS). The authority of Sar Sanghchalak beginning from Dr. Keshav Baliram Hedgewar to M.S. Golwalkar or Guruji, Bala Saheb Deoras, Rajendra Singh or Raju Bhaiya and K.S. Sudarshan is unquestioned and unquestionable. Maurice Durverger in his seminal work on *Modern Political Parties* alerted us that the Twentieth Century parties are different from factions or parties or groups of the Nineteenth century because of their party organisations. Robert K. Merton, an American sociologist, informed us that political parties are fully controlled by organisation which he termed 'machine politics'. RSS is the real controller of the BJP and it is not an accident that during the cabinet formations of 1998 and 1999, the BJP team of Council of Ministers was cleared and approved by the RSS leadership. BJP is the political wing of the RSS and it is not without reason that during Janata Party rule of 1977-79, the BJP nominees in the government were Atal Bihari Vajpayee and L.K. Advani, the two important members of the RSS. The same story was repeated when the BJP formed a coalition government at the centre in 1998 and 1999. Anderson and Danle observe that :

> "However, the RSS—the major socialising agency for the cadre in the Jana Sangh and the BJP (as well as for other RSS affiliates) — has exerted influence over both policy and personnel selection without abandoning its apolitical orientation. Full-time RSS workers (i.e. the pracharaks) delegated to the affiliates maintain effective control by determining who will be recruited and advanced up the ranks......
>
> "The Swayamsevaks ...tended to perceive political participation as an extension of their former RSS activities....The political task, like the 'Cultural' task in the RSS, was to mobilise people to support the belief system of the RSS".[21] If RSS is the 'gate-

keeper' of all affiliates of the Hindutva, its ideology from Hedgewar to Sudarshan has to be spread by the RSS Pracharaks and their ideology in the words of Sudarshan is that :

"This is Hindu Rashtra. It is based on *dharma*. Its identity lies in one Motherland, one Sanskriti, common ancestory and heritage and the unity in diversity. It is these three that constitute the national culture".[22]

The Akhil Bharatiya Pratinidhi Sabha of the RSS is the all-India representative policy making body and *Shakhas* of the RSS are the places where the ideology is taught and preached. M.S. Vaidya, a member in of the RSS national executive maintained in an interview that "in the north-eastern region of the country...the Baptist Church was behind the insurgency in the region". In the same tone he alleged that Christian missionaries were aggressively involved in 'conversion activities'. Further he said that despite unsympathetic governments and various odds, the RSS had spread far and wide with 30,000 branches all over the country.[23]

The RSS organisation is hierarchical and it is established on the principles of military hierarchy and discipline where superior-subordinate relationship is well defined and well-observed. The RSS organisational chart clearly tell us about the linkages of one level of hierarchy with the other. The *Shakha* and the *pracharaks* spread the message of Hindu Rashtra and Malkani comments that '*Shakha* training produces 'certitudes' — and the RSS does not encourage 'doubting Thomases'.[24]

The RSS, like Indian army, has a flag. It conducts daily *Shakhas*, and it has a prescribed dress for the Swayamsevaks. The Swayamsevaks have to bow their head before the Guru and worship the flag. Further, the organisation celebrates Hindu religious-ritualistic festivals to inculcate the spirit of Hindu Rashtra among the Swayamsevaks. The hierarchical steel frame of the RSS is like the following:

The Sar Sanghchalak (The Chief)

↓

Sarkaryavakak (General Secretary)

↓

Prachar Pramukh (Chief Organiser)

↓

Pracharaks

Everyone mentioned above in the hierarchy is a full-time cadre with defined role and relationship with others in the RSS hierarchical organisation. The Sangh Parivar has established special organisations in every important segment of public life and its Bharatiya Mazdoor Sangh, a trade union of workers established on July 23, 1955 claims a membership which is more than the combined strength of the two Communist Party all-India trade unions. Hindu saints and priests are actively associated with the activities of RSS and its affiliates. Hindu festivals, Hindu rituals, and Hindu scriptures are the reference points of the RSS leadership. The target groups of Hindu organisations which work together are workers, students, women, Hindu refugees and special targets are Scheduled Castes and Tribal populations. Craig Baxter, Jafferlot, Andersen and Damle, and Graham in their study of the early phase of Bharatiya Jana Sangh provide us with great details about the close relationship between RSS, Jana Sangh, Bharatiya Janata Party and other Hindu organisations. Not only this. Jafferlot informs that :

> "The Jana Sangh adopted a similar pattern of party-building in the 1950s since its organisation relied primarily on a hierarchy of RSS trained-cadres".[25]

Another important organisation of the forces of Hindutva is Vishwa Hindu Parishad and it is RSS which played a 'leading role in founding the VHP in 1964'.

The upshot of above discussion is that the ideology of Hindutva is the mainstay of the BJP and its organisational mainstay is RSS and its other affiliates. BJP has a commitment to the ideology of Hindu Rashtra and it has a committed and army-like trained and disciplined cadre of the RSS to spread and propagate this ideology. The above discussion clearly brings out the ideological puritanism of the Sangh Parivar including the BJP and the role of committed cadre for the promotion and propagation of the ideology of Hindu Rashtra. The BJP is different from every other political party of India because of its exclusivist Hindu ideology and its capacity to mobilise its well-trained and ideologically committed cadre to work for the party of Hindus. The real backbone of the BJP is the RSS and other numerous Hindu organisations like the VHP, Bajrang Dal, etc. The above discussion puts at rest the controversy that BJP is separate from the RSS and RSS is only a 'cultural' organisation. BJP is the political face of the believers and practitioners of Hindu Rashtra and RSS is the real controller of the BJP MPs, MLAs, Ministers and Prime Minister. Anderson and Damle observe that "This study focusses on the 'family' of organisations around the RSS, especially its political affiliate. The affiliates all have a centralised authority structure very similar to that of the RSS. All of them recruit their cadre largely from the RSS, and the RSS trained cadre occupy the key organisational positions".[26]

RSS and BJP are indistinguishable both at the level of organisation and ideology because they are two sides of the same coin of Hindu Rashtra.

BJP-ELECTORAL PERFORMANCE:
Political Strategies and Changing Social Base

The BJP and every affiliate of the Sangh Parivar has expanded and extended its area of influence during the last fifty years and at the end of the Twentieth Century the Central government of India is controlled by a coalition led by the BJP, and the state governments of Uttar Pradesh, Himachal Pradesh, Gujarat and Orissa are managed by the BJP or BJP and its allies. Further, the BJP is the main opposition party in Rajasthan and in Maharashtra State Assembly the opposition consists of Shiv Sena and BJP alliance. It is worthwhile to describe the story of political journey of BJP by dividing it into some phases of politics of India.

BJP in the 1950s and 1960s

The Congress party of India had a formidable presence in the 1950s and it dominated the electoral scene in the Lok Sabha and state assembly elections of 1952, 1957 and 1962. Every opposition party including the Jana Sangh/BJP had to reckon with the all-India presence of the Congress. In spite of the emotive appeal of Hindu communalists in post-Partition independent India, the Jana Sangh could get only three Lok Sabha seats and obtained 3.06 per cent of the national votes during the 1952 Lok Sabha elections. Its presence in the State Assemblies was also marginal because it obtained only 35 seats and could secure only 2.76 per cent of the votes polled during the State Assembly elections of 1952. India had been partitioned in 1947 and India and Pakistan had witnessed worst kind of communal holocaust and ethnic-cleansing during 1947-1950 and in spite of the atmosphere of inter-religious hatred, the party of the Hindutva could not cut any ice with its so-called Hindu constituency of voters and secular parties and groups like the Congress, the Communist party of India and socialists established their effective relationship with the Indian voters.

The Table 5.1 of electoral performance of the Jana Sangh shows that its expansion was quite slow. It began its Lok Sabha journey with 3.06 popular vote in 1952 and increased it up to 7.37 per cent in 1971-72. The story is same in the State Assembly elections where it obtained 2.76 per cent votes in 1952 and increased it to 8.56 percent in 1971-72. In the 1950s and 1960s, the Lok Sabha and State Assembly elections of 1967 are a watershed in Indian politics because the voters punished the Congress for the first time and the party suffered serious electoral defeats in the

Table 5.1: Jana Sangh Electoral Performance: Parliamentary and State Assembly Elections

Year of Election	*Parliament*			*Assembly*		
	% of	*No. of Seats*		*% of*	*No. of Seats*	
	Votes	*Contested*	*Won*	*Votes*	*Contested*	*Won*
1952	3.06	92	3	2.76	725	35
1957	5.93	130	4	4.03	606	51
1962	6.44	195	14	6.07	1177	119
1967	9.41	250	35	8.80	1702	257
1971-72	7.35	159	22	8.56	1233	104

Source: *'The Brotherhood the Safform'* by Walter K. Andersen Shridhar D. Damle.

Lok Sabha and State Assembly elections of 1967. The tallest leaders of the Congress like K. Kamaraj, Atulya Ghosh, S.K. Patil and others were rejected by the Indians voters, and after the elections of 1967 the Jana Sangh formed many short-lived, unstable but important coalition governments in many states of India. The Jana Sangh share of national vote had increased in 1967 elections, and many political parties and groups were willing to share power with the Jana Sangh in various state governments. The Jana Sangh leadership had always been open to the idea of forming coalitions with other opposition parties and groups for confronting the Congress party which was a 'single dominant factor' in Indian politics. Dr. S.P. Mookerjee, the founder of Jana Sangh, organised the National Democratic Front of 32 opposition MPs in December 1952. The idea of an 'opposition bloc' was concretised by Mookerjee in the very first Lok Sabha. All important leaders of the Jana Sangh/BJP like Dr. S.P. Mookerjee, Deen Dayal Upadhya, L.K. Advani and Atal Bihari Vajpayee have joined different political groups to displace Congress from its position of dominance. The post-1967 election developments and formation of many Samyukta Vidhayak Dal (SVD) governments witnessed the marriage of all kinds of political antagonists who formed governments alongwith the Jana Sangh. This story of the 1967 immoral marriages of political convenience have continued till the end of Twentieth Century and political parties have made all kinds of ideological compromises to share power with the Hindu communalists.

BJP in the 1970s and 1980s

Indian politics took a turn in 1971 and 1972 when Indira Gandhi won the Lok Sabha and State Assembly elections in a very convincing manner. The Jana Sangh obtained 7.35 percent of the national vote in the Lok Sabha elections of 1971 and 8.56 percent of votes in the State Assembly elections of 1972. The Congress party under the leadership of Mrs. Indira Gandhi established its pre-eminent position in Indian politics in 1971 and 1972. The Hindu 'joint family' or Sangh Parivar continued its intervention in public affairs and it very actively participated and promoted Jayaprakash Narayan's Movement against Mrs. Indira Gandhi's Congress party governments in Gujarat and Bihar in 1974 and 1975. Jayaprakash Narayan and leaders of the Congress (Organisation) like Morarji Desai accepted the great contribution of the RSS in launching anti-Congress Movements of 1974-75. During the Emergency phase of Indian politics of 1975-77, the Sangh leaders and activists were arrested or they became politically passive to escape any punishment from the Government of India.

The Lok Sabha elections of March 1977 brought the Congress (O) the Jana Sangh, the Congress for Democracy, the Lok Dal and Socialists to power at the Centre and it is for the first time that the Jana Sangh leaders became ministers of the central government of India. It was a dream of Dr. S.P. Mookerjee in the 1950s and it became a reality in the 1977, Lok Sabha elections. The victory procession of the Jana Sangh continued in the State Assembly elections during the post-Emergency phase of Indian politics. The Jana Sangh and affiliates of the RSS were found exercising governmental power either as Ministers in the Central government or Chief Ministers and Ministers in important states of India. Within two decades, Jana Sangh had become an important political formation in India.

A few salient features of Jana Sangh-in-power during the so-called Janata Party rule of 1977-79 may be mentioned to understand the real activities of the party in power. First, the Jana Sangh Chief Ministers or Ministers or MPs and MLAs, especially in the state governments of Rajasthan, Uttar Pradesh, Madhya Pradesh and Himachal Pradesh, implemented Hindu cultural agenda, and as partners in the central government, its spokesmen launched a movement for the withdrawal of "history textbooks written by secular historians and published by the National Council for Educational Research and Training". Second, the Jana Sangh and RSS spearheaded a strong movement for the spread of Hindutva through government controlled educational institutions. Madhu Limaye and a few others realised that the presence of Jana Sangh in the corridors of political power had provided it with a great opportunity to penetrate its Hindu ideology among government institutions and functionaries and they raised a question about the 'dual membership' of the Jana Sangh representatives in the Morarji Desai Council of Ministers. A demand was made that Atal Bihari Vajpayee and L.K. Advani should resign from the membership of the Rashtriya Swayamsevak Sangh as a pre-condition for their continuation as Minister of External Affairs and Information and Broadcasting in the Council of Ministers. Atal Bihari Vajpayee and L.K. Advani resigned from the Council of Ministers because they refused to delink themselves from their parent organisation, i.e., the RSS. Loyalty to the RSS and commitment to the ideology of Hindu Rashtra as defined and propagated by the RSS is a pillar of the belief system of Vajpayee and Advani. How could they severe their relationship with the RSS? Vajpayee and Advani were representatives of the RSS and its ideology in the Council of Ministers of Morarji Desai. This episode establishes once for all that Jana Sangh/BJP is a political extension of the RSS and political control over Prime Minister or Ministers or MPs or MLAs is exercised by the RSS leadership.

BJP in the 1980s and 1990s

The Janata Party experiment of 1977-79 came to an end and Congress party under the leadership of Mrs. Indira Gandhi returned back to power in the Lok Sabha elections of 1979-80 and State Assembly elections of 1980. The Lok Sabha elections of 1984 were contested under very exceptional circumstances because India's Prime Minister became a victim of political assassination and the Congress party led by Rajiv Gandhi won the elections of 1984. The Lok Sabha elections of 1989, 1991, 1996, 1998 and 1999 witnessed the stabilisation and expansion in the electoral support of the BJP both at the Centre and in the State Assemblies of India. Hence the 1990s has been a real decade of the Parivar and the BJP. The BJP obtained 85 Lok Sabha seats in 1989, 119 seats in 1991, 160 seats in 1996, 180 seats in 1998 and 182 seats in 1999. The BJP and Sangh fraternity practiced the strategy of Hindu mobilisation on the issue of Ram Janmabhoomi.

The Sangh fraternity has always maintained that Ram Temple at Ayodhya was destroyed by the Mughal King Babar and a mosque was constructed at the site of Rama's place of birth and Hindu Samaj has to reconstruct the Ram Temple at the same place where it originally existed and which was then occupied by Babri Mosque. This Temple-Mosque controversy was completely mishandled by the Congress party under the leadership of Rajiv Gandhi and P.V. Narasimha Rao because they did not confront the RSS affiliates like Vishwa Hindu Parishad, Bajrang Dal and others who were mobilising the masses and Hindu saints and priests for the 'liberation' of the place of so-called Birth of Lord Rama. The Hindu organisations launched movements like *Shila Pujan, Shilanayas, Rath Yatra* and the BJP contested the Lok Sabha elections of 1991 on the issue of construction of Ram Temple at Ayodhya. This was not the first time that the 'joint family' of Sangh had mobilised Hindus around Hindu cultural symbols for gaining political mileage during the elections. The RSS had mobilised large number of Hindu saints in 1967 and they had demonstrated in Delhi in support of their demand for a ban on 'Cow slaughter' in India. Mrs. Indira Gandhi, as Prime Minister of India, took very serious note of Hindu mobilisation on the issue of 'cow' and she confronted the Sangh and the priests by alleging that their religion-based political mobilisation is a great threat to secular and culturally plural India. On the contrary, Rajiv Gandhi and P.V. Narasimha Rao as Prime Ministers and Congress party leaders made compromises with militant Hindu organisations on Temple and Mosque controversy and this encouraged the Sangh fraternity and they succeeded in destroying the Mosque on December 6, 1992. It is wrong to maintain that the Hindu organisations had immense support of the Hindu masses behind the Ram Janmabhoomi movement because after the events of December 6, 1992, the BJP-led state governments of Uttar Pradesh, Madhya Pradesh, Himachal Pradesh and Rajasthan were dismissed by the Central Government and the State Assembly elections of 1993 decisively proved that the Hindu voter did not vote for the so-called party of Hindus which had destroyed the Babri Mosque. The BJP was decisively defeated in the State Assembly elections of North India where it was expecting that it would return to power with the enthusiastic support of the Hindu voter. The State Assembly elections of 1993 in Madhya Pradesh, Rajasthan, Uttar Pradesh and Himachal Pradesh exposed the myth that Hindu voters would support a Hindu party which had destroyed the Mosque at Ayodhya.

The BJP has risen to power not by just exploiting Hindu religious symbols but because of the open or clandestine support it has always received from so-called secular leaders and secular political parties. The Samyukta Vidhayak Dal governments were formed in some states in 1967 and many secularist and radical political groups enthusiastically shared power with the Jana Sangh. Jayaprakash Narayan's 'Total Revolution' of 1974-75 was actively supported by the RSS and 'J.P.' expressed his gratitude to the RSS for extending its support to the Movement. Morarji Desai became Prime Minister in 1977 with full support and participation of the Jana Sangh. The Jana Sangh which was formed in 1950 took only twenty seven years to share power with other secular parties at the Centre in 1977. V.P. Singh became Prime Minister of India in 1989 with the full backing of the BJP and he followed the dictates of BJP while dealing with Kashmir problem in 1989-90. The BJP leadership is correct in maintaining that before the Lok Sabha elections of 1998, they were working as king makers and in 1998 other parties are rushing towards the BJP for making alliances and coalitions. It may be mentioned here that BJP's political success is only partly on the basis of its own strategies of

Hindu mobilisation. Its real success lies in making the secularists as its allies, promoters and supporters. Jayaprakash Narayan, Morarji Desai, V.P. Singh and other secular parties and groups have helped the Sangh fraternity to rule over India and implement its programme of Hindutva. The party of Hindu Rashtra has obtained only 25 percent of the votes during the Lok Sabha elections of 1998 and 23.6 percent in 1999. Are the majority of Hindus voting for the party which claims to speak on behalf of the Hindus of India? The success of BJP to a large extent is the result of support extended to it by pseudo-secular parties, groups and leaders in India. While the BJP and RSS have been always involved in spreading the ideology of Hindu Rashtra of 'one culture, one nation and one country', the so-called secular and socialist parties have surrendered themselves before the powerful 'logic of power' for the sake of power and office and in the process, they have legitimised the forces of Hindutva by seeking their cooperation in struggles or by sharing power with it in the government.

Nehru and Hindutva versus Opportunistic Alliances and Hindutva

The Constitution of India provides some constitutional basic rights to religious minorities to promote, profess and practise their religion and minority cultural rights have also been safeguarded by the Constitution. Further, Jawaharlal Nehru confronted the forces of sectarian and irrational Hindutva by mobilising the common masses of India and during the Lok Sabha and State Assembly elections of 1952, 1957 and 1962. Nehru specifically targeted the ideology and politics of Hindutva and the so-called Hindu voter did not oblige the Jana Sangh which remained at the margins of Indian politics during Nehru phase. The average national vote polled by the Jana Sangh, which includes every state of India, was 2.76 per cent in 1952, 4.03 in 1952, and 6.07 in 1962. The moral of above description is that Hindu communalism can be contained and marginalised if the secular forces are determined to challenge it at political and ideological level. Nehru's phase of politics substantiates the argument that the Hindutva has extended its areas of influence in public life because either the secular forces are not ready to confront it or they are willing to extend it an active or passive support. Hindutva is marching on not only on its own steam, it is also gaining in strength and influence because many social and political groups which claim to be secular have extended full support to Hindutva and also secular forces have not effectively and unitedly challenged the politics and ideology of Hindu Rashtra.. This thesis can be proved by dividing politics of India during Nehru and post-Nehru phases because Hindutva was effectively contained during the Nehru phase of politics and Hindutva has gradually marched on during post-Nehru phase of politics. How did Nehru confront the forces of Hindutva from 1947 to 1964?

After the independence of India, the struggle in defence of secular Nationhood was led by Jawaharlal Nehru and many worthwhile lessons can be learnt from Nehru's methods of fighting against very powerful forces of communalism. Nehru in his Letters to the Chief Ministers wrote that "India will disintegrate as a nation-state if religion based parties are in power". Nehru firmly believed that Indian democracy will be a sham and India will not survive as a Nation because "communalism will break up India if allowed free play". Thus, Nehru's struggle against communalism was not tactical or just for the sake of the winning of an election. The essence of Indian nationhood was its cultural diversity, and he asked the people of India to develop "an outlook which embraces all this variety and considers its very own."

The Congress party had its own quota of Hindu conservatives and believers of soft Hindutva. Many a time Nehru came into serious conflicts with his own comrades-in-arm who were not convinced about Nehru's definition of secular India. Nehru was engaged in a struggle against communalism at every fora of public and political life and in this he had to fight many battles within his own party. A few facts may be mentioned to substantiate that Nehru fought at many fronts to defend and promote the idea of secular and plural Indian Nation.

Nehru contested the first Lok Sabha elections of 1952 and he made it as a fight between secular politics versus politics of Hindutva as represented by the Hindu Mahasabha, the Jana Sangh and the Ram Rajya Parishad. The Lok Sabha elections of 1952 were contested around the issues of secular politics versus religion based politics and Nehru campaigned in the whole country against the forces of Hindutva. On political level Nehru targeted Hindu Mahasabha, Jana Sangh and Ram Rajya Parishad and voters were asked to vote against these political formations. The election results of Lok Sabha and State Assemblies of 1952 went in favour of the secular parties like the Congress, the communists and the socialists, and the parties of the Hindutva were marginalised and effectively defeated. It does not mean that secular democracy became firmly established because of electoral victories. The real significance of Nehru's political agenda of confronting the forces of Hindutva during the elections of 1952 was to fight against the whole social milieu of communal hatred and divisions which had plagued India in its early years of freedom. Indian society was quite vitiated by the propagandists of Hindutva whose one plank was reunion of India and Pakistan by the establishment of an Akhand Bharat. The President of Hindu Mahasabha at its Calcutta session in December 1949 made a policy statement that the objective of the Sabha was to establish an Akhand Bharat and Nehru immediately contradicted it by describing such a statement as 'most irresponsible'. Nehru could not have allowed the demand for Akhand Bharat to go unchallenged and uncontested because the Hindu Mahasabha was involved in playing a Hindu card against the Muslims of India and Pakistan, and making every effort to make Indian Muslims feel guilty for the partition of India. Nehru's contribution in the making of secular Nationhood is quite significant if the context of pre-partition and post-partition events is kept in mind because communalism had captured the hearts and mind of large number of people of undivided India, and feelings of communal hatred had to be fought if independent India had to become secular state.

A few facts may be mentioned to support the argument that Nehru had to confront the Hindu conservatives and believers of soft Hindutva within the Congress party. A very controversial issue before the Constituent Assembly was the choice for a National language for a multi-lingual country and Hindu conservatives within the Congress led by Purushottam Dass Tandon, Seth Govind Das and others championed the cause of Hindi as a national language for India. Gandhi-Nehru version about linguistically diverse country was that Hindustani which is a spoken language of large number of people should become India's lingua-franca. This was not acceptable to Hindi enthusiasts who started describing Urdu '*as a symbol of secession*'. The Congress party was polarised on the issue of pure Hindi versus every day spoken Hindustani and on the basis of a secret vote of the Congress Legislative party 78 votes were in favour of Hindi and 77 votes were for Hindustani and thus the defenders of Hindi within the Congress and outside celebrated it as a victory for Hindu culture whose medium is Hindi. Nehru was defeated by his own party but he continued to fight against his colleagues within the Congress on issues which had communal overtones. Dr. Rajendra Prasad, as the President of India, wanted to attend the consecration at Somnath Temple and Nehru advised him that it would give wrong signals because Head of a secular state should not openly identify himself with purely Hindu religious ceremonies and rituals. Similarly, Nehru government's effort to reform Hindu laws on the basis of Hindu Code Bill met with stiff opposition both from Congress leaders and other important Hindu leaders. Nehru was opposed by leaders like Alladi Krishnaswami Iyer, Bakshi Tek Chand, Pattabhai Sitaramayya and on December 17, 1949, Nehru appealed that just the "principle of the Bill could be accepted" and Dr. Rajendra Prasad categorically stated that "any attempt to pass this Bill without first educating the electorate and getting a mandate from it" was just not acceptable. Not to be left behind, Swami Karpatriji Maharaj, President of the Hindu Dharma Sangh, addressed a letter to members of Parliament that "to make a piece of social legislation, on which the electorate had no chance to express its will, a matter of confidence in the government, is to perpetuate a constitutional outrage". Hindu conservatives within the Congress were quite disturbed with Nehru championing progressive secular causes like Hindu Code Bill or Hindustani instead of Hindi and they decided to tame him by putting Purushottam Dass Tandon as the Congress party elected President. How could Nehru function with a party President whose social outlook was fundamentally opposed to his social philosophy? Hindu conservatives within the Congress wanted to capture the party apparatus because nominations for the first Lok Sabha and State Assembly elections were to be made by the party organisation and with Tandon at the helm of party affairs, Hindu conservatives would have a field day in getting their candidates nominated for contesting the elections. Nehru confronted Tandon and his Hindu conservative supporters within the Congress party and forced him to resign from his position of party President.

It is worth mentioning that Nehru wrote to Govindvallabh Pant, the then Chief Minister of Uttar Pradesh, that alarming news was coming from Faizabad (Ayodhya) on a controversy between Temple and Mosque and it should be nipped in the bud otherwise it would flare up into a communal question. Nehru was not satisfied with the assurances of Pant and suggested that he may personally visit Faizabad to assess the situation at the grass roots level. Pant obstructed Nehru's efforts to resolve this so-called Temple-Mosque dispute in the early 1950s and it exploded when the Babri Mosque was destroyed on December 6, 1992 by the Hindu Parivar fanatics.

Nehru's task was not only to fight against the ideology of Hindutva, soft or full-fledged; Muslim minorities had also to be given a sense of confidence that after Partition of India they were full-fledged citizens of a secular state and this country belonged to all irrespective of caste, colour, creed or faith. Nehru fulfilled this psychological need of the Indian Muslims who felt insecure by the atmosphere of hatred created by the forces of Hindutva. Nehru's struggles against Hindutva and Hindu social reactionaries occupied his seventeen years of leadership of India from 1947 to 1964. Hindi became an instrument in the hands of believe of Hindutva and Hindu social reactionary forces to propagate Hindu cultural values. B.V. Keskar, the then Information and Broadcasting Minister of Nehru government, sanskritised Hindi language of the All India Radio and even banned the playing of songs of Indian movies by the Radio. Nehru himself came out openly against the sanskritised Hindi which became the medium of All India Radio. Incidentally, socialists led by

Ram Manohar Lohia castigated Nehru for his anti-Hindi stance. The issue for Nehru was that in the formative years of secular republic of India, Hindi language was likely to become an instrument in the hands of Hindu cultural revivalists and this would provide a fertile social milieu for the strengthening of the ideology of Hindutva. Nehru targeted both the ideology and practice of Hindutva because he was firmly committed to the values of secular society for India. This description should help in understanding the reasons for strong anti-Nehru feelings and sentiments among the leadership and followers of the Hindu 'joint family'.

The contemporary fighters against Hindu communalism should learn a few lessons from Nehru's approach and struggles in defence of secularism. First, secularism is not a verbalised belief-system to get Muslim votes during the elections. Tactical political secularism cannot confront the ideology of Hindutva. Second, if Congress leadership is committed to the ideology of secularism, it has to do a lot of cleansing within its own organisation. Nehru's fight was not only against the puritanical forces of Hindutva, he also fought Congress Hindu conservatives who were providing legitimacy to Hindutva by promoting policies like sanskritised Hindi or opposition to the Hindu Code Bill. The collapse of Babri Mosque on December 6, 1992 clearly established that Congress leadership had not taken care of their own soft Hindu elements and this was completely un-Nehruvian way of doing things. In summation, it may be mentioned that Nehru has left a clear message to the defenders of secularism that any compromise with Hindutva, soft or hard, will weaken and ultimately destroy secular India. Nehru succeeded in containing Hindutva because, unlike his successors, he refused to make any compromise with Hindutva.

Story of Opportunistic Alliances

Hindutva has grown because Nehru's secular politics in the real sense of the term has been abandoned by his political successors. Nehru could never think of forming any coalition governments with the help of Jana Sangh or its later *Avtar* BJP. Politics of Hindutva has been legitimised by political leaders and groups who have always projected themselves as secular forces in society. A few facts may be mentioned to substantiate the argument that Hindutva has been on the 'march' because post-Nehru political leadership has made 'historic compromises' with the forces of Hindutva. First, the Lok Sabha and State Assembly elections of 1967 are a watershed in Indian politics because the Congress party's monopoly of power was broken and political space vacated by the Congress was occupied by the Jana Sangh and many other social groups who very enthusiastically shared political power with the Sangh Brotherhood. The

Jana Sangh secured 67 seats in the Lok Sabha elections of 1967 while it had only 14 members in 1962 and its percentage of vote increased from 6.44 in 1962 to 9.41 percent in 1967. The party also won 261 seats in State Assemblies which was much more than its tally of 119 in 1962. Not only this. The Jana Sangh actively participated in the 'United Front governments' of Bihar, Haryana, Madhya Pradesh, Punjab and Uttar Pradesh. Jana Sangh/BJP has not looked back from that moment of glory of 1967 and whenever opportunity arose either at the Centre in 1977, 1998 and 1999 or in any State of India from 1967 onwards, it has formed coalition governments with the help of every so-called national or regional secular party. The Vajpayee-led National Democratic Alliance government has active support and participation of 24 parties like the DMK, the Telugu Desam, the Biju Janata Dal, the socialists like Ram Vilas Paswan, George Fernandes, Shard Yadav or the Akali Dal or secularists like Farooq Abdullah of National Conference. Similarly, the Jana Sangh/BJP has been able to form coalition governments in the States, whenever the need has arisen from 1967 to 2000. A secular Naveen Patnaik of the BJD has legitimised the BJP in Orissa State and the Bihar socialists are happy to walk hand in hand with the BJP. Km. Mamata of the Trinamool Congress, A.K. Ghani Khan Choudhri, a veteran Congress leader, are engaged in saffronising the secular Bengal by floating a grand alliance alongwith the BJP to confront their enemy number one, i.e., the Communists. What a great achievement of secularists who were in the Congress? Thus politics of coalitions has benefited the BJP by establishing its political credibility in public life. Second, every important extra-parliamentary struggle launched by secular leaders like Morarji Desai or Jayaprakash Narayan or others welcomed the Sangh family to participate as comades-in-arm in mass struggles of the 1970s or of the 1990s. The *'Nav Nirman Samiti'* of Gujarat launched its struggle in 1974 and Jayaprakash Narayan launched his struggle in Bihar in 1975 and in these mass struggles the RSS workers were invited to play an active role under the umbrella provided by secular leaders. Incidentally the 'power bloc' constituted by the ruling classes of India had started fragmenting when Jayaprakash Narayan launched his movement in 1974-75, and an intense struggle among factions and strata of the ruling classes has not come to an end. Not only this. None of the factions and strata of the ruling classes have taken to armed struggle in their inter-class and intra-class conflict. Factions and strata of the ruling classes are fighting their battles against one another within the frame work of parliamentary democracy. Hence even opposites can form coalition governments to consolidate their power within the state.

It is not without reason that 'J.P.' publicly praised the RSS and its 'family' members at the annual Jana Sangh session in March 1975 by dismissing the charge that the Jana Sangh was 'fascist'. Walter K. Anderson and Shridhar Damle in their *The Brotherhood in Saffron The Rashtriya Swayamsevak Sangh and Hindu Revivalism (1991)* and P.N. Dhar in *Indira Gandhi the 'Emergency' and the Indian Democracy (2000)* have marshalled great facts to validate the argument that the Sangh 'family' provided shoulders to leaders of secular movements and in return the Sangh gained in legitimacy in public life.

Nehru's project of secularism was integrally linked with his larger project of modern secular nation-building on the basis of economic planning and eradication of poverty and economic and social backwardness. The whole society was mobilised around the larger goals of building a new India. Nehru clearly realised that the poor masses of India who lived without any hope could fall prey to the tricks of irrational sectarian Hindu ideology. Nehru gave hope to the poor of India and made them identify with the building of a new and prosperous India. The post-Nehru political leadership especially of the 1990s abandoned the project of nation-building for the whole society and adopted a project of free market economy for the benefit of the propertied classes; more than 500 million people who are still living below the poverty line and at a subsistence level do not occupy any place in their schema of economic development of the country. The new slogan of the withdrawal and retreat of the State has created social and psychological anxieties among the poor masses who feel left out of the fruits of economic development. On the one hand, Hindutva has appropriated the upwardly mobile consumerist middle class Hindu by promising him the freedoms of market economy and on the other, it is exploiting and manipulating the anxieties and insecurities of the poor by mobilising them on the platform of politics of targeting of Muslim and Christian minorities. The RSS chief K.S. Sudarshan is preparing the Hindus for fighting a big 'epic battle' against the non-Hindus. The ascendancy of Hindutva in the 1990s is closely linked with the project of private market economy in which the absolute majority of poor find themselves completely abandoned by the State. This social milieu provides great space to Hindutva to exploit the insecurities of the vulnerable strata of society by projecting all non-Hindus as a great threat to the so-called Hindus.

Politics of Hindu versus the 'other' has been examined by placing Nehru in the centre-stage of our discussion to suggest that Hindu communalism can be contained and marginalised as was done by Nehru. The Hindu Right-wing politics can also become a permanent feature of India if pretenders to secularism like Morarji or V.P. Singh, Narasimha

Table 5.2: Occupations of Madhya Pradesh BJS and BJP MLAs 1957-90

	1957	*1962*	*1967*	*1972*	*1977*	*1980*	*1985*	*1990*
Agriculturalists[1]	2	15	12	14	23	21	27	99
Merchants, Industrialists	4	7	8	6	12	11	10	29
Lawyers	1	2	8	9	22	14	6	37
Medical practitioners	—	3	3	1	9	3	2	12
Teachers	—	—	1	6	7	1	1	6
Clerks, executive	—	1	6	1	4	2	3	9
Workers, craftsmen	—	6	2	1	3	2	2	5
Social workers	1	1	1	2	9	1	1	5
Pujaris, Sadhus		1	1	—	1		—	—
Journalists	—	1	1	1	—	—	2	1

1. The figures in this category must be considered as approximate because 'agriculturists' seem to designate cultivators as well as land owners. The biographical data do not permit differentiation of the intermediate status, even though education led me to reclassify some individuals (e.g. an 'agriculturist' with an L.LB. has been considered a 'lawyer'). This table remains relevant for visualising the balance between MLAs from a rural background and the others. As far as politicians are concerned, they have been classified according to their original professions.

Sources: Jafferlot.

Rao, the Congress leaders, or George Fernandes or Ram Vilas Paswan, the socialist leaders, or Karunanidhi and Naidu, the regional leaders, or Jayalalitha and Mamata Banerjee are ready to openly embrace the politics of Hindutva as they have been doing from 1967 to 2000. The post-independence history of India clearly shows that Hindu communalism has thrived with the connivance and collaboration of free market wallahs who also pretend to be secularists.

Further, the growth of a party can be understood if it is able to expand and extend its social base among multiple groups of the society. The Jana Sangh and RSS had a very narrow social base among Brahman and Bania castes of urban areas of North India. The social reach of Jana Sangh was very narrow in terms of Hindu castes and in class terms it attracted mercantile capitalists and lower, middle and rich traders. The Hindutva did not have any rural social constituency in the 1950s, 1960s and 1970s. Has the BJP and Sangh family extended its social constituencies?

The Table 5.3 by Jafferlot while limited to Madhya Pradesh clearly tells us that political leadership of the BJP is in the hands of middle class professionals.

While the Table 5.4 about social base of parties provided by Mitra and Singh clearly tells us that the image of Congress party as a 'coalition of minorities' is still true, the BJP is a party of Hindu upper castes. It

Table 5.3

Caste and Community based distribution of Jana Sangh and B.J.P. MLAs in Madhya Pradesh, 1952-93

Caste groups and communities	*1952*	*1957*	*1962*	*1967*	*1972*	*1977*	*1980*	*1985*	*1990*	*1993*
Upper caste	2(40)	3(30)	11(29.7)	31(42.5)	25(49)	57(48.3)	18(32.7)	19(34.5)	71(32.5)	42(36.8)
Brahmin	2(40)	1(10)	7(18.9)	14(19.1)	7(13.7)	32(27.1)	8(14.5)	11(20)	(31(14.2)	22(19.2)
Rajput		1(10)	7(18.9)	14(19.1)	7(13.7)	32(27.1)	8 (14.5)	11(20)	31(14.2)	22(19.2)
Kayath				4(5.4)	4(7.8)	4(3.3)	1(1.8)		3(1.3)	1(0.9)
Banya		1(10)	1(2.7)	5(6.8)	4(7.8)	10(8.4)	4(7.2)	4(7.2)	16(7.3)	7(6.3)
Khattri						2(1.7)	1(1.8)		1(0.4)	1(0.9)
Sindhi				1(1.3)		1(0.8)	1(1.8)		2(0.9)	1(0.9)
Intermediate castes			2(5.4)	—		2(1.7)	1(1.8)			1(0.8)
Maratha			2(5.4)			2(1.7)	1(1.8)			1(0.8)
Other backward classes		2(20)	3(8.1)	9(12.3)	8(15.6)	11(9.1)	10(16.2)	15(27.2)	48(21.7)	21(18.4)
Jat				1(0.8)	1(1.8)		1(0.4)	1(0.9)		
Yadav				1(1.9)	1(0.8)	1(1.8)	1(1.8)	5(2.3)	3(2.7)	
Kurmi		1(10)		2(2.7)	1(1.9)	3(2.5)	2(3.6)	3(5.4)	8(3.6)	3(2.7)
Teli				2(2.7)	1(1.9)		1(1.8)	3(5.4)	5(2.3)	1(0.9)
Kira				1(1.3)	1(1.9)	2(1.7)	1(1.8)		4(1.8)	2(1.8)
Panwar					1(1.9)	1(0.8)	3(5.4)		5(2.3)	2(1.8)
Gujjar			1(2.7)	2(2.7)	2(2.7)	2(3.9)		1(1.8)		
Raghuwanshi			2(1.3)					3(1.3)		
Pokhal									1(1.4)	
Others			2(5.4)	1(1.3)	1(1.9)	3(2.5)		8(14.5)	16(7.3)	9(8.1)
Scheduled castes	1(20)	1(10)	8(21.6)	16(21.9)	8(15.6)	20(16.9)	12(21.8)	7(12.7)	36(16.5)	27(23.6)
Scheduled tribes		1(10)	9(24.3)	13(17.8)	11(21.5)	17(14.4)	10(18)	10(18.1)	53(24.3)	16(14)
Jains	2 (40)	2(40)	3(8.1)	4(5.4)		10(8.4)	4(7.2)	3(5.4)	8(3.6)	7.(6.1)
Muslims								1(1.8)	2(0.9)	
Sikhs						1(0.8)			1(0.4)	
Total	**5(6)**	**10(10)**	**37(41)**	**73(78)**	**51(51)[1] 118(128)**	**55(60)**	**55(58)**	**218(219)**	**114(117)**	

1. The Jana Sangh won only 48 seats in 1972, but the party succeeded in winning three more in subsequent by-election.

NB. We have not been able to identify the caste of some MLAs; the last line indicate the total number of those whose caste was known and the total of MLAs in parenthesis.

Source : Jafferlot

Table 5.4
Social Bases of Political Parties (1996 and 1998) (in per cent)

Background Characteristic	*1996 INC+*	*BJP+*	*1998 NF*	*LF*	*BSP*	*INC*	*BJP+*	*UF*	*BSP*
All-India Average Gender	**27.5**	**24.9**	**10.1**	**7.5**	**3.4**	**27.3**	**32.9**	**19.2**	**2.9**
Female	27.6	23.0	9.4	7.6	3.1	28.0	29.5	19.6	2.8
Male	27.4	26.8	10.8	7.4	3.6	26.5	36.3	18.7	3.0
Locality									
Rural	28.1	22.6	10.6	8.8	3.8	27.0	31.8	19.6	3.1
Urban	25.6	32.2	8.7	3.4	2.0	28.2	36.3	17.7	2.4
Age									
Up to 25 years	25.7	27.0	10.2	6.9	3.8	24.4	35.0	17.8	4.3
26-35 years	27.1	25.5	9.9	7.7	3.5	27.5	33.9	18.6	2.6
36-45 years	28.8	25.1	9.7	8.1	2.9	27.4	32.4	20.5	2.6
45-55 years	27.0	23.6	10.2	8.4	3.5	28.2	32.0	21.5	2.2
56 years and above	30.0	21.3	10.9	6.4	2.9	29.7	29.9	18.2	2.6
Education									
Illiterate	28.6	21.1	12.3	6.6	5.0	29.1	28.9	18.3	4.0
Up to middle	28.4	23.8	9.2	8.9	2.8	26.9	34.3	20.8	2.4
College, without degree	25.8	31.3	8.0	7.7	1.6	25.7	36.5	19.1	1.8
Graduate and above	21.1	36.7	6.1	6.0	0.9	21.5	42.5	16.6	1.6
Occupation									
Unskilled worker	30.6	17.0	9.9	10.8	5.2	34.6	23.0	21.4	4.1
Agricultural and allied worker	28.4	17.8	11.5	8.9	5.2	26.2	26.2	24.5	4.5
Artisan and skilled worker	27.3	24.1	9.3	7.7	3.0	26.9	30.6	23.1	2.1
Cultivator (> 5 acres)	26.1	26.2	14.0	6.4	4.9	21.7	32.8	18.3	3.1
Cultivator (< 5 acres)	29.7	34.6	8.2	1.6	2.5	31.1	41.9	10.8	2.0
Business	23.3	33.0	10.1	7.6	0.7	26.2	37.9	21.5	1.5
White collar and professional	26.2	30.8	5.6	8.0	0.3	24.3	39.6	15.7	1.0
Caste									
Scheduled Caste	31.6	14.4	5.6	11.0	12.1	29.6	20.9	22.2	11.2
Scheduled Tribe	39.2	19.0	6.2	6.5	1.0	41.9	25.6	11.6	0.4
Other Backward Caste	21.7	23.6	16.3	5.9	2.3	22.5	34.6	21.0	1.6
Upper caste	28.4	33.6	7.1	7.3	0.4	28.1	38.5	17.4	1.1
Religion									
Hindu	26.2	28.9	8.4	7.4	3.7	25.6	37.4	17.4	3.0
Muslim	35.3	3.1	25.3	10.1	1.2	35.1	6.8	34.4	1.3
Christian	39.9	3.0	2.0	5.6	—	42.1	9.1	18.6	0.4
Sikh	18.3	14.3	16.7	2.4	5.6	21.9	39.8	18.0	10.2
Other	26.5	6.0	12.0	2.4	4.8	39.5	19.7	3.9	10.5
Economic Class									
Very poor	29.6	16.0	10.7	11.3	4.4	27.3	27.1	23.7	2.7
Poor	28.3	23.1	10.5	6.7	4.7	27.4	31.8	19.0	3.3
Middle	26.1	31.1	10.9	5.6	2.2	26.9	37.3	16.6	2.7
Upper	22.4	40.1	7.9	3.4	0.4	28.3	38.9	14.3	1.9

Note: Parties here represent pre-poll alliances.
1996: INC+ INC + AIADMK
BJP+ BJP + Samata + Shiv Sena + Haryana Vikas Party
NF + JD + Samajwadi Party

LF + CPM + CPI + RSP + FBL
1998: BJP+ BJP + Samata + Shiv Sena + Haryana Vikas Party + AIADMK + Akali Dal + Trinamool Congress + Lok Shakti + Biju Janata Dal + TDP (NTR)
UF + Janata Dal + SP (Mulayam) + TDP (N) + AGP + TMC + DMK + MGP + CPI + CPI(M) + RSP + FBL

Source: Subrata K. Mitra & V.B. Singh *Democracy and Social Change in India : A Cross-sectional Analysis of the National Electorate*, New Delhi, Sage Publications, 1999.

deserves to be mentioned that the Ram Janmabhoomi movement of the Sangh family paid dividends to the BJP because it could mobilise other backward castes also. The vote of no-confidence of the minorities in the BJP is quite clear from the above Table because it has a notional and nominal presence of Muslims and Christians within the party. The presence of minority communities in the BJP is only a case of 'show boys' for publicity purposes.

In summation, it may be mentioned that during the last fifty years Sangh family has emerged as a central factor in Indian politics on the basis of its own steam and it has also gained in strength because of the opportunistic politics of alliances and coalitions made by the so-called secular parties. Finally, in terms of social base BJP is a party of, by and for Hindus and its goal is to establish Hindu Rashtra.

BJP-IN-GOVERNMENT

The Atal Bihari Vajpayee-led coalition governments of 1989-99 and 1999-2000 have enthusiastically followed and implemented 'economic policies' of globalisation, liberalisation and privatisation. The Jana Sangh was always opposed to the policies of economic planning followed by the Nehru-Indira governments which were characterised as 'licence-permit Raj' by the RSS Brotherhood. Economic policies followed by the Vajpayee government are a continuation of IMF-World Bank consensus on India. The global aid-givers have maintained that economic development is obstructed by an interventionist and regulatory State and economic growth can take place if market is allowed to play its natural role and the State is rolled-back. The Vajpayee government is actively pursuing policies for the opening of economy to foreign private investors in industrial, financial, insurance and trading sectors of the economy. The Vajpayee government has made many new laws which are required to attract foreign investors especially in the field of insurance and industrial and consumer sectors of the economy. The Vajpayee government is implementing every commitment which it has made with the World Trade Organisation. Yashwant Sinha, the Finance Minister of the Vajpayee government, is focussed on containing fiscal deficit of the Indian government by either cutting some 'subsidies' or by mobilising financial resources by undertaking disinvestment of public sector undertakings. The BJP and Swadeshi Jagran Manch of the Sangh Brotherhood were critical of the economic policies followed by the Congress party under the leadership of P.V. Narasimha Rao during 1991-1996. The BJP in opposition critised economic policies which it has been aggressively implementing while it is in power at the Centre. The Vajpayee government has constituted a very high power 'Economic Advisory Committee' in which members of the political class and leaders of Indian capitalist classes sit together and evolve policies for the capitalist development of India in the age of New Global Capitalism. A real and significant development in the phase of BJP-in-power in the Central Government is the complete integration of the Indian State and the Indian capitalist classes within the country and externally the Indian State is integrating itself with world monopoly capitalism. The Indian capitalist class is now sitting within the Indian State apparatus and it is actively involved in decision-making institutions of the State. The Vajpayee government's path of development was elaborated in the President, K.R. Narayanan's address to the joint sitting of the two Houses of Parliament on October 25, 1999. The President observed :

"Experience, both domestic and international, suggests that rapid and multi-sector growth is possible only by pursuing a bold strategy of economic reforms. The nation's re-oriented strategy of development will have to rest on a *triad* in which the government provides a strong policy and regulatory leadership, the private sector brings the dynamism and efficiency of the competitive environment, and, local democratic institutions and the civil society brings enthusiastic participation by the people". What is the reality of this rhetoric?

Table 5.5
Foreign Direct Investment in India

Year	*FD Approval*	*Actual Inflows*	*Realisation Rate*
1991	534	351	65.73
1992	3888	675	17.36
1993	8859	1787	20.17
1994	14187	3289	23.18
1995	32072	6820	21.26
1996	36147	10389	28.74
1997	54891	16425	29.92
1998	30814	13340	43.29
1999	28367	16868	59.46

The actual flow of foreign direct investment in India does not match with the enthusiasm of the Vajpayee government. India is not a great destination for foreign investors in spite of the fact that in February 2000 the Vajpayee government placed about all items "under the automatic approval route for FDI and NRI/OCB investment". It was claimed that the Vajpayee governments' new thrust on liberalisation was "aimed towards increasing the present inflow of FDI to an annual figure of $10 billion which would imply a jump of nearly two and half times from $4.02 billion in January/December 1999". These hopes of the Vajpayee government have not been fulfilled. On the contrary, the policy of liberalisation has distorted economic development of the country because every decision of the government is guided by the need of 250 million middle and upper middle class consumers of India. S. Balakrishnan in his *"FDI or Fast Depleting Independence"*?[27] draws attention to the socially disastrous consequences of economic policies pursued by the Vajpayee government. He observes :

> "A glaring and tragic example comes to mind immediately. The roads are narrow, badly laid and ill-lit", the traffic, as it is, is chaotic and ill-disciplined and the spiralling bill for import of crude eats up a sizable part of our foreign exchange earnings. Yet models after models of new cars, of various sizes and powers, with vaunted new features and accessories, with different price tags, from well-known foreign stables, are hitting the roads everyday." The worst part of the 'opening of economy' to the foreign investors is that India has not gained in getting new technologies from foreign investors. The most telling example of India's failure to get any technological benefits from foreign investors is our Maruti Udyog where government of India is a partner. Suzuki has not 'shared with India its steering road technology' nor it has permitted export of Maruti cars with Suzuki identification."

The Ninth Five-Year Plan document of April 1997 was launched on the premise of 'growth with social justice and equity'. The only beneficiary of social justice oriented governments of H.D. Deve Gowda, Inder Kumar Gujral and Atal Bihari Vajpayee have been government employees on whom the Central Government spent Rs. 18,000 crore and the State Governments had to spend Rs. 35,266 crores because the Fifth Pay Commission had recommended pay revisions and the governments implemented these recommendations. In the name of 'national security' the Vajpayee government has increased defence expenditure to more than additional Rs. 23,000 crores in the budget of 2000-2001. The 'holy cows' of India, i.e., the political class, the bureaucracy and defence sector are the main culprits for the rising fiscal deficit of the country and this is precisely the social constituency of the forces of Hindutva. The forces of Hindutva are operating the Indian economy for industrial capitalist classes, business classes, middle class professionals, bureaucrats, entrepreneurs and middle and upper middle class urban and rural populations of India. The BJP does not have any economic programme either for rural development or for the generation of employment in a labour-surplus economy. Since the social base of Hindutva is very narrow, it is operating the economy in the interests of its narrow class base. This is the crisis of India. With hardly 20 million income tax payers, the fiscal crisis of the Indian State is the product of social arrangements of a capitalist-landlord controlled society. The appropriators of social surplus with the full support and protection of the Indian State are not ready to share their wealth with the real producers in society. The working classes of India have become victims of increasing income disparities in the phase of liberalisation of Indian economy and the BJP does not have any economic programme for the working classes of India. The BJP at the Centre has followed economic policies which clearly reflect its class character which primarily lies in traders, merchants, upper and middle class professionals and self-employed rent-seekers. This is the essence of its economic policies. It has no answers for the problems of either the rural or the urban poor and unemployed youth of India.

Foreign and Defence Policies of the BJP-Led Government

Jana Sangh/BJP have always advocated a very tough foreign policy against Pakistan and China on the basis of a premise that Pakistan as a Muslim country can never be positive towards a Hindu majority India and China as a communist country is a rival of India in the Asian continent. Anti-Muslim and anti-Communist ideology of the Sangh Brotherhood is fundamental principle of their foreign policy. The Jana Sangh leadership had always opposed India's foreign policy of Non-alignment because they alleged that Indian policy was tilted in favour of Soviet Russia and Atal Bihari Vajpayee as Minister of External Affairs in the Morarji Desai government proclaimed that India would pursue a policy of 'genuine non-alignment' without any tilt in favour of any power bloc, western or eastern communist countries. Since Russian system has collapsed and global power equations have changed, anti-Communist foreign policy orientations of the Sangh Brotherhood are now focussed against China. The Jana Sangh/BJP has been consistent supporters of Israel in India because Israel was fighting against the Arab countries and anti-Islamic Sangh Brotherhood viewed Israel as a natural friend of their anti-Muslim ideological and political plank.

Further, the Sangh Brotherhood has always supported the idea of militarily strong Hindu India and a nuclearised India has been always on the agenda of the forces of Hindutva. A militarised and nuclearised India has been the ideal of Indian nationhood among the believers of the RSS and its multiple affiliates. The BJP got an opportunity to follow an anti-Pakistan and anti-China foreign policy and an aggressive military based defence policy when it came to power at the Centre in 1998. The BJP celebrated as a day of great national achievement when nuclear device was exploded on May 11, 1998 at Pokharan. The Vajpayee government proclaimed from the house top that India has become a 'Nuclear Power State'. In a confidential letter written by the Vajpayee government to President Clinton of the United States it was mentioned that India exploded nuclear device because its security was threatened by Pakistan and China. Since the United States' administration decided to leak the contents of the government of India's letter, Indians came to know that BJP's defence and foreign policies were directed against China and Pakistan. Indian jubilations came to an end when at the end of May 1998, Pakistan followed suit and exploded its nuclear device. The United States, European Union and Japan disapproved this action of the Vajpayee government and all of them imposed 'economic sanctions' against nuclearised India. The government of India in post-Pokharan phase became active in convincing the powerful western countries about its security threat perceptions and the five nuclear power states demanded that India should sign Comprehensive Test Ban Treaty before economic sanctions imposed on India could be withdrawn. The BJP-led coalition government was unable to accept the demand of nuclear power states for signing the Comprehensive Test Ban Treaty because many opposition parties in India did not support the idea of the signing of the CTBT. In the absence of political consensus in India, the Vajpayee government could not have signed the CTBT and the United States would not remove economic sanctions against nuclearised India without it putting its signatures on the CTBT.

The worst aspect of nuclear explosion was that India announced that Pakistan and China were threats to our security and Pakistan equalised with India by exploding its nuclear device and India's diplomatic relations with China became a serious bone of contention between the two neighbouring countries. Since the United States had declared nuclear South Asia as the 'most dangerous region in the world', the government of India was under immense global pressure to mend its fences with Pakistan. Since the economic sanctions were like a sword of democles hanging over the head of Indian government, Atal Bihari Vajpayee undertook a visit to Pakistan on February 20, 1999 which is known as

Bus Journey to Lahore. It was expected that India and Pakistan would start moving towards peaceful co-existence after the meeting at Lahore between Atal Bihari Vajpayee and Nawaz Sharif. On the contrary, a war broke out at Kargil in Kashmir in May 1999. Under pressure from the government of United States, Pakistan ended its Kargil misadventure and relationship between India and Pakistan was completely frozen. The so-called victory of India in Kargil war became an issue during the Lok Sabha elections of September-October 1999 and BJP asked the voters : "The leader you can trust in War : In Peace-Proven experience or proven inexperience"? Hindutva survives and thrives on anti-Muslim and anti-Pakistan sentiment and Pakistan's misadventure in Kargil gave a great handle to the BJP campaigners during the elections who successfully projected India's victory in Kargil as an accomplishment of the leadership of Atal Bihari Vajpayee.

Pokharan II, victory in Kargil, shooting down of Pakistan's aircraft Atlantique by the Indian forces at Rann of Kutch on August 22, 1999 were highlighted by the BJP during the election campaign for the Thirteenth Lok Sabha elections. The National Democratic Alliance Manifesto of August 29, 1999 gave a slogan that 'India shall be built by Indians' and on national security, it observed that "The 13 month long Vajpayee government had brought about a paradigm shift in national security, ...The NDA promises to allocate adequate funds to "correct the imbalance and budgetary neglect of Defence needs".[28] The BJP-led coalition government congratulated itself on a very successful five days visit of President Bill Clinton of the United States to India from March 20 to 25, 2000 A.D. The government of India has proclaimed that "a new page has turned in the US-Indian relationships after the visit of President Bill Clinton." While the Government of India has publicly stated that its foreign policy is operated in the frame-work of a 'multi-polar world' and not a 'unipolar' world dominated by the United States, in reality, the BJP-led government is enthusiastically pursuing a pro-United States foreign policy. The Ministers of the Government of India like Pramod Mahajan of Information Technology or Yashwant Sinha of Finance and others are leading delegations of government officials and business and industrial groups to the United States for securing economic and trade benefits from that country. A news item in the *Economic Times "CII in pursuit of free trade pact with US*" mentioned that in the first week of June 2000, a select group of Indian industrialists, including Arun Bharat Ram, Narayanan Murthy, Ajay Piramal, K.V. Kamath, Jamshyd Godrej and Tarun Das will visit San Francisco and Washington to look at ways to enhance business links. "Heading the road show will be finance minister Yashwant Sinha and PMO secretary N.K. Singh".[29]

Tarun Das, a member of the delegation, observed that the "Lobbying will intensify during their interactions with select Congressmen and senators led by Jim McDermott of the Indian caucus". The ruling classes of India and political class led by the BJP-National Democratic Alliance is making every effort to strongly link India with the United States for the building of Indian economy and national security. On the advice of the United States, the Vajpayee-led government has opened a dialogue with Hurriyat leaders in Jammu & Kashmir. On the one hand, the Sangh Brotherhood is opposed to the economic policies of globalisation, on the other, social classes supporting the BJP and RSS affiliates are working for close alliance with the United States which is the leader of world capitalism. This is the class reality of BJP and its pro-United States foreign policy is in accord with class interests of its social constituency. This reality was expressed in the *Organiser* of April 30, 2000: "A new globally minded yet spiritually based Hindu intelligentsia is the need of the hour to deal with the challenges from the west. One of the great debacles of modern India is that the Marxists captured the intellectual elite of the country and turned them into mouth piece of anti-Hindu attitudes".[30]

To sum up, pillars of India's foreign policy under Atal Bihari Vajpayee are anti-Pakistan and anti-China and pro-United states. Defence build-up for the security of India has been always a policy plank of the forces of Hindutva because they equate a highly militarised and nuclearised India as a real strong point of the Hindu Rashtra. The grandeur of greatness of the Hindu is the mind-set of the Sangh Brotherhood and in this perspective Hindu state has to be a formidable military power. On the occasion of 'anniversary' of Pokharan II, George Fernandes in a meeting of the National Democratic Alliance observed that "India is strong because of Operation Shakti thanks due to Vajpayee's leadership."[31]

Not to be left behind, Vajpayee observed that : "Our rivals did not hope that India would emerge a global power. But today we have done it. The world has undisputedly accepted India as a global player. Today we are successfully challenging the world in trade, science and technology as well as other fields. There is no doubt we would come out victorious. The country is transforming into a global power as there is a definite policy which had made our enemies envious."[32] The *Organiser* paints Pakistan as real villain of the piece and warns Hindus that it is 'Hindu cowardice' which has been responsible for our humiliations at the hand of others and a patriotic Hindu should be ready to fight an 'epic war' as demanded by K.S. Sudarshan of the RSS. The hate campaign against Muslim Pakistan is a staple diet for the Sangh Brotherhood. "There is no system in Pakistan for the news to appear freely. Doordarshan shows music, dance and glamour. Pakistan cannot, owing to the religious construction", proclaims *Organiser*.[33] It is not surprising that after Kargil war of May-July of 1999, the government of India has stopped any negotiations or dialogue with the government of Pakistan on the plea that general Parvez Musharraf should first ask the so-called *Jihadis* to stop cross-border terrorism and only then talks between India and Pakistan can be resumed. Many a time in the past the government of India had held serious talks after military misadventures by Pakistan. The BJP has a new 'foreign policy doctrine' towards Pakistan and the result is a complete breakdown of any foreign policy dialogue between the two quarrelsome neighbouring countries.

Domestic Governance for Hindutva

The BJP has vigorously pursued its own agenda while leading the coalition governments at the Centre from 1998-99 and 1999-2000. Atal Bihari Vajpayee while campaigning during the Lok Sabha elections of 1998 proposed a 'Presidential System' instead of the chronic 'instability of parliamentary democracy'. The BJP in the Lok Sabha elections of 1999 made a proposal for the 'Review of Constitution of India' in the Manifesto of National Democratic Alliance, and the government of India has given top priority to this programme of the NDA by setting up a Constitution Review Commission.

It must be stated here that the RSS had never agreed with the democratic, republican, federal and secular Constitution of India of 1950. The believers of Hindutva had not accepted any of the basic premises of the Indian Constitution. Hensen states that:

> "Political power understood as sovereignty and national strength was, nonetheless, always crucial to Golwalkar's vision of a Hindu nation. In the 1950s Golwalkar advocated a strong 'Unitary State' and opposed the reorganisation of the Indian states into linguistic units, which he believed would weaken the cohesion of Hindu society and set in motion centrifugal forces. Instead, the country should move toward 'One Country, one State, one Legislature and one Executive' in order to strengthen itself and be able to counter foreign aggression."[34]

The RSS Hindu 'joint family' had always opposed the essential principle of pluralism as enshrined in the Indian Constitution by propagating the ideology of "One people, one culture, one nation". Atal Bihari Vajpayee, L.K. Advani and every important decision-maker of the BJP is firmly committed to the Unitarian doctrine for the governance of Hindu India as propagated by Guru Golwalkar and this is the reason that the Vajpayee government has appointed an eleven member Constitution

Review Commission in 2000. The ultimate source of truth for every member of the Sangh fraternity is Sar Sanghchalak of the RSS and K.S. Sudarshan while taking over the office of Sar Sanghchalak in 2000 from Rajendra Singh observed that :

> "The post of Sar Sanghchalak is like the legendary throne of Vikarmaditya. Whosoever sits on it is bound to do justice to the cause".[35]

Atal Bihari Vajpayee, L.K. Advani, Murli Manohar Joshi and every important leader of the BJP was trained by Guru Golwalkar and everyone of them is pursuing the goals of Hindu Rashtra as laid down by Golwalkar and successive Sar Sanghchalaks whose authority over the Sangh 'family' is complete. The RSS demands obedience from its members; otherwise, even Balraj Madhok, President of the BJP, was shown the door for differing with the dominant view point of the RSS leadership. The agenda for Constitution Review of the Vajpayee government is in reality the agenda of RSS as laid down by Sar Sanghchalak M.S. Golwalkar and the target of Review of the Constitution is Chapter III of Fundamental Rights of citizens which guarantees cultural rights to multiple and diverse communities of India. On the eve of Golden Jubilee celebrations of the Republic of India in the Central Hall of Parliament on January 27, 2000 Atal Bihari Vajpayee observed :

> "Our constitution has served the needs of both India's diversity and her innate unity. It has strengthened India's democratic traditions.
>
> "But even in the mightiest fort one has to repair the parapet from time to time, one has to clean the moat and check the banisters. The same is true about our Constitution.
>
> "Five decades after the adoption of the Constitution, India is faced with a new situation. The need for stability both at the centre and in the states has been felt acutely".

This rhetoric of Vajpayee could not conceal the truth because in the name of achieving the so-called political stability, an attempt may be made by 'nominated' members of the Constitution Review Commission to give a seal of approval to the Unitarian and centralised system of governance for India as desired by the RSS leadership from the times of Sar Sanghchalak M.S. Golwalkar.

K.R. Narayanan, the President of India, in the Central Hall of Parliament on January 27, 2000 observed that :

"Our recent experience of instability in government is perhaps not sufficient reason to discard the parliamentary system in favour of presidential or any other system."

President Narayanan expressed the view point which was reflected in the philosophy of our Constitution Fathers that India is a unique mosaic of 4,635 communities and 325 languages written in 24 scripts. India is a country of diversities without any parallel and this pluralist democracy with secular and federal system of governance can keep the country together and any attempt to impose Hindu hegemony in India will destroy the unity of the country.

The eleven member Constitution Review Committee 'nominated' by the Vajpayee government consists of Justice M.N. Venkatachaliah as Chairman, and its other members are Justice R.S. Sarkaria, Attorney General Soli Sorabjee, former Attorney General K. Parasaran, former High Court Judge K. Punniah, Journalist C.R. Irani, former diplomat Abid Hussain, former Lok Sabha Secretary General, Subhash Kashyap, former BJP MP Sumitra Kulkarni, former Speaker of the Lok Sabha P.A. Sangma, and Justice B.P. Jeevan Reddy. This Constitution Review Commission is handpicked by the Vajpayee government and it is a mixture of former members who have been active in public services and politicians fully acceptable to the BJP including a former BJP MP. This Commission does not have any legitimacy because 'nominees' of the government cannot be accepted as legitimate instrument for the Review of the Constitution which is a fundamental basic law of the country. In its first meeting on March 23, 2000 11-member nominated Constitution Review Commission decided the items for scrutiny and they were listed as follows :

(a) Menace of defections;
(b) Constitutional provisions on removal of poverty;
(c) Working of Article 356;
(d) Appointment and removal of governors;
(e) Decentralisation of powers and strengthening of Panchayati Raj;
(f) Enlargement of fundamental Rights,
(g) Effective enforcement of directive principles/fundamental duties; and
(h) Provisions relating to fiscal and monetary policies.

It may be mentioned here that none of the above listed topic for the Review of Constitution deserves a new National Commission because during the last fifty years many Commissions have gone into the working of many aspects of our Constitution and an elected Parliament of India has many a time amended the Constitution and made suitable changes on the basis of democratic principle of legislative debate on the nature of change in the Constitution of India. The spokesman of the Review Commission Justice B.P. Jeevan Reddy has maintained that they "would only review the working of the constitution and not rewrite it completely". It deserves to be mentioned that review of the working of the constitution has been an ongoing process during the last fifty years and there is absolutely no role for a Commission appointed by the Vajpayee government unless its task is to redefine the Constitution for a '*Unitary Hindu India*' as desired by the RSS founding fathers. The BJP published a 44 page brochure on 'Constitutional Study and Review' in which it maintained that the Constitution has been frequently amended and nothing new is being done by appointing a Constitution Review Commission and "nobody can doubt that the composition of the review panel is broad-based and totally a political and non-partisan in character. It is headed by Justice Venkatachaliah, a former Chief Justice of the Supreme Court and a highly respected authority on legal and constitutional matters."

The ruling classes and political parties are concerned about the growing political instability in India. The Constitution of India is neither responsible for fragmentation of politics nor it can offer any remedies.

The fault does not lie with the Constitution of India. Adolf I Hitler blamed the Weimer Republican Constitution for all the ills and crises of Germany and after burning the Reichstag in February 1933, he forgot about the Constitution and established a fascist government. Hitler had delegitimised the Constitution of Germany by making the people believe that it was the sole source of Germany's crisis and once people had lost their trust on the Republican Constitution, Hitler did not face any difficulty in subverting it. This is the lesson of History. Indian Constitution has been amended on the basis of proper procedures laid down in the Constitution itself and the Vajpayee government is going beyond these constitutionally laid down procedures for demanding its review. Electoral reforms can be undertaken by amending the Constitution on the basis of political consensus. The crucial distinction is between review of Constitution by 'nominees' of the government of India or amendments of the Constitution, as they have happened in the past on the basis of procedures laid down by the Constitution itself. The Sangh fraternity wants to generate a controversy on the viability and suitability and mutability of the Republican Constitution of India for governance of the country on the basis of a report by its nominated 11-member Commission. The so-called inadequacies of the Constitution will become a very contentious issue in India because the Sangh 'joint family' somehow wants to stabilise itself in power by pushing a Review of the Constitution. After all Atal Bihari Vajpayee has highlighted the issue of political instability and the Review Commission will have to suggest mechanisms so that the

BJP-led coalition can remain in power for five years. The Sangh joint family has shown its contempt for democracy by not going to Parliament for any discussion on the Review of Constitution and this has brought the cat out of the bag because the agenda of Hindu Rashtra cannot succeed on the basis of Parliamentary approval in India.

The Vajpayee Government and Minority Communities

While the BJP obtained less than 25 percent of votes during the Lok Sabha elections of 1998 and 1999, the minorities of India have kept themselves away from the BJP. It is for the first time in the history of democratic India that a Prime Minister does not enjoy the confidence of Muslim and Christian communities. Minorities are not feeling safe in India because the BJP-led Central Government and Uttar Pradesh, Gujarat State Governments of the BJP and Orissa coalition government of BJP and Biju Janata Dal have failed to protect the rights and interests of the minorities. The Sangh 'joint family' especially its affiliates like the Vishwa Hindu Parishad and Bajrang Dal have targeted Christian missionaries on the basis of an allegation that these missionaries are actively involved in 'conversion' of poor Hindus especially Dalits and tribals into Christianity. The Sangh functionaries have spread a 'hate campaign' against Churches and schools maintained by Christian missionaries as a part of their Hindu agenda and a protective umbrella provided by the BJP governments has encouraged the Hindu lumpen organisations to target the Christian minority. A few facts may be mentioned to substantiate the argument that the BJP governments have made minorities feel insecure and unsafe in the country.

Visit by Pope : the Akhil Bharatiya Pratinidhi Sabha of the RSS passed resolutions on the visit of Pope, cow protection, cultural invasion from West etc. In a resolution on the visit by Pope, it observed that :

> "The ABPS appeals to all Vedic, Jain, Buddhist, Sikh and all other Hindu religious organisations to reach the poor and illiterate people, especially those living in tribal belts and slums, educate them about the 'Church-sponsored conspiracy of evangelism...".[36]

When Pope John Paul II visited India from November 5 to 7, 1999, the Sangh functionaries became very active in propagating that the visit of Pope was linked with the conversion activities of Christian missionaries in India. With the expansion in the strength of Sangh family in the 1990s, the agenda against all institutions of civil society of Christians has become the object of hostile targeting by its functionaries and other affiliates of the Sangh. Educational institutions, Churches and hospitals maintained and managed by the Christian community have been attacked by the workers of Sangh 'joint family' and these institutions of civil society of Christian community have been labelled as the centres for religious conversion. The Sangh leadership has appealed to the Triumala Tirupati Devasthanan that it should use some amount from its annual income of Rs. 400 crore for Hindu uplift as is done by the Church for welfare of the Hindus. Hindus have to be protected from religious conversion activity undertaken by the church, and Atal Bihari Vajpayee, as Prime Minister of India, has asked for a 'national debate' on the issue of religious conversion indulged in by Christian churches. Since the BJP is in the Government in the Centre and in some States of India, Sangh functionaries and its affiliates feel fully protected while campaigning against Christian minorities and their institutions. The BJP government in Gujarat and the BJP-BJD coalition government in Orissa have not been able to control the hate atmosphere created by the Sangh fraternity against Christian minority and its institutions because Chief Ministers and Ministers of the BJP governments themselves believe that Christian church in India is a great threat to Hinduism because it is successful in converting a section of Hindus into Christianity. Further, the Sangh affiliates have launched a campaign that churches in India are funded from foreign countries for undertaking activities leading to religious conversions. Acharya Giriraj Kishore, senior Vice-President of Vishwa Hindu Parishad observed that "..., the foreign missionaries have brought funds to the tune of Rs. 50,000 crore in the North-East for conversion purpose".[37]

The Sangh Parivar has launched a big campaign against Christian community and its institutions who have been described as 'conspirators' against Hinduism in India and they have been emboldened in undertaking their activity of targeting the Christian institutions because BJP is in the government and the Prime Minister himself desires that the issue of religious conversions indulged in by Church deserves a public discussion. The Sangh 'joint family' has indulged in violence against some members of the Christian community after accusing them of indulging in conversion of tribals in Orissa, Gujarat and North-East India. The Sangh functionaries could take law into their hands because they felt protected by the presence of BJP in the government.

While the Sangh 'joint family' is targeting Christian missionaries for indulging in religious conversions, the 'reconversion' from Christianity to Hinduism is publicly acclaimed and celebrated. In a 'reconversion' ceremony in Orissa on June 18, 2000, the VHP described "...the reconversion as a home coming for the family and added that several families have shown interest to return to Hinduism."[38]

Who has given this license to Hindu organisations to convert Christians into Hinduism ? If the activity of 'reconversion' of religion is undertaken openly, conversion to another religion should also be considered a legitimate right of any individual citizen of India. Hindu organisations cannot appropriate a right for themselves and level allegations against others on issues concerning religious conversion and reconversion. Since the Sangh 'joint family' has launched a campaign against Indian Christians and their institutions, the All-India Christian Council has catalogued "300-odd incidents of violence against Christians and churches in India in the last two years...". Not only this... In 1998, 400 copies of the Bible were burnt in Rajkot and three dozen churches were burnt in the Dangs. Christian preachers have become target of Sangh functionaries and a kind of All-India anti-Christian movement has emerged during the last two years. The All India Christian Council observed that: "The ominous mass violence is meant to terrorise the Christian community, to stop people coming to Churches, to frighten away students from our schools and the ill, the weak and the marginalised from our outreach programmes."[39]

While the *Organiser* of June 18, 2000 quotes D.B. Thengadi on its front page in bold letters that '*Conversion is anti-national*;' L.K. Advani, the Home Minister of India, has a readymade reply that the Inter-Services Intelligence Agencies of Pakistan are involved in the current anti-Christian activities and he does not see anything wrong with the climate of hatred created by the Sangh 'joint family'. Advani is busy in arming himself with new draconian 'laws' and 'new techniques', which he has learnt from the Israelis, to contain the ISI activities in India but who will contain his own 'Sangh fraternity', from attacking and targeting the minorities.

The BJP has risen to power because of its involvement in Ram Janmabhoomi Movement by targeting the Muslim community which was made responsible for the construction of a Babri Mosque over Ram Temple by Mughal Emperor Babar. L.K. Advani's Hindu Symbolism of Rath Yatra from Somnath to Ayodhya was a clarion call to Hindus to defend their religion and places of worship from Muslims. When the Sangh Hindu 'joint family' destroyed the Babri Mosque on December 6, 1992, a message was given to the Muslims of India that Hindu Rashtra has avenged its humiliation inflicted by Muslim rulers. The BJP government in Uttar Pradesh had a legal responsibility to defend the Babri Mosque and for its failure to perform its constitutional responsibility the President of India dismissed the State government under Article 356 of the Constitution of India. The election results of U.P. State Assembly in 1993 surprised the BJP because it had obtained an absolute majority in the elections of 1991 and it could obtain only 175 seats out of 425 in the post-Babri Mosque demolition elections of 1993. The real message of BJP-in-government is that it will not uphold the law of the land in any situation which concerns Muslim minority. Every hero of the VHP connected with Ram Janmabhoomi Movement like Uma Bharati, Jaibhan Singh Pahwaiya, Vinay Katiyar, Yogi Adityanath, Swami Chinmayanand and others are members of Parliament of India. The believers of Hindu Rashtra are now legislators and Ministers, Chief Ministers, MPs and MLAs, and under their benign protection sometimes Christians are targeted and some other times Muslims are made victims. The Uttar Pradesh BJP government has a new law to regulate 'places of religious worship' and a plea has been made to regulate the construction of religious places because mosques of Muslims have become places of refuge of anti-national agents of Inter-Services Intelligence of Pakistan. The Home Minister of India, L.K. Advani, himself alerts the country every day that the ISI agents are very active in India and the needle of suspicion naturally is against Muslims of India. While participating in the Debate on demand for Grants of the Home Ministry, Advani, said that "Pakistan which suffered humiliating defeat in 1971 had called for a *Jihad* against India and now 'Indian Muslims' should reply to this call".[40] Advani represents a mind set of every member of the Sangh Parivar which believes that Hindu is separate from Muslims and Muslims of India are expected to '*Reply to Pakistan*'. If a Home Minister of India expects a special role by Muslims as Muslims while dealing with Pakistan, and the U.P. government wants to supervise the construction of every mosque by Muslims, the message and meanings are very clear that under the BJP government Hindus and Muslims and Christians are separate categories on the basis of which BJP governments would treat them either by showing preferences or discriminations.

Neena Vyas in '*Now, a party with difference*' catalogues some important minority community linked events during the 24 party BJP-led government at the Centre

(a) October-December 1998—Attacks on more than a dozen Churches in the Dangs area of Gujarat. Advani warns against growing attacks on Christian minority;
(b) January 1999—Prime Minister tours the Dangs and gives a call for a national debate on conversions;
(c) January 23, 1999—Missionary Graham Staines and his two young sons are burnt alive in Orissa, allegedly by Dara Singh, a Hindu fanatic;
(d) Attacks on nuns, Christian schools and churches continue through 1999.

(e) February 13, 2000—Nityanand Swami, Chairman of the U.P. Legislative Council, warns of a 'check' on 'Convent Schools'.

(f) February 13, 2000—Tirade against the visit of the Pope by the VHP and the Organiser.

(g) April 22, 2000—A Gospel team from Hyderabad attacked in Agra.[41]

The above catalogue of incidents clearly establishes that an anti-minority atmosphere has been created during the BJP-led government in India.

Special Patronage for Hindus

BJP-in-government has been engaged in making every government or quasi-government or autonomous cultural organisation of India like the Indian Council of Social Science, Indian Council of Historical Research, National Book Trust, Sahitya Academies or Indira Gandhi National Centre for Arts as instruments for the promotion of the ideas of Hindu Rashtra as defined by the Rashtriya Swayamsevak Sangh and its affiliates. Further, Brajesh Mishra, of the Prime Ministers Office plays an influential behind-the-scene role for promoting the bureaucrats who have Hindu belief systems or links with the RSS. Keshubhai Patel, the Chief Minister of Gujarat, not only openly attends public functions of the RSS, he also wanted that membership of the RSS should not be a disqualification for public servants. Since the RSS is the fountain source of doctrinaire Hindutva, its members entering the public services will definitely convert the Indian State apparatus as *Hindu State*. Many political parties opposed the idea of BJP state government of Gujarat to allow RSS membership into the public services and because of very stiff opposition of political parties, the state government of Gujarat withdrew its notification for permitting the RSS members to enter the public services. If on the one hand, the Uttar Pradesh state government of BJP wants to enact a law for the Regulation of Public Religious buildings and places of worship especially of the Muslim community, on the other, Hindu places of worship are getting special attention of the government of Hindutva. Since Orissa suffered huge losses because of super-cyclone, the government decided to increase its annual grant to the Lord Jagannath Temple of Puri from Rs. 6.38 crore to Rs. 6.94 crore for the year 2000. *The Hindustan Times* of May 3, 2000 in a news report mentioned that Urban Development Minister, Jagmohan has evolved 'a grand multi-crore project for the development of a residential pilgrim centre near the Laxmi Narayan temple, popularly known as Birla Temple of Delhi". Jagmohan, the Urban Development Minister has been willing to always provide facilities to Hindu pilgrims whether in Vaishno Devi or Delhi from the public exchequer of the Indian State. If on the one hand the BJP government has frequently announced special financial grants for facilities for Hindu pilgrims attending religious functions like Kumbh Mela, on the other "Bajrang Dal of the Hindu fraternity attacked Christians in Ahmedabad on May 6, 2000, who were distributing copies of the Bible and other evangelical literature".[42]

The above narration of a few significant events and developments of the last three years of the BJP government at the Centre clearly points out to the emergence of a new tendency in India where the Indian State is openly tilted in favour of Hindus and it has shown biases and discriminations against minority communities. The BJP governments of Atal Bihari Vajpayee or Ram Prakash Gupta of Uttar Pradesh or Keshubhai Patel of Gujarat are behaving in a partisan manner for the promotion of the concept of Hindu Rashtra, and under BJP governments minorities of India are feeling insecure.

The Vajpayee-led coalition government at the centre has aggressively pursued agenda of the Sangh Parivar both in domestic and foreign policies. A nuclearised India which can confront hostile Pakistan and China has always been the goal of Sangh 'joint family'. Dr. S.P. Mookerjee of the Jana Sangh had contested against Jawaharlal Nehru's Kashmir policy in the 1950s. Pokharan II, victory of India in Kargil over Pakistan and the strengthening of defences of India have been claimed as great achievements of Vajpayee-led coalition government and Sangh 'joint family' is celebrating the emergence of strong Hindu Rashtra under the BJP leadership. Within the country, Hindus have received special attention by the BJP government and minorities have been shown their place by the Sangh functionaries. Guru Golwalkar had always opposed the Republican Constitution of India, and the Vajpayee government has fulfilled the desire of Sar Sanghchalak by appointing a Constitutional Review Commission. Guru Golwalkar did not believe in the states' reorganisation of India on linguistic basis in the 1950s; the Vajpayee government has begun the exercise of redrawing the boundaries of the Indian states and Bills for the creation of Uttarakhand, Chhattisgarh and Jharkhand are ready to be introduced in the Lok Sabha during 2000. L.K. Advani, Home Minister of India, made a public statement on May 14, 2000 that "the Ayodhya movement retains its relevance in the current political context in term of its ability to curb caste-driven politics". An integrated and homogenised Hindusim remains the goal of Sangh family and movements for the liberation of Ayodhya or Kashi or Mathura continue to be an integral part of the forces of Hindutva whether within the government or outside the government. This is the essential reality of BJP-in-government. It is for the first time that a Central Government is pursuing policies which are directed towards the promotion and strengthening of Hindu Rashtra in India.

EXPLANATIONS FOR THE GROWTH OF BJP IN THE 1990S

The BJP has witnessed a phenomenal growth during the decade of 1990s. It succeeded in obtaining 89 Lok Sabha seats in the Ninth Lok Sabha elections of 1989, 119 seats in the Tenth Lok Sabha elections of 1991, 160 seats in the Eleventh Lok Sabha elections of 1996 and 180 seats in the Twelfth Lok Sabha elections of 1998 and repeated the same performance in the Thirteen Lok Sabha elections of 1999. Further, the party has increased its share of national votes; it peaked in 1998 Lok Sabha elections when it secured 25 percent of the national votes and in 1999, 23.4 per cent of the voters opted in favour of the BJP during the Lok Sabha elections.

The BJP formed three coalition governments at the Centre—in 1996 for thirteen days, in 1998 for thirteen months and the BJP-led National Democratic Alliance is continuing in power under the leadership of Atal Bihari Vajpayee. The BJP MPs represent every state of North and North-Western India, Karnataka and Andhra Pradesh in the South, and even in Assam the party obtained one Lok Sabha seat in 1998 and 2 Lok Sabha seats in the 1999 elections.

It is important to explain the growth of the BJP in the 1990s because in the first Lok Sabha elections of 1952 it obtained only three seats and it was a very marginal player in Indian politics. It seems paradoxical that the party of Hindutva could not get the support of Hindu voters even when the post-Partition Hindu-Muslim divide was quite deep because of post-Partition tragedy of Hindu-Muslim migrations. It looks quite paradoxical that Hindutva has come to occupy a central position in the Indian public life after four decades of Indian Independence at a time when inter-community relations had improved as compared with the situation of 1947-1950.

Does an Explanation Lie in the Strategies Adopted by the Sangh Joint Family

The Hindu 'joint family' of RSS, VHP, Bajrang Dal, ABVP and others brought the issue of *Hindu identity* in a big way in the 1980s. The Hindu 'joint family' launched mobilisation Hindus on the basis of their religious and cultural symbols, and Hindu saints and seers were involved in motivating Hindus for asserting their Hindu identity. In a multi-religious country like India, Hindu identity was constructed by targeting other religious communities like Muslims and Christians.

The theme of humiliation of Hindu Rashtra by foreign Muslim invaders was brought in public discourse and symbols of humiliation like Ram Janmabhoomi or temple at Mathura or Kashi were projected as standing monuments of historical wrongs done against the Hindus by foreign Muslim invaders. The concept of the 'other' is fundamental for the spread of the message of Hindu identity and K.S. Sudarshan, the present Sar Sanghchalak observed in a meeting of Swayamsevak that :

> ".....the Muslims kept themselves away from the national mainstream because the religious fundamentalists want to keep them isolated".

That every community should be in the national mainstream has a special meaning when RSS leaders talk about the idea of 'mainstream' because for them Hindu constitutes the mainstream of India.

Sudarshan observed that "....Hindutva was not the name of any community in particular — it is the concept of cultural nationalism. Hindus have always worked for world peace and unity. Only the Hindutva has the capacity to accept, imbibe and absorb all religions". Sudarshan asserts that Hindus are tolerant and he observed "...that India gave permission to Pope John Paul to visit India although Hong Kong and Sri Lanka had refused his visit. Pope came and promoted Christianity".[43]

That Muslims are not joining the Indian mainstream; tolerance is a special virtue of Hindus and Christianity is involved in religious conversions of innocent poor people of India: these are the main talking points of the Hindu 'joint family'. These statements of Sar Sanghchalak create a wall of distance between Hindus, Muslims and Christians. The Sangh 'joint family' has created the image of wounded Mother India (Bharat Mata). It formed a Shri Ram Janmabhoomi Mukti Jagna Samiti (the committee for the liberation of Lord Ram's Birthplace) and from 1984 the RSS, BJP, VHP, Bajrang Dal launched a large-scale mobilisation of Hindu saints and seers for propagating the idea of liberation of the place of Birth of Lord Rama. Dharam Sansad, Sadhu Sammalans and many such movements were launched for the liberation of Ram Janmabhoomi at Ayodhya. Every trick of the trade was played and Yatras in the mould of Hindu religious tradition were organised to purify the bricks with holy water for the Temple at Ayodhya. L.K. Advani in the tradition of old mythical Hindu kings took a Yatra from Somnath to Ayodhya in 1991 and Hindu mobilisation became the major political and religio-cultural activity of Hindu 'joint family' from 1984. Many activists of Ram Janmabhoomi belonging to VHP and Bajrang Dal contested the Lok Sabha elections of 1989 on the basis of nomination by the BJP. On December 6, 1992 L.K. Advani, Murli Manohar Joshi, and every leader of RSS, VHP, Bajrang Dal with a crowd of 200,000 destroyed the Babri Mosque at Ayodhya. An aggressive and militant political Hinduism had announced its arrival on the Indian political scene after the demolition of the Mosque at Ayodhya.

Is Hindu mobilisation launched by the Hindu 'joint family' on Ram Temple an adequate explanation for the expansion of BJP in the 1990s? Why the appeal of Dr. S.P. Mookerjee of the Jana Sangh or V.D. Savarkar of Hindu Mahasabha or leadership of the Ram Rajya Parishad did not cut any ice with the so-called mythical Hindu voter in the Lok Sabha elections of 1952? If an appeal to Hindu sentiment on the basis of history of humiliations suffered by the Hindus is a sufficient cause for Hindu assertion, it should have been an effective instrument for the mobilisation of Hindus in the 1950s. Why has the appeal to Hindu religious symbols succeeded only in the 1990s? Hindu 'joint family' has been consistently taking an aggressive anti-Pakistan stand and it has always projected Muslims as the 'Other', and suddenly they could succeed in these efforts in the 1990s because of Ram Janmabhoomi movement. Hansen observes:

> "The sharpest edge of the entire Ram agitation, which sought to create a collective Hindu subjectivity as it spoke, by exactly in the constant drawing of the external boundaries of the Hindu-community-becoming-nation".[44]

It cannot be denied that the growth of BJP and other members of its 'joint family' in the 1990s can be explained on the basis of Ram Janmabhoomi movement and other related developments among the Hindu community which were exploited by the forces of Hindutva. At the same time, the limitations of this explanation about the growth of BJP and other Hindu organisations in the 1990s also deserve to be noted. First, the BJP state governments of Uttar Pradesh, Madhya Pradesh, Rajasthan and Himachal Pradesh were dismissed in December 1992 after the demolition of Babri Mosque and in the elections of 1993, the BJP got 96 seats out of 200 in Rajasthan, 117 seats out of 320 in Madhya Pradesh and only 175 seats out of 425 in Uttar Pradesh. Why in these elections did the Hindu voter refuse to provide an electoral legitimacy to the party of Hindutva in the State Assemblies?

Second, Hindu religious symbols were employed for the mobilisation of Indians on many occasions during the Twentieth Century especially during anti-colonial struggles of India. Bal Ganga Dhar Tilak's Ganesh Pooja festival is prominently referred by some scholars that leaders of Indian national movement made use of Hindu religious idiom during the anti-colonial struggle. Some of these facts have led Peter van de Veer to argue that religious language and idiom is crucial in India because it brings together very effectively 'discourse on the religious community and discourse on the nation" and religious nationalism has played a significant role during India's anti-colonial struggles.[45]

Peter van der Veer is making a mechanical relationship between anti-colonial Indian nationalism with religiosity and religious belief system of the people of India. Gandhi launched powerful Non-Cooperation Movement, Salt Satyagrahya-Dandi March, Civil Disobedience Movement, Quit India movement, and mobilised masses in a purely secular manner on the secular issue of anti-colonialism. The essence of Indian nationalism during its anti-colonial phase lies in its contest against purely religious based mobilisation Hindu Mahasabha and Muslim League. Nationalist leaders launched many secular struggles but religious idioms were never used for popular mobilisation. Not only this. Tilak's Ganesh Pooja festival celebration was confined only to Maharashtra and many a time, local leaders of the national movement mobilised people on the basis of local religious traditions but all-India anti-colonial movement mobilisation was always organised on the basis of secular idiom and symbols. While it is not denied that sometimes religious symbols were employed by the nationalist leaders for local mobilisations, the basic thrust of anti-colonial movement was on secular issues through secular slogans of mobilisation.

Does an Explanation Lie in the Strategy of Coalition-Making by the Hindu Party?

Many scholars specially Jafferlot have maintained that the BJP has come to power because it has deftly and intelligently used the strategy of coalition-formation with many secular parties during last four decades and it has been the beneficiary of this strategy of coalition-making with secular leaders and secular parties. A few facts may be mentioned to substantiate the argument that BJP has grown in strength on the basis of its capacity to make alliances with others. First, whenever Indian voters failed to give a clear verdict for a single dominant party either during the Lok Sabha or State Assembly elections, the Bharatiya Jana Sangh and its present Avatar Bhartiya Janata Party was available either to participate in the coalition governments or it supported a party of its own choice by remaining out of power. The BJP participated in the Morarji Desai-led government in 1977 and it supported the V.P. Singh-led government in 1989-90 without sharing power with it. Even when the BJP was supporting the V.P. Singh government by not sharing power with it in a direct manner, the party exercised immense influence over the decisions of the V.P. Singh government. Jagmohan of the BJP was appointed governor of Jammu & Kashmir by the V.P. Singh government on the basis of a demand from the

BJP. The Lok Sabha elections of 1996 again witnessed that no single party had a majority to form the government at the Centre and the President of India invited Atal Bihari Vajpayee to become the Prime Minister because the BJP had obtained 160 seats and it formed a bloc of 194 with the support of Shiva Sena, Akali Dal, Haryana Vikas Party etc. Vajpayee failed to receive a vote of confidence in the Lok Sabha in 1996 but a point was made that BJP can form coalition government at the Centre and in the States of India. This story was repeated by the BJP in 1998 and 1999 and BJP-led coalition governments were formed at the Centre.

Second, the Hindu 'joint family' of RSS, VHP, Bajrang Dal, Akhil Bharatiya Vidyarthi Parishad have actively participated and supported movements and struggles landed by opposition parties and opposition leaders. Gujarat and Bihar Movements of 1974-75 were openly and enthusiastically supported by the Sangh Fraternity.

Jayaprakash Narayan felt obliged to the RSS during his struggles against Mrs. Indira Gandhi's government in 1974-75 and 'J.P.' publicly proclaimed that "RSS workers are devoted nationalists". The RSS strategists have never missed any opportunity to participate in any mass movement whenever an occasion arose from the 1970s to the 1990s.

Third, it has been suggested that the most important asset of the BJP has been its highly committed and motivated RSS cadre. Since BJP is a cadre-based party, this asset of the BJP has been loaned to many parties and leaders either during the elections or whenever they decided to launch any anti-government struggle. Anderson and Damle have devoted full attention to the internal organisation of the BJP and RSS cadre for understanding the strength of the forces of Hindutva.

The BJP has gained in strength because it has successfully practiced the strategy of coalition-making in politics and its devoted and committed cadre has proved a great asset for the survival and expansion of the BJP. While many political parties or groups or leaders have refused to enter into any alliance with the BJP, many others have legitimised it by working together with the BJP. BJP has never considered any party or group or leader as 'untouchable in politics' and every such association with them has brought political dividends to the party.

If strategies of coalition-making followed by the BJP have brought it great political dividends, the Communist parties should not have been left behind by the BJP. BJP and Communists have been great champions of coalition governments but at the end of the Twentieth Century it is the BJP-led coalition which is in government at the Centre while Communist parties are still struggling to form a viable alternative of Third Front. It is also true that strategies of the Communist parties succeeded in 1989-90 and 1996-98 when Third Front groups could keep away the Congress and BJP from political power in the Central government. This is only one part of the story of coalition-making strategies of the BJP and Communist parties. BJP has expanded its electoral base in India by following the politics of strategic alliances, and it has succeeded thrice in leading a coalition government at the Centre but the Communists have not been able to expand their electoral base in India. Hence any explanation for the growth of BJP on the basis of its strategies of coalition-making has its own limitations because electoral and political strategies are necessary but not sufficient explanations for the growth or decline of parties.

Explanation for the Growth of Hindutva Lies in the India of 1990s

Craig Baxter (1969), Bruce D. Graham (1990), Walter K. Anderson and Shridhar D. Damle (1987), Christopher Jafferlot (1996), Peter van der Veer (1996) and Thomas Blom Hansen (1999) have in their scholarly studies offered explanations either by looking into the internal organisation and strategies of the BJP and its cadre or they have explained the growth of BJP by linking it with political process and Hindu cultural ethos of India. These scholarly studies provide lot of insights into the internal dynamics of 'Joint Hindu Family' and they have linked their explanations by bringing out the changing dynamics of Indian politics which has facilitated the growth of BJP.

The focus of any study on the phenomenal growth of BJP and various Hindu religious organisations should be in finding an explanation for the need of Hindus to accept the party of Hindutva in the 1990s. Hindus of India did not show any preference for the Jana Sangh in the 1950s and 1960s when memories of Partition and post-Partition events were quite fresh within the country. The Jana Sangh, Hindu Mahasabha and Ram Rajya Parishad failed to win public space on the basis of their appeals to Hindus. Hindus were not convinced that they needed a Hindu religion-based party to defend their interests in India.

How could Hindus of the 1980s and the 1990s respond positively and enthusiastically to the appeals of Hindu religion-based party and organisations? Why did Hindus embrace politics of Hindutva in the last decade of the Twentieth Century when they had earlier rejected it in the 1950s and the 1960s? The so-called Hindu India was not at all threatened by any outside country in the 1980s and 1990s but even in the absence of any threat to the security of India, the Hindu party could create an acceptability for itself by playing on the so-called feelings of insecurity among the Hindus of India. How could a Hindu majority country become a fertile ground for the propagandists of Hindu Rashtra? The idea of Hindu identity suddenly became attractive to the Hindus in the 1990s and the party of Hindus succeeded in positioning itself as a great defender and promoter of Hindu identity. What is the explanation for the search for Hindu identity in a Hindu majority country? The growth of BJP and the expansion of Hindu 'joint family' of organisations in the 1990s can be explained by identifying the causes which have made Hindus assert their 'identity' in a Hindu majority country. Why have the Hindus felt the need for the construction of religious Hindu community national identity? Why have Hindus chosen to identify themselves as Hindus at the close of the Twentieth Century? A community may construct its own identity if it feels threatened by any other community. Who is a threat to the majority community in India? How have Hindus come to believe that their identity is under threat from other communities? Hansen is the only Western scholar who has attempted an explanation on the growth of BJP in the 1990s by referring to the new aspirations and anxieties of 'the large middle class and dominant communities' who have been exposed to new 'global cultural and economic flows' at the end of Twentieth Century. Hansen observes that "...it was the desire for recognition with an increasingly global horizon, and the simultaneous anxieties of being encroached upon by the Muslims, the plebeians, and the poor that over the last decade have prompted millions of Hindus to respond to the call for Hindutva at the polls and in the streets, and to embrace Hindu nationalist promises of order, discipline, and collective strength".[46]

Hansen's line of argument about the rise of Hindutva is correct and carries conviction but fault lies in his narrative; he has not been able to properly contextualise the crisis and specific political developments of the decade of the 1990s for properly explaining the linkage between economic globalisation and the politics of Hindu identity. Yogendra Yadav with Sanjay Kumar and Oliver Heath in their very valuable election analysis published in the Frontline (Madras) of November 19, 1999 talk about '*The BJP's New Social Bloc*'. The first important finding of Yogendra Yadav *et al* election Survey of 1999 Lok Sabha is that: "Most of the gains made by the BJP-led front came from the erstwhile United Front and the allies of the Congress (I). But these votes did not flow directly to the BJP : they accrued to its allies".[47] An analysis of Andhra Pradesh elections of 1999 has also mentioned that an election alliance between BJP and Telugu Desam proved beneficial to both the parties and because of this alliance, Congress party in Andhra Pradesh suffered an electoral defeat. The second significant finding of their analysis is that: "It may be an exaggeration to say that the BJP represents the rebellion of the elite, but it is nevertheless true that its rise to political power has been accompanied by the emergence of a new social group that is defined by an overlap of social and economic privileges".[48] Third, Yadav *et al* have shown that a positive correlation exists between 'the poorer the voter, the lower the vote for the BJP', 'Caste and class hierarchy reinforce each other in favour of the BJP' and 'both caste and class converge in BJP's support base'. The authors conclude that:...., the highest chances of voting for the BJP obtain in the group that is both upper class and upper caste, and the lowest among the lowest class Dalits".[49]

Since India is witnessing a 'Grand Transition', the above findings make an important revelation about the social profile of the BJP inspite of the fact that many distinctions or social categories are blurred and in a state of flux.

A few salient features of politics and economics of the 1990s may be briefly mentioned to show that this was a decade of special crisis for India. First, V.P. Singh was involved in a factional conflict with some leaders of his own party and to divert public attention, he announced the acceptance of the Mandal Commission recommendations on reservations in public services in August, 1990. If on the one hand, the V.P. Singh governments' action on Mandal Commission led to serious caste versus caste conflicts in North India, on the other, the BJP and every member of the Hindu 'joint family' jumped into public activity to protect united Hindus identity by launching mobilisation for Ram Janmabhoomi. The ideologues of Hindu 'joint family' launched a counter offensive against the divisive caste politics of V.P. Singh and other supporters of Mandal Commission by mobilising the Hindu Samaj on a common platform of liberation of Ram Janmabhoomi with a programme for the construction of Ram Temple at Ayodhya.

India of the 1990s witnessed the emergence of powerful struggles on the basis of assertions of identity and manipulative politics of identity occupied central public space in India. V.P. Singh, Mulayam Singh Yadav of Uttar Pradesh, Lalu Prasad Yadav of Bihar mobilised the backward caste peasant classes on the basis of their distinct caste identity, Kanshi Ram and Mrs. Mayawati of the Bahujan Samaj Party mobilised 'other Dalit castes' on the basis of their Dalit caste identity. Identity versus identity politics was on the run and the forces of Hindutva jumped into the ocean of identities with a goal to protect and project an integrated Hindu identity. Politics of identity is always based on the concept of the 'other' and for the Sangh fraternity the 'other' was Muslim and Christian and also Hindu caste system. The Hindu organisations were involved in the manipulation of Hindu identity for maintaining the inner unity of Hindus by focussing on their 'other', i.e., Muslims and Christians. Mandal versus Mandir, or Reservations versus Ram occupied pubic space in the beginning of the 1990s.

Second, alongwith these political developments of the 1990s, Indians were caught in serious fiscal crisis in 1991 and India was on the verge of an economic collapse. The fiscal crisis of the Indian state was reflected by the balance-of-payments crisis of 1991 when the P.V. Narasimha Rao government approached the World Bank and International Monetary Fund and Western industrial countries to launch a 'rescue operation for Indian economy'. The Narasimha Rao government announced a New Economic Policy for India whose major components were opening of the economy to foreign investors, and privatisation and deregulation of the highly regulated domestic economic regime. Globalisation, liberalisation and privatisation of Indian economy was undertaken as a response to the serious fiscal crisis faced by the Indian state in 1991. The Indian ruling classes and political and bureaucratic governing classes[50] opted for foreign capital to resolve the fiscal crisis of the Indian State which was the product of many wrong policies followed by the Indian State from 1950 to 1990. The Indian state and the ruling classes were not ready to learn from their own failures at the domestic economic front; many corrective measures could have been undertaken to resolve the fiscal crisis of the Indian State if the ruling classes and political and bureaucratic governing classes had agreed to set the house in order. In a country of one Billion people, only 20 million of Indians pay income tax. Many private corporate industrial and trading groups pay 'zero tax' to the State. Further, the Indian state allocates a large share of its annual budgeted expenditure for the salaries and benefits to the members of the political and bureaucratic governing classes. While the ruling classes of India do not contribute to the exchequer of the Indian State, the governing classes take away a lion's share from the limited fiscal resources of the State. Fiscal crisis of the Indian State is a logical product of the class action of accumulators of economic surpluses who are reluctant to be taxed and of the governing classes who act as co-shareholders with the ruling classes in exercising control over the fiscal resources of the state.

India opened its economy to foreign investors in the 1990s to overcome its own crisis and once the economy was opened to the foreign investors and rolling back of the state became the new mantra of international and Indian capitalist classes, a large domestic social constituency of middle and upper middle class Indians extended full support to the idea of free market economy, free foreign investments, competition in market, and production of quality consumer goods. The functionaries of the state, leaders of private corporate sector and opinion-makers joined together to project that India was a big market of 250 million buyers of quality goods. It deserves to be mentioned that professional middle and upper middle classes, the middle class entrepreneur, the managers of service sector of economy and surplus generating middle class peasantry were very important beneficiaries of the post-independence economic development of India. This social group, which is broadly the 'petit-bourgeoisie' of India, enjoys great social status and power within the country and these social groups of society are completely linked with the industrial and agrarian capitalist classes.

The decade of 1990s witnessed serious fiscal crisis of the state and also the emergence of identity politics in a big way. Large social solidarities of workers or peasants were all broken into fragments on the basis of caste versus caste, sub-caste versus sub-caste in the Jati system, religion versus religion and region versus region. Many new social movements took birth in the 1990s dealing with the problems of 'Environment' or 'Child labour' or 'Women questions' but all these movements were focussed on 'single issue programmes' and one movement had no linkage with any other movement and larger issues of society were broken into particular issues for mobilisation. Particularism and fractionalisation of society became a distinctive feature of the politics of the 1990s. Political mobilisation on the basis of caste or religion or region in the 1990s disintegrated and fragmented party system and caste-based parties and religion-based parties on the basis of sectional representation emerged on the scene in politics. The construction of all-India Hindu identity which transcended fragmented caste identities assumed great significance for the BJP, and the Hindu 'joint family' popularly known as *Sangh Parivar* rallied Hindus on the slogan of Hindu unity against Muslims and Christians.

Hindu religion-based politics with a goal to establish a powerful Hindu identity replaced an all-India secular democratic politics in the 1990s because secular parties could not create a powerful united movement of the exploited classes which could be perceived by the people as an alternative to the social goals offered by the believers of Hindu Rashtra or Jati Raj. The quest for Hindu identity in the crisis stage of globalisation succeeded because other secular political parties could not offer any alternative social goal for the poor of India. The decade of 1990s has witnessed the deepening of social and economic disparities in India and neither globalisation nor Hindu or caste identity can offer any solution to the basic problems of the marginalised strata of society. The Hindu 'joint family' has acted as a dream merchant by providing a religion-based slogan for mass mobilisation during the elections. The dream of great and powerful Hindu India has been effectively and successfully sold by the Hindu 'joint family' to the upcoming rural and urban middle and upper middle classes who on the one hand have global aspirations and on the other they aggressively identify themselves with Hindu rituals, temples, and other religious symbols. Hinduism has been offered to the 'lumpen and unemployed poor' who are mobilised by the Hindu 'joint family' to target the Muslim and Christian minorities. Hindu 'joint family' has given a common social goal to different strata of Hindu society and it has succeeded in rallying Hindu groups for the protection and promotion of Hinduism in India.

Hindu middle classes were attracted towards consumerism and open identification with Hindu religions became obvious in the early 1970s when two Bombay made movies like 'Bobby' on the one hand and 'Santoshi Ma' on the other became a craze with the viewers. The message of 'Bobby' movie was that dreams for worldly success can be fulfilled and achieved, and 'Santoshi Ma' attracted great attention because worldly success without 'religious feelings of prayers' was inadequate. These two movies gave a message that 'Complete Hindu' is one who is 'successful in life' and who practices Hindu religion for his salvation. Hindus have not turned their back either on the goal of economic success or in their practice of Hindu religion. Coloured television sets were symbols of economic success and television serials of 'Ramayana and Mahabharat' fulfilled the religious need. Karl Marx had clearly alerted us to the powerful appeal of religion for the insecure and the poor masses in a society. While describing religion as an 'Opiate' of the people because it strengthens 'false consciousness' Karl Marx also maintained that it provides 'hope' to the hopeless and frustrated masses: "Religion is the sigh of the oppressed creature, the heart of a heartless world, just as it is that spirit of a spiritless situation. It is the opium of the people".[51]

The Congress party of Indira practiced 'soft Hindutva' while contesting the BJP politics of militant and aggressive Hindutva. V.N. Gadgil, a senior leader of the party, observed that the Congress "depends on the support of Muslims and other minorities and ignores the interests of the majority". When a leader of a secular party like the Congress is taking cognisance of the Hindu identity, it substantiates our argument that Hindu factor in Indian politics has emerged in a significant manner in the 1990s. The upwardly mobile middle and upper middle class Hindus are economic globalisers and supporters of Hindu-religion-based politics because it helps them to reconcile 'consumerism' with 'Hindu religious identity'. Since middle class politicians, bureaucrats, professionals, technocrats, entrepreneurs, intellectuals and articulators of ideas occupy a special position of power and influence in Indian society, their ideological beliefs become the representative ideas of the whole society. The ruling classes of India have taken good care of the economic interests of the middle classes because of obvious reasons. First, the Indian middle class identified itself with the aspirations of property owing exploiting classes and second, the middle class of India is a believer and practitioner of social statusquoism which ends up in supporting the ruling classes and ideology of Hindu conservatism. In summation, it may be mentioned that crisis-ridden India is finding answers in the ideology of free market economy and construction of political Hinduism.

Finally, the economic integration of India with global capitalism has sharpened economic disparities within the country. It is instructive for Indians to see social reality in the United States which is the real centre of global capitalism. Americans are worried about growing inequality in their society. "....... The National Centre of Policy Analysis noted recently...that the share of total income to the top 20 percent of American households is increasing while the share going to the lowest 20 per cent is falling. The Federal Reserve Board has found that, while the median family's net worth rose 17.6 per cent between 1995 and 1998, the richest families reaped most of the gain and the poorest families' wealth actually shrank."[52]

If this is the social consequence of capitalism in the most important capitalist country of the world, in India with the exception of 250 million absolute majority of our people are involved in severe struggle for subsistence and survival. While 'working' America and 'corporate' America is sharply divided on the opening of economy for free trade, Indians have become the champions of free market economy. Global capitalism divides every country because it is concerned only with the buyers of quality consumer goods and the majority of population of every country under the impact of global economic integration is ejected out of the market because their share of income is so low that they cannot participate in the market which caters to the needs of the prosperous only. The Wretched of the Earth of India have been left to their own resources, if any, and at the mercy of God, if any. The opiate of Hindutva does not provide jobs to the jobless. The International Labour Organisation at its 55th International Labour Conference stated that: The world is "still a long way from universal acceptance of these fundamental principles and rights in practice", and globalisation has not helped in improving the social situation for the working classes. "On the contrary, with the internationalisation of production the power of collective bargaining has been seriously reduced as corporations have the capital that gives them the ability to exist when and where they want". Further, "The labour market is getting segmented with restructurisation of production, technological innovation, the advance of privatisation on a large-scale, and labour markets thus getting segmented, part-time work is increasing. Firms are increasingly sub-constructing to cut costs, therefore workers find it more difficult to organise themselves to fight for their interests. The benefits of globalisation have not benefited everyone and everywhere, and global inequalities are growing and many economics becoming increasingly marginalised, ..."[53]

The main victims of globalisation, liberalisation and privatisation are the working masses of India and its real 'beneficiaries' are a minority of Indians who consist of 250 million consumerists and corporate sector. The working classes which were always locked in an unequal class relations have reentered a new relationship where a united working class struggle for the defence of their rights has been crippled by the penetration of caste versus caste, religion versus religion and region versus region clash of identities in the all-India Trade Unions and All-India Kisan Sabhas. A report by the Associated Chamber of Commerce (ASSOCHAM) has revealed that the loss of mandays due to strikes/lockouts in 1999 stood at a whopping 24.5 million compared to 22.6 million in 1998. The CITU Secretary, W.R. Varada Rajan observed that : "Privatisation, liberalisation and globalisation—which brings with it retrenchment and sickness/closures in uncompetition units—is inflicting horrendous damage on the quality of life of workers."

The Assocham's study reveals that the 'wage loss on account of industrial action nearly doubled to Rs. 103.06 crore in 1999 from Rs. 54.14 crore in 1998.

The growing social frustrations of the absolute majority of working India during the 1990s have found an expression in street action by Hindu lumpens represented by the Bajrang Dal and others, and the forces of Hindutva have gained in strength because they have successfully played on the fears of the poor by identifying Muslims and Christians as targets of hatred. L.K. Advani keeps on raising the spectre of 'illegal Bangladeshis' in India and according to him Muslim Bangladeshis and Pakistani Inter-State Intelligence Agencies are threatening Hindu India's Unity. The Uttar Pradesh state government has a new law so that mosques can be controlled because they have become the headquarters of ISI of Pakistan. Similarly, Christian missionaries have to be targeted because they are involved in religious conversion activities and they are a threat to Hindu India. Hindu India is under 'siege' and it has to be defended from its internal and external enemies. While anniversary celebrations of nuclear explosion of Pokharan II were marked by the assertion of strong India L.K. Advani is taking care of internal enemies of Hindu India by the Criminal Law Amendment Bill 1995 which is a new version of maligned and completely misused earlier Terrorist and Disruptive (Prevention) Act (TADA) which was allowed to lapse. Advani not only needs a new law to deal with domestic 'enemies' of India, he wants his police force to learn lessons from Israelis who smashed the Palestinians.

The focus of our explanation is on the linkage between the fiscal crisis of the Indian State and the emergence of Hindutva as a strong force in Indian public life in the 1990s. The upshot of our narrative is that

Indian society has been sharply divided and fragmented around 'exclusivist identities' and the ruling classes and political and bureaucratic governing classes do not feel compelled to restructure fundamental social and productive arrangements in India because the identity politics of targeting the 'other' has weakened the united working class challenge in the 1990s. The Hindu majoritarian identity politics is a response to the deep social and economic crisis of India. The politics of Hindutva is playing an important social role in the situation of deep crisis of Indian economy.

It is a well known fact of history that any powerful 'ideology' or 'social idea' can become acceptable only when social situation is ripe for it. Hitler and Mussolini found a positive response because in the phase of crisis of German and Italian capitalism, fascist ideology of anti-Semitism could be effectively sold to the insecure poor of these countries. This is actually happening in India. Nehru's socialism provided futuristic 'hope' to the Indians in the 1950s and 1960s and in a contest against Nchruvian goals of nation-building the ideology of Hindutva had no takers. The 1990s have witnessed the collapse of East European communist state system, and Indians have also experienced that the communist and socialist parties could not successfully confront extremely divisive politics of identities, and in this situation of crisis of India social space was occupied either by Hindu communalist or casteists or regional chauvinists who are very comfortable in each others company. Political bloc of casteists, regionalists and the party of Hindus is a reflection of fragmentation of the ruling classes in crisis ridden India. Identity politics has weakened or destroyed large social solidarities of the working classes who could challenge the exploiting propertied classes of India. This is the social reality of India in the beginning of the Twenty First Century. The growth of Hindutva can be understood and explained by establishing proper linkages between politics of classes and fractions in the age of crisis of capitalism when exclusivist 'identity' politics is legitimised by the political and intellectual representatives of the exploiting classes. The ruling classes always feel threatened by large social solidarities of the working classes and Hindutva serves class interests by its politics of group versus group, and community versus community.

NOTES AND REFERENCES

1. Michael Minkenberg: "The Renewal of the Radical Right Between Modernity and Anti-Modernity": Government and Opposition: Volume 35, Number 2, pp. 174-75, see pp. 170-88 Also see Jurgen Falter and Siegfried Schumann "Affinity Towards right-wing Extremism in Europe" in Klaus von Be Yme

(ed.) Right-Wing Extremism in Western Europe, London : Frank Class 1988, pp. 96-110.

2. Charles Taylor: "The Politics of Recognition", in A. Gutmann (ed.) *Multi-culturalism*, Princeton, Princeton University Press, 1994.
3. Harish Khare, "Borders cannot be redrawn on religious basis : P.M." *The Hindu*, New Delhi, August 16, 2000, p. 1.
4. Martin E. Marty and R. Scott Appleby (eds.) *Fundamentalisms Observed*: *Chicago* : Chicago University Press 1991, p. ix.
5. Daniel Gold, "*Organised Hinduism from Vedic Truth to Hindu Nation*" in Martin E. Marty and R. Scott Appleby (eds.) *op. cit.*, p. 567.
6. M.S. Golwalkar: Bunch of Thoughts and Spotlight, Bangalore, Vikarma Prakashan, 1966 and Sportlights: Guruji Answers : Bangalore : Sahitya Sindhu : 1974 : Quoted by Daniel Gold, *ibid*, p. 567.
7. V.D. Savarkar : Hindutva : Bombay : Veer Savarkar Prakashan, 1969, p. 1.
8. Antono Gramsci : Selections from the Prison Notebook : edited and translated by Quinton Hoare and Geoffray Nowell Smith : New York : International Publishers : 1971, p. 172.
9. Ranjit Guha: (ed.) Subaltern Studies: Delhi : Oxford University Press, 1982, pp. 5-6.
10. Peter van der Veer: Religious Nationalism : Hindus and Muslims in India. Delhi: Oxford University Press, 1996.
11. *Ibid.*, p. 28.
12. *Ibid.*, p. 28.
13. V.D. Savarkar: Hindutva : Bombay: Veer Savarkar Prakashan, 1969, pp. 3-4.
14. M.S. Golwalkar, (We, Our Nationhood Defined) 1938-39, pp. 52, 56 quoted by Thomas Blom Nansen: The Saffron have: Democracy and Hindu Nationalism in Modern India : Delhi, Oxford University Press, 1999, p. 81.
15. Ram Sharan Sharma : Advent of Aryans in India, New Delhi, Manohar, 1999, pp. 99-10.
16. Pomila Thapar, "Some Appropriations of Theory of Aryan Race Relating to the Beginnings of Indian History" in Daud Ali (Ed.) Invoking the Past : The Uses of History in South Asia, New Delhi, Oxford University Press, 1999, p. 35.
17. Organizer, "BJP-then and now", New Delhi, April 23, 2000, p. 2.
18. BJP celebrates '20th Anniversary' *Organizer*, New Delhi, April 23, 2000, p. 7.
19. Christofa Jafferlot: The Hindu Nationalist Movement and Indian Politics, 1925 to 1990s strategies of identity—Building Implantation and Movilisation (with special reference to Central India): New Delhi, Viking, 1996, p. 9.
20. Jaffarlot, *ibid.*, p. 522.
21. Walter, K. Anderson and Shridhar, D. Damle, *The Brotherhood in Saffron: The Rashtriya Swayamsevak Sangh and Hindu Revivalism*, New Delhi, Vistaar Publications, 1999 (Seventh Printing), pp. 251-52.
22. K.S. Sudarshan, Sar Sanghchalak's Interview: *Organizer*, New Delhi, March 19, 2000, p. 5.
23. *The Indian Express*, New Delhi, May 24, 2000.

24. Quoted by Tapan Basu *et al.*, : Khaki Shorts and Saffron Flags: New Delhi: Orient Longman, 1993, p. 38.
25. Jafferlot, *op. cit.*, p. 522.
26. Anderson and Damle, *op. cit.*, p. 4.
27. S. Balakrishnan: "FDI or Depleting Independence?" *The Hindu*, New Delhi, May 24, 2000, p. 21.
28. Manifesto: National Democratic Alliance, April 29, 1999.
29. Indrani Bagchi : "C11 in pursuit of free trade pact with us", *The Economic Times* : New Delhi, May 31, 2000.
30. *Organizer*, New Delhi, April 20, 2000, p. 2.
31. "P.M., allies became friends again" *The Hindustan Times*, New Delhi, May 12, 2000, p. 8.
32. A.B. Vajpayee "Spread Indian Culture to Counter Cultural Invasion" *Organizer*, New Delhi, Vol. 1, No. 46, June 4, 2000, p. 20.
33. *Organizer*, New Delhi, Vol. No. 41, April 30, 2000, p. 19.
34. Thomas Bloom Hansen : The Saffron Wave : Democracy and Hindu Nationalism in Modern India. New Delhi, Oxford University Press, 1999, pp. 83-84, quoted from M.S. Golwalkar : Bunch of Thoughts, Bangalore; Jagaran Prakash, 1966, p. 299.
35. *Organizer*, New Delhi, March 19, 2000.
36. *Organizer* : New Delhi, March 26, 2000, p. 9.
37. "Construction of Rama Mandir begins in Jan. : VHP", *The Economic Times*, New Delhi, June 5, 2000, p. 2.
38. "VHP reconverts tribal family in Orissa village" : *The Hindustan Times* : New Delhi, June 19, 2000.
39. "Sangh Parivar behind the hate campaign, says Christian council" : *The Hindustan Times*, New Delhi, June 19, 2000.
40. "Muslims, reply to Pak : Advani", *The Indian Express*, New Delhi, April 27, 2000, p. 1.
41. Neena Vyas, "Now a Party with difference", *The Hindu*, New Delhi, May 7, 2000, p. 14.
42. Rathen Das, "Treating minorities, Gujarat style", *The Hindustan Times*, New Delhi, May 7, 2000
43. Manik K. Kher, "Muslims should join the mainstream", K.S. Sudarshan. *The Organizer*, New Delhi, June 11, 2000, p. 8.
44. Thomas Bloom Nansen : The Saffron Wave 1999, p. 177.
45. Peter *van der* Veer: Religious Nationalism : Hindus and Muslims in India : Delhi, Oxford, 1996.
46. Thomas Bloom Hansen, 1999, p. 5.
47. Yogendra Yadav et al : "The BJP's New Social Block", *Frontline,* Madras, November 19, 1999, p. 32.
48. *Ibid.*, p. 32.
49. *Ibid,* p. 38.
50. Note: French Marxist N. Povlantz made an important distinction between the 'ruling classes' and the 'governing classes' in capitalist society. The governing classes manage the class state and they also have a share in the accumulated surpluses.

51. Marx's writing: Contribution to the critique of Hegel's philosophy of Right: Karl Marx and Frederick Engels: On Religion (Second Impression): Moscow, Foreign Languages Publishing House, 1955, p. 42.
52. Geneva Overholser "The unfairness of Income Inequality", *International Herald Tribune*, New York, March 25, 2000, p. 6.
53. Shiela Mathurani, "This bargaining right affected by globalisation, ILO": *The Economic Times*, New Delhi, June 8, 2000.

6

The United Progressive Alliance Government

The Congress-led United Progressive Alliance government at the Centre was formed on May 22, 2004 and it was for the first time that the Congress party formed a coalition government at the Centre. The BJP-led National Democratic Alliance government at the Centre had exercised power for more than six years from 1998 to 2004 and its electoral defeat was welcomed by secular political forces in the country because BJP-in-power at the Centre had assaulted the secular fabric and democratic ethos of plural and diverse society of India. It has been suggested that the replacement and displacement of the BJP-led NDA government by the Congress-led UPA government at the Centre has liberated India from the forces of Hindutva and the votaries of Hindu Rashtra have been ejected from state power. It deserves to be clearly stated that an interpretation of electoral verdict of 2004 Lok Sabha elections cannot be dichotomised or even simplified by asserting that the voters during the elections showed their clear preference in favour of secularism and against the Hindu Rashtravadis. The Congress had mobilised the voters on the plank of 'vote for Hand which stands for *aam Admi*[1] and the BJP asked the voters to renew their confidence in the party/government which had created a 'Shining India'. Can it be stated that the Congress and the BJP were clearly identified by the voters on the basis of their ideology of secularism versus Hindutva, and other issues mentioned in the election manifestos of these two parties did not carry any conviction with the voters? It deserves to be clearly stated that electoral verdict cannot be interpreted on the basis of a single factor especially when victory and defeat of the two major contenders for power is extremely narrow. The Congress-led

UPA government at the Centre has to follow and implement 'secular agenda for governance' because Congress is ideologically committed to 'secularism' and it has replaced the BJP-led government which is firmly committed to the ideology of Hindu Rashtravad. The only significance of the Lok Sabha elections of 2004 is that a party with an agenda of religion-based politics has vacated the office for a party which is practitioner of secular-based politics. A government-in-power can not be analysed and evaluated on the basis of just one agenda because multiple and diverse social groups look towards a government for the satisfaction of their specific demands. Not only this. A coalition government at the Centre has to accommodate diverse demands of different groups because partners in a coalition government represent the interests and demands of different social constituencies. The Congress-led UPA government at the Centre has to harmonise the conflicting interests of fourteen groups which are represented in the government along with the demands of the Communist parties which are 'outside supporters' of the government at the Centre. It was alleged that the Congress would not succeed in managing a coalition government at the Centre because it did not have any experience of working with diverse coalition groups at the Centre. The opponents of the UPA government, especially the BJP, were extremely skeptical about the survival of a coalition government led by the Congress but the Congress has belied the expectations of its critics and opponents and the UPA government has continued to remain in power at the Centre. The UPA government is working on the basis of a National Common Minimum Programme which has been agreed by all the coalition partners including the Communists, who are the 'outside supporters' of the government. It does not mean that the implementation of the Common Minimum Programme can be a smooth affair because in spite of agreements on the CMP, different coalition partners have different priorities of their own and different groups will like to push their agenda through the government. The upshot of above description is that coalition government at the Centre, whether led by the Congress or the BJP, is always at the tenterhooks because it has to accommodate diverse and competitive demands of its supporters in the government.

The UPA government has evolved a mechanism of Coordination Committee for dealing with the issues raised by the Communists who are its 'outside supporters'. It deserves to be clearly stated that the Congress and the Communists have never agreed to share power either at a formal or informal levels and it is for the first time in post-Independence India that Communists are 'supporting' the Congress-led UPA government. The Congress and the Communists represent different social constituencies and interests of different social classes and this is the reason that they have never cooperated with one another in the task of governance of the country. The Communists are supporting the Congress-led UPA government with a view to keep the forces of Hindutva out of governmental power. The Congress is a lesser political evil for the Communists because a full-fledged party of the Hindutva has to be kept out of power with a view to defend the secular fabric of India. Hindutva is the greatest threat to the democratic Republic of India because its ideology of religion-based politics is a complete negation of the philosophy of secularism which is the foundational philosophical principle of Communists and for this purpose, they are extending support to the Congress at the Centre. Communist parties are extending support to the Congress to keep the BJP miles away from state power, it does not mean that the communists have abandoned their pro-poor ideological baggage in favour of pro-rich economic policies of the Congress party. The Communists have applied pressures on the Congress in every Coordination Committee Meeting with a view to keep it under check so that it does not violate the Common Minimum Programme which is the guiding framework of the UPA government. It is worthwhile to mention a few important differences which have emerged between the Congress and the Communists and both of them have tried to resolve contentious public policy issues on the basis of hard bargaining with a spirit of give and take. Communists and the Congress have been opposed to one another on economic and foreign policy. The Communists have opposed economic liberalisation and pro-American policies of the Congress and many a time, both of them have found themselves at loggerheads and a situation arose when the Communists 'decided to walk out' of the Coordination Committee meetings.

The Congress-led coalition has worked very smoothly, because except the Communists who have public policy differences with the Congress, other regional and sub-regional groups have cooperated with each other and the government has been able to project its United image. It does not mean that fourteen groups do not have inter-group or intra-groups tensions but the functioning of the government has not been adversely affected by inter-group conflicts. The State Assembly elections of 2005 in Bihar witnessed that Lalu Prasad Yadav of the Rashtriya Janata Dal and Ramvilas Paswan of the Lok Jan Shakti party were not able to work together at a common electoral platform in spite of the fact that both these parties are part of the UPA government at the Centre. Not only this. Sonia Gandhi also failed to reconcile the differences between these two groups during Bihar State Assembly elections of 2005. The same story was repeated in 2006 and in Tamil Nadu Vaiko decided to form an electoral alliance with Km. Jayalalitha of the AIADMK against M. Karunanidhi's DMK in spite of the fact that Vaiko and the DMK are present in the UPA government at the Centre. The state level political contradictions do not get resolved in spite of the fact that some political opponents have decided to sit around the table as comrades-in-arm at the Centre.

If the above story of relationship between Communists and the Congress and the Congress and other regional partners of the UPA government leads us to conclude that coalition government at the Centre is an 'alliance of convenience', the problems which exist within the Congress also can not be wished away or put under the carpet. What is the relationship between Sonia Gandhi, the Congress party President, and Manmohan Singh, the Prime Minister of the Congress-led UPA government at the Centre? Manmohan is a nominee of Sonia for the office of Prime Minister of India. Sonia abandoned her claim to accept the office of Prime Minister in spite of the fact that her own party and every alliance partner represented in the UPA had shown a clear preference for Sonia's candidature as Prime Minister. It deserves to be clearly stated that Sonia has revived the Congress party and from 1998 to 2006, the Congress party has been led by Sonia who is an 'unchallenged' leader of the party. Sonia's political opponents like the BJP had to eat an humble pie because the voters have shown complete confidence by electing and re-electing Sonia for the Lok Sabha. The Lok Sabha elections of 2004 brought back Sonia-led Congress to power because her party could form a coalition government at the Centre. Sonia's pre-eminent position in the Congress has remained intact in spite of the fact that she has not accepted to be the Prime Minister of India. Sonia Gandhi decided to constitute a National Advisory Council under her Chairmanship and the constitution of such a NAC has given rise to a controversy that the UPA government has created 'dual centres of power' because in a parliamentary system, it is the Council of Ministers which is the real repository of 'executive powers' and Sonia's NAC is either redundant or 'extra-constitutional centre of power'. The fact of the matter is that Sonia shall continue to occupy a 'pre-eminent' position in the UPA government because of the 'pre-eminence' in the Congress party.

How does one evaluate the performance of UPA-in-Government irrespective of the fact that Sonia or Manmohan or both of them occupy equal or more than equal status in relation to one another? The Communist parties have a yardstick for the evaluation of the UPA government and they have maintained that it is a government with 'secular agenda' but its economic and foreign policies are flawed because they are pro-Big Business, Indian and foreign, and pro-America. The role of Communists is to apply 'correctives' and 'brakes' over pro-global capitalist policies of the government. Further, except the Communists, other allies of the

Congress in the UPA government, have maintained smooth relationship with one another because every regional partner of the coalition government at the Centre does not have any clear cut ideological agenda of its own. Every group in coalition government is guided by the interest of its own social constituency.

It is not enough to maintain that the UPA government at the Centre is guided by secular ideology because its track record on socio-economic issues facing the country deserves to be clearly scrutinised. A few facts may be mentioned to highlight the essentials of socio-economic challenges faced by India in 2006. The Economic Survey of the Government of India (2005-06) has highlighted the reality of economy of the country. While the government has projected a rosy picture of 'economic growth', the Economic Survey on the basis of National Sample Survey Organisation has mentioned that "The Survey had estimated a reduction in the incidence of poverty from 36 percent in 1993-1994 to 26.1 percent during 1999-2000."[2] If one-fourth of the population is still under the poverty line as defined by the government, the UPA government has to play an 'activist' role in attacking directly the issue of mass poverty. Not only this. Agrarian crisis is a reality and marginal farmers have taken recourse to 'suicide' because they cannot face economic distress suffered by them. How can rural poverty be tackled if investment in agricultural sector has been on the decline? The Economic Survey of the Government of India has itself referred to the basic cause of agrarian crisis.

Capital Formational in India Agriculture

The decline in the share of the agricultural sector's capital formation in GDP from 2.2 percent in the late 1990s to 1.7 percent in 2004-05 is a matter of concern. This declining share was mainly due to the stagnation or fall in public investment in irrigation, particularly since the mid-1990s. However, there is indication of a reversal of this trend with public sector investment in agriculture reaching its highest level of Rs. 12,591 crore in 2004-05 since the early nineties. The share of public investment in gross investment increased by over 11 percentage point to reach 29.2 percent in 2004-05 relative to 1990-2000.

Further, India is facing grave crisis of rising 'unemployment' and in a labour surplus economy, the growth of unemployment gives rise to social conflicts and violence

The economic thinking in the UPA government is clearly anti-poor and the Economic Survey while dealing with a serious issue like growing unemployment focuses its attention on reform of 'labour laws' to eject the workers who are already employed.

Gross Capital Formation in Agriculture**

Year	*Investment in Agriculture (Rs. Crore)*			*Share in Agricultural Gross Investment (percent)*		*Investment in Agriculture as a percent of GDP at Constant Prices*
1990-91	14836	4395	10441	29.60	70.40	1.92
1995-96	15690	4849	10841	30.90	69.10	1.57
1996-97	16176	4668	11508	28.90	71.10	1.51
1997-98	15942	3979	11963	25.00	75.00	1.43
1998-99	14895	3870	11025	26.00	74.00	1.26
1999-00	17304	4221	13083	24.40	75.00	1.37
New Series (at 1990-00 prices)						
1999-00	43473	7754	35719	17.8	82.2	2.2
2000-01	38176	7018	31158	18.4	81.6	1.9
2001-02	46744	8529	38215	18.2	81.8	2.2
2002-03	45867	7849	38018	17.1	82.9	2.1
2003-04	47833	12809	35024	26.8	73.2	2.0
2004-05	43123	12591	30532	29.2	70.8	1.7

* Quick Estimates.

* *Source*: CSO.

** *Economy Survey*, 2005-06, pp. 169-70.

"Some salient features of the trend of unemployment rates in the country are:

> The unemployment rate went up between 1993-94 to 2004. On the basis of current daily status (unemployed on an average in the reference week), during the reference period, unemployment rate for males increased from 5.6 percent to 9.0 percent in rural areas, and from 6.7 percent to 8.1 percent in urban areas.

Similarly, unemployment rate for females increased from 5.6 percent in 1993-94 to 9.3 percent in 2004 in rural areas and from 10.5 percent to 11.7 percent in urban areas.

Furthermore, unemployment rates on the basis of current daily status were much higher than those on the basis of usual status (unemployed on an average in the reference year) implying a high degree of intermittent unemployment. This could be mainly because of the absence of regular employment for many workers.

Urban unemployment rates (current daily status) were higher than rural unemployment rates for both males and females in 1993-04. however, in 2004, rural unemployment rates for males was higher than that of urban males.

Unemployment rates varied sharply across States. States, where wages are higher than in neighbouring ones because of strong bargains or social security provision, such as high minimum wage; had high incident of unemployment, in general."

Unemployment Rates**

Year	*Investment in Agriculture (Rs. Crore)*			*Share in Agricultural Gross Investment (percent)*		*Investment in Agriculture as a percent of GDP at Constant Prices*
1990-91	14836	4395	10441	29.60	70.40	1.92
1995-96	15690	4849	10841	30.90	69.10	1.57
1996-97	16176	4668	11508	28.90	71.10	1.51
1997-98	15942	3979	11963	25.00	75.00	1.43
1998-99	14895	3870	11025	26.00	74.00	1.26
1999-00	17304	4221	13083	24.40	75.00	1.37
New Series (at 1990-00 prices)						
1999-00	43473	7754	35719	17.8	82.2	2.2
2000-01	38176	7018	31158	18.4	81.6	1.9
2001-02	46744	8529	38215	18.2	81.8	2.2
2002-03	45867	7849	38018	17.1	82.9	2.1
2003-04	47833	12809	35024	26.8	73.2	2.0
2004-05	43123	12591	30532	29.2	70.8	1.7

** *Economic Survey*, pp. 207-09

Indian Labour Laws and Labour Market

"Indian labour market is characterised by a sharp dichotomy. A large number of establishments in the unorganised sector remain outside any regulation, while the organised sector has been regulated fairly stringently. It can be reasonable argued that the organised sector has provided too much of job security for too long, while the unorganised sector has provided too little to too many.

Various studies indicate that Indian labour laws are highly protective of labour, and labour market are relatively inflexible. These laws apply only to the organised sector. Consequently, these laws have restricted labour mobility, have led to capital-intensive methods in the organised sector and adversely affected the sector's long-run demand for labour. Labour being a subject in the concurrent list, State-level labour regulations are also an important determinant of industrial performance. Evidence suggests that States, which have acted more pro-worker regulations, have lost out on industrial production in general.

Perhaps there are lessons to be learnt from China in the area of labour reforms. China, with a history of extreme employment security, has drastically reformed its labour relations and created a new labour market, in which workers are highly mobile. Although there have been mass layoffs and open unemployment, high rates of industrial growth especially in the coastal regions helped their redeployment. In spite of hardship workers in China seems to have benefited from wage growth, additional job creation and new opportunities for self-employment.[3] "

The UPA government at the Centre has become quite aware of the prevailing grave economic crisis in the country and its response has been in the form of National Rural Employment Guarantee Scheme. This is not only the response of the UPA government to resolve the crisis prevailing in the country. The Central Government has decided to 'modernise' paramilitary armed forces to tackle the so-called Naxal problem facing thirteen states of India. Naxalism is a consequence of the prevailing social discontent in the country and the UPA government does not have any strategy to eliminate the causes of social discontent and it has decided to take recourse to police oppression. India has been moving from crisis to crisis and the UPA government, whether Sonia-led or Manmohan-led, has not come forward with any policy package to tackle the prevailing social crisis in India.

The upshot of above description is that India has abandoned National Project for the Development of the whole country and every all-India and regional party represented at the Centre is implementing pro-rich and anti-poor public policies and Sonia Gandhi's Congress is the major carrier of the agenda of globalisation, liberalisation, deregulation and privatisation. The poor masses of India are not in the reckoning in the economic and political agenda following by the pro-rich liberalisers and it is not surprising that the BJP and the Congress have continued to follow the same economic strategy while in power at the Centre. The UPA government has saved India from the forces of fanatic Hindutva and Narendra Modi could not dare to repeat his performance in Vadodra in 2006 because instead of his protector Atal Bihari Vajpayee, Manmohan Singh is the Prime Minister of India. The UPA has liberated the central government from the stranglehold of Hindu Communal forces, it has not risen to the occasion while dealing with the problems faced by *Wretched of the Earth* of India.

DO WE HAVE A PRIME MINISTER?

Parliamentary democracy in England or Canada or Australia has in reality become a prime ministerial government; the office of the PM has evolved from the status of primus inter pares or first among equals to the present position of the leadership of the Cabinet and elected House of Parliament.

The council of ministers is collectively responsible to the elected House of Parliament, but in reality the writ of the PM runs over all the members of his Cabinet. Not only this. The PM can ask for the resignation or even the dismissal of a dissident member of his council of ministers because appointment of a minister is his sole prerogative. The PM can act as an unquestioned leader of his council of ministers if he enjoys the unquestioned political authority over his own party.

Unfortunately, Manmohan Singh is a PM nominated by Sonia Gandhi, who is the real and unquestioned leader of the Congress Party which is leading the UPA government at the Centre. Singh is not even a light weight leader of the Congress; the real repository of power is Sonia Gandhi who is the president of the Congress and the chairman of the National Advisory Council. Not only this, every coalition partner of the UPA looks towards her as the final arbiter of disputes or differences between the Congress Party and its coalition partners. The Communist parties, supporting the Congress-led UPA government from outside, look towards Sonia for their coordination with the Singh-led government.

It is noteworthy that Pranab Mukherjee, or P. Chidambaram or Arjun Singh, or Kamal Nath of the Congress Party care for the opinions and wishes of the PM because Sonia Gandhi, the supreme leader of the Congress, is supporting Singh in his present position. The Congress CMs too look towards Sonia Gandhi and not Singh, for guidance, advice, instructions and orders. It is Sonia Gandhi who decides to hold meetings of Congress CMs and they have to explain their record of activities to her and not the nominated PM. A telling example is provided by the manner in which Natwar Singh, the former external affairs minister, was made to 'quit' the Cabinet because Sonia Gandhi had got annoyed with her own favourite minister in the Volcker Affair. Natwar Singh was shown the door not by Singh but by Sonia.

The upshot of the above description is that the PM has no authority or freedom to exercise his real prerogative of either appointing a minister or in asking for his resignation. The Congress party representatives in Singh's Cabinet can continue at the 'pleasure' of Sonia and not on the basis of choice or goodwill of the PM. The essential point to be noted here is that Singh is shinning in the reflected glory of Sonia. He is in office because of his 'loyalty' to Sonia.

Jawaharlal Nehru or Indira Gandhi or Rajiv Gandhi or Narasimha Rao or Atal Bihari Vajpayee were not only PMs in their own right, they controlled the party organisation. Complete support of a party is a precondition for becoming a PM in a parliamentary democracy. It is not without reason that Jawaharlal Nehru threatened to resign from the CWC if Purushottam Das Tandon continued as party president. The clash and conflict between these two personalities was resolved in favour of the PM and the party president was made to quit his elected office.

Indira Gandhi decided to 'split' the Congress party in 1969 when the party president Nijalingappa had ganged up against her on the choice of the party nominee for the post of President of India. Indira Gandhi again 'split' the party in 1978 because a powerful section within the party was 'hostile' to her. In fact, every Congress PM, except Singh, had been either the unquestioned and unchallenged choice of the party or managed and manipulated party support in his/her favour.

A PM has to 'control' his party for his authority to be fully accepted by every minister in his Cabinet. Indira Gandhi fought against her opponents within the party because her authority as PM would have been completely diluted, even eroded, if she had allowed parallel or 'dual' centres of power. It is not without reason that V.P. Singh or Chandra Shekhar or H.D. Deve Gowda or I.K. Gujral could remain PMs only for a very short period because none of them had either firm support of a party or a coalition of parties. Vajpayee could remain PM from 1998 to 2004 because he was fully supported not only by the BJP but also other coalition partners. In other words, a PM is effective only on the basis of his own political strength within the party of which he is the leader.

Singh is not the leader of the Congress or of the UPA and hence he cannot lead the council of ministers. It has been observed that every pubic controversy involving the UPA government is resolved by the active intervention of Sonia Gandhi and not the PM. He does not have any role in the party's internal affairs because Sonia has the real power. The functioning of the government is also affected by such an unnatural 'dual control system' because every party or group in the UPA looks towards Sonia for the final word. The Left parties had walked out and boycotted the coordination committee meetings in the middle of 2005 because they had developed serious differences with the UPA government on economic policies of liberalisation, globalisation and privatisation and it was Sonia Gandhi's intervention which bought back the Left to the co-ordination committee meetings. Sonia Gandhi's National Advisory Council carries more weight in decision making than Singh and it had become clear on the issue of National Rural Employment Guarantee Scheme and the Right to Information Act 2005.

It deserves to be reiterated that the office of the PM in the UPA government has been completely devalued. It is not only that Singh owes his job to Sonia, all Congress ministers look towards Sonia for their continuation in office. Sonia has power without responsibility and Singh is shouldering responsibilities without real power.

—*The Economic Times,* 21 January, 2006

OFFICIALLY THE WEAKEST?

Parliamentary democracy revolves round the personality and leadership qualities of the Prime Minister, who is nearly always the sole spokesperson of the country's foreign and domestic policies. Manmohan Singh's press conference on February 1 was therefore a significant aid to understanding the policies of the UPA Government.

The Prime Minister chose to address the media at a time of sharp divisions within the country not only on the issue of foreign policy, but also on questions being raised regarding his own leadership qualities. It is not surprising that the country is debating the issue of Manmohan Singh's political authority, thanks to the circumstances that made him the Prime Minister in May 2004. The Congress had elected Sonia Gandhi to lead the Government at the Centre after the electoral debacle of the BJP-led NDA in the 2004 Lok Sabha election. Sonia Gandhi, however, 'nominated' Manmohan Singh to lead the coalition Government at the Centre.

Manmohan Singh has been the Prime Minister for 20 months and his press conference was an appropriate forum to clarify the issues that are in people's minds. The crux of the matter is the relationship between Manmohan Singh and Congress president Sonia Gandhi. After all, the UPA Government is led by the Congress, which is fully controlled by her.

Is the Prime Minister leading the Government without any authority? Manmohan Singh dismissed L.K. Advani's allegation of being the 'weakest Prime Minister' by observing: "If I am a weak Prime Minister then how strong was Advani when he went to Jinnah's mausoleum and had to resign as party president because the RSS didn't like it?" It was easy for Manmohan Singh to dismiss Advani's charges because the BJP-led NDA Government was dictated to by the RSS.

The BJP is the political front of the Sangh parivar. K.S. Sudarshan, the RSS sanghchalak, not only guided the BJP Government, but also ensured that both Atal Bihari Vajpayee and Advani were reduced to insignificance after the 2004 Lok Sabha election. It was, therefore, quite easy for Manmohan Singh to tackle the BJP at his press conference. If Sonia Gandhi is perceived as an 'extra-constitutional centre of power', the Vajpayee-led Government too was subservient to the RSS. Also the Manmohan Singh Government is far more stable than the regimes of V.P. Singh, Chandra Shekhar, H.D. Deve Gowda and Inder Kumar Gujral.

The Congress has always provided prime ministers who have governed the country without any other power centre, thanks to their control over party apparatus. In the current scenario, however, Manmohan

Singh is the head of the Government while Sonia Gandhi is the leader of the party. Little wonder, Manmohan Singh observed in the press conference: "She (Sonia Gandhi) is a source of strength for me. I'll probably be less effective in many of the tasks she has to perform as UPA chairperson and Congress president."

Sonia Gandhi is aware of the Congress's culture of backstabbing. The party leaders have perfected the art of duplicity and, to quote Rajiv Gandhi, "They are power brokers." P.V. Narasimha Rao, during his prime ministership, provided enough opportunities to Sonia Gandhi to come to the conclusion that traditional Congress leaders did not have the virtue of loyalty or even political integrity.

During the Rao regime, Arjun Singh and N.D. Tiwari walked out of the Congress to float a new party, the Congress (Tiwari). If party leaders could walk out of the Congress at the behest of Sonia Gandhi and betray Narasimha Rao, they would not hesitate to do the opposite for profit. Manmohan Singh is not like a traditional khadiwala politician. Not surprisingly, Sonia Gandhi trusted him over others in May 2004.

A storm broke out soon after the Prime Minister's press conference when a television channel showed a series of letters written by the PMO and the Cabinet Secretariat over the past 20 months, pleading the ministers to keep the Prime Minister in the loop about various policy decisions taken by their respective departments. It can be argued that the UPA allies are not following the principle of collective responsibility. Every party or group considers itself as an 'equal partner of the Congress'.

The UPA came into existence to keep the BJP out of power. Except this binding principle, the UPA partners have nothing in common either among themselves or with the Congress. The lack of coordination in the Government, therefore, could easily be attributed to the lack of commonality within the UPA.

On the issue of the PMO letter, BJP president Rajnath Singh observed: "We feel sorry for the Prime Minister's helplessness. It would not be off the mark to say that Manmohan Singh is indeed the weakest Prime Minister our country has ever had." It seems Rajnath Singh has forgotten RSS's interference during Atal Bihari Vajpayee's regime. In fact, Rajnath Singh has succeeded L.K. Advani as BJP president because of the Sangh's disapproval of the latter.

As far as the role of the Leftist parties is concerned, Manmohan Singh said, "I do not think they (the Left parties) will do so (stall policy-making). In the long run, some pressure does perform a useful function in a democracy. We will complete five years and with regard to pressure from Left, it is not unexpected." It is not only Manmohan Singh but every Prime Minister of a coalition Government who has to work under 'constraints'.

Parliament holds the Prime Minister responsible for the acts of the Government. Sonia Gandhi and her party cannot pretend on the floor of the House that the Government's authority is not exercised by the Prime Minister. Manmohan Singh is in the seat of the most powerful office of the Government and this role provides him with enough room to exercise discretionary powers. Manmohan Singh is not just primus inter pares in his Council of Ministers; he is also not in the category of other Congress prime ministers like Jawaharlal Nehru, Indira Gandhi, Rajiv Gandhi and Narasimha Rao. Also, he does not belong to the category of stop-gap prime ministers like Chandra Shekhar, H.D. Deve Gowda and Inder Kumar Gujral.

If Manmohan Singh is constrained by Sonia Gandhi's role in politics and Government, he is only emulating Atal Bihari Vajpayee. After all, Vajpayee too was held in check by the RSS and other outfits of the Sangh parivar. —*The Pioneer*, 7 February, 2006.

CONGRESS SEARCH FOR DIRECTION

The forthcoming Assembly elections in Maharashtra, Haryana and Arunachal Pradesh, the completion of 100 days of the Congress-led United Progressive Alliance Government at the Centre, and the All-India Congress Committee session held in Delhi on August 21, 2004, provide an opportunity to analyse and understand the working of Congress party organisation and the actual performance of the UPA Government. These are all inter-related issues because the Congress organisation and the coalition Government are on test and any failure or weakness within the party will provide opportunity and political space to its main political rival, the BJP.

It deserves to be mentioned that both the Congress and the BJP, the main contenders for all-India political space, are very much in the reckoning for political power on their own at the Centre. This is because the electoral verdict of the 14th Lok Sabha elections has neither completely weakened the BJP nor has it given a pre-eminent position to the Congress. The BJP-led NDA Government lost because its major coalition partners like the TDP, the AIADMK and the INLD suffered electoral setbacks. The Congress allies like the DMK or the RJD et al achieved electoral victories and that made it possible for the Congress to form a coalition Government at the Centre.

The Congress is still in a bad shape as compared to its glorious past and the BJP is looking for an opportunity to displace it from power. The Congress has to tackle this new political situation by clearly articulating its ideology and by reviving its extremely sick grassroots organisation.

Sonia Gandhi, the sole architect of the Congress's revival, brought to the attention of party leaderships on August 21, 2004, at the AICC session, that the core issue before the party is 'Government-organisation relations'. She clearly stated: "It generally happens that in the wake of a party's victory in election and the establishment of Government, the organisation takes a back seat."

Sonia Gandhi unambiguously told factional warhorses of the party: "This has also been a reason behind our electoral defeat in some states where the Government had eclipsed the organisation. This should not be repeated in future." Sonia Gandhi's call for 'revival and rejuvenation of the party organisation' seems to be a will-o'-the-wisp because the organisation's office bearers, including the PCC presidents, are themselves reluctant to serve the organisation and instead prefer to wallow in the luxury of their ministerial chairs. The Congress has lost the culture of dedicated organisation workers because ministerial berths are too profitable to be sacrificed at the altar of faceless party organisation.

It is not without reason that important ministers of the Manmohan Singh Government like Natwar Singh, Shivraj Patil, Arjun Singh et al, are given ministerial berths without being members of the Lok Sabha. Shivraj Patil, the Home Minister, was defeated in the elections. The BJP-led NDA, too, had ministers from the Rajya Sabha because they could not be elected to the Lok Sabha. Sonia Gandhi thus gets the credit for reminding every Congress leader about the need for renewal of the party organisation.

A committed party organisation is necessary but not a sufficient condition for the survival and success of the party in a democracy where alternative ideologies and policies compete against one another. Sonia Gandhi's second theme at the AICC session was to bring into sharp focus her party's differences from its main competitor, the BJP. The Congress resolution said that "the political fraud resorted to by the BJP in trying to camouflage its narrow, communal beliefs and attitudes, inspired and directed by the RSS, behind a facade of a variety of pseudo-political issues almost derailed the country from its secular foundations". This anti-BJP resolution of the Congress may remain a paper document because the party's commitment to secular politics does not go deep down the line within the party organisation.

Also, the Congress has recognised and reiterated its belief that "India has entered the era of coalition Government". If this is so, coalition partners have also to be committed to the ideologies of secularism as expounded by the Congress. The UPA Government is known more for its internal differences among its partners than a united front of anti-communal parties and groups. The mudslinging between Lalu Prasad

Yadav and Ram Vilas Paswan has not brought any credit to the Singh Government in its first 100 days. If one part of the story is the deadlock in Parliament because of the BJP's 'negative tactics', the other is the Congress chief ministers of Punjab and Manipur who have shown that neither the Congress nor the UPA Government has any semblance of unity.

Is it the 'coalition dharma' to witness Cabinet ministers charging one another in pubic as to who is more dishonest? Can any party be taken seriously in which its own chief ministers act like 'regional barons'? The Congress should also learn the lesson that its allies cannot be taken for granted, especially the Left which stands for programme and policies. The UPA ministers have forgotten that in a coalition Government, policy announcements like the hike in FDI in insurance, telecommunication and civil aviation require the consent of all partners in the Government.

The Congress should learn to practice coalition dharma and 'coordination' with allies and partners, which is the foundational principle of coalition politics. Further, the performance of the UPA Government would also be noticed in the forthcoming Assembly elections in Maharashtra, Haryana and Arunachal Pradesh. Maharashtra is ruled by a coalition of the Congress and the NCP, and both these parties are sharing power at the Centre. Therefore, it is natural that the BJP-Shiv Sena alliance will raise issues about the functioning of not only the State Government but also the Central Government. Similarly, in Haryana, Om Prakash Chautala will hammer the point about Captain Amarinder Singh's decision in Punjab to abrogate all water sharing agreements with neighbouring states.

A unilateral action by a Congress Chief Minister without caring for neighbours' projects a pan-Indian party like the Congress in very poor light. Sonia Gandhi called upon the Congress governments in the states to ensure that 'organisational workers' are not alienated, but the signals from Punjab and Manipur have proved that the all-India Congress party's writ does not run over its own chief ministers. It is also true that in any competitive political system, a political party has to project its own achievements as well as the failures of the Opposition. The Congress and the BJP are ideologically poles apart, their competition is unlike other sectarian, regional chauvist casteist parties and both of them are suffering from internal party factionalism.

It is a fact that in its behaviour, the BJP has not been any different from the Congress, though it still has a solid organisation to support it during the elections. Sonia Gandhi is making Herculean efforts to rejuvenate the Congress's sick organisation and provide direction to the party that has become 'directionless' because of loaves and fishes of office.

She must remember that Rajiv Gandhi was not only attacked by 'power brokers in the Congress', he was also destroyed by the same power brokers as well as professional factionalists. The euphoria of forming a Government at the Centre is attracting Congressmen to Sonia Gandhi and she has to guard herself against such forces within the party.

The upshot of above description is that the Congress is involved in a struggle to come to grips with the new political situation and one hopes that Sonia Gandhi may be able to inject some vitality into this slow, dying party. —*The Pioneer*, 28 August, 2004

CONGRESS ON TIGHT RED LEASH

Prakash Karat, General Secretary of the CPI(M), and Jyoti Basu have demanded that the UPA-led Coordination Committee meeting should be held after the State Assembly Elections in Assam, West Bengal, Kerala, Tamil Nadu and Pondicherry because the government is 'deviating' from common minimum Programme.

Karat during Kerala elections on April 24, 2006 stated that, "After the elections, we are going to examine which Common Minimum Programme the Manmohan Singh Government is going to implement – the one of the UPA, or the one dictated by George Bush. We would like the Government we support to implement the former." Karat observed that "India had thrown to the wind the basic tenets of non-aligned movement" and this is the compelling reason for holding the Coordination Committee meeting after the elections of May 2006.

Prime Minister Manmohan Singh while campaigning in Kerala stated on April 19, 2006 "we are implementing the CMP of the UPA of which CPM is a very important and valuable partner. We have absolute commitment to the CMP in its entirely and it guides the future direction of all our politics".

The real contentious issue that divide the UPA government and the Communist parties is the Pro-American foreign policy pursued by the Central Government. The Communist parties had organised anti-Bush demonstrations in March 2, 2006 and it was alleged that India should not support an anti-Iraq and anti-Iran policies of the American aggressors. The Left parties have also organised public meetings against the Central Government on its support to the Americans on dispute with Iran on nuclear issues. The Communists are also opposed to the India-US agreement on nuclear cooperation for civilian purposes.

Why are the Communists supporting the government with which they have basic differences both on domestic and foreign policies? Is common secular agenda of the UPA government and the Communists enough to sustain such a political arrangement at the centre? The Communists parties have a minimalist commonality with the Congress and this is the reason that these two political formations are finding it difficult to cooperation with one another at the level of Central Government. A common struggle against religion-based politics as practiced by the BJP can be a necessary but not a sufficient condition to sustain any kind of 'alliance' between historically well-known opponents like the Congress and Communists. Communists are not only committed anti-religion based politics of the forces of Hindutva, they are also fundamentally opposed to the economic and foreign policies of the Congress party. The Common Minimum Programme was agreed in May 2004 and every Coordination Committee meeting ended up in a patch work and they have temporarily agreed to work together on the plant of defence of secular agenda for Indian politics.

Sonia Gandhi, the real centre of power in the Congress party, during election campaign in Kerala stated on April 18, 2006 that "The United Democratic Front alone can ensure social harmony and development" because "only the UDF has a positive agenda for the state". Communists and Congress are not only electoral opponents, these two political formations represent two different social polls in Indian politics and this is the reason that Chandrababu Naidu of the TDP. Jayalalitha of AIADMK, Mulayam Singh of the Samajwadi Party *et al.,* have been asking the Communists to follow their traditional politics of forming an anti-BJP and anti-Congress alliance at the Centre. Prakash Karat, in People Democracy, the official organ of the party, has stated that the Third Alternative will emerge on the basis of 'joint action' by parties "believing in secularism, pro-people economic policies and anti-imperialism." This according to Prakash Karat "will lead to the emergence of a common platform and ultimately a third alternative". The main purpose of attack by the left parties against the Congress and demand for a meeting of the Coordination Committee after the state Assembly elections on May 8, 2006 is to effectively 'intervene' in the economic and foreign policies of the UPA government, and also apply 'Correctives'; whenever possible, in the directions of policies followed by the Central Government. It does not mean that the Communists have closed their political options by supporting the UPA Government because it has an 'open alternative options' of aligning with strong regional parties against the BJP and the Congress. The Communist parties are working on 'Two options' i.e. continue to support the Congress-led UPA government in common struggle against the BJP and also keep their doors and windows open for anti-Congress and anti-BJP political alliance. The primary purpose of the communists at the present is to weaken and defeat the forces of Hindutva represented by the Sangh Parivar and in this political enterprise either ally with the Congress or opt out of the Congress and form a third political alliance to continue struggle against BJP and the Congress. It is a well-known fact that the Congress and the BJP, the only two claimants for all Indian political space, seen to be in an extremely vulnerable political position and possibilities of revival of the Congress and the BJP as formidable all India political force are quite remote. The Congress and the BJP are witnessing a phase of political exhaustion and both these so-called all India parties need allies to form any government at the center. And the Congress with just 146 Lok Sabha Members is not in any position to form any government without allies. Are Communist parties awaiting for political developments, which may necessitate the formation of anti-BJP and anti-Congress third alternative alliance of parties. The main strategy of Communist parties is to keep 'pressure' on the Manmohan Singh Government by remaining 'outside the UPA government'. The Communists are overtly or covertly working to create a Third Alternative Alliance and withdraw the support from the Congress-led UPA government. This is the explanation for the Communist parties demand for the holding of Coordination committee meeting after the State Assembly elections of May 8, 2006 because they want to exert maximum pressure on the UPA government to follow the CMP in letter and spirit. It is also very clear that the Communists are not closing any 'option' and the present 'marriage of convenience' between the Congress and the Communists may end any time and lead to political divorce.

—*Sahara Time*, 6 May, 2006

AN INHERENTLY WEAK COALITION

The UPA government at the Centre has completed 18 months in office. Its journey has, however, not exactly been smooth. The UPA is much more than a coalition of 14 parties, groups and individuals, though. Apart from managing its disparate constituents, it also has to do business with Mulayam Singh Yadav's Samajwadi Party and the Communists on whose outside support it depends heavily for its survival.

It is obvious, therefore, that such a coalition would have a rather rough ride. Manmohan Singh, in an interview to Rajat Gupta of McKinsey, had stated: "We are a coalition government and that limits our options in some ways.... Privatisation happens to be one such area." He went to say, "I must confess to you that in the prevailing milieu, the thinking in our coalition is that for enterprises that are doing well under competitive conditions, we must have a special justification to prove to our coalition colleagues that there is need for privatisation." But has the PM given us the whole truth about his predicament?

Each of the 14 parties, groups, which constitute the coalition, evidently want to use their presence in the government to promote their own interests, which often enough have little or no correspondence. The blame for all the government's acts of omission and commission, as a consequence, has become the Congress's headache.

That is the story from inside the coalition. The government's dealings with its 'outsider' supporters, mainly the Left parties, have turned out to be no better. The Left and the UPA have in place a 'panel' to jointly oversee the implementation of the Common Minimum Programme (CMP), which was forged on a supposed consensus between the various outfits that constitute the alliance and its outside supporters. The actual working of this panel, however, has not only been smooth, but appears to have brushed consensual functioning against its grain. Recently, there was a deadlock in the coordination panel after the Communists walked out of it because of serious differences with the government on disinvestment and privatisation of profit-making PSEs.

The essential reason for such paralysing acrimony is not far to be found. Congress, the principal player in the UPA, and the Communists have fundamentally different ideological approaches and social constituencies. Thankfully, though, the Left 'boycott' of the coordination panel has ended, and it is back to business as usual. The routine of coordination committee meetings, between the government and the Left parties, has been restored. Nevertheless, the gulf between the two on crucial economic issues, as also the orientation of foreign and defence policies, has remained as unbridgeable as ever.

To figure out the origins of the UPA government's current predicament, it is important that one examine the various coalition experiments that India has seen. The country has been witness to some successful coalition governments, especially in states. A coalition can survive well only if parties that constitute it form a pre-election alliance on the basis of a well defined common minimum programme. It's precisely this that is responsible for the enduring success of coalitions in West Bengal and Kerala.

Other more recent instances of similarly successful coalitions have been the Nationalist Congress Party-Congress government in Maharashtra, which rode to power and has retained its grip on it, by basing its unity on a cogent and programmatic opposition to the BJP-Shiv Sena alliance. Nitish Kumar of the Janata Dal (United) and the BJP routed Lalu Yadav in Bihar by evolving consensus on an agenda of governance that it has projected as an alternative to Lalu's populist misrule.

The one common lesson that all these coalition experiments offer is that partners in a political alliance must have ideological convergence on some key and fundamental issues if they are to remain united in power. The UPA government, unfortunately, fails to fulfil even the most basic pre-condition of a durable coalition; it is not a product of any pre-poll alliance of parties and groups. It is more akin to the freak phenomenon that various so-called United Front coalition governments of the 1990s epitomised. All those governments were products of accidents of India's political history, and their political transitoriness is best captured by their rather short-lived tenures. The UPA government, by the look of it, is destined to either follow its freakish predecessors in having a rather short life, or, live longer by lurching precariously from one crisis to another.

That a Congress-led government is cooperating with the Communists for the first time in the history of post-Independence India must, nonetheless, be underscored here. That it is largely because they want to keep their common enemy, the Hindutva-peddling BJP, out of power should, however, be equally emphasised. The Left parties of India are unambiguously committed to fight the vicious and dangerous politics of the forces represented by Hindutva, and this has been a compelling enough reason for them to come together with the Congress. It does not, however, mean that the Communists are ready to sacrifice their fundamentals while supporting an anti-BJP government. The Congress and the Communists know all too well that the issue that unites them is as important as the ideological fundamentals which divide them, and which have kept them apart for more than 55 years.

The real weakness of the UPA government, in such circumstances, lies in the incapacity of the Congress to truly fulfil its role as leader of the coalition. That it has 144 MPs in a house (Lok Sabha) of 543 members has not helped matters.

The crisis-ridden UPA government's weakness certainly stems from the fact that it is a conglomeration of disparate groups. And the Congress's inability to demand its right of leadership from its partners, because of its precariously small numerical presence in Lok Sabha, has further complicated matters. Manmohan Singh is handicapped, not so much by the diverse clamour of his partners and supporters, but because the Congress, no thanks to its below par electoral performance in 2004, is not in the driver's seat. —*The Economic Times*, 24 December, 2005

POLITICS OF TIRED FRONT

A sizeable section of the political class has always been engaged in creating a Third Front political alternative which is anti-Congress and anti-BJP. Notable among them are the Left parties. Indeed, V.P. Singh, Chandra Shekhar, H.D. Deve Gowda and I.K. Gujral could become prime ministers because the Left was able to keep the Congress and the BJP out of power. Incidentally, these freak governments at the Centre survived with the 'outside' support of either the BJP or the Congress. And whenever these parties withdrew support, the governments fell.

In 2005, the Left changed its policy and announced that it would not forge an alliance with a party that did not subscribe to its ideology. This decision was a result of its experience with Third Front allies. The Left found out that its so-called Third Front allies were political opportunists. This shift in policy has compelled other anti-Congress and anti-BJP parties to reconsider their strategies for the formation of a Third Front alternative in the future. The Left has sent a clear message that it will not be party to opportunistic and shifting Third Front alliances just to keep the Congress or the BJP out of power.

Samajwadi Party chief Mulayam Singh Yadav stated on June 5 that "it was time the Left gave a lead to provide an alternative combine at the national level". He said that an alternative Third Front should be available to the voters and that such an alliance would consist of regional parties.

Sharad Pawar of the NCP, in its convention on June 10 at Surat, announced his party's opposition to the disinvestment policy of the UPA government. He is a part of the Congress-led Government, but his political ambition to emerge as a leader of future 'alternative' depends on his acceptability to the Left. This is why he is opposing the disinvestment policy of the UPA government.

L.K. Advani's comments on Mohammed Ali Jinnah and the subsequent political crisis within the BJP and the Sangh parivar have activated some of the allies of the BJP-led NDA because developments within the BJP and the Sangh Parivar have a direct bearing on the political future of the NDA. George Fernandes and Nitish Kumar of the Janata Dal (United) made public statements in support of Vajpayee-Advani leadership because any continuing crisis within the BJP would have a direct impact on the future of JD(U)'s leadership.

Chandrababu Naidu of the TDP had announced that his party could not get the support of Muslim voters because of its association with the BJP-led NDA Government at the Centre. He is now distancing himself from the BJP. Naidu said on June 9 that he, like Advani, wanted a debate on Jinnah. In his opinion, Mr. Advani had done nothing wrong by making statements on Jinnah during his visit to Pakistan. The NDA consists of only those parties which can never be with the Congress in their states. This is the logic of anti-Congress or anti-BJP alliances because these two national parties are in competition not only against one another, but also against regional parties.

Secular versus communal politics is the agenda of the Congress, the BJP and the Left. For every other regional party, ideological issues like secularism are simply political tactics.

What this means is that both Mulayam Singh Yadav and Sharad Pawar are looking for an 'alternative' to replace the Congress as the leader of the UPA and establish a non-Congress, non-BJP Third Front to replace the shaky Manmohan Singh Government. Incidentally, a Third Front government, if it gets formed, too will be unstable and temporary.

What is the explanation behind the formation of alliances at the Centre and why are these alliances farcical and temporary? The compulsion of forming alliances at the Centre is that the electoral verdict is completely fragmented. Neither the all-India parties nor the multiple regional parties are getting enough seats to form a stable government.

The UPA consists of major, minor and insignificant parties with a view to creating a workable majority in the Lok Sabha. The publicly-stated goal of the Congress and other groups in the UPA is to keep the "communal" BJP out of power. But past record of regional parties is not at all encouraging because a majority of such parties have never hesitated to form alliances with the BJP.

Not only this. If, on the one hand, some regionalists have felt comfortable in the company of the BJP, others, which are secular pretenders, have extended clandestine support to the party. For instance, Mulayam Singh Yadav in U.P. is a great champion of non-Congress and non-BJP third alternative, but he is keeping intact his line of communication with the BJP. Further, the socialists and other varieties of Jayaprakash Narayan-inspired Janata Dals have never hesitated in forming alliances with the BJP. Mr. Fernandes is the best example of a socialist sitting comfortably with a communal BJP.

At the national level, anti-Congressism is more important than anti-BJPism because every regional party from Arunachal Pradesh to Jammu & Kashmir has to reckon with the Congress and not the BJP on its home turf. The Akali Dal in Punjab, the National Conference in Jammu & Kashmir, the Janata Dal (Secular) in Karnataka, the TDP in Andhra Pradesh, the DMK and ADMK in Tamil Nadu, the AGP in Assam are all contenders for power and everyone of them has to confront the Congress in the State.

This is why anti-Congressism has greater appeal to the regional parties. The Communists are supporting the Congress-led UPA government for the first time because they are ideologically committed against the BJP's politics of Hindutva. The BJP of 2005 is not the Jana Sangh of 1952. BJP-in-Government from 1998 to 2004 has alerted the Communists that Hindutva is a force to reckon with. The party has polarised politics of Himachal Pradesh, Rajasthan, Madhya Pradesh, Jharkhand, Chhattisgarh and Gujarat.

The BJP's growing political influence cannot be contained without involving the Congress in a struggle for anti-communal politics at the national level. The Congress has made subtle concessions to the Hindu sentiment, but it has consistently fought against the Jana Sangh/BJP, and the Communists, as committed anti-communalists, need a national level ally. The Congress is the only available option.

The Congress and the Communists are simultaneously competing and cooperating with each other because of the logic of the growing strength of the BJP in 2005. The Congress and the Communists can be comrade-in-arms on an ideological platform of anti-communalism; the rest of the regional and sub-regional parties have flexible ideologies. Politics of opportunistic alliances is the guiding principle of the regional forces. Every regionalist has tasted the fruits of political power at the Centre and this is the only compelling reason for them to make alliances at the Centre.

The regional and national parties do not have any common cementing factor. This is the reason why the DMK and the AIADMK feel comfortable with both the Congress and the BJP at the Centre depending on their need of the hour. For instance, M. Karunanidhi's DMK has been a comrade-in-arms of both Atal Bihari Vajpayee's NDA and Manmohan Singh/Sonia Gandhi's UPA.

The upshot of all this is that politics of alliances, coalitions and fronts is based on pure opportunism and self-advancement. Thus all the political alternatives in the 1990s and the 2000s have been farcical political marriages of convenience. —*The Pioneer*, 16 June, 2005

HAMMER AND TONGS: LEFT MEANS BUSINESS

The Manmohan Singh led-UPA government celebrated one year of its rule with great fanfare mid-May. And hardly a month after their self-congratulatory functions, the Congress has received a stern message from the Communists who have said they would abstain from the UPA-Left front Coordination Committee meetings indefinitely.

The proposed boycott of Coordination Committee meetings by Communists has rattled Sonia Gandhi and Manmohan Singh who immediately began negotiations with the Left Front leaders to be assured of the latter's active support to the UPA coalition. Prakash Karat, the general secretary of CPI(M), announced on June 26 that the boycott of the Coordinating Committee meeting was because of serious policy differences.

In a letter to the Prime Minister, the Left Front stated, "Right now we want to give a serious message to the coalition leadership that we cannot be taken for granted on economic policies, especially disinvestment." The announcement by the Government that "it will go ahead with disinvestment in Bharat Heavy Electricals Limited and other public sector undertakings" was the last straw which completely alienated the Communists from the UPA.

The Left Front is concerned that Manmohan Singh, P. Chidambaram, Montek Singh Ahluwalia and other reformers in the Congress, by policies of disinvestment of the navratnas, are laying the foundation for "gradual privatisation" and the Left cannot accept this 'creeping privatisation' of profit making public sector units. Not only this; the Communists have let known their unhappiness with the UPA government on price hike of petroleum and its dilly dallying on National Employment Guarantee Scheme which has yet to receive parliamentary sanction.

All this led Prakash Karat to state that disinvestment of BHEL was "the first serious violation of the common minimum programme." He concluded his stern statement saying the Left "will continue to extend support to the Government but we do not want to give an impression that there is coordination because there is none." The crux of the matter is that the political understanding between the UPA Government and the Communists has reached a yield point.

It is wrong to conclude that the Communists are distancing themselves from the Congress because in the forthcoming 2006 State Assembly elections in West Bengal and Kerala, the two have to contest against each other. This interpretation shows an ignorance of Communist economic philosophy which is fundamentally different from 'Manmohanomics'. Decisions of globalisation, liberalisation and privatisation have directly hit the poor workers and peasants who happen to be the main constituency of the Communists. At no cost can a political group be indifferent to the concerns of those who play the main role in bringing it to power one election after another.##

How can anti-poor and anti-labour class policies of this Government be accepted by a political group representing the poor of India? Unlike the Congress and other bourgeois parties, the Communists cannot act as the gatekeepers of capitalists. The Prime Minister in the National Development Council meeting on June 27-28 admitted that the country was facing serious agrarian crises. The Communists cannot rest assured merely with verbal rhetoric unlike the Prime Minister, seeing that the plight of the rural poor is still not being redressed.

It is not only starvation deaths or the suicides committed by small and marginal indebted farmers which are a testimony to the deep agrarian crisis, it is complete callousness and inaction of the Congress-led UPA government towards these suffering classes that the Communists cannot accept. It is an overall disenchantment with the Congress on basic economic policies that has brought about the current impasse.

It must be clearly stated that the Communists follow principled national and international policies and their ideological commitment to fight against the forces of Hindutva is the only rationale behind their 'outside' support to the Congress-led UPA government. Religion-based politics is diametrically opposite to the communist ideology of dialectical materialism and secularism.

The opposition of the Communists to religion-based politics is based on their firm commitment to secular and social values. The outside support by Communists to the Congress-led UPA was basically at keeping the forces of Hindutva out of power. Communists are now faced with a predicament. They must support the Congress to keep BJP out of the corridors of power. But at the same time they cannot be taken for granted. This time they mean business. —*Sunday Pioneer*, 3 July, 2005

WHAT IS THE BJP'S POLITICAL FUTURE?

The BJP's electoral defeat in the Lok Sabha elections in April-May 2004 and in the Maharashtra assembly polls of October 2004 has stirred a hornet's nest. The party of fanatic Hindutva is now completely preoccupied with trying to formulate future strategies of political revival. In short, it's worrying itself over how it would stage a comeback at the Centre. The BJP has undertaken an internal cleansing process by holding *chintan baithaks*. And the organisational reshuffle that it conducted recently, with old warhorse L.K. Advani being brought in once again as party president, is with the express purpose of rejuvenating its political machine. The question, however, is, has the BJP introspected enough and properly ascertained the reasons behind its electoral defeats? Would a simple leadership change be enough to restore its electoral health?

It is essential to state here that the BJP is not like any other centrist or regional party, and any meaningful understanding of its future prospects is possible only by locating the salient features of this 'party with a difference'. The BJP, the Sangh parivar's political mask, is involved in electoral politics with a clear goal of establishing what it calls Hindu Rashtra. Every activity of the Sangh fraternity, including the BJP, is directed towards capturing state power and the transformation of civil society with the sole purpose of refashioning India into a Hindu nation. And BJP-led governments, both at the Centre and in states, have used governmental authority to effect the Hinduisation of civil society.

The greatest achievement of BJP governments has been to convey a clear message to minority communities that they have to accept the definition and practices of Hindutva as laid down by the parivar and its governments. It is not without reason that Atal Bihari Vajpayee, as prime minister, had declared that the construction of Ram Temple, an integral part of the parivar's agenda, was a 'national sentiment', because in its scheme of things the Indian nation can't be anything else but Hindu. It is not surprising that Advani, in his coronation ceremony as party president on October 27, 2004, declared that Ram temple will be constructed. He also stated that this goal of Hindutva would have been achieved if the BJP had been re-elected.

Vajpayee, as prime minister, desired a national debate on religious conversions, a pet theme with fanatic Hindus, to confront the Christian missionaries. It is erroneous to maintain, therefore, that the BJP becomes moderate while in power and a militant fanatic force while mobilising voters for elections. The shadow-boxing among the various fraternal constituents of the Sangh is for the mass media's consumption. An electoral defeat for the BJP is just a temporary set-back, because every member of the parivar, the BJP included, inside or outside the government, are always engaged in strengthening the roots of their ideology of Hindutva in every institution of civil society. Democratic elections are a 'necessary evil' for the Sangh, because the Constitution, though not to its liking, is a fundamental law of the land. Governance, therefore, is not the be-all and end-all as far as the parivar is concerned. Its final aim is Hinduisation of civil society.

The Sangh parivar is a whole and while some of its parts manage *shisu mandirs*, others work towards the Hinduisation of tribals. There are yet others, *pracharaks* like Narendra Modi, who have been assigned the responsibility to man the levers of governmental power. Hence it would be quite misleading to maintain that Vajpayees or Advanis or Modis are 'moderate' while in government and turn their coats when in Opposition. It is no accident that Vajpayee and Advani, as leaders of the central government, attended the public coronation of Narendra Modi after he had been re-elected as chief minister of Gujarat. The message is loud and clear: the Supreme Court's indictment of the Modi government "as Neros" during the post-Godhra riots in Gujarat in 2002 has no significance for Vajpayee, the prime minister of the Sangh parivar.

Hindutva stands for a 'polarised India, and every *swayamsevak*, whether prime minister or chief minister, has to work for it. That is the real face of the BJP and its prospects for electoral victories are bright if social cleavages are widened and sharpened by the parivar.

—*The Economic Times*, 2 November, 2004

WHITHER BJP

The real agenda of the meeting of the National Executive of the BJP held from September 16 to 18, 2005 at Chennai was to deal with the controversies around its Party President L.K. Advani which had arisen during his visit to Pakistan in June 2005. The major issue raised by the RSS against Advani's statements in Pakistan was of 'ideological deviation' by the BJP President who not only projected Mohamed Ali Jinnah as 'secular' but also committed a great ideological sin by abandoning the Sangh Parivar's ideology of Akhand Bharat by stating that Pakistan was a reality. Advani's statements in Pakistan in June 2005 and strong reactions from the RSS and other 'outfits' of the Sangh Parivar like the VHP, Bajrang Dal et al about his 'ideological deviations' has led to a great public debate on the real significance of Advani's attempt to distance himself and the BJP from crude and militant Hindutva of the RSS and other shops of the Sangh Parivar. It deserves to be stated that Advani and the BJP had unambiguously implemented the agenda of Hindutva during Vajpayee-led National Democratic Alliance coalition government from 1998 to 2004. It has been suggested that electoral defeat of the BJP in the Lok Sabha elections of 2004 prompted a section of the BJP leadership to project itself as a right-wing and socially inclusive party instead of its image of a fanatic Hindu party which is anti-minority and anti-equality of every citizen before the law of the country. Was it an attempt by the BJP to reinvent itself and abandon its core agenda of fanatic Hindutva with a view to broaden its political and electoral reach to communities which had kept themselves away from the Hindu BJP? It has been surmised that Advani and a section of the BJP leadership realised that a liberal Hindu face is electorally more beneficial than the present ideology of fanatic Hindu Rashtravadis. Political parties in any competitive democratic electoral system try to shift their position on the basis of new challenges and also with a view to respond to the perceptions of the voters. If the BJP has to reinvent itself and Advani's effort is to project a 'liberal BJP' before the voter of India, it has to carry conviction with its parent organisations like the RSS and fanatic fraternal organisations like the VHP, Bajrang Dal et al. The BJP is not a 'Normal democratic party' like the Congress.

The BJP is a party with a difference because it is a political instrument of the RSS and any ideological change with a view to win an election cannot be carried out by Advani or others without the full approval and consent of the RSS. The BJP is just an extension of the RSS and it is a big zero without the RSS and it becomes amply clear from the statements of Advani himself at Chennai meeting where he announced his decision to step down from the post of President of the BJP in December 2005. Advani said that ideologically, RSS and BJP, have 'symbiotic relationship' and "Both the organisations have benefited immensely from this relationship and together they have succeeded in bringing out ideology of cultural nationalism to the centre stage of India" Advani believes that the RSS and the BJP are 'equal' and 'comrade-in-arms' for the promotion of Hindutva but as a political party, the BJP should enjoy 'autonomy' from its sister organisation. Did Advani get any support from anyone within the National Executive of the BJP on his clarion call for 'autonomy' from the RSS? The answer is a big no. Not only this. Atal Bihari Vajpayee publicly stated at Chennai that the RSS is "an exceptional organisation, unequal in the world". Vajpayee observed that the bond between the RSS and BJP is 'unbreakable' and the Jan Sangh/BJP was 'established by the RSS'. Advani himself admitted that the RSS should stick to its mission of 'man-making and nation-building' and also 'train BJP functionaries for politics'. Thus the cat is out of the bag and the argument that the BJP under the leadership of Advani has tried to project a new face of liberal Hindu is unsubstantiated and ill-founded because Advani's departure itself has been commanded by the RSS. A party of the Hindus, for the Hindus and by the Hindus has no capacity to abandon its hardcore ideology because the BJP is just one arm of the RSS and all outfits of Hindutva have to work for the implementation of the ideology of Hindutva as laid down by the RSS. The BJP is an empty balloon without the organisational network of the RSS and it has no independent capacity of its own to mobilise the voters without the *swayamsevaks*. The Congress party still continues to win elections in some states and regions in spite of the fact that its party organisation is in a shambles. It is an irony of Indian politics that the Congress without a well-knit party organisation still has electoral and political presence from Kashmir to Arunachal Pradesh and the BJP/RSS, in spite of committed cadre cannot win an election on all India basis. Not only this. The BJP will be reduced to political cipher without RSS cadre while all regional and casteist parties are able to win region-specific elections on the basis of their 'leaders' or appeal of caste or region. Lalu Yadav or Mayawati or Chandrababu Naidu and other regional and caste leaders are able to mobilise social constituencies on the basis of their social agenda and as leaders of their parties, they have enough flexibility and manoeuvrability to extend their social reach by making multiple social alliances. The BJP is constricted and constrained because Muslim and Christian minority communities are persona non-grata to Hindutva and a vast majority of secular Hindus keep away from fanatic Hindutva of the BJP. The BJP is unable to motivate and mobilise many social constituencies and groups because it has socially and culturally exclusive agenda and all other parties, all-India or regional or casteist, are open fronts for multiple social groups. It is possible Advani and other leaders of the BJP understood this logic and compulsion of democratic politics and perhaps Advani attempted to broaden and widen the reach of party of Hindutva. But Advani himself is a cog in a wheel and part of a machine and the organisation has clearly shown him the door and made him a zero. The upshot of above description is that competitive democratic politics provides great learning opportunities to parties to adapt and adjust to the new demands of electoral politics. Politics of Hindutva as practiced by the Sangh Parivar has reached a dead end and it cannot cross 20 per cent of national votes limit. Hindutva itself is a limiting factor and the BJP cannot 'reinvest' itself on the model of other parties or groups in India. —*Sahara Time,* 1 October, 2005

AMERICA'S KISS OF DEATH

A second term for President George Bush in the White House has led Indian foreign policy-makers to dream of occupying a high seat in the United Nation's Security Council (UNSC). Prime Minister Manmohan Singh and his Foreign Minister Natwar Singh have made this issue the primary objective of India's foreign policy. To achieve this goal, Indians have started knocking at the door of the White House because without US support, the existing arrangements in UNSC cannot be altered.

Indian foreign policy makers have not hesitated to beg for support for a permanent seat in the UNSC from a country which has shown nothing but contempt for the UN—including the Security Council—while pursuing its imperialist agenda in Iraq. The UPA government, like the previous NDA government, is following a foreign policy which is completely pro-US, irrespective of its imperialist doctrine.

In this context, the visits to the US by Indian foreign and defence policy-makers assume significance; they will be setting the agenda of the forthcoming July 18 summit between President Bush and Manmohan Singh in Washington. The US has committed itself to making India a major power in the 21st century, and the Indian ruling class is ready to do anything to please the Americans. The Indian Parliament passed the Weapons of Mass Destruction Act as demanded by the Americans in return of defence deals.

The signal is clear: If India wants access to US's civil nuclear technology or if it wants the US to lift its embargo on high-tech defence supplies, Parliament will accept any 'conditionality' laid down by the superpower.

It is not incidental that a major Indian newspaper published a survey on June 23/24 that Indians were more pro-America than citizens of any other country. The message was that the US has a very powerful social constituency in India and that the Indian Government is in tune with the sentiments of pro-US feelings of the Indian elite.

Foreign Secretary Shyam Saran, in his meeting with US Under-Secretary of State for Political Affairs Nicholas Burns on June 24 and 25, cleared the "contours of Singh's upcoming visit to the US". While many bilateral agreements are under discussion, Indians want cooperation from the US in civilian use of nuclear energy. The US is asking for "additional non-proliferation commitments by India".

Indian foreign and defence policy-makers are zealously pursuing their goal of establishing close relationship with the US for supplying the latest weapons system so that India can build a powerful modern war machine to establish its status as a major power in the 21st century.

British Prime Minister Tony Blair has said that Europe faces 'grand strategic future' if it shies away from 'urgent economic reforms' while "emerging giants like India and China power ahead". Blair added, "The USA is the world's only superpower. But China and India, in a few decades, will be the largest economies, each of them with populations three times that of the entire EU."

The Indian ruling elite is possessed by the idea of an 'emerging great power of the 21st century' because US and UK are certifying our future 'greatness'. They desire 'symbols' of national power like nuclearisation, permanent UNSC membership, and a powerful war machine. These symbols can be obtained only with US support. Manmohan Singh's forthcoming visit to the US is one more attempt to seek concessions and cooperation from the global superpower.

It is clear that India is making every effort to curry favour with the superpower, but Indians seem to be pretending that the US is not seeking any special role from India to promote and defend US's national interests. Bilateral relations between India and US are not between equals, and expectations of reciprocity are also based on unequal power relations between these two countries.

The US treats Pakistan as a 'frontline state' and, in spite of frequent protestations from India, the US can never abandon Pakistan just because it is hostile to India. The US can be a facilitator between India and Pakistan in their dispute over Jammu & Kashmir, but it will never impose a decision on Pakistan because it needs it for its larger strategic interests in the oil rich Islamic countries of the Gulf and Central Asia.

The logic of bringing US-Pakistan relations into this discussion is to establish a point that if the US is helping Pakistan on the basis of 'reciprocity', Indo-US relations cannot be an exception to this general rule of foreign policy based on bilateralism of 'unequal' powers. Hence, the attempt by Indian foreign policy-makers to keep under the carpet the 'conditions' under which the US is willing to help India in achieving its national goals. The foreign policy establishment is evading this important issue from public scrutiny.

US Secretary of Defence Donald Rumsfeld, during the Asian Security Conference held in Singapore on June 3 to 5, expressed his country's "threat perception from China". He elaborated that China's defence expenditure is much higher than what its official document claims. "Since no nation threatens China, why this growing investment in defence?" A pillar of US foreign and defence policy has been to identify an 'enemy' country and make alliances to confront it. Post-Cold War phase, China has emerged strong. Hence, the US is firming up 'alliances' to deal with an emerging China.

Is India a candidate for US strategies against China? This question cannot be ignored because the Vajpayee government had identified China and Pakistan as India's enemies in an official communication to President Bill Clinton while explaining the nuclear tests conducted by India in 1998. Is the Manmohan Singh government brushing this issue of China-US-India relations under the carpet? The Indian Parliament should seek a public statement from the Prime Minister about the quid pro quo for US generosity towards India.

The story does not end with this. The US is violating every international law while dealing with prisoners of war from Iraq and Afghanistan at Guantanamo Bay. Vice-President Dick Cheney said on June 14 that there was no plan to close the prison. The Indian Parliament should ask the Government to make its position clear on serious violations of international law by the US.

Petroleum Minister Mani Shankar Aiyar is making every effort to ensure that the Iran-Pakistan-India gas pipeline project takes shape. However, US National Security Adviser Condoleezza Rice told him on June 13 that this project could violate the Iran and Libya Sanction Act (1996) of the US. Rice's statement was reiterated by US Under-Secretary of State for Political Affairs Nicholas Burns on June 25 in Delhi. He said, "Our problem is with the Government of Iran. We believe that Iran, as a state founder of terror, has been extremely unhelpful in the Middle East."

Has India succumbed to US pressure and abandoned the project? After all, the American friends of India consider Iran 'a founder of terrorism'. The political framework of India's foreign policy needs to be clearly spelt out by the UPA Government. It is to be hoped that the Congress of today will follow Nehru's tradition of foreign policy and take Parliament into confidence on the concessions given to the US by the Government. —*The Pioneer*, 28 June, 2005

SYMBOLS OF NATIONAL POWER

The first official visit of prime minister Manmohan Singh to the United States from July 18 to 20, 2005, preceded by defence minister Pranab Mukherjee's signing of a 10-year defence agreement between India and the US on June 29, 2005, deserves to be understood and analysed in the context of changing perceptions of the ruling classes about the status of India in the 21st century.

The Indian ruling elite seems to feel that India has arrived as a 'middle power' in the international arena and now it should not play the role of just a developing country, dependent on concessions given by the super powers. Indians are not alone in their perception that their country is an 'emerging power' of the 21st century. President George Bush and Secretary of State Condoleezza Rice have made public statements testifying that India is a new 'emerging power' in Asia. The latest World Bank report issued on July 13 has also declared that India has 'arrived' by joining the 'league of the world's biggest 10 economies.'

It is a well known fact that nation-states search for new 'symbols of power' to assert their economic status among nations of the world. The world capitalist system is based on the structures of hierarchy because of the distribution of unequal economic power. Countries with great economic strength have to achieve new distinctive symbols of power with a view to differentiate themselves from the absolute majority of economically backward and disadvantaged category. Hierarchy of economic power has to be translated into hierarchy of military power among the unequal nations of the world.

The Indian ruling classes are involved in 'acquiring' national status symbols which they consider are commensurate with their new economic status of the 'league of 10 economic powers' in the world. Hans J. Morganthu in his classic had long ago stated that 'power among nations' is determined by their military and economic capacity to influence and dictate policies to other nation states. Indira Gandhi was an eminent student of Morganthu school of 'power among nations' when, in 1974, she served notice to the super powers that India is a new nuclear power. The first Pokharan nuclear explosion in 1974 was a symbol of national assertion by Indira Gandhi. This journey of nuclearisation of India was completed by the Hindu Rashtravadis in May 1998 with Pokharan II.

The Indian elite, along with Hindu chauvinists and militarists, have never forgotten that China militarily humiliated India in 1962 and this powerful lobby in politics and society has created the concept of expenditure on defence 'as a holy cow' for Indians. India asserted its military power in 1971 by helping to dismember Pakistan. Every weapon of war available in international market has witnessed buyers from the Indian state and this urge for the acquisition of latest 'defence technology' has been concretised by Pranab Mukherjee who on June 29, 2005, signed an important defence agreement with the US. Military might is a symbol of national power and India's increased purchasing power is used for strengthening its military standing among the nations.

Further, the Congress-led UPA government, following in the footsteps of Indira Gandhi's quest for 'symbols of national power' has made a permanent seat in the UN Security Council as the goal of its foreign policy. The desire of India to occupy the high table of permanent membership in UN Security Council is an agenda of the 'emergent economic power' of the 21st century.

The Union government has not fought for the restoration of the status of UNSC, which was totally ignored by the US when it launched a war against Saddam Hussein in 2003. Neither have the policy-makers in India objected to the Bush declaration that "Americans will launch a pre-emptive war against any country". India cannot oppose US military interventions because it cannot reach the SC status without the consent of the sole super power.

The upshot of above description is that adventurist nuclearisation and militarisation of India and its struggle to become a permanent member of the UNSC and other related goals of foreign and economic policy are based on the premise that India has arrived on world stage. It must be stated that the quest of Indian ruling classes to receive international recognition as an emergent economic and military middle power depends on the patronage of Americans.

The Indian ruling and political classes represented both by the BJP and the Congress have recognised the fact that without the consent of the US, India will remain a toothless paper tiger. The Americans seems to be acceding to the wishes of the Indian state leaders for allowing them to play a global role. The US has announced its love for establishing 'democracy from above' in feudal, military and authoritarian countries in the Islamic world and Indians are projecting their democratic credential before the new Messiah of global democracy. Americans have a very hospitable climate in India because every influential class, strata, group or lobby is willing to do 'business with America'. Anti-Americanism is a thing of the past and prosperous social groups in India identify themselves with a prosperous and powerful America.

Will America respond to the desires of their friends in India? The pro-American powerful social constituencies are a necessary but not a sufficient reason to motivate the US to patronise India of the 21st century. If Indians have new dreams of grandeur of regional power status,

Americans are unabashed interventionists and adept at playing one country against the other. In a 2003 report by American Council on Foreign Relations on South Asia, it has been clearly stated that the US has an opportunity to influence major regional developments and India-US should work on 'genuine partnership'. In other words, India can depend on US friendship and generosity if India supports American 'interests' in Asia; unstated but well known fact is that India versus China is the American national goal in this part of the world. So India has apparently opted for a pro-American stance since without US support India cannot play its desired role of a middle power.

—*The Economic Times*, 19 July, 2005

MORTGAGING INDIA'S SOVEREIGNTY

Prime Minister Manmohan Singh made a statement in the Rajya Sabha on March 14 that India would not surrender the autonomy of its decision-making process regarding 'nuclear deal' with the US. He observed: "Any notion that the new deal we have with the US amounts to surrender is totally misplaced." Indeed, brave words from the Prime Minister, who is an architect of the erosion of India's sovereignty on the basis of disingenuous plea of the adaptation of Indian policies to the requirements of a 'changing' world order. The pillar of this new world order, according to Manmohan Singh, is that the US is 'a super power' and a 'prominent market economy'.

The nuclear deal with the US has been necessitated because India is forced to look towards countries that could 'export capital and new technology'. The basis of the UPA government's foreign policy is that India requires the American support not only for 'nuclear energy for civilian purposes', but also 'capital' and 'technology' for economic development. India's 'enlightened national interest' can be pursued by aligning with the sole super power of the 21st century. The UPA think tank believes such an alignment is beneficial to the country, though there seems no alternative available for the country either.

President George Bush has introduced the Indo-US Civilian Nuclear Bill in the US Congress. He has to seek the sanction of the Congress for treating India as an 'exception', since the latter is not a signatory of the Nuclear Non-Proliferation Treaty. Manmohan Singh's claim that India had not surrendered its 'autonomy' was exposed when the US State Department expressed its 'disapproval' of Russian fuel supplies for the Tarapur reactors.

The Bush Administration argued that the timing of the Russian announcement was inappropriate, as the US Congress was engaged with the details of the Indo-US nuclear deal. Russian Prime Minister Mikhail Fradkov, during his visit to India on March 16, announced that the Tarapur reactors would be supplied fuel. Manmohan Singh had justified the nuclear deal with the US on the basis that the nuclear energy was required for India's economic growth. But the Russian offer seems to have upset the Americans because, for them, the Russians have jumped the queue in India. While President Bush could negotiate on the issue of nuclear cooperation, it seems Fradkov is not 'autonomous' to strike any nuclear energy deal with India. Manmohan Singh's phoney claim of India's 'autonomy' has been exposed by America's mild 'veto' to the Indo-Russian agreement on Tarapur. It seems India is expected not to negotiate with any friendly supplier of nuclear reactor and fuel, till the US Congress gives green signal to the Indo-US nuclear deal. It is just the beginning of the so-called autonomous relationship between the two unequal allies. The phoney claim of India's autonomy cannot be accepted on its face value without identifying the reasons behind America's decision to provide a 'special and exceptional status' to India. What is the compulsion for President Bush to provide exceptional nuclear status to India, and not to Pakistan? After all, Pakistan has been a tried-and-tested ally of the US. Former President Bill Clinton had described Pakistan as an ally in the war against terrorism, which is a common goal of Washington and Islamabad. What has happened between the presidency of Clinton and Bush that made the US abandon Pakistan in favour of India?

President Pervez Musharraf and the people of Pakistan are feeling let down by the special nuclear status accorded to India. It will be enlightening to understand the security interests and goals of the US vis-a-vis India in the 21st century. It does not require a prophet to predict that the US must be expecting a pound of flesh for extending concessions to India. Also, the nuclear deal has put the American seal of approval on India's nuclear weapon state status. Why has the US abandoned its anti-nuclear proliferation regime for India?

The cat is out of bag and the US National Security Strategy Document of March 17 mentions: "India now is poised to shoulder global obligations in cooperation with the United States in a way befitting a major power." On page 49, President Bush describes India as a "major power that shares our commitment to freedom, democracy and rule of law". Bush further observes: "India is a great democracy, and our shared values are the foundations of our good relations." He has referred specifically to the nuclear agreement as "a roadmap to realise the meaningful cooperation that had eluded our two nations for decades".

The document clearly shows that the US has patronised India as a part of its global strategic goals of the 21st century. In the document, President

Bush lauds India and expresses concern over the Middle Kingdom's (China) "continuing military expansion in a non-transparent way". He expects that China "must act as a responsible stakeholder that fulfils its obligations". Do we get any message from the American Security Strategy Document? The message is loud and clear that the Americans are in the business of forming alliances in Asia to contain the emerging China.

Pakistan has been left high and dry because the US is not sure about the future direction of the relationship between Islamabad and Beijing. The Bush Administration cannot trust Pakistan as far as China is concerned, but it has high expectations from the powerful anti-China social forces in India. Therefore, India can be a credible ally of the US against China along with Japan and South Korea.

It is easy for us to celebrate our nuclear weapon state status, but difficult to preserve national sovereignty, as India's growing economic dependence on 'capital exporting countries' will turn it into a camp follower of imperialism. Meanwhile, China and Pakistan will adapt their strategic and security goals in the light of the Indo-US alliance. Therein lies our problems. Unlike the Cold War era, India has opted to align with the US. At the same time, it needs to be stated that the foreign policy of country is closely integrated with its economic path.

The Jawaharlal Nehru-Indira Gandhi phase of politics has come to an end. The Congress, fully backed by the BJP and India's military-industrial establishment, has buried the country's autonomous national political development. In the early 1990s, India witnessed a complete break with the past by taking the path of economic liberalisation, which led to its integration with global capitalism. The economic policy of global integration was further pursued by the BJP along with its Pokharan misadventure in 1998. Thereafter, India began its full-scale search for foreign capital and technology, along with the desire to pursue nuclear aspirations. Both these goals have brought India under the American shadow.

The upshot of the above description is that the convergence of India's economic and foreign policies has led to a situation where both the Congress and the BJP are not worried about its autonomy in international relations. Where is the social constituency for the defence of nation-to-nation autonomous relationship in international relations? The UPA Government has fully consented to mortgage India's sovereignty.

—*The Pioneer*, 28 March, 2006

INDIA-US STRATEGIC RELATIONS

The public discourse on the significance of the 'strategic partnership' between India and the United States has been trivialised by its supporters who have characterised it as the 'building partnerships for the development of India-US civil nuclear cooperation,' emphasising the agreement as going a long way in helping India meet its energy requirements for economic development. One the other hand, the military-industrial-nuclear weapon lobbies represented by Atal Bihari Vajpayee have criticised the US-India nuclear deal', quoting the US Assistant Secretary for South Asia, Richard Boucher, that "India would be urged to further define its minimum credible deterrent to facilitated amendment of the US Atomic Energy Act" according a 'special waiver' to India. The Hindu Rashtravadi, Vajpayee, representing the sentiments of India's nuclear bomb lobby, issued a stern warning that, "The nation shall pay a heavy price in future by closing its options on the size of its credible minimum nuclear deterrent. Our nuclear armed neighbours shall face no such constraints…India should retain the right to conduct nuclear tests if any other country, such as China or Pakistan, were to do so."

It needs to be clearly stated that the public discourse on the India-US nuclear deal should be liberated from the narrow and limited interpretations of the defenders of nuclear energy resources or the champions of the nuclear bomb. The real significance of the new economic, foreign and strategic policies pursued by India can be appreciated and analysed only by linking the so-called 'India-US Partnership' with the 'New National Model of Development' followed by India from the beginning of the 1990s, wherein India willingly and voluntarily decided to 'integrate and link itself' with global imperial centres of capitalism led by the sole military super power of the 21st century.

Immanuel Wallerstein in his After Developmentalism and Globalisation, What? (2004) has indulged in wishful thinking that "…the triadic struggle between the United States, Western Europe and Japan/East Asia is the principal locus of capital accumulation in the capitalist world economy…', as if the so-called triad are roughly equal contestants in the attempt to reorganise the global production and financial systems. Wallerstein appears to have missed the reality of American-led NATO military bloc, which has made America a pre-eminent power for the whole of the European Union even as American military alliances with Japan, South Korea and other East Asian capitalist economies have brought these countries under the shadow of American hegemony. Is Japanese military involvement in Afghanistan and Iraq at the command of the Americans as accident? Similarly, American and Europe are working together in dealing with Iran's nuclear problem, substantiating the argument that the 'triad' of capitalism is not engaged in any meaningful inter-capitalist struggles or conflicts. No wonder the Indian ruling classes are agreed that the pre-eminent global status of America should be recognised for it will be beneficial and desirable for India to become an 'ally' of the sole global super-power.

The military-industrial complex which rules America has described India and China as two powerful emerging economies and is convinced that a militarily strong China is a 'competitor' to American hegemony, especially in Asia. Evidently, this situation is not acceptable to imperialist America. Both Strobe Talbott and Robert J. Einhorn stated that "The US by acknowledging India as a major power and a strategic partner, has finally given India the recognition it has wanted for so long. The onus is now on India to live up to the trust that the Americans have placed in them and show the world that it is a responsible nuclear nation." The only amendment which should be made to the Talbott-Einhorn formulation is that America's new and special emerging relationship with India is not merely confined to the nuclear deal but is a comprehensive and all-embracing 'alliance' between a real super-power and a country which wants to establish 'regional pre-eminence' with the support of America. Hence the question: what does America expect from India?

Condoleezza Rice, in her testimony before the Senate Foreign Relations Committee on 5 April 2006, stated the nuclear deal is a 'strategic achievement for both countries' and that India has agreed to the Missile Technology Control Regime and safeguards under International Atomic Energy Agency. She continued, "We believe this initiative will unlock the progress of our expanding relationship in other areas and lead to expanding business opportunities for both countries." The cat was out of the bag when Rice said that "India was the only non-aligned country to vote for the referral to the UNSC on the Iran nuclear issue." The three pillars of foreign policy issues as represented by George Bush are (a) export of democracy; (b) unilateralism, and (c) pre-emptive military action to safeguard American national interests. India has accepted to be a partner in the US project of the 'export of democracy' by contributing to Kofi Annan's Democracy Fund. Nor has India launched a campaign against America for misleading the entire world on Iraq, even when no weapons of mass destruction were found. India has remained a mute spectator to American military adventurism and unilateralism in the name of restoring or projecting democracy in Iraq and Central Asia. This clearly indicates that India as a 'junior alliance partner' of the US has not only abandoned the Nehru-Indira model of relative autonomy of the state in relation to other states, including the super powers, but has fully accepted American hegemony in global affairs.

Is there a social explanation for the complete break with its own past in the Indian national model of deployment? It does not require a genius to see that India is suffering from a deep crisis of capital accumulation because of the narrow social base of its market. The new economic policies of imposed fiscal structural adjustment along with a package of liberalisation, privatisation and deregulation of capital markets were not only a response to the balance of payment crisis. Even after a decade and half of the new economic policy regime, the Indians can only claim the 250 million new middle class as their social constituency for market and if this structurally 'limiting' factor has to be overcome to help accumulation, the only option is to integrate India with other centres of global imperial capitalism. The political and bureaucratic class along with the big industrial groups and the surplus generating rural and urban petite bourgeoisie seem to have arrived at an agreement to integrate India with global capitalism led by the United States. America is a 'giver' and India is a 'taker' and a quid pro quo among unequals is always in favour of the 'donor' or 'giver'. This is the reality of India's relationship with the US and it is a misnomer, even misrepresentation of facts, so characterise such a relationship as 'Building Partnerships' (*Seminar* 560, April 2006).

The emerging US-India alliance has to be seen in the broader political economy of global-imperial capitalism and the politics and economics of a developing capital is country like India. Hence the issue is not only 'nuclear energy for civilian purposes', but India's place in the world capitalist system led by American hegemonic power. India is also concerned with China's rising economic and military power and given the history to Sino-Indian mutual mistrust, it is plausible to argue that India would like to counterbalance China with the support of the United States. Moreover, since the United States has open targeted China, India as China's competitor can be a reliable ally even though it is negotiating with China at a bilateral level. India's ambition as a nuclear weapon state cannot be limited to just decorative and protective goals. India versus China is a plausible game plan of the Indian nuclearists and India cannot meaningfully compete with China without the protective umbrella of America. In effect, India's ambition to play the role of a South Asian policeman while containing Chinese power has brought it under the umbrella of the real super power. It is this emerging 'alliance' between a real super power and an ambitious regional power that lies at the heart of the matter. Other issues are peripheral. —*Seminar,* May 2006

NOTES AND REFERENCES

1. Party claimed to stand for the cause of Common Man/Woman.
2. *Economic Survey* (2005-06). Government of India, Ministry of Finance, Delhi, p. 17.
3. *Economy Survey*, p. 209.

7

The Indian State

CHANGING CONTEXT AND NEW CHALLENGES

Many social scientists who have studied the formation of new States which emerged during the post-World War II phase of decolonisation have examined the story of the working of these States on the basis of following six issues:

(a) What is the identity and ideology of these new States?
(b) What is the legal, constitutional and political system of these States?
(c) What kind of foreign policy has been pursued by these States ?
(d) What have been the national security concerns of these States?
(e) What kind of path of economic development has been followed by these States?
(f) How is civil society functioning in these States?

Further, these scholars are now focussing their attention on crisis facing the new States of Asia, Africa and Latin America. It has been suggested by a group of scholars that States of the decolonised countries have invited crisis because all of them followed the statist model of economic development and these interventionist States collapsed under the unbearable burden of their activities. *Law and State:* has focussed attention on *Development: Old Issues—New Problems*[1] where the problem of *Good Governance* facing the Third World has been highlighted as the central issue facing the newly independent States. Not to be left behind the supra-States like the IMF, World Bank and the WTO are also offering suggestions to Third World States for improving their system of governance if they want to participate actively in the new globalised order[2]. These studies undertaken by the Western scholars or supra-State organisations are examining the 'crisis of governability' in the Third World. Such approaches for the study of Indian State have been employed by Atul Kohli or Aysha Jalal or Paul Brass and others. Theoretical framework of all these Western scholars has been fixed around 'modernisation of traditional societies' and the success or failure of the functionaries of the State in meeting the challenges of modernisation of old societies. H.C.F. Mansilla in 'Development: Old Issue—New Problems' observes:

"Development is now understood as a complex phenomenon which is based on the achievement of modernisation, urbanisation, and industrialisation, and simultaneously on the strengthening of the nation-State, the reaching of a general high standard of living and the adoption of contemporary consumption levels". This was the emphasis of studies of all modernisation theorists beginning with Sammuel J. Huntington and all of them began to view the failure of the experiment of modernisation because of the "crisis of institutions of governance of the State". Not only this. With the collapse of Berlin Wall and the unification of Germany in 1989 began the process of disintegration of the whole East European Socialist State System in 1991. President George Bush declared that the cold war had ended and a New International Order had emerged in the 1990s because the communist system had collapsed and the market-led democracies of capitalist countries had emerged as successful model for the whole world. During the 1990s, democratisation of Third World States became the focus of scholarly writings of the Western countries. The last decade of the Twentieth Century signified the end of the Interventionist welfarist State and the emergence of market-led democracies. Pranab Bardhan, while applying this dominant American social science framework, argued that India was deadlocked because the Indian State was fully derailed because of the stranglehold of powerful pressure groups in society. Thus dominant bourgeois western social science as represented by scholars of the metropolitan capitalist countries and their Indian intellectual translators are engaged in the study of Indian State from the point of view of its failures in dealing with the multiple problems of Indian society and the root cause of such failures of the Indian State lies in its complete lack of institutional capabilities and resources in performing functions for societal development. It has been argued that the Indian State, having failed, should 'retreat' from its expanded spheres of activities and allow markets and voluntary associations of civil society like the Non-government organisations to deal with societal problems. Since the Indian State has failed to deliver the goods because of its interventionists policies of the era of economic planning, it should give place to 'markets' to perform their legitimate role in economy, and to autonomous and voluntary associations of civil society to resolve social problems. The upshot of above description is theoretical frameworks of the Western social scientists as applied to the study of Indian State have undergone a change during the last fifty years depending on the shifts in the perspectives of their State systems. During the 1990s, managers of the capitalist world have promoted market-led democracies for the whole world and western scholars have argued that the over-burdened States of the Third World have broken down under the weight of rent-seeking bureaucratic Leviathan and they should be cut to size and market forces should be allowed to play their legitimate role in managing the affairs of society. Democratic States are now completely equated with capitalist State system. Universalisation of market-led democracy and capitalist State system have emerged the focal points of reference of western State systems, supra-State global organisations, western scholars and intellectual translators of their ideas in India.

Marxist theoretical framework rejects all the premises and assumptions of bourgeois social science, whether practiced by the western scholars or their intellectual translators in India. Since the social essence of every State lies in its class character based on property determined social relations in every society, the meaningful study of State has to be undertaken on the basis of its class ideology and the role of State institutions for the promotion and protection of interests of the dominant classes in society. On the basis of class theory of Karl Marx, the first question which deserves attention is : How has the democratic State of India responded towards dominant propertied social classes of the country? Not only this. How have dominant propertied social classes responded towards universal adult franchise based democratic State of India? How have the exploiting classes operated the levers of power of the Indian State after occupying a central position in the corridors of State power? Within the power bloc of social classes, different fractions of the bourgeosies and the landlords and capitalist farmers have been involved in mutual cooperation, competition and conflict among themselves for controlling the power of Indian State. How has the uneasy coalition of fractions of dominant exploiting classes managed the affairs of the State for the appropriation of surplus value?

During the Indian struggle for independence, a few questions and doubts had arisen about the essential nature of the functioning of Indian democratic State. More than 562 princely States during British rule over India wanted to keep away from the future democratic State of India because the march of democracy would be extremely harmful to the class interests of the hereditary monarchical-feudal princely States. Not only the Indian princes feared and opposed the emergence of a democratic State of India, the feudal-landlord classes were absolutely apprehensive of their own class future under a democratic State.

Along with feudal-landlords, rulers of princely States, Hindu, Muslim communalists, leaders of Scheduled Castes, a section of neo-colonial Indian elite were dead-set against the emergence and establishment of a democratic State after Independence of India. V.D. Savarkar of the Hindu Maha Sabha was a champion of Hindu State and Mohammad Ali Jinnah rejected the idea of democratically elected majority rule because he equated the principle of democratic-majoritarianism as a Hindu rule which will be always discriminating against the Muslim minority community, and Dr. B.R. Ambedkar, leader of the Scheduled Castes, contested the idea of Indian independence because, according to him, it would lead to the rule by Brahmans and upper caste Hindus who would dominate and exploit the Dalit castes in the name of power given to them by universal adult franchise-based democracy. An important section of anglicised and neo-colonial elite was distrustful of democracy where illiterates will rule over men of merit because an illiterate voter will elect his representatives during elections irrespective of their hereditary gifted merit and talent. Western scholars were also distrustful about the idea of political democracy in India where all "essential pre-requisites of democracy were conspicuous by its absence". S.M. Lipset or Barrington Moore Jr. and others have argued that democracies in Western capitalist countries have succeeded only in the 20th century because of the emergence of extremely modern and enlightened middle class or because of the demands of the proletariat classes which were accommodated by the capitalist classes. How will democracy succeeded in a country like India where important social groups committed to democracy do not exist? In a largely feudal-landlord dominated agrarian country, social soil is fertile for 'authoritarianism' and it is not at all suitable for the functioning of competitive political democracy.

It is worthwhile to examine the role of multiple social groups on the basis of their actual participation in parliamentary democracy of India. India has conducted thirteen Lok Sabha elections from 1952 to 1999 and voters participation in elections has been quite encouraging and the level of voters turnout has disproved the fears of different power groups about the functioning of democracy in India. The Table 7.1 clearly shows that the level of voters participation has gradually increased beginning with low vote percentage of 45.7 in 1952 to more than 60 percent during the other Lok Sabha elections.

Every social group beginning from erstwhile rulers of princely States to feudal landlords, peasants and other strata of society have actively contested in democratic elections and as candidates during the elections, they have mobilised voters for the winning of elections.

Table 7.1: Voters Turnout

Year	*Voters Turnout %*
1952	45.7
1957	47.7
1962	55.4
1967	61.3
1971	55.3
1977	60.5
1980	57.0
1984	64.1
1989	62.0
1991	56.7
1996	57.9
1998	62.0
1999	60.0
2004	58.1

In a society where male completely dominate over women, women had successfully contested during every election and because of a poor picture of successful women in Parliamentary elections, a demand has emerged to reserve 33 per cent of all elected seats for women only.

Muslim representation in elected Lok Sabha, while limited, has disproved the fears of the founders of Pakistan that Muslims will be treated as second-class citizens in Hindu dominated majoritarian political democracy.

To sum up every social group has emerged as an active participant in Indian democracy, and during the 1990s, the Dalit castes have asserted their right to contest the elections and they have begun to participate very actively during elections. Since politics is a dialectical activity, the positive and the negative features of Indian democracy have been clearly observed.

Since Dalit castes are asserting their right to vote, the established dominant and exploiting classes and castes are indulging in large-scale violence against the Dalit voters. In spite of the terror created by the powerful exploiting strata of society, Dalit voters are coming forward to exercise their right to vote and even get killed for performing their duty as a citizen.

At the close of the Twentieth Century and beginning of Twenty-first Century, democratic State of India is confronted with assertive citizenry and the downtrodden and exploited masses are demanding protection of their rights from the State. A new India has been born as a result of the functioning of universal adult franchise for fifty years, and new social assertions of the exploited classes have created serious situations of social conflict and violence in society.

An important question that emerges from the above description is : How have the dominant social classes, groups and castes exercised the levers of power of a democratic State of India? The dominant exploiting classes and strata are sitting within the State and all institutions of governance, and these classes are legitimising the exercise of State power on the basis of their electoral victories.

State from Above and State from Below

Indian State has built capitalism in India and it has evolved institutional mechanisms of harmonising the conflicting interests of multiple strata of the exploiting classes and in the process the Indian State has helped in establishing the hegemony of the exploiting classes over the whole society. Nicols Poulantazs has made an important distinction between the 'ruling classes' and the 'governing classes' in the late capitalist industrialising countries of the West and this distinction is very vital for understanding the relationship between the Indian ruling exploiting propertied classes and the governing classes as represented by the political executive and bureaucratic apparatuses of the State. Every important capitalist of India can walk into the corridors of power and functionaries of the State behave as willing collaborators of the capitalist classes. Further, functionaries of the State take advice from Birlas, Tatas, Bajajs and their organised associations like the Federation of Indian Chambers of Commerce and Industry, Confederation of Indian Industry and Association of Chamber of Commerce and Industries. Thus the 'ruling classes' operate through 'governing classes' of the State and both work in harmony of the basis of mutuality and reciprocity. This mutuality between the ruling propertied classes and governing classes of the State benefits both of them because State facilitates the accumulation of surplus which is shared both by the ruling classes and the governing class. Resources of the State are invested in the development of Indian capitalism and a part of these resources are taken away by the functionaries of the State. This is the reason that private capitalism has come of age during the last fifty years because State of the capitalists has followed policies and programme which have helped in the growth of capitalism.

'State from Below' is also a class State because the landlord classes have used democratic-electoral path to capture the apparatuses of the State to protect their property interests. The real issue before the feudal-landlord classes was about their land ownership and they had serious apprehensions that the emerging democratic State of India will alter agrarian property relations because peasant classes will get enfranchised and they will use their political power for land reforms. Agrarian land reforms' agenda was scuttled by the landed gentry and rich peasant classes who were fully represented in all the institutions of governance at the level of State governments in India. P.S. Appu in his book on *Land Reforms in India* (1996) describes in details the sorry State of affairs regarding laws for the abolition of parasitic intermediaries like Zamindars, Talukdars, Jagirdars, Malguzars, Jamies etc., and the worst situation was faced in the implementation of law concerning the reform of tenancy and the imposition of ceilings on agricultural holdings. While some security was granted to the 'tenants' because of Land Reforms, "resourceful Zamindars succeeded in ejecting some of them…Everywhere the reform led to the large-scale ejectment of tenants-at-will, under-tenants and share croppers."[3]

Landed property interests remained protected under Indian democracy and the pre-independence hostility of rulers of princely States, feudal-landlord classes towards democracy was replaced by their active participation in democratic governance because Indian democracy did not pose any threat to the class interests of these classes. On the contrary, economic and political power got integrated in a manner that State power and interest of the classes became inter-changeable and serious skepticism of the feudal-landlord classes was replaced by enthusiasm for democracy. Class interests were protected and promoted under the new democratic State of India both from '*above*' and also from '*below*'.

An Assessment of State-from-above and State-from-below

The above narration brings out a clear picture of many positive and negative features of the actual functioning of democratic State of India during the last fifty years. While democracy in India was launched from 'above', it has spread itself to every part of the country irrespective of rural-urban divide in society. Every section of society is actively participating in democratic politics including rulers of the erstwhile princely States, feudal-landlords, capitalist farmers, middle and marginal farmers alongwith the landless agricultural workers have exercised their vote during the elections. Members of every community and castes and sub-castes have been active in exercising their right to vote. Since the process of the growth of democratic consciousness in India has been incremental, the 1990s has witnessed the emergence of an activist Dalit participation in elections.

The other side of the story is that democratic State has been gradually losing its 'relative autonomy' from dominant and exploiting propertied-classes which had been a feature of '*State from above*' during Nehru-Indira Gandhi phase of politics. Democratic '*State from below*' was always, speaking relatively, an instrument in the hands of landlords, capitalist farmers and surplus-appropriating peasant classes and State power was used for the protection and promotion of the interests of land-owing classes. Kripa Shankar, while writing in 1999 on '*Tenancy Reforms: Rhetoric and Reality*' observes:

> "In India 40 percent of the rural households are either landless or own less than 0.2 hectare (ha) of land. Less than 1 (0.88) percent of the household own 14 percent of the land. In such a situation the poorer households lease in land. Even though leasing has declined 15 percent of the households continue to lease in land according to NSS Report 1992... .
>
> "Given the reality that the number of landless and sub-marginal farmers is rising fast and the lessors have the option to switch over to cash or fixed produce contract it seems very difficult that any measure can be effectively implemented to either give them security or raise the share of produce in their favour."[4]

Social dialectics of Indian democracy during the last fifty years has disproved David Ricardo or Karl Marx or Barington Moore that landlord classes (including surplus generating peasantry) do not accept democracy because in India, all classes and strata have accepted and participated in democracy. Since dialectical process reveals positive and negative features of society, the exploiting classes have captured the State apparatuses by following democratic route. Further, increasing level of electoral participation of the voters has emerged as a threat to the power of exploiting classes, and hence the rigging of elections and terrorisation of voters is becoming a new norm of behaviour of the exploiting classes during the elections. Politics of ballot and politics of bullet are coexisting in Indian democracy because dominant social classes have shown little concern about the exploited strata of agrarian and urban society. Unlike, the Western capitalist countries, the idea of welfare State in India, has not been accepted as a firm pillar of democratic capitalist State. Every welfare programme for the deprived and exploited section of society is implemented half-heartedly because the ideology of welfarism in a class-divided society is not an integral part of the strategies of exploiting classes.

This is the reason that Indian democratic State is facing a serious crisis because more than half of the Indian population has been left completely deprived of the fruits of capitalist development. This retarded development of Indian capitalism is acting as a brake over overall economic development of the country because Indian market has been limited by the absence of large majority of participants in market transactions. If half of the population does not have purchasing power, country's economic growth gets limited. Hence crisis of the Indian State is not because of its institutional incapabilities to govern as suggested by western writers on India. Indian State has failed to practice any meaningful distributive agenda for the whole society. While 350 millions people are still officially declared as living below the poverty line in 1999 another 250 million are also living on very low subsistence levels. This situation has not changed even at the beginning of Twenty-first Century. While fiscal resources of the State are appropriated by the exploiting propertied classes in the name of economic development, functionaries of the State also appropriate a lion's share in the fiscal resources of the State for rendering services to the propertied classes and this leads to fiscal crisis of the State because surplus investible resources for the development of India are not with the State because they have been appropriated by the 'ruling classes' and the 'governing classes'. This fundamental fiscal crisis of the Indian State compelled the political and industrial capitalist classes to approach Western capitalist countries and supra-State institutions of global capitalism to bail out India from its deep crisis in 1991.

New Context and Challenges

Fiscal crisis of India burst in the 1990s and it was manifested in the form of balance of payments crisis, but the form reflected the real substance of fiscal crisis of the State. It is also during the 1990s, the ruling classes and strata, revealed their inter-class and intra-class conflicts which were concretely represented by the new assertions of middle peasantry and development of aggressive and violent Hindutva. During the 1990s, India witnessed the politics of targeting of social groups and the '*concept of the other*' emerged as the idiom of Indian politics. In a crisis situation, either societies find basic solutions to problems or they want to maintain the social status quo by finding scapegoats like race versus race, caste versus caste, religion versus religion etc. This is the present political reality of India. The Indian State and all the fractions of the ruling classes are protecting and preserving the present social status quo, and reasons for basic social crisis are not responded. If on the one hand, globalisation, privatisation and liberalisation are viewed as solutions for crisis of retarded Indian capitalism, on the other, social violence is emerging in a big way around the politics of targeting of ethnic groups, caste, and religious communities. L.K. Advani, the Home Minister of India, observed on December 17, 1999 that "violence has increased in Indian society during the last twenty years", but he did not mention that his own politics of Hindutva has also contributed to the growth of social violence.

India has entered the Twenty-First Century with unresolved social crisis which is quite deep because status quoist social forces have complete control over the State apparatus and the path of globalisation will further accentuate social disparities in India. How can such a level of inequality and social disparities prove functional for any democratic State, and least of all, for India where poverty and exploitation is quite widespread. The greatest challenge before the Indian State is that an awakened and socially assertive Indian voter is demanding social equality. Indian has become conscious of his rights and this is the achievement of our democratic experiment. Since responses of the State are based on class interests, the deprived and exploited social groups are struggling to be heard in the apparatus of the State. Democracy has provided social spaces to all social groups to contest and compete for their rights and launch struggles for social equality. This is a new India because Indian society had never accepted even at an abstract level, the principle of social equality among human beings. Democratic experiment of India, with all its positive and negative features, has generated a new feeling of demand for rights among the exploited classes. This is how the Indian State entered the 21st Century.

THEORETICAL PERSPECTIVES ON POLITICAL CHANGE

Political institutions, with a proper system of checks and balances, are established to regulate and manage the exercise of power in a society. The complex industrial societies of today, as differentiated from the early peasant societies, have created a complex web of institutions to manage their public affairs. The institutional arrangement in a political community is reflective of the values cherished by its members. Any change in value perspective or value preferences of members of the political community poses a serious challenge to its institutional arrangement for the management of public affairs. In the face of such a challenge, either the old institutions are replaced because they are not in conformity with the new value cherished by the political community or the institutions break down because they lack in adaptive capacity. Any 'lag' between values and institutions precipitates a serious societal crisis characterised by movements of protest or dissent in society.[5]

Further, the actual processes of politics make a significant impact on the functioning of political institutions. Political institutions interact with the macro and micro processes in society at both the formal and informal levels. The actual dynamics of politics creates harmony or disharmony between the actual forces of politics and the institutional arrangement for governance in society. Many a time societies face challenges of dissonance between the forces of the major politics and the governmental institutions. A situation of stabilised harmony among all factors of politics in society is rarely found to be a reality. Political institutions may show capability of adaptation to the challenges posed by the actual processes of politics, or they may break down and create a crisis situation in society. Such a crisis situation in its turn may act as the midwife of political change. In short, there is an interaction between political institutions, values, and processes of politics. The behavioural implications of such an interaction are not always in the direction of a proper equilibrium of forces. One often finds a gap between values and institutions, or between institutions and processes of politics, and forces of change emerge from such gaps. The motive force of change in society is dissatisfaction with the existing social order; and such dissatisfaction is maximum when the values are in conflict with the institutions or when the institutions are in conflict with the political processes. In other words, change is an integral part of social and political reality. There is a consensus among social theorists that society is not a static but a developing and evolving system. The consensus breaks down when questions regarding the nature, content, and direction of social and political change arise.

(a) Does social and political change mean slow and gradual adaptation to the environment or a fundamental break with the past and creation of a new social environment?
(b) Is change quantifiable? Can its indicators be identified and quantified? Or is change qualitative in nature? Does change mean going from lower to higher (qualitative change), or is it a measure of the capacity of the system to respond within given parameters of societal values? Does change mean a destruction of the past and the building of a distinctly new present, or is it just piecemeal social reconstruction?
(c) What are the instruments of change? How do we identify such instruments? Do we analyse the instruments of change by their role, or social existence, or level of social consciousness, or by the goals which they want to achieve? The forces and factors making for change in society have to be properly located and perceived. We cannot make change or study it if we fail to distinguish between appearance and reality in society. Any analysis of reality entails a probe into the basic factors of change in society.
(d) What is the method of bringing about political and social change? Gradualism is the keyboard in the dictionary of liberal political theorists. Marxists believe that change is not possible without struggle. It is stated that the history of mankind is the history of class struggle, and nothing can be achieved without class struggle. Thus strategies of change depend on the meaning of change attributed by the instruments of change.

Acceptance or rejection of violence as a method of social change is untenable. Method of change is closely linked with the content and meaning of change.

(e) Who oppose change in society? How can one make change or study it without locating the forces and institutions opposed to change? If change means that some established sections of society are to be disestablished, opposition to change is natural.

The above questions focus our attention on the complexity attached to political and social change in society Social theorists in history have been sharply divided on the nature, content, instrumentalities, and strategies of change. In this chapter our purpose is to examine the theoretical standpoint of Anglo-American political science, as well as the Marxian approach, to the above-mentioned questions regarding political change. Illustrations to prove or disprove the theoretical perspectives of the above two schools of writing would be provided from the concrete experience of India.

I

Liberal Democratic Theoretical Framework on Political Change

Theories in social sciences grow in the context of prevailing social beliefs; and they draw their frames of reference from their historical experience. The reality of the universe for a social theorist is coterminous with his own experiences and exposures, which are conditioned by the structure of the society in which he grows. City-States were the points of reference for Plato and Aristotle; and capitalism in the nineteenth century provided the basis for Karl Marx's social and political analysis.

George H. Sabine rightly observes:

> It cannot be supposed that any political philosophy of the present time, more than those of the past, can step out of the relationships in which it stands to the problems, the valuations, the habits or even the prejudices of its own time. A writer of history, at least, ought to avoid the egoism that makes every generation fancy that it is the heir of all the ages.[6]

Sabine further underlines the relationship between environment and the social theorist thus:

> Modern political ideals—such, for example, as justice, liberty, constitutional government, and respect for the law—or at least definitions of them, began with the reflection of Greek thinkers upon the institutions of the city-state. But in the long history of

> political thought the meaning of 5Uc terms has been variously modified, and always that meaning has to be understood in the light of the institutions by which the ideals were to be realised and of the society in which those institutions did their work… . In order to understand it all accurately what their theories meant, it is necessary first to realise at least roughly what kind of institutions they had in view and what citizenship connoted as a fact and as an ideal, to the public for whom they wrote.[7]

Moreover, the social theorists conditioned by the existing structure of society develop a corpus of knowledge either to defend the existing social order or to change it. Whether a social theorist is an apologist for the existing social order or a revolutionary his starting point is the given premises of the environment. A perceptive social theorist relates his experience to the history of societies, and develops a universal world perspective. Some social theorists examine the present in the context of the past and develop a paradigm for the future, while others view 'present' as present and recommend the value Premises of the present to their contemporaries.

Social theorists who believe in the premises and postulates of the liberal democracies of the capitalist countries of the West have a theoretical framework in which to study political and social change. Since such theorists have made a great impact on the writings and researches of Indian political science,[8] it is worthwhile to examine their approach to political change.

Contemporary political theory in the United States of America has developed in the environment of a highly developed and complex capitalist society. A large majority of American social theorists accept that the basis of American society (*viz.* capitalism) is sound and that its institutional arrangement has stood the test of time as, for example the two World Wars and the serious economic depression of the nineteen thirties. The economic arrangements in society, they further believe, provide for upward mobility, social justice, and welfarism. They also argue that capitalism in the United States has developed its human and spiritual content. According to Talcott Parsons, that capitalism is on the verge of being transcended:

> Democratic government, the welfare state, trade unionism… education, science, and even humanistic culture play such important roles that calling (the United States) 'capitalistic' in anything like the classical Marxian sense seems increasingly forced.[9]

Writing about the advanced capitalist societies in his "*The Coming of Post Industrial Society*", Daniel Bell highlights the great flexibility and adaptability of capitalism in ensuring social justice and welfarism. He observes:

> If an industrial society is defined by the quantity of goods as making a standard of living, the post-industrial society (like the USA) is defined by the quality of life as measured by the services and amenities—health, education, recreation, and the arts—which are now deemed desirable and possible for everyone.[10]

There is no crisis of capitalism in the Western societies. On the contrary, goods are being replaced by services, and the quality of life is improving.

What is the nature of the State in such a society? The State is a neutral arbiter among the contending social forces. Society has many organised functional and political groups which compete to influence the decision-makers, and the State mediates to provide justice to the various sections of society. Participatory democracy operates on the basis of competition, bargaining, and consensus politics. Politics as an activity is concerned with reconciliation of antagonistic interests; and various alliances and coalitions are formed to resolve conflicts through the politics of bargaining and pressure. The social situation never deteriorates so far as to touch breaking-point, because attempts are continually made to evolve compromises. Thus the rules of the game in democratic politics ensure that the extremes are avoided and a working compromise is available. For the last two hundred years, democratic politics has delivered the goods in managing public affairs in the advanced capitalist societies of the West. As S.M. Lipset writes:

> Democracy is not only or even primarily a means through which different groups can attain their ends or see the good society; it is the good society itself in operation.[11]

Politics of compromise functions because of the following reasons:

(a) People have a pragmatic approach, and ideological cleavages in society have come to an end. Antagonistic ideologies which divide societies and lead to serious conflict situations have ceased to be relevant in an advanced capitalist society like the American society.[12] Further, the advanced capitalist societies of the West have entered upon the post-industrial stage; and questions of management and bureaucracy have acquired greater relevance than issues of ideology.[13]

(b) The politics of consensus and compromise has created an atmosphere in which violence as a method of resolving public issues is rejected by the overwhelming majority of the people.

"Where is the legitimacy of violence in a participatory democracy?", argue the Liberals. A very important premise of democratic theory in the capitalist countries is the capability and resilience of its institutional arrangement to resolve or reconcile social contradictions. This is what makes the Liberals reject the legitimacy of violence in society

(c) The democratic societies of the West have survived many challenges because social and political change in these societies is incremental, not catastrophic. Gradualism is the keynote of change; and Karl Popper argues that "piecemeal social engineering" is a sure mechanism for developing.[14]

Society develops to higher level of 'harmony' gradually because there is 'no war of all against all'. *Thus the goal of change is harmony; the process of change is gradual.*

Thus, is a competitive political system, which is exposed to pressures and counter-pressures, the State mediates but does not deal with all aspects of social life. In the democratic political system power is diffused and deconcentrated, and it is wrong to ask "who" governs such societies. There is no one focal point of governance, and participation is encouraged.[15]

Such a political system has stability and institutional resilience because political and social change is incremental. Its proof is that the advanced capitalist countries of the West have not faced revolutionary upsurges but have resolved social conflicts in a spirit of give and take. Thus, the theoretical perspective of liberal democracy on political change is based on the belief in gradualism, incrementalism, and constitutionalism.[16]

US scholars owing allegiance to the above-mentioned theory of political change for their society turned their attention in the nineteen fifties and sixties to the great experiment of nation-building and problems of change in "developing societies.[17]

The theoretical framework for the study of developing societies was built around the American paradigm in political science, *viz.* "behaviouralism, systems approach, and structural functionalism." One basic feature of this approach was a rejection of history as a frame of reference for the study of societies. The new political science in the United States of America developed by borrowing ideas, concepts, and methods from psychology (Harold Lasswell in the nineteen thirties), social psychology (David Truman and group approach of the late nineteen forties), sociology (structural-functionalism of the nineteen fifties), and economics (equilibrium, input-output, the game theory, etc. in the nineteen sixties). The methodological stress of the new political science was on the collection of data, interviewing, and participant observation. The term 'State' disappeared from the vocabulary of political science, and professional attention was concentrated on the study of political systems, structures, roles, communication, political culture, and political socialisation. All this was called a 'revolution' in political studies. The new political scientist examined the complex reality of developing societies with concepts, tools of analysis and belief systems developed in their societies. They applied these categories to compare their societies with the developing ones, and evolved a theoretical framework for the study of political modernisation of the societies of Asia, Africa, and Latin America.

Robert E. Ward and Rustow provide a check-list of differences between modern and traditional politics. They are:

"(1) a highly differentiated and functionally specific system of governmental organisation;
(2) a high degree of integration within this governmental structure;
(3) the prevalence of rational and secular procedures for the making of political decisions;
(4) the large volume, wide range, and high efficacy of its political and administrative decisions;
(5) a widespread and effective sense of popular identification with the history, territory, and national identity of the State;
(6) widespread popular interest and involvement in the political system, though not necessarily in the decision-making aspects thereof;
(7) the allocation of political roles by achievement rather than by ascription; and
(8) judicial and regulatory techniques based upon a predominantly secular and impersonal system of law."[18]

The secularisation of politics, the governmentalisation of society, the institutionalisation and routinisation of political authority, the subordination of primordial loyalty structures to civil authority, and the legitimisation of governmental authority by people's participation differentiate modem societies from the traditional ones.

The goal of political and social change in traditional societies is to achieve the values embodied in the modern political systems. Political change in traditional societies means that the societies should be modernised and establish participatory democratic systems. As Edward Shils wrote:

> A modern society is not just a complex of modern institutions. It is a mode of relationship between the centre and the periphery

> of the society. Modern society entails the inclusion of the mass of the population into the society in the sense that both elite and mass regard themselves a member for the society and, as such, as of approximately equal dignity. It involves a greater participation by the masses in the values of the society a more active role in the making of society-wide decisions, and a greater prominence in the consideration of the elite.[19]

Taking his argument further, Shils states that the new states do not form a single civil society, because they rest on the pre political matrix of constellations of kinship groups, castes, tribes, and feudalities.[20]

For Samuel P. Huntington the critical issue in developing societies is the relationship between participation and political institutionalisation. Political participation is a new feature of developing societies. What is its impact on political institutionalisation?[21]

In a detailed article on change, Huntington recommends that the study of political change can be said to involve "(1) focussing on what seem to be the major components of the political system; (2) determining the rate, scope and direction of change in these components; and (3) analysing the relations between changes in one component and changes in other components."[22]

Theories of political change should tackle the above questions mentioned by Huntington. He elaborates his argument further by conceiving five components of the political system, and changes in these components should be the focus of analysis in theories of political change. The components of the political system are:

(a) Culture, that is, the values, attitudes, orientations, myths, and beliefs relevant to politics and dominant in the society;
(b) Structure, that is, the formal organisations through which the society makes authoritative decisions, such as political parties, legislatures, executives, and bureaucracies;
(c) Groups, that is, the social and economic formations, formal and informal, which participate in politics and make demands on the political structures;
(d) Leadership, that is, the individuals in political institutions and groups who exercise more influence than others on the allocation of values;
(e) Politics, that is, the patterns of governmental activity which are consciously designed to affect the distribution of benefits and penalties within the society.[23]

II

Critique of the American Social Science Approach

A flood of literature has gushed forth from the United States on the problems of developing societies. The authors of this literature have tried to develop theoretical perspectives on political and social change. They do differ among themselves on the various aspects of the theories of change and modernisation, but they have brought out all the salient features in their writings and highlighted the concerns of the dominant academic culture in the United States. We offer a few criticisms here of the major assumptions of the dominant academic writings on the theories of political change.

(1) Social science theory in the United States seeks to generalise from the unique and specific experiences of the United States. In their attempt to universalise their knowledge the theorists project a history of the development and achievements of their own society as a model for emulation for others. One dominant belief of these theorists is in the gradualness of change. In this belief universally applicable? If the advanced capitalist societies have had smooth sailing, relatively speaking, in public affairs, and have developed institutions in a gradual manner, it is because they have functioned in a specific kind of environment which may not be available in other societies. Societies where an industrial revolution comes first have a distinct advantage over those where it comes belatedly. New power to control and harness nature with the help of the machine opened up new vistas of human development in the industrial West. History provided the West with great opportunities for development without any serious competition from large areas of the world. The Industrial Revolution in the West was a unique event, and it afforded unique opportunities to the West to develop economically and mould the life of the people in a gradual manner. It is a serious weakness in any theoretical framework to universalise from the limited and unique experience of the theorists.

Further, the industrially advanced societies of the West have not faced any breakdown and can, therefore, face the challenges of time successfully. This is in fact what constitutes the basis of the confidence of the theorists of the West in their values and political institutions. Absence of serious breakdown is again a unique experience. How can it be concluded from this that societies do not breakdown? Theories of change as developed by political and social sciences in the Anglo-American universities today are of limited relevance because they are projections of the specific but limited historical experience of the West, which is not shared by other political communities.

(2) The theorists in the West are broadly satisfied with the basic premises of their political system, and their concern is how best to effect a gradual adaptation of the system to new demands. The major concern of the theorists is about 'change in the system' and not about a 'change of the system'. They feel that the foundations of their society are on sound principles, but marginal issues always arise, and the system, though sound, may need to change in some respect in order to respond to demands and challenges. The system should be capable of managing conflicts. What is the nature of such conflicts? It is suggested that in the developed capitalist societies, there are no antagonistic and irreconcilable contradictions. The working class has accepted the values of the system, and the capitalists have accepted the principle of collective bargaining and strikes. The State has accepted the role of mediation between the working class and the capitalists. Welfarism and democracy are working well. Occasionally there are crisis situations, and challenges are posed by deviant and marginal groups. The theorists in the West, therefore, concentrate on the theories and techniques of 'conflict resolution'. Fundamentally 'conflict resolution' takes place in conformity with the premises of the system. Theorists of 'conflict resolution' view the problem as one of a 'change in the system', not as destructive of the system.

Theories of social and political change as expounded by the social scientists of the United Kingdom and the United States are inadequate for an analysis of change in societies where the political system is on trial and is confronted with serious challenge by forces which want to replace it by an absolutely different system. Theories of change concerned with 'change in the system' are only partly useful because they cannot explain the macro processes of fundamental change in society. Political change can mean a break with the past and the establishment of a system that is absolutely new. Social theories of the West dealing with 'change in the system' do not have the necessary explanatory capability and methodological competence to explain "change of the system".

(3) What is the standpoint of dissidents in the United States about the theories of social change propounded by the dominant group of social scientists? We would briefly refer to the views of Alvin Gouldner and Irving Horowitz. In his book The coming crisis of Western Sociology Gouldner is critical of the conservative sociology of Talcott Parsons and the structural functionalists. After critically examining Parsons and functionalism, he points out the strains and tensions of the functionalists specifically. He suggests two tensions in functionalism. One is that it is in its treatment of social change that Parsonsianism will most likely abandon some of its most fundamental domain assumptions and that, especially, it is likely to manifest a tendency to shift abruptly direr to

radically different domain assumptions, particularly those of Marxism. Second, the pressure for this shift is mounting and it may mount to the point where the functionalists will feel the need to attempt, explicitly and openly, to solve problems in the analysis of social change by deliberately borrowing from Marxism. In short, the analysis of social change is increasingly leading functionalism toward a convergence with Marxism.[24]

The main thrust of Gouldner's critique is that functionalism, which is based on an assumption of the stability of society, is inadequate as a theory for analysing and explaining political and social change. The failure of the functionalists to explain social change is compelling them to accept Marxism, their fundamental enemy in social theory.[25]

Horowitz gives four reasons for the failure of the social Sciences to study social change in a fruitful manner. These reasons are as follows:

> First, sociology has so sundered separated history from the social sciences that development is considered an accoutrement rather than a necessary aspect of the study of any society. Second, empirical sociological studies tend to focus on internal structure and consistency, stressing pattern maintenance, models of equilibrium, consensus system, structural hegemony, etc. This approach leaves little place for conflict situations, forms of radical change, spontaneous and unstructured behaviour, and other 'unstable' forces producing change and development alike. Third, there is a fear that to discuss human development leaves one open to charges of utopianism. This is an age which takes forward strides self-consciously. Fourth, there is a widespread doubt that the concept of development is scientifically definable since it has for so long exclusively been the rallying cry of political ideologists.[26]

To sum up, contemporary political theory in the United States has not proved adequate to study the processes of political change in developing societies.[27]

Many developing societies the facing challenges from forces which are against the existing social and political system. Many movements are afoot for the destruction of the existing social order and its replacement by a new system. Social theories of the West are not able to explain why such movements have arisen because they have never grappled with questions of fundamental change of the system. The social reality from which the social sciences of the West have abstracted their formulations cannot be replicated in the complex situation obtaining in developing countries today.

III

Marxian Framework for the study of Political Change

The Marxian theory of change has fundamental differences with the dominant social theories of change propounded by the Anglo-American social scientists in the advanced capitalist countries of the West. The very starting point of Karl Marx is different. Marx believed that the duty of social theorists is to find out the laws of social development and make generalisations and abstractions by studying the forms of interconnection within the processes of the world. Further, the social theorist should not only interpret and explain the concrete conditions of social life but also involve themselves in the struggle for change. Not only this. Marx held that the test of the validity of a theory is in practice.

He wrote:

> The question whether objective truth belongs to human thinking is not a question of theory, but a practical question… . The truth, i.e. the reality and power of thought must be demonstrated in practice. The contest as to the reality or non-reality of a thought which is isolated from practice, is a purely scholastic question… .

Philosophers have only interpreted the world in various ways, but the real task is to *alter* it.

Marx also not only wrote a theory of change but also actively participated in the revolutions of his time, so that he was banished from Germany and France. Isaiah Berlin is wrong when he characterises Marx as follows:

> He (Marx) was by temperament a theorist and an intellectual, and instinctively avoided direct contact with the masses to the study of whose interests his entire life was devoted.[28]

Marx not only recommended mass struggles for political and social change but also actively participated in them and arrived in London in 1849 as an exile. Berlin has misrepresented the life history of Marx.

A few aspects of Marxian theory would be highlighted here to make his perspective on change clear. There are three important intellectual sources of Marxian thought, i.e. German philosophy, British capitalism (political economy), and French radicalism. He took the cudgels against some of the main currents in philosophical and economic thinking of his time, wrote powerful indictments of his adversaries, and laid down guidelines for action for bringing about change in society by analysing the dialectical relationship of social forces.

(1) The starting point of Marx's science of society is that men must associate themselves to produce their means of subsistence. If men do

not produce, they perish. And production is a social activity. The tools, the implements, and the skill and knowledge needed for production are 'forces of production'; and while men are involved in social activity of production they enter into multiple 'relations of production'. Social life develops only when people adapt their relations of production to their forces of production, and work out ideas and organise themselves in suitable institutions to that end. The two indivisible sides of social production are productive forces and the relations of production; and in Marxist terminology this is known as "mode of production'. Mode of production is the determinative basis of the social system. Society and its dominant ideas, political views, and institutions depend on the mode of production. If the mode of production changes, and it has continually changed since the inception of human society, the entire social system changes. Every new and higher mode of production signifies a new and higher level in the history of man's development. The change in the forces of production brings about qualitative change in society. If, however, the change in the relations of production bears no relation to the change in the forces of production, social development is retarded. Any want of harmony between the two (i.e. between the forces of production and the relations of production) leads to acute conflict; for then a contradiction arises between the new forces of production and the old relations of production and leads to a social revolution in antagonistic socio-economic formations. Social antagonisms and contradiction can be resolved by a revolution, and only a successful revolution can usher in the necessary social change needed for harmonious life. Marx explains this as follows:

> In the social production which men carry on they enter into definite relations that are indispensable and independent of their will, these relations of production correspond to a definite stage of development of their material powers of production. The sum total of these relations of production constitutes the economic structure of society—the real foundation, on which rise legal and political superstructures and to which correspond definite forms of social consciousness. The mode of production in material life determines the general character of social, political and spiritual processes of life. It is not the consciousness of man that determines their existence, but, on the contrary their social existence determines their consciousness.

The materialistic interpretation of history and the identification of social contradictions of an antagonistic character are both essential to revolutionary consciousness. Without them basic change in society cannot come.

(2) Since nineteenth century capitalism was the essential reference point of his critique, Marx examines in detail the contributions of capitalism to social development. He also scrutinises its negative aspects, including its basic tendency to accumulate surplus value and exploit and oppress the working class. The laws of capitalist accumulation lead to a serious exploitation of the working class by the capitalists. Marx suggests that it is only by struggle that the working class can liberate itself from the shackles of capitalist exploitation. He is clear that social and political change cannot come about without struggle. He declares: "The history of all hitherto existing society is the history of class struggle." If struggle is the motive force of change, a few pertinent questions arise here: (a) Who would struggle, and against whom? (b) Are there any stages in the struggle? (c) Does the theory and practice of Marxism suggest any strategies for the struggle for social change? (d) Does the Marxian methodology of social analysis help identify the situations and the nature of the struggle for social change?

Marx is a theorist of social transformation. For him the purpose of change is a qualitatively higher social life. His attention is focussed on the factors inherent in the death of a society. According to him, a new society can be born only when social contradictions have been resolved. For contradictions to be resolved, they have to be properly identified and a struggle Waged against them. The exploiting class in its hands all the instruments of coercive power. The exploited classes need to organise themselves in order to conduct their struggle against the exploitative social system. Class struggles take place only when the masses are conscious about exploitation and the causes of it. As the level of consciousness rises, the struggle intensifies. For Marx, social and political change is achieved through conscious struggle of the working class against capitalism.

(3) Marx emphasises that societies ties contain within themselves the causes of their decay and death. Social contradictions get resolved only when the society concerned undergoes a qualitative change. Marx emphatically declares that a revolution capable of changing a society cannot be manufactured to order. The most important prerequisite for revolutionary change is that the forces of production should exhaust all their potential of growth and that a serious antagonism should develop between the relations of production and the forces of production. To see whether such an antagonism exists or not, one should examine the nature of the epoch concerned. In understanding the nature of the epoch for revolutionary action, it is essential to remember that at the various stages of history of development of societies, different modes of production may co-exist.[29]

As societies develop, a dominant mode of production emerges—either the slave, the feudal, or the capitalist mode of production. The moral is that the historical forces should be properly identified. One cannot wish away a particular phase in history and its proper meaning for social change. Marx says in *Das Kapital*:

> Just as it would be impossible to arrive at a correct judgment about an individual by noting only his own view of himself so it is impossible to judge whole revolutionary periods by the conscious way in which they see themselves, for on the contrary such consciousness must be explained as the product of the contradictions of material life of the conflict between the forces of social production and their actual relations. No social order ever disappears before all the productive forces for which there is room in it, have developed, and the new higher relations of production never appear before the conditions of their existence have matured in the womb of the old society… the problem itself only arises when the material conditions necessary for its solution already exist or at least are in the process of formation.

Marx advances a philosophy of history and a theory of society on the basis of which the correlation of social forces in a society at any given time is to be examined and interpreted for the purpose of waging a struggle for revolutionary change. Marx states this very clearly as his distinctive contribution in the *Communist Manifesto*:

> What I did that was new was to prove (1) that the existence of classes is only bound up with particular, historic phases in the development of production; (2) that the class struggle necessarily leads to the dictatorship of the proletariat; (3) that this dictatorship itself only constitutes the transition to the abolition of all classes and to a classless society.

(4) What is the nature of the State in Marxian analysis? Any theory of political change must at the very start come to terms with the question of the place of the State in society. In his book *The Origin of the Family, Private Property, and the State*, Friederich Engels, a long time friend and collaborator of Karl Marx, describes the State as a "power, arisen out of society but placing itself above it". Its first "distinguishing characteristic… (is that) the State is distinguished by the grouping of its members on a territorial basis"; it holds sway over a definite territory. Its second feature is 'the institution of a public force' which "consists not merely of armed men, but also of material appendages, prisons, and coercive institutions of all kinds". The officers of the State, who are 'in

possession of the public power', act as 'officials of society standing above society'.

The State is a coercive instrument in the hands of those who own property; and it is not a neutral agency in society. In history the need for the institution of State was first felt by the propertied classes; for the State could help the propertied classes in the accumulation of surplus value and suppress the real producers of surplus who resist such exploitation. The executive power of the State with its enormous bureaucratic and military organisation could be used to establish or preserve security for capital investment. The State originated when the classes emerged in society No one talks of the States of the North American Indians or other primitive communities. As Engels writes:

> An institution that lent the character of perpetuity not only to the newly rising division into classes, but also to the right of the possessing classes to exploit and rule the non-possessing classes. And this institution was found. The State arose.

To sum up, Marx's attempt is to find law of social development (like Darwin's law of evolution of species by natural selection), and in this attempt he follows the method of a materialistic interpretation of history. Society undergoes a qualitative change when the mode of production changes. Social classes which play a progressive role in changing society create their own powerful negations, and through class struggle the exploiting classes get liquidated. Being involved in the struggles in capitalist societies, Marx examines the laws of capitalist development and the processes of capitalist accumulation in detail and works out their social implications.

Many contributions have been made to the Marxian theory of social and political change, one of the most important of such contributions being that of V.I. Lenin. Lenin deals with the phase in which competitive capitalism is about to enter upon the stage of monopoly capitalism, and develops a very exhaustive theory of imperialism and its consequences for the societies of the world.[30]

Lenin points out five essential features of imperialism. They are:

(1) The concentration of production and capital has, developed to such a high degree that it has created monopolies which play a decisive role in economic life;
(2) the merging of bank capital with industrial capital and the creation, on the basis of this 'finance capital', of a financial oligarchy;
(3) the growth of the importance of export of capital, as distinguished from export of commodities;

(4) the formation of international monopoly combines of capitalists which divide up the world; and
(5) the completion of the territorial division of the world among the greatest capitalist powers.

The ideology of imperialism is dominance and regimentation. Since it cannot stand the anarchy of competition, it uses the power of the State to subjugate and regiment other societies. State interference in the economic life of society under monopoly capitalism assumes great significance. And to protect and promote the interests of monopoly capitalism, the State involves itself in the subjugation of other societies and territories.

The result of imperialism is that an international division of labour is forced on a world scale, and colonies are reduced to the position of producers of raw material and importers of finished products from the metropolis. The social and economic development of the colonies is arrested and hindered by the operation of imperialism. Colonies become appendages of the metropolis and suffer underdevelopment, deprivation, and stagnation. Underdevelopment of the colonies is forced by the mediation of the colonial State. The contemporary forms of this dependence of the developing countries on the Western capitalist societies, including the 'development of underdevelopment', peripheral industrialisation and economic blockages, the internal disarticulation of social relations, etc. have been widely studied in recent years. It is Lenin who has laid the theoretical foundations of these studies. Lenin's contribution to the analysis of imperialism is being highlighted here because it is very relevant to an understanding of the processes of social and political change. What is the nature of change in colonies as differentiated from the developed capitalist societies? Are processes of change universal in all societies? The answer is definitely no. Processes of social change depend on the historical stage on which a particular society has (or a number of societies have) entered.

The material foundations of society and the existing correlation of class forces help in understanding the stage of development of society. To understand any specific society, the relations of societies among themselves on a global scale should also be examined. And concretely speaking, the capitalist societies practised large-scale exploitation of extensive areas of the world and precipitated a situation of underdevelopment in those areas. Hence theories of political and social change have to examine the role of imperialism and its impact on various societies. Marxism-Leninism sharply focuses attention on the exogenous and endogenous factors of social change.

IV

Relevance of Competing Theoretical Perspectives for the Study of State and Political Process

Our description of the major theoretical perspectives in contemporary social science on political change shows that such perspectives are of competitive character. They view change from wholly different angles, and they are for either 'Change in a System' or 'Change of the System.' A meaningful theoretical perspective for the study of political change in India should include the following approach.

In identifying the basic processes of change in India, the starting point has to be the impact of British imperialism on Indian society. The mediation of the colonial State was responsible for the arrested and uneven growth of Indian society. The exploitative policies of British imperialism reduced Indian economic and social life to the subsistence level. The policy of free trade while dealing with a poor and underdeveloped country proved disastrous for India. The British needed India as a source for the raw materials needed for their domestic industries and as a market for their finished products. The consequence of this policy was the destruction of the flourishing cottage industries of India, unemployment of artisans and craftsmen and extreme strain on the rural resources to feed the natives and produce raw materials for the industrial prosperity of Britain. The phenomenon of serious famines recurring in a predominantly agricultural country like India is due to the British policy of de-urbanisation and de-industrialisation of India.[31]

During the late nineteenth century a small and dependent capitalist class emerged in India. This class received the necessary impetus for development during the inter-war periods in the twentieth century. Pockets of industrialisation developed in the twentieth century leading to the emergence of the small Indian capitalist class.[32]

British imperialism created its own negation in the form of a national liberation movement. The national movement was led by the middle class, and the capitalists joined the bandwagon of this movement. Large areas of feudal India were untouched, in qualitative terms, by this patriotic struggle against imperialism. Hence when India achieved freedom, it had all the features of a transitional society. Modern India being a product of colonial rule, there is a situation of co-existence of feudal and capitalist modes of production. India is multi-structural society in which semi-feudal and rich peasantry in the rural areas exists with medium and monopoly capitalism. In a multi-structural society, multiple loyalty structures from the most traditional to the most modern co-exist and compete.

India is a society in transition, and the existence of various social formations is one of the concrete realities of this society. When a society is in a transitional stage, the 'old' and the 'new' may be either in conflict or in temporary alliance. The theorists of change have to identify the forces which stand for a break with the past and for the establishment of a new social order in a transitional society. Further, a transitional society is not a polarised society. In the absence of a polarisation of forces, the conflicts in the various modes of production are sought to be explained away by studying peripheral or transitory features of society. A deep study of changing role of caste, and its adaptive capacity can show how distorted the theoretical framework of scholars is. Caste is a part of reality but not the total reality. Caste is valid because the agrarian structure has features of semi-feudalism. Instead of studying the political forces which maintain semi-feudal relations, the symbols of feudal and semi-feudal ways of life, *viz.* caste, becomes important for study. The distinction between the wood and the trees gets obliterated in the study of political change in India. A transitional society witnesses conflicts between the entrenched and the emerging forces; and study of political change demands that the nature of such conflicts should be examined.

A theoretical framework for the study of political change in India can emerge only from an examination of the nature of the State in a large agricultural country that is on the road to capitalist industrialisation. It is a complex social situation. Industrialisation cannot take place unless classes and groups which stand for industrialisation are enabled to play the leading role. In order to perform such a role these classes and groups try to capture the State power. But the logic of participatory democracy in a big agricultural country is that the rural interests are both numerically and socially very significant. Such a situation can lead to serious conflict between the landed interests and the leaders of industry; or there can be an alliance between them to influence State power. If the landed interests and the industrial classes enter into an alliance, the pace of industrialisation is bound to be slow. If they enter upon a path of conflict, society gets involved in struggle. What role does that State play in a situation of conflict or alliance between the landed interests and the industrial classes? It is necessary to note here that class alliances in a transitional society are not very neat and clear. To analyse the shifts in alliance is a continuing task for the scholar.

To sum up, a developing society is involved in a network of external and internal linkages which help or hinder change. Only that theoretical perspective is valid for the study of change which can expose the nature and consequences of such linkages.

IMPERIALISM-LED GLOBALISATION: A PERSPECTIVE

The capitalist mode of production as distinguished from its predecessor the feudal mode of production is 'expansioninst' because 'capital accumulation' begins with the territorial boundaries of a nation-state but capital's great need to 'accumulate' cannot be fulfilled without colonies and unequal trading partners for the assured supply of raw material for constantly 'expanding' markets. This inherent logic in the dynamics of capitalist expansionism has led many scholars to maintain that the new development of capitalist globalisation is not a new one. Since capitalism has been always international, current phase of capitalist globalisation is not something different from the ongoing process of internationalisation of capitalism beginning with 1500 AD to the present decade of the twenty-first century. Even Eric Hobsbawm states that 'Pax Americana,' is an echo of 'Pax Britianica' just as the latter had been an echo of 'Pax Romana'.[33] The ongoing debate on globalisation is centred around the validity and relevance of capitalist nation-state systems which were formally recognised in the Treaty of Westphalia in 1648. It is maintained that the current stage of 'finance capital' which means globalisation of finance capital along with its centralisation has broken geographical and territorial boundaries of the nation-state system because 'globalisation-cum-centralisation' of capital has completely weakened the 'capacities' of nation-states to control the fast mobility of finance-capital across the whole world. Two fundamentally opposite view points have been expressed about the viability of nation-states to control their national economies in the age of globalised-cum-centralised finance capital. William I. Robinson and Jerry Harris observe: "...globalisation involves an 'epochal shift' in the development of the world capitalist system. Specifically, it represents the transition from the nation-state phase to a new transnational phase of capitalism'.[34] George Soros, a self-confessed speculator, proved that the global mobility of capital was much 'faster' than abilities of the national federal banks and other financial control mechanisms to control and regulate the 'flight' of capital?[35] Eric Hobsbawm, on the other hand, has a much more 'nuanced' understanding of the role of nation-states in the phase of transnationalised finance capital. Hobsbawm observes:

> "We have a globalised economy, we can aspire to a globalised culture, we certainly have a globalised technology and a single global science, but politically speaking, we have a world that remains in reality pluralist and divided into territorial states."[36]

It is a hurried conclusion that national territorial states are things of the past in the present era of globalisation. In spite of the fact that nation-states, especially of the South, are under great pressure from the capital and technology exporting states of the North, the local populations look only towards their own states to act as a 'buffer' against interventionist imperialist states and also manage domestic affairs for the satisfaction of domestic populations. Since capitalist crisis is an inherent and integral part of capitalist system of private accumulation and social production, it is the local state which is expected to find solutions to the 'crisis' created by capitalism at the global level as witnessed by the East Asian capitalist countries from 1997 to 2000. Eric Hobsbawm draws attention to the social dialectics of globalised capital and 'domestic states' while dealing with the 'conflicts' created by global capitalist crisis. He observes : "This brings us back to the great question of the conflict between the forces of capitalism, which are in favour of removing all obstacles, and political forces, which basically operate through nation-states and are either obliged or deliberately choose to regulate these procedures. This is a conflict because the laws of capitalist development are simple : maximise expansion, profit, and the increase of capital. However, the priorities of governments and people organised into societies are different by their very nature, and to some extent they are in conflict."[37]

While the idea of the 'retreat of the state' and autonomy for markets lies buried after the warnings by Hobsbawm and others, it is not to suggest that the state is only a 'regulator' of free market and competitive economy as desired by the capitalist globalisers.

Another question may be raised here to deepen our understanding of the role of the state under the present phase of globalised-cum-centralised finance capital. Is globalisation inevitable and is it not reversible to some extent? This question has to be faced squarely because from the beginning of 1980s the model of free market economy has been sold in a fundamentalist manner. Hence, globalisation in the last decade of the Twentieth Century rests on an ideology of American model of free market capitalism in which the role of the state is that of a 'facilitator' and 'regulator' of the rules of the game for managing an efficient free market economy. The state has not only to act as an executive agency of its own ruling classes and corporate houses, it has also to play the role of a good 'host' for transnational capital. The votaries of globalisation have maintained that the state is the real villain and it should be ejected from the centrality of position it occupies in the national economy and replaced by a friendly 'host' state for domestic and global capitalism. In the Introduction to the World Bank Policy Research report entitled '*Bureaucrats in Business : The Economics and Politics of government*

Ownership', Michael Bruno, Vice President, Development Economics and Chief Economist of the World Bank, observes :

> "Yet in many countries, particularly the poorest, some parts of the economy have remained stubbornly resistant to reform. This report deals with one of the more important of these : the inefficient, loss-making state-owned enterprises that are a significant burden on government budgets and scarce resources in many countries. These enterprises hinder growth, impede market liberalisation, and thus both directly and indirectly limit efforts to reduce poverty."[38]

Further, the report points out: "However, we have presented evidence that SOEs are less efficient than the private sector in competitive markets and, with effective regulation of private firms, in monopoly markets as well. Finally, we have shown that large SOE sectors can be a drag on the economy because of the aggregate impact of inefficient operation at the micro-economic level and because large SOE sectors are typically associated with large fiscal and current account deficits, which in turn have negative repercussions on growth."[39] Thus, the ideological recipe of antistatist neo-liberal classical economics is sold to the new liberalisers in the Third World that the post-Independence project of state-led model of economic growth followed by these countries has been completely flawed and the model of free market capitalism of the United States of America is recommended for achieving goals of economic growth, which these countries have missed during the period of interventionist state-led economy.

It deserves to be stated that assumptions underlying the neo-liberal free market ideology, sold by the Americans and global institutions like the World Bank and IMF controlled by them, have been proved empirically wrong and as Hobsbawm observes : "In theory, economists believe in the complete triumph of the free-market ideology, but in practice no country has ever tried to go all the way down the road, partly because of political impediments."[40]

Contradictions of this Model of Globalisation

Historically, capitalism has developed and expanded internationally with the help of its own national states. Harry Magdoff brings out this aspect:

> "While the expansion of capitalism has always presupposed and indeed required cooperation among its various national components—with respect to transportation facilities, weights and measures, monetary and credit arrangements, etc.—there never has been a time when these national components ceased to struggle each for its own preferment and advantage."[41]

Hobsbawm and Magdoff have alerted Third World globalisers that the state still remains the site of social contest both against local ruling classes and the external imperialist ruling classes. Further, many social conflicts emerge within countries of the South if they follow policy prescriptions of free market fundamentalists, and it is only the local state which has to deal with social conflicts which are the product of exported global ideology of free competitive market capitalism. Stephen Gill in '*Structural change and global political economy : Globalising elites and the emerging World Order*' observes:

> "Nonetheless, trends in the ownership, location, and nature of economic activity suggest that the identity and allegiance of firms have taken on a less and less territorial aspect in the 1990s. This indicates potential contradictions between globalising and more territorially bounded social forces and institutions, and between economics and politics at the global level. The economic system is one of increasingly planetary reach, whereas political authority is still primarily constituted at the national level,... states are being recast into a kind of transmission belt for globalising forces—a transformation that has been developing since the 1990s, and that accelerated in the 1980s, especially in the third world."[42]

The most important implication is the birth of a 'new contradiction' between the demands of global finance capital for the restructurisation of the state systems to implement the neo-liberal classical economic ideology and the pressures of local populations on their states to fulfill their 'basic demands'. The impoverished majority of masses especially of the South will be involved in struggles against their own states due to failures of these states to meet legitimate demands of their poor citizens. This will weaken the democratic legitimacy of every state under neo-liberal umbrella. Further, socially unstable countries cannot have stable democratic states. Since different fractions and strata of the ruling and non-ruling classes will be differentially impacted by economic arrangements under free market capitalism, society will be seriously fragmented because intra-class, and inter-class struggles will take place to assert their rights over the size of the economic cake and in such an unstable social situation, the state will be continuously involved in fire fighting activities.

In summation, it may be mentioned that the new imperialism-led capitalist globalisation will consolidate the 'core' capitalist countries of the North and marginalise and exclude the developing countries of the South on whose shoulders super-capital accumulation is going to take place. It is not without reason that Bukharin characterised the imperialist state as a 'robber state.'[43] Polanyi had warned that 'market mechanism' would 'result in the demolition of society'.[43]

Politics and Economics of Imperialism-led Global Capitalism

The internationalisation of production and globalisation of finance has also happened at a time when Pax Americana had become a reality in the last decade of the Twentieth Century and the beginning of the Twenty-First Century. Every countervailing force and every system of balance of power among the nation-states has come to an end with the collapse of socialist state systems and the last decade of the Twentieth Century has witnessed the emergence of a hyper-super economic and military power. The implications of sole super-power-led New Global Order deserve to be mentioned because economics and politics of the new epoch of globalised-cum-centralised finance capital cannot be clearly comprehended without analysing the arrival of imperialist America on the world scene. President George Bush Sr. declared that the decade of 1990s has begun with the emergence of a New International Order which in reality meant unipolar world in place of a post-World War II situation of bipolarity where space was occupied by two super-powers and the two alliances—North Atlantic Treaty Organisation and the Warsaw Pact. The collapse of Soviet Russia provided full space for American hegemony to emerge which was asserted during the American war on Iraq in 1991 on the pretext of liberating Kuwait from Iraq. This caravan of hegemonic America is unstoppable. It has been legitimised by George Bush Jr. by launching his so-called global war against terrorism in the form of a response to the terrorist attack on World Trade Centre on September 11, 2001. Americans have changed regimes in Afghanistan and Iraq between 2001 and 2003 on the pretext of fight against global terrorism. Even George Soros, who built his reputation as a great speculator and launched US $5 billion project to promote democracy at the global level, observes: "America, under Bush, is a danger to the world"[44], and he has announced he would distribute funds to democratic forces in America for the defeat of George Bush in the forthcoming presidential election.

A very dangerous doctrine has been advanced by neo-conservative forces ruling over America that the post September11, 2001 events of terrorism against America demand a 'pre-emptive' war against any sovereign state suspected to be supporting terrorism against America. This doctrine of 'pre-emptive war' against any country by America means that except the American state, no other state is sovereign and every nation-states' sovereignty is at the mercy of America.

The America's war against Iraq in 2003 was launched under the doctrine of 'pre-emptive' strike against the most dangerous enemy of America. This new threat to the sovereignty of every state in the 1990s deserves a little elaboration. Strobe Talbott, an important policy-maker in America, observes : "Along with the expansion and adaptation of international institutions in the Nineties came the establishment of a new principle. It was agreed that there are limits on the sovereignty of the nation-state : national governments are subject to international sanction if they violate certain basic norms within their own borders,'[45] and hence war against Bosnia (1995), Ksovo (1999), Afghanistan, (2001/2), Iraq (2003) et al. The only exception to the general rule of the end of state sovereignty theory is that America is super-sovereign state and pre-eminent power in the world. It has the license and the responsibility to act as a global policeman and punish the errant nation-states. Not only this. America is above any international obligation and it showed a contempt for the Security Council of the United Nations when it unilaterally declared pre-emptive war against Saddam Hussein of Iraq in 2003. America has not only shown contempt for the United Nations, it has, at its sweet will, refused to be a party to the Kyoto Treaty on Global warming or international treaty 'on Ozone-destroying chemicals' (1989).

The arrogance of power by the sole policeman has been stated by Tabott: "Virtually all previous watersheds in the evolution of the international system had entailed the repudiation of specific empires. Cumulatively, they amounted to a repudiation of imperialism in general. Westphalia marked the end of the Holy Roman Empire, the Congress of Vienna carved up the Napoleonic one, Versailles did the same to the 'Habsburgs' and 'Ottomons'; the 'Romanous' was by then already on the ash heap of history. The allies in the Second World War defeated the Third Reich and the Empire of the Rising Sun, and the sun began to set on the British empire not long after. Throughout the 20th century the US was an opponent of empire and a champion of decolonisation. The fading of the cold war was made possible by the collapse of what was often called the world's last Empire, with Moscow as its metropole. Yet a decade later, in 2001, theoreticians for a new administration in Washington toyed with the idea of imperialism as a model of American foreign and defence policy."[46]

The Bush regime and the American neo-conservatives have made American imperialism not only 'fashionable' but also profitable because wars are profitable for the imperialists. Shripath Ramphal, a former Secretary-General of Commonwealth of Nations, gave a warning that "The ambition for world domination has ever been a global curse. September 11 is not the origin of present dangers. As many understood, and said, at the time, it was an enormously criminal act of terrorism; it was also enormously stupid. What it did was to provide a new imperialism to emerge with plumes of virtue and trumpets of righteousness."[47] Listen to the language of US President Bush in London who "...defended the war against Iraq as necessary to confront repression but also for 'effective' multilateral institutions, and for the Global expansion of Democracy".[48] What is the US record while dealing with international democratic obligations? Americans have refused to endorse (a) the Kyoto Protocol; (b) the International Criminal Court; (c) the Anti-Ballistic Missile Treaty; (d) the Landmine Treaty; (e) the Biological and Toxin Weapons Convention; (f) the UN Agreement to Court Agreement to curb the International Flow of Illicit Small Arms *et al.*

War for Profit

Harry Magdoff has alerted us that the sluggish Japanese economy was the only beneficiary during the Korean war; Korea's misfortune between 1950 and 1955 brought great fortune to the Japanese "first as suppliers of war materials and services for United Nations and after the July 1953 armistice as suppliers of materials needed for the reconstruction of South Korea".[49] The same story of profits from war is repeating in the case of America's war on Iraq.

On the plea of fighting international terrorism in the post-September 11, 2001, the United States, at the end of year, invaded Afghanistan, in early 2003 it attacked Iraq and on May 1, 2003, declared that the war against Saddam Hussein was over.

But there is another side of the story. After destroying polity, economy, and society in wars of 'aggression', American's hearts are bleeding for the economic and political reconstruction of 'destroyed' Afghanistan and Iraq. Incidentally, Osama bin Laden's Al-Qaeda and the Taliban regime in Afghanistan were created and destroyed by America and Saddam Hussein's most dangerous weapons could not be traced in Iraq, and still the aggressive war was launched against these two countries. It is the post-war scenario which has to be brought into sharp focus around a question : Who will be the real beneficiaries of post-war reconstruction in Afghanistan and Iraq. A few facts may be mentioned to substantiate the argument that 'profit' is the driving force of war mongers in America. First, on October 18, 2003, the United States' Congress sanctioned US $87 billion for the ongoing reconstruction of Afghanistan and Iraq. Has the American Congress sanctioned more than US $80 billion to establish democracy in Afghanistan and Iraq or to control Afghanistan for Central Asian oil resources and Iraq, an oil rich country?

Second, the World Bank was asked to study vital sectors of Iraqi economy which were to be re-constructed. Americans assembled seventy countries including tiny Sri Lanka to act as 'donors' for the reconstruction of Iraq's economy and the Madrid Conference was held on October 23-24, 2003 to legitimise American game in Iraq. Incidentally, such a *Tamasha* was also enacted in January 2002. A Conference of 'donors' for Afghanistan was held to pledge US $5 billion for reconstruction of that country. The Vajpayee government also stood in the queu at both these American-led conferences and made financial contributions for the reconstruction of war destroyed economies. Every important multinational corporation from road builders to hospitals which is closely linked with the higher echelons of the neo-Conservative lobby of President Bush has been given a lucrative contract for the reconstruction of these two countries. A non-partisan Centre for Public Integrity has maintained in a report in Washington DC on October 31, 2003, that the first US $8 billion in contracts have been awarded to 71 companies by the Pentagon, the State Department and the US Agency for International Development. Charles Lewis, while releasing this report in US, said "There is a stench of political favouritism and cronyism" in awarding contracts. Further, it is well known that Bush Administration has strong linkages with private corporate sector, and this is the reason that private sector companies like Engineering giant Batchel or Halliburton, an oil services and logistic company, formerly led by Vice-President Dick Cheney *et al* are blue-eyed boys for the award of every new lucrative contract. The puppet Iraqi Governing Council in September 2003, on the eve of G-7 meeting in Dubai announced a so called policy that 'except for oil' foreigners/ Americans were welcome. The Council said "Foreign investors were to be given highly favourable terms in which to take over banks, insurance, pharmaceuticals, health care, power, telecommunications *et al*."

The 'Business' of America has always been to earn profits even out of every human destruction, especially wars—global or local. Americans have learnt from experience that wars bring huge profits by selling arms for reconstruction in post-war destroyed societies. Marshall Plan President Truman of America for the reconstruction of war devastated Europe paid rich dividends to the American Big Business, after which the Americans have never abandoned such golden opportunities for earning profits. Prof. John K. Galbraith has authoritatively told us that it was not New Deal policies of President Roosevelt which pulled America out of its great economic depression of the 1930s, but the profits earned during the World War II that brought economic boom to the depressed American economy of the 1930s.[50] An important lesson was learnt by the American capitalist classes that while capitalism goes through cyclical crisis even leading to economic depression and stagnation, the 'defence production sector' of the capitalist economy will always earn profits and keep the crisis-ridden economy an ongoing activity. USSR collapsed because it could not bear the economic burden of the Warsaw Pact and cold war competition with America. As a result of the uneven and unequal competition between the two super-powers, America emerged as the sole-super-power on the scene in the 1990s and converted a bipolar world into a unipolar New International Order. Both India and Pakistan have been involved in military competition since independence, and every defence related purchase brings profits to defence sector of the capitalist countries. As late as October 30, 2003 US Assistant Secretary of State Christina Rocca, while testifying before the House Committee on International Relations Sub-Committee on Asia-Pacific and International Terrorism observed : "Both India and Pakistan are responsible for the impasse over Kashmir". American policy of 'equating' dispute-related neighbouring countries has created a situation of 'competition for arms for security'. Every developing country visits Arms Bazzar of the Western Capitalist producers and suppliers of arms. Every local war in any region of the world brings 'profits' to the arms industry of the west. It is not without reason that Dwight Eisenhower in his Farewell Address on January 17, 1961, stated:

> "We now stand ten years past the mid point of a century that has witnessed four major wars among great nations......... until the last of our world conflicts, the United States had no armaments industry....We annually spend on military security more than the net income of all United States corporations....
>
> "This conjunction of an immense military establishment and a large arm industry is new in the American experience.
>
> "In the councils of government, we must guard against the acquisition of unwarranted influence, whether sought or unsought, by the military-industrial complex. The potential for the disastrous rise of misplaced power exists and will persist."

Much water has flown down the Atlantic and Pacific when Eisenhower warned about 'military-industrial complex' influencing the corridors of power. The present establishment of America under President Bush is consciously and actively pursuing the interests of 'military-industrial complex of America' which is earning profits out of every local war and the so-called post-war reconstruction whether in Afghanistan or Iraq or from dispute between India and Pakistan.

India Trapped

The Indian governing classes with the active and enthusiastic approval and consent of the ruling classes have integrated themselves with the American imperialist-led New Global Order. The decade of 1990s was a kind of probationary period for the Indian state and different fractions of the bourgeisie and the capitalist farmers and they slowly and steadily moved towards global integration. The beginning of Twenty-First Century has witnessed 'over enthusiasm' in Indian political, administrative, oppressor and exploiting ruling classes because they have willingly joined the 'bandwagon' of George Bush Jr.'s 'alliance of fight against terrorism' after the events of September 11, 2001. India has accepted the right of Americans to launch preventive and pre-emptive wars against any sovereign state on the plea of a fight against terrorism.

A few facts may be mentioned to substantiate the argument that India has abandoned its national project of self-reliant economy led by a relatively autonomous state, both internally and externally, in favour of a New Economic Policy based on globalisation, liberalisation and privatisation. Not only this. The national project of self-reliant economy was firmly situated on the principle of sovereignty of the nation-state but the project of New Economic Policy of the 1990s is based on the doctrine of subordination of the Indian state to global capitalist-cum-imperialist countries. The whole programme of structural adjustment and control over fiscal deficit has been carried out by the Indian state at the behest of capital exporting countries of the North and the global institutions like the International Monetary Fund, and World Bank. It is imperative to find out *social explanations* for India becoming a willing candidate for global integration. The leading strata of the Big Bourgeoisie is actively supporting the New Economic Policy because if transnational corporations are entering the Indian market, the Indian Big Business is also going abroad to launch its own businesses either through investments or acquisitions. Tata Steel is working on mergers and acquisitions in China, South East Asia, Far East for the emerging markets of Rs. 25,000 crore where demand for steel is potentially possible. "In the next few years, global demand for steel will come mainly from China and the Southeast Asian countries. It is hence important for us to establish a presence in these regions." "We are not looking at acquiring small units : Tata Steel has already begun (to look) in some of these countries for available opportunities."[51]

If Tatas are going abroad for accumulation and profits, Indians are reciprocating it by allowing foreign investors in its own firms. 'FIIs now own an average of 30% stake in 10 top Indian Corporates, reflecting the growing role of foreign investors in driving investments. Their stake in the top 50 companies is now put at an average of more than 17.5% up from 15% just two years back." Further, Morgan Stanley informs that foreign institutional investors "have pumped in over US $1 billion in mid-cap stocks, allocating nearly 36% of total inflows to the smaller cap companies."[52]

The Tata Motors have also tied up with Daewoo commercial vehicles, Korea, and signed the 'acquisition' of company for US $118 million.[53] The Reliance group, the Aditya Birla group, and IT companies like Wipro and HCL *et al.* are scouting for business in foreign markets. It is estimated that Indian Corporate businessmen have invested US $1048.78 million (Rs. 4,813 crore) abroad during 2002-2003 as reported by the Reserve Bank of India on September 30, 2003.[54]

The Indian Commerce and Industry Secretary R.R. Shah informed the Indian Economic Summit organised jointly by the World Economic Forum and CII on November 24, 2003 that the 'acquisition' by Indian companies abroad during the last three and half years involved nearly 124 companies. Warning the Indian Big Business, D.S. Brar, Ranbaxy Laboratories CEO&MD, said it means nothing if 'domestic strength' of a company is weak. He said : "In India we are used to a lot of short cuts to get our work done but such measures would not deliver in other countries. This is one area where we can stumble in the global market."[55]

Here is a testimonial from a representative of capitalist class that in the age of globalisation, 'state and capital' get fully integrated and the corporate houses achieve free entry to the corridors of political and bureaucratic decision-makers, and so, Karl Marx is vindicated that the state is an executive agency of the bourgeoisie including global ruling classes. The Foreign Financial Institutional Investors are full of liquidity and they have pumped Rs. 23,000 crore into Indian Equity market.[56]

A timely warning has been given by T.N. Ninan to globalised India that "This year's stock market boom has been fuelled essentially by the dramatic increase in FII inflows, a consequence of the excess money sloshing around in the rest of the world." But how many among us understand the drivers of this global liquidity, which determines our stock prices? As the international hedge funds have moved in for the first time, India's stock market could get more volatile. "So, it matters to Indian businessmen and investors what is the rate of recovery in the US,......... These changes reflect the changes in the corporate sector. Between a third and a half of the 100 largest American corporations have set up their tents in India; a decade ago, there would have been barely 10 or 15 of the top 100. Our largest companies in some field are now Korean (white and brown goods). All but one or two (crore) companies are foreign-owned. So when Daewoo goes belly up in Korea, Indians lose their jobs in UP. Insurance, telecommunication and other sectors have been opened up, the international presence is significant, if not dominant."[57]

The implications of global integration of India are clear. Any crisis in the centre of capitalism would have very adverse and serious consequences for India. It should not be forgotten that the much maligned Nehru-Mahalanobis model of planned economy, saved India from 'debt trap' of the 1970s when 'oil shock' pushed almost every developing country under the burden of 'debt'. A little less globally integrated India escaped the adverse impacts of East Asian crisis of 1997. Globalisation has increased the vulnerability of Indian market to external economic crisis. The Mark & Spencer closed its shops in Paris, France, and the French workers employed by Mark & Spencer were shown the door and it was left to the Parisian workers to fend for themselves. Foreign firms can withdraw from the 'host' country without notice. Alongwith Indian big business, new entrepreneurial strata of the bourgeoisie are supporters of global integration of India because it has opened new opportunities for lucrative profits and incomes for them. The upwardly mobile entrepreneurial, and business managerial class, the product of the institutes of technology, the institutes of managements and business, are a very critical social constituency for the integration of India with global capitalism. Not only this.

The entrepreneurial and business managerial strata of the bourgeoisie attitudinally love to imitate American life styles and socially feel happy to identify themselves with the American material comforts of life. They are socially delinked with the India of artisans, factory or farm workers or daily wage earners, i.e., the Wretched of the Earth of Fanon. While bourgeoisie is going global, the middle class professionals in bureaucracy, media, advertisement and intelligentsia is behaving like typical 'moneyed middle class' whose sole goal is to maximise incomes. In every Third World country, the middle classes exercise great influence over every level of social power and the rising Indian middle class has abandoned every important social project in preference to 'money making' project including 'voluntary sector' (the NGOs) which has also become profitable for the greedy middle class. Since 'accumulation' has become the sole goal of the lower middle class the petit bourgeoisie and the big bourgeoisie, these sole beneficiaries of globalisation are social legitimisers of the global integration of India.[58]

India Sitting on a Time Bomb

It deserves to be stated that the Indian ruling classes are enthusiastically integrating themselves in world capitalist system from a position of weakness and any weak peripheral capitalist country is certain to become victim of very powerful imperialist exploiters.

The first weakness of the Indian capitalist system lies in its 'underdeveloped' character which is proved by the limited resource base of the Indian state. The revenue collection from income tax and corporate tax is estimated as Rs. 1,35,000 crore[59] for 2004-05. The Central Board of Direct Taxes reported that tax payer base is expected to post a 22 per cent growth to touch 5 crore payers in 2004-05.[60] If 50 million out of a population of one billion are in the tax net of the Central Government of India, its serious fiscal weakness is quite clear. If income tax, excise tax, customs tax and corporate tax are not yielding enough fiscal resources for the Indian state, it has direct implications for the state and the national economy. It is not only that the Indian capitalist state has its serious domestic fiscal weaknesses, in the decade of 1990s, it was under great pressure from powerful countries of the North to reduce its tariff rates and income tax rates. At the India-ASEAN free trade meeting the World Bank directed India to lower its tariff and remove non- tariff barriers. The World Bank consultant Garry Pursell observed : "India has to bring down its tariff drastically before it signs the FTA with ASEAN".[61] India is not only expected to lower its tariff rates, it is not allowed even to raise its income tax rates because neo-classical liberal economic policy promoters are for the downward revision of income tax as practiced by George Bush Jr. of the United States. Mukul G. Asher observes : "Globalisation and international trends have substantially curtailed the autonomy of the Asian countries to raise income tax rates. Intense competition brought about by excess capacity and deflationary tendencies are likely to restrain profit shares in national income in most Asian countries. This avenue therefore also will not be available for mobilising additional resources."[62] In this new globalised regime of fiscal ideology, the Indian State will be always compelled to follow the suit and implement the taxation and tariff policies as suggested by the capitalist countries of the North.

The second structural weakness of Indian economy is 'demand constraint' because it has not been able to deepen and broaden its market for production and consumption. India remains primarily an agrarian country and if the economic health of rural society is not sound, 'demand constraint' will remain a specific feature of India which will put a brake over its total economy. D.H. Pai Panandikar informs that "Agriculture contributes about 25 per cent to our GDP. This is not so in other emerging economies which have already left agriculture way behind and depend mainly on exports to drive industrial growth." Panandikar continues : "Since 1996 both agriculture and industry have lost steam, the first because the demand emanating from the agricultural sector was not enough to support larger industrial production. Agriculture will remain a bottleneck for industrial growth."[63]

Third, the decade of 1990s has witnessed neglect of rural India because gross capital formation in agriculture and Allied sector has declined interestingly in a few years of the 1990s and it is the private investment which has outstripped the public investment in rural capital formation.

Table 7.2: Gross Capital Formation in Agriculture and Allied Sector (at 1993-94 prices)

	Public Sector	*Private Sector*	*Total (Rs. Crore)*
1981-82	7130	6499	14079
1991-92	4346	10589	14965
2000-01	4520	14931	19451
Pre-reform (Average)	6212	8289	14502
Post-reform (Average)	4777	12589	17366

Source: Department of Agriculture and Cooperation, GOI.

The above Table clearly tells us that the situation between 'pre-reform' and 'post-reform' period is different. In 1981-82 public sector investment led private sector in agrarian capital formation, but from 1991-92 to 2000-01 the private sector investments were leading. Such an investment has its own priorities for its own specific needs. While Indian agrarian weaknesses are growing, the doctrine of structural adjustment and control over fiscal deficit is directed against the 'regime of subsidies' at a time when developed capitalist countries practice huge subsidies for their agriculture. The Cancun Conference of the World Trade Organisation 2003 brought into sharp focus this aspect of International Farm Economy where only 3-4 percent of total European Union–American population is in the farm sector, and these farmers get domestic and export subsidies amounting to US $300 billion. Allan Wheatley observes : "Rich countries spend some US $300 billion a year on farm subsidies, about six times more than on development aid. The European Union Cow is the most pampered....The United States funnels more than $3 billion a year in subsidies to its cotton farmers, three times its aid to Africa."[64] The rice producers of Japan and the cotton producers of America get 700 per cent subsidency in US $3 billion subsidy respectively in a world where 2.7 billion poor people have to live on an average of US $2 a day or less.

Fourth, the inherent logic of the pattern of growth in India under the new globalised capitalist system is leading to alarming levels of social inequality and the minority of the consuming very rich, upper middle class and the petit bourgeoisie live in an island of vast destitute and deprived social setting. The social distinction between the minority population which has control over surpluses and the absolute majority of the labouring classes gets widened when the state abandons its role of social equaliser, and this reality of great social inequality has emerged with new vengeance. Lijee Philip divides social classes into three categories : "Consuming 'n' very rich, aspirants class and the destitute class", and he maintains that the first two class categories will remain the key focus for consumption of most consumer products. It is maintained that during the financial year 2002 the consuming class contributed to 29 per cent of incomes of Indian household which is set to increase to 40 per cent in financial year 2007. While the climbers class (Rs. 20,000 to Rs. 45,000) will remain stagnant at 40 per cent. The aspirants and the destitute classes see a decline from 16 per cent and 13 per cent to 9 per cent and 8 per cent respectively. Further, by financial year 2007, income levels of 85 million will be a little more than US $5000.[65]

Alongwith growing social inequality and disparity in the regime of free competitive market economy, the employment position for the unskilled workers, who are a majority of the Indian work force is creating serious social discontent in the country. Under the caption 'Demolishing myth' *The Economic Times* made a plea for the need for an increase in public investment in the country : "It is equally, if not more, important that employment opportunities for unskilled workers grow as well. Unfortunately, thanks to policy-induced rigidities in our labour market, liberalisation has seen a sharp fall in employment in the organised sector. With the share of agriculture in GDP falling over 20 per cent this has meant larger and larger numbers becoming dependent on smaller and smaller share of the economic pie. Inevitably, income disparities will grow and with that, social unrest, unless public investment comes to the rescue by creating demand for unskilled labour."[66]

Alas, the state is not listening to these warning signals and 'unemployment related riots' have already begun in the country.[67]

The Decade of 1990s: Emergence of Right Wing Politics and Social Violence

The above description clearly validates the argument that a State, which is under dictations from the global capitalists and domestic strata of exploiting classes, has created a social situation which is volatile and violent protests. It is a well known fact that deep economic crisis either leads to the emergence of rightwing fascist/authoritarian politics or anarchic violence by disorganised deprived social groups. The forces of Hindutva have exploited this explosive social situation to win over the 'unemployed' and the street urchins to defend Hinduism against its enemies. If the ideology of Hindutva has found a fertile social soil for growth in a highly discontented society, many disorganised groups are also indulging in politics of bullet.

Social Violence in India

The greatest challenge to the democratic state of India has emerged from powerful individuals, Mafia groups, land grabbers and phoney pretenders of ideologies of religion or communist revolution who believe that instead of democratic dialogue, disputes will be settled with the power of gun. Any minor dispute between any two communities or between the police forces and a crowd immediately creates a violent situation as it happened in Bihar on January 3, 2003, when people came on the roads to protest against the killings of three young men by the Bihar police in an alleged 'fake encounter'. Bihar witnessed large-scale violence which was 'spontaneous' because people perceived that the so-called democratically elected Government follows 'undemocratic' methods to deal with its citizens. L.K. Advani, the Home Minister of India, observed on December 24, 2002, before the BJP Executive that India was facing serious threats from Islamic Terrorism and Left Extremism because both these groups practiced the politics of bullet and pretended to believe in an ideology which justifies the role of violence in society. Trinath Mishra, the Director General of Central Reserve Police Forces, observed on December 26, 2002 that "Left wing terrorism poses a bigger threat than Islamic terrorism. It has its roots in social and economic issues, and is, therefore, much more difficult to put down. Left wing extremism will only spread and grow." The CRPF D.G. Mishra identified 'nine states' like Orissa, Andhra Pradesh, Bihar, Maharashtra, Jharkhand, Chhattisgarh, Madhya Pradesh and West Bengal where the Left Extremist groups like the Maoist Communist Centre or People's War Groups are taking recourse to violence while dealing with their perceived 'enemies' whether exploiters of the poor or oppressive state functionaries. President A.P.J. Abdul Kalam, while addressing the Governors of the Indian States on January 11, 2003, asked them to play a "*positive role*" in bringing about unity of minds and he asked everyone "to collectively fight and eliminate communal differences and insurgency in the country". Thus, public policy-makers are concerned with the growth of social violence on the basis of ideologies which believe in dividing the society or by groups and individuals who gain personal benefits in an atmosphere of general and large-scale social violence.

An important issue which has emerged in public discourse is about the role of 'foreign supported cross-border terrorism' in Jammu and Kashmir or in some other states of India. But we have also to consider 'domestic factors' which give birth to serious social discontent, deprivation and alienation and create a hospitable social situation for violent group activity. The Sangh Parivar has identified Pakistan as the 'nerve centre of Islamic terrorism' and L.K. Advani, as Home Minister, has committed the Government of India to fight against Pakistan supported violent Islamic activities in our country. This is an unexceptionable position because a neighbouring country's state cannot be allowed to destabilise Indian society by arming violent groups in the name of religion and *Jihad*. Not only this. A complete national consensus exists that Pakistan's inspired cross-border terrorism has to be effectively contained with the help of the Indian security apparatuses. Difficulties arise when the Sangh Parivar and the BJP governments make the threat of Islamic terrorism as their single point political agenda because of their own ideological position where Pakistan's involvement gets equated with anti-Indian Muslim agenda.

An active and persistent involvement of Pakistan's Inter-State Intelligence agencies (ISI) in spreading violence in India is recognised and accepted by every political formation but identifying, without any evidence, the involvement of ISI and Muslim *Jihadis* in the burning of railway compartment at Godhra on 27 February, 2002 was enough to burn Gujarat. Communal riots were the logical product of Sangh Parivar's statements about 'Muslim Community' beginning from February 28, 2002. A country which has a Muslim population of more than 150 million cannot remain peaceful and free from violence if every activity of the Pakistan State has to be equated with the conduct of Indian Muslims. Why should the Indian Muslims as citizens of this country be accountable for the misdeeds and misconduct of Muslims in any other country, including Pakistan? Why should the Hindus of India be held responsible if any Hindu violates the law in some other country? The tragic events of Godhra and post-Godhra violence remain relevant for the analysis of Sangh Parivar's attitude towards Indian Muslims because distrust of Muslim community gets extended to violence against the community. Hence it came as a surprise when the Prime Minister, Atal Bihari Vajpayee, observed on December 16, 2002, while celebrating BJP's electoral victory in Gujarat that "It saddens me that not many from the Muslim community are stepping forward to say that they are repentant for Godhra. Even now no one (from Muslims) is saying that whatever happened was wrong and that we have to live together". If a Prime Minister has such feelings, in spite of the fact that many Muslim organisations had condemned the Godhra tragedy of February 27, 2002, one can imagine the attitude of Bajrang Dal or Vishwa Hindu Parishad or RSS towards the Muslims in Gujarat.

The upshot of above description is that India has become violent society because the foundational principle of Islamic or Hindu fundamentalism is around the politics of targeting the opposite religious community. The Islamic fundamentalists believe in their religious superiority and it is inherent in their logic of religious Puritanism that believers of other religions like Hindus or Christians have to be taught a lesson because they are 'religious enemies'. This logic applies also to Hindu fundamentalists who publicly charcterise Muslims as *Jihadis* and enemies of Hindus. Further, Pakistan can create difficulties for India in Jammu and Kashmir or in some other cities, but if the social climate within India is hospitable, inter-religious violence cannot take place. The 'external' factor in the creation of violence in Indian society is not sufficient to institutionalise inter-community violence or regular violent confrontations between the security forces of the Indian State and groups which believe in the doctrine of violence. This is true even in Kashmir where Pakistan is actively involved but no Indian Muslim group has volunteered to be a *Jihadi* in Kashmir. Local discontent is a necessary condition for the success of foreign inspired violent terrorism. Mufti Mohammed Sayeed, who is himself involved in the battle in J&K as Chief Minister, observed on January 8, 2003, that "..., one should not blame the other side always. It is we who have to address the internal dimensions. We have to address the alienation of people. We have to try and win the hearts and minds of the people... If the internal discontent was over, no force can ignite the fire from outside." Indira Gandhi as Prime Minister had popularised the conspiracy theory of 'foreign hand' for every difficult problem of India but it was sheer escapism from domestic challenges to her government.

Moreover, religious-based political ideology is not the only 'mother' of social violence. The Naxalite groups, who are openly following the path of violence, are the product of social-economic conditions in the states which have a large discontented 'tribal population' or states which have neglected the rural poor. The Naxalite groups (like the MCC or PWG) have not achieved legitimacy in the whole of India. This question has to be answered. It is a well known fact that Bihar has an 'unfinished' agenda of land reforms and the oppressor and the oppressed groups and classes are confronting one another with private armies. The state of Bihar is witnessing the phenomenon of emergence of '*State within State*' where opposite groups are involved in their own violent battles and democratically elected state has been completely marginalised in dealing with the politics of bullet. There is no 'foreign hand' or 'external factor' in the violence-ridden society of Bihar because Naxal groups are products of pure 'Swadeshi' social milieu based on institutionalised system of social injustice. Vinod Mishra, an authentic Naxal leader, made a statement that 'violence' cannot bring agrarian transformation and he abandoned the path of violence for the resolution of agrarian restructuring. If in spite of such a realisation by a tall Naxal leader, Naxal groups are still busy in confronting the state police forces and indulging in the politics of bullet versus bullet, the explanation lies in the prevailing social inequalities. A mix of law and order approach and social programme for the eradication of poverty of the exploited classes can effectively contain the Naxalite violence. A visit to tribal belts in Orissa or Bastar in Chhattisgarh or in Madhya Pradesh etc. will clearly show that the tribals are victims of a nexus between local politicians, local bureaucrats and contractors and hapeless tribal men and women have become victims at the hands of this powerful Mafia and Naxal groups are able to play on the emotions of the *Wretched of the Earth.*

Further, non-ideological violence in urban areas has increased because every big city has 'islands of prosperity' and 'ghethoised slum or quasi-slum population'. A large-scale semi-working class migrant population is an important segment of population of every urban city. It is not "*A Tale of Two Cities*" of *Charles Dickens* but of many cities in each mega city. In such a situation social discontent is the order of the day. Urban social discontent arising out of growth in the number of poor migrants and 'pockets of richness' can be contained if public services are efficient and service-oriented. In the 'age' of privatisation of public services their 'affordability' is the only criterion and in such a situation the majority of urban poor are left to depend on their own very meagre personal and individual resources. It is a socially volcanic situation and any rumour regarding the destruction of a mosque or a Dargah or a Temple or the killing of a cow brings lumpen groups on the streets who express their own frustrations by killing others. Joseph E. Stiglitz in his seminal work on '*Globalisation and its Discontents*' (2002) warns governments that "adverse social situation leads to civil strife". Stiglitz observes that : "Civil strife in Africa has been a major factor setting back its development agenda. Studies at the World Bank show that such strife is systematically related to adverse economic factors including unemployment that can be produced by excessive austerity. Moderate inflation may not be ideal for creating an environment for investment but violence and civil strife are even worse".

In summation it may be suggested that efficient coercive apparatus of the state is not the only answer to the growing levels of multidimensional social violence in India where democratic elections cannot be held without large-scale presence of para-military forces. It is a warning to the Indian ruling classes that ideologies of religious hatred and social divide have given birth to social violence, and combined with socio-economic discontent prevailing in the country India has become a headquarter of domestic social violence. Religion is a private affair and public services are meant for building a just social order. This is the only recipe for Indians if they wish to protect democracy from crowd or mob indulging in violence in the name of religion or economic deprivation. Undettered by the right wing authoritarian forces of Hindutva, the Hindu unemployed indulged in a riot against Hindus. India is sitting on a volcano which is already erupting.

Riot of the Unemployed

The self-appointed ideologues of *Akhand Bharat*, i.e., believers of one culture, one nation and one country, miserably failed to tackle November 2003 violence in Bihar and Assam which was caused by serious public policy actions of the Central government. The Central government completely failed to understand the grave social implications of growing 'unemployment' in the country when it received more than 70 lakh applications for only 38,000 railway jobs in the 'D' category. The very fact that the railways received 70 lakh applications for limited openings should have alerted any democratic government to realise the gravity of unemployment situation in the country and any competitive examination for such a limited number of opportunities had the potential and possibilities of generating social conflicts and discord among seven million candidates spread over the whole of India. Not only this. The BJP-led central government always makes tall claims about running a coalition government of one major party along with 24 regional parties and groups but it is extremely sad that such a government does not understand the specific serious economic problems of backward states and regions of India and a policy for recruitment is announced without taking political precautions to deal with any inter-regional conflict among the backward regions where opportunities for jobs are very scarce and limited. Since the central government did not prepare itself to deal with any abnormal situation which was likely to arise because of very volatile social situation in backward states, the very first test held for 'D' category jobs on November 9, 2003, led to a chain of violence.

A few facts may be mentioned to substantiate the argument that the Indian political class simply failed to rise to the occasion to deal with emotive issues around '*identity*' because the first warning had come on November 9, and it was a Napoleonic blunder of the Indian state that the killings and violence against ethnic groups had continued for three weeks. First, on the very first day at Guwahati 2 lakh candidates from the whole of India, especially Bihar, came to appear for the examination. Since the local unemployed youth thought that the jobs would go out of their hand if the '*outsiders*' were allowed to grab them, they reacted violently against the outside competitors. Second, the moment violence began the Railways and the Government of India, as guardians of an all-India national labour market, completely failed to protect either the Assamese travelling through Bihar or Bihar candidates who had gone to appear in the examination to Mumbai. While irritated and angry persons who returned from Guwahati to Bihar, ransacked the railway passengers of the North-East in the train, the Shiv Sainiks captured all trains leading to Mumbai and tore away the 'examination letters' of candidates from Bihar and all candidates from Bihar were packed back from Mumbai. It deserves to be stated that neither the Rabri Devi government nor the Gogoi's government are responsible for creating an atmosphere of inter-ethnic hate, but the Shiv Sena, which is a partner of the Vajpayee-led National Democratic Alliance at the centre, directly contributed to Maharashtrian versus Bihari discord on Railway's recruitment. It is for the Prime Minister to answer about his political association with regional chauvinists like the Shiv Sainiks.

It has 'been a great achievement that during the last fifty-five years of post-independence India Article 16 of the Constitution which guarantees employment rights of every Indian '*irrespective of place of birth*' of any citizen has been gradually implemented. The Supreme Court of India has also put its seal of approval that all-India jobs are for everyone irrespective of region or state or city of birth. It is a great success of Indian democratic national-integration process that in every long distant train, peoples from different regions are travelling from their homes to distant places for work. Every metropolis, every industrial, commercial and specific commodity production city like diamonds work in Surat or small shopkeepers in Kohima, is an evidence of mixed populations from far off places. Migration always raises difficult issues, because social and cultural 'dissimilarities' lead to social reluctance for mutual acceptability by diverse ethnic groups and India has enough experience of dealing with inter-ethnic conflicts.

Further, regional identity is a real fact of plural and diverse India and national politics has to create hospitable conditions for inter-regional harmony and fraternity. If on the one hand regional chauvinists have been playing the politics of 'sons of the soil' on the other, the national leadership has tried to create a complex network of 'accommodative' federalism. Region and nation in a multi-regional and multicultural country get integrated only if interdependencies are strengthened and this is precisely the role of the Central Government of India and whenever social fabric breaks down and a situation of region versus region emerges, it is only the Central Government which has to provide healing touch and intervene positively and effectively in intra-region and inter-regional conflicts. The Vajpayee government totally failed to deal with anti-Bihari violence in

Assam. It is sad to mention that neither the Prime Minister nor the Home Minister of India, *the 'political face' of Indian nationhood*, felt the need to visit the troubled and disturbed Assam to give a clear 'political message' that the whole nation stands behind the victims of ethnic violence.

It is not a new discovery of India that the United Liberation Front of ASOM (ULFA) or National Democratic Front of Bodoland (NDFB) would be happy to fish in any troubled waters, and it is also well known that extreme chauvinists like ASOM Gana Parishad would also play with fire and it is not surprising to secular national forces that the local BJP of Assam would try to make it Hindu versus Muslim issues and link it with their anti-Bengali and anti-Bangladeshi plank of political platform in Assam. The most shocking statements came from the State Minister of Home Affairs, and the BJP President Venkaiah Naidu that Bangladeshis are involved in current anti-Bihari violence in Assam. Is Bal Thackeray a Bangladeshi who is also creating anti-Bihari sentiments in Maharashtra? It goes to the credit of much maligned Lalu Prasad Yadav who rushed to Guwahati and met migrant workers and addressed intellectuals on November 25, 2003. Lalu Prasad gave a clear political message that in Bihar, the anti-Assamese mischief was curbed in one day, and the Bihari migrant labourers like push-cart pullers, milkmen, masons, barbers, cobblers et al have been serving the Assamee society for generations and all of us are workers. After this appeal, Lalu in Guwahati "...warned for the upteenth time that if violence against Biharis in Assam continued then the state may have to starve for essential items as truckers will not come here in fear." The Centre and state government of Assam are busy in mutual blame game, while the need of the hour was for the Centre to understand the special semi-disturbed situation of the Assamee society where a claustrophobic attitude exists for the 'outsiders' and any trouble spot in Assam has always taken a violent turn.

The All Assam Student Union is continuing with a struggle for the reservation of all-India jobs for the 'locals.' Is it the way to build a nation of great diversities and pluralities? The Sangh Parivar and its political arm, the BJP should get a clear message from the sad and tragic events of November 2003 that their definition of Hindu Rashtra is completely flawed because real Indian nationalism is based on a 'sentiment of living together' by multi-cultural, multi-lingual, multi-religious and multi-regional communities. A government which does not accept this real definition cannot be democratically responsive to diverse needs and sentiments of the peoples of India. The explanation for the complete failure of the Vajpayee government to mediate successfully among people from Bihar, Assam and Maharashtra flows from their understanding that Indians do not have very diverse goals and aspirations which are defined by their specific religion, or region, or language or culture. Globalisation, liberalisation and privatisation of economy during the decade of 1990s has helped in the growth of highly skilled jobs in information technology, automobile industry or other service sector of economics. India of 1990s has failed to create jobs for the unskilled poor workers, because 'public investment' in the areas of economy which generate jobs for the millions of unskilled labour force has lagged behind the requirements of expanding Indian labour market. In such a grim economic situation, the practitioners of Hindutva will not be able to stop violence by poor Hindus against Hindus whether in Assam or Maharashtra or Bihar.

The only option before the State alongwith the ruling classes, in a situation of serious social turmoil, is either to practice the ideology of Hindutva and play on the insecurities of the majority by making them believe that all social ills are a product of Muslims and Christians of India as Nazis did by targeting the Jews or tinker with democracy and take course to Draconian laws like the Prevention of Terrorist Act. India at the beginning of the Twenty-First Century is witnessing the rapid growth of anti-democratic social and religious forces as a result of deep social crisis created by the current New Economic Policy regime of the 1990s. The Hindutva has consolidated itself by propagating the ideology of 'hate' against minorities and this ideology of the politics of targeting is always of the ruling classes during the phases of serious social discontent. Its carriers are 'village vagabonds' and 'lumpen' elements of towns and cities who are operating under the protective umbrella of the state. The Bajrang Dal, the Vishwa Hindu Parishad, the Shiv Sainiks have attracted the semi-skilled or unskilled frustrated and unemployed army of aggressive and violent youth who have been given an anti-minority cause by the Sangh Parivar. India of the 1990s has witnessed recurring inter-community riots as a result of the ideology of hatred against the minorities practiced and preached by the Sangh Parivar. The divisive ideology of Hindutva is the mother of violence and it also keeps busy the army of lumpens recruited by the Sangh Parivar.

India is witnessing a social logic of globalised capitalism where the 'accumulators' have abandoned the poor and the poor have been rejected by the state, controlled by the exploiting classes. Jeremy Seabrook in '*Ironies of history*' observes: "The global defeat of socialism and the victory of 'globalisation'—that contemporary *avatar* of capitalism and imperialism—led to the 'liberalisation' and 'opening up' of India. Today's young generation is more likely to be studying business studies, a master's in management, personnel or business administration. They have turned away from any sense that the world can, or indeed, needs to be changed, and seek principally personal ambition, their place in an expanding and highly prosperous middle class."[68] In this situation of social Darwinism, it is not surprising that 'the right of the political spectrum' in India has deftly used Hindu religion to pursue their 'antistatist neoliberalism where state power is meant for controlling social discontent through 'regressive ideology' and brute coercive power of military and para-military forces.

NEW GLOBAL CAPITALISM AND DEMOCRATIC STATE

The modern historical epoch of science, technology, communications and information led—capitalism has given birth to its own antagonistic social contradictions. The end of Twentieth Century is witnessing a socially concrete contradiction between transnationalised and globalised capitalism and the nation-state system which is expected to manage public affairs within its own well-defined territorial boundaries. The ongoing process of centralisation and Globalisation of capital has sharpened the cleavages between the powerful state system of the 'Centre' of world capitalism and the 'peripheral' developing capitalist state-system of the post-World War-II decolonised countries. The social contradiction between the real centers of capitalist power and peripheral capitalist state systems has not polarised the capitalist global system into two sharply divided and antagonistic blocs of countries especially after the collapse of the erstwhile East European socialist state systems. On the contrary, it has been suggested that during the 1990s the world has witnessed the triumph of market-led capitalism of the advanced western capitalist countries and every other nation-state has to come to terms with the demands of the capitalist dominated New World Order. Eric Hobsbawm concludes his *Short Twentieth Century* by maintaining that the 'spectre of communism does not haunt Europe'; instead, it is the "spectre of globalisation" that haunts the earth and has raised new doubts about the relevance, role and even the need for nation-state at the end of the Twentieth Century.[69]

A few obvious stylised facts may be mentioned to properly situate the changes that have taken place during the last decade of the Twentieth Century. First, global capitalism has always functioned under the direction and leadership of a dominant capitalist power like the Pax-Britianica before and Pax-Americana after World War-II. Further, the post-World War-II global capitalism has operated on an institutionalised basis for the regulation of global political economy. The major institutions for the management of global political economy are:

(a) The Organisation for Economic Cooperation and Development (OECD);

(b) International Monetary Fund (IMF);
(c) International Bank for Reconstruction and Development (i.e., World Bank);
(d) Commission of European Community;
(e) General Agreement on Trade and Tariffs/World Trade Organisation; and
(f) United Nations Conference on Trade and Development.

Anne O. Krueger informs us that the World Bank, the IMF and the WTO are expected to work in a coherent manner for dealing with global economy. She observes:

> "The World Bank, IMF and WTO are instructed by their governments to achieve 'coherence' in economic policies between trade, financial and development issues, and the WTO has a mandate in this direction."[70]

It is worthwhile to refer here to some of the distinctiveness of the WTO which was the result of Uruguay Round of Multilateral Trade Negotiations which were formally adopted in Marrakesh in April 1994. Every member of the WTO has to accept "in its entirety a common set of rules and disciplines covering goods, services, and intellectual property (the so-called single undertaking)".[71]

The WTO has legal and institutional foundation for enforcement of its decisions on disputes in the area of goods, services and the protection of intellectual property rights. The Article VI of the WTO agreement states: "The General Council shall make appropriate arrangements for effective cooperation with other inter-governmental organisations that have responsibilities related to those of the WTO." While World Bank, IMF and WTO are expected to work together, many other international organisations and agencies operate to regulate global political economy on the basis of agreements made by the nation-state. They are:

(a) World Intellectual Property Organisation;
(b) International Organisation for Standardisation;
(c) Coadex Alimentarious Commission;
(d) International Office of Epizootics; and
(e) International Plant Protection office.

All above organisations have to work in a particular global context which consists of a real center of capitalist economic power and a vast global village of peripheral, under-developed/developing capitalist countries. Democracy, market, civil society, and borderless global village have emerged as the focal point of analysis during the 1990s. This happened because the whole word order built during the post-World War-

II phase of international development collapsed in 1990 because one pole of the polarised cold war bloc politics suddenly collapsed and disappeared and a new world order of non-bloc politics emerged at the global level. These fundamental changes at the global level had their direct bearing on the issues of governance and management of inter-governmental relations especially between the powerful countries of the west and the weak but emerging peripheral nation-states of Asia, Africa and Latin America.

The upshot of above global developments is that the distinction between external and internal or foreign and domestic political processes and institutions for governance has been fully obliterated and a dynamic interaction has come into existence between the politics of western countries and the politics of developing countries. This is a compelling reason and any study of the social essence of democratic state of India during the 1990s will be uncomplete and inadequate without situating it within the dynamics of the new global capitalism of the 1990s. A few illustrations may be given to substantiate that 'powerful capitalist countries' are able to determine and decide many things for or on behalf of the peripheral democratic/authoritarian weak state systems of the 'other' side of the globe.

(a) The election of the WTO Director-General in 1999 resulted in a contest between Mike Moore of New Zealand and Dr. Supachai of Thailand. The US maintained that Mike Moore of New Zealand (the US supported candidate) was more acceptable to the US NGOs, the labour unions and the Congress.[72]

In this contest, the will of the US prevailed and the New Zealander was appointed as Director-General of the Council of WTO. Since, WTO is a "quasi-judicial body, an embryonic world government, whose rulings on world trade are supposed to be binding even on America and European Union", the appointment of Director became a bone of contention in the 1999 elections.

(b) Political power and capacity to decide on behalf of global community is with the western world because of the serious 'unequal' nature of distribution of economic power among the nation-states.

UNDP informs us that, ... "between 1960 and 1991 the share of the richest 20 percent rose from 70 percent of global income to 85 percent while of the poorest declined from 2.3 percent to 1.47 percent". And by 1999 the poor "more than 85 percent of the world's population received only 15 percent of its income" and "the net worth of the 358 richest people, the dollar billionaires, is equal to the combined income of the poorest 45 percent of the world population 2.3 billion people".[73]

(c) With the collapse of the erstwhile USSR, its Warsaw Pact also came to end, the Western Countries under the leadership of United States have strengthened their collective military might under the expanded North Atlantic Treaty Organisation. The United Nations and its Security Council have become 'handmaidens' of the Western Countries as dramatised during the events of Kosovo and East Timor. The State sovereignty of Serbia and Indonesia was ignored and decisions were taken by the Western states with rubber stamp of the Security Council of the UNO. The growing military power of the Western-led NATO has attracted many erstwhile East European countries to become its members. Hungary, Poland and Czechoslovakia have been admitted in this military club.

(d) The new global capitalism of the 1990s is characterised by the mobility of finance (or capital) and the main actors are supra-state transnational organisations which are also establishing production bases in the peripheral capitalist countries for inter-firm and intra-firm export and trade purposes.

The Table 7.3 clearly tells us that there is a great concentration of capital/finance, trade and technology with supra-national corporations with whom peripheral nation-states have to negotiate and bargain from a position of weakness. This is the reason that Human Development Report, 1999, has attracted attention to some of the startling features of new global capitalism whose impact is felt by the democratic state of India.

These facts may be re-capitulated for the purpose of framing an analytical structure for study of the impact of new developments on Indian democracy:

(a) "More than US 1.5 trillion dollars circulate in the world's currency markets each day. Finance capital is the moving force behind new global capitalism of the 1990s".

(b) Since global capital is concentrated in G-7 countries like United States, Canada, France, Germany, England, Australia and Japan and their transnational Corporations, inequalities between countries have increased. Human Development Report of 1999 states: "The income gap between the fifth of world's people living in the richest countries and the fifth of the poorest was 74 to 1 in 1997, up from 60 to 1 in 1990."[74]

(c) "OECD countries with 19 percent of the global population, have 71 percent of global trade in goods and services, 58 percent of foreign direct investment and 91 percent of all internet users."

Table 7.3: World Top Twenty TNCs

Corporation	*Country*	*Industry*	*Total*	*Foreign*	*Total*	*Foreign*
General Electric	USA	Electricals	272.4	82.8	79.1	21.1
Shell Royal Dutch*	USA	Petroleum	124.1	82.1	128.3	71.1
Ford Motor Company	USA	Automotive	258.0	79.1	147.0	65.8
Exxan Corporation	USA	Petroleum	095.5	55.6	117.0	102.0
General Motors	USA	Automotive	222.1	55.4	158.0	50.0
IBM	USA	Computers	081.1	41.4	75.9	46.6
Toyota	Japan	Automotive	113.4	39.2	109.2	51.7
Volkswagen Group	Germany	Automotive	060.8	–	109.3	51.7
Mitsubishi Corporation	Japan	Diversified	77.9	–	64.4	41.0
Mobil Corporation	USA	Petroleum	46.4	31.3	80.4	53.1
Nestle SA	Switzerland	Food	34.0	30.9	42.8	42.0
Asea Brown Boveri	Switzerland	Electrical Equip	30.9	–	33.8	32.9
Eif Aquitaine SA	France	Petroleum	47.5	29.3	44.8	26.6
Bayer AG	Germany	Chemicals	32.0	29.1	31.4	25.8
Hoechst AG	Germany	Chemicals	35.5	28.0	33.8	18.4
Nissan Motor Co. Ltd.	Japan	Automotive	58.1	27.0	53.8	29.2
Flat Spa	Italy	Automotive	70.6	26.9	51.3	19.8
Unilever	Netherlands UK	Food	31.0	26.4	52.2	45.0
Daimler-Benz AG Philips	Germany	Automotive	65.7	–	70.6	44.4
Electronic NV	Netherlands	Electronics	31.7	24.5	40.9	38.9

* Foreign sales are outside Europe.

" Foreign assets and sales are outside the UK and the Netherlands.

*** Data on foreign assets are either suppressed to avoid disclosure or they are not available in case of non-availability, they are estimated on the basis of the ratio of foreign total sales or similar ratios.

Source: UNCTAD, Human Development Report/II

(d) The world's 200 richest people more than doubled their net worth in the four years to 1998, to more than US $1 trillion. The assets of the top three billionaires are more than the combined GNP of all least developed countries and their 600 million people.

(e) "The recent wave of mergers and acquisitions is concentrating industrial power in mega-corporations at the risk of eroding competition. By 1998 the top 10 companies in pesticides controlled 85 percent of a US $131 billion dollar global market, and the top 10 in telecommunications 86 percent of a US $262 billion dollar market."

(f) "In 1993 just 10 countries accounted for 84 percent of global research and development expenditures and controlled 95 percent of the US patents of the past two decades. Moreover, more than 80 percent of patents granted in developing countries belong to residents of industrial countries."[75]

(g) "Foreign direct investment topped US $400 billion in 1997, seven times the level in real terms of the 1970s."

(h) "International bank lending grew from US $265 billion in 1975 to US $4.2 trillion in 1994."

Global inequality has become quite acute at the close of the Twentieth Century because of the current capitalist mode of development, and this structural inequality of power between the few developed centers of capitalism and a large majority of peripheral developing capitalist state systems has changed the whole agenda of contemporary discourse where the very relevance of nation-state as a center of decision-making for national management has become questionable. Pearson Commission had attracted the attention of developed countries by pointing out that "the widening gap between the developed and the developing countries has become the central problem of our times" and this gap has been further widened because of the concentration of finance capital in a 'few capitalist countries.'[76]

Dynamics of Democratic State of India: Domestic Scene

India was structurally linked with world capitalism as a British colony, and the new state of India after independence from the colonial rule on August 15, 1947 launched its journey for the making of an economically developed country on the basis of active state involvement for dealing with the present and future of country. India adopted a path of economic development on the basis of 'import substitution industrialisation' which was directed and managed by the Indian state. Social and political explanations for state-led model of economic development of India may be mentioned for understanding the rationale behind state-led capitalist development of the country. Indian state earned its democratic legitimacy by organising participatory and competitive elections on the basis of universal adult franchise based on secret ballot and multi-party system. Democratic legitimacy of the state strengthened its functionaries while dealing with local capitalist, industrial, entrepreneurial and landlord classes of the country. Indian state became relatively autonomous of the power of social classes and strata of society because it was based on democratic verdict of the people who wanted the state functionaries to implement development agenda for the whole society. Since the new state of independent India had emerged after struggling against British colonialism, the leaders of new state acted as jealous guardians of their new freedoms from foreign intervention and for this, they adopted a "relatively autonomous path of self-reliant economic development" on the basis of negotiated transactions with global capitalist countries.

Democratic state of India followed a path of relative autonomy from the local and global centers of power and it successfully laid down the foundations of heavy industries, machine tools, steel plants, heavy electricals, petro-chemicals and others from 1947 to 1970. Such a path of relative self-reliant development could not have been smooth because the need for investible capital and technology could not have been met only by domestic resource mobilisational capability. Further, democratic state of India had to organise policies for the distribution of the gains of economic development across varying social classes and strata of society. The Indian dream was shattered when a Ford Foundation study by Rath and Dandekar on Poverty in India, came to a sad conclusion that the fruits of economic development have not reached the poor and the belief of the public policy makers that social benefits of development will 'trickle down' to the poor sections of society failed to come true. Since the 1970s, ambivalence emerged in social thinking about the path of state-led capitalist development followed by the country and ad hoc solutions were worked to jump over the balance of payments crisis. In 1991. the leaders of Indian state opted to follow a new path of capitalist development because the 'old state-led path' had come to a grinding halt and the country was involved in a serious balance of payments crisis. It is sheer coincidence that the Indian crisis of the 1990s came on the global scene at a time when the new global capitalist order of the 1990s had emerged in a triumphant manner by proclaiming that 'market-led democratic state' can manage public affairs and the old state centred model of development had been proved wrong. The global capitalist order of the 1990s projected the ideology of political democracy and replacement and displacement of the state by the 'market'. While the 1960s social science of the western countries struggled with the identification of social pre-requisites for democracy (Lipset 1958), in the 1990s western scholars like Huntington (1991) were writing about the onward march of successful democracy and the demise of communism, and state-led economic development.[77]

India-met with all the requirements of democracy as proclaimed by the Western capitalist countries because Huntington suggested that "Alternation of parties is a good index of consolidation of democracy"[78] and Prizeworski (1991) suggested that the real test of a democracy is "a system in which parties loose elections."[79]

India has regularly held highly competitive elections and political parties have alternated smoothly in holding reins of power and the verdict of the ballot has been always respected by every major contender for power. The only point of departure in the Indian perspective from the neo-liberal economic ideology of world capitalism of 1990s was the role of state in economic development. The Indian model of the engagement of the democratic state in the shaping of 'present' and 'future' of the country was challenged by the supporters of the ideology of market regulation of economy. The World Bank brought out its *World Development Report* of 1997 dealing with "The State in a Changing World"[80] in which it brought the debate into sharp focus on 'state-led' and "market-led" models of development. India has witnessed three phases of liberalisation in 1966-68, 1985-87 and in post-1991. The last phase is a break with the past because state regulation of economy has become villain of the piece for the exporters of neo-liberal ideology. of market and the Indian supporters of 'state-failure' in India who succeeded with plea for deregulation, Globalisation and privatisation for the capitalist development of India during the 1990s.[81]

It needs to be emphasised here that the ideologically loaded new globalised capitalism found great acceptance in India because the 'crisis' of 1991 provided a fertile social ground for "external" and 'internal' social groups to promote the ideology of an open national economy based on 'market autonomy' and abandon the old path of relative autonomous state acting as a leader of economic development of the country with a capacity to negotiate with foreign capital exporting countries on the basis of maintaining a defence of relative national sovereignty of India. In the 1960s, Geogre Wood, President of the World Bank, organised a mission, known as Bell Mission, to persuade India to "free up the industrial sector, to free up prices and allow market incentives to work". Then this prescription of the aid World Bank did not carry conviction with the leaders of Indian state.[82]

The critical question is why are the boundaries of the sovereign nation-state of India are getting dissolved in the sea of global capital flows and ideology of market-led and business-led economic model of development? Why is the Indian democratic state operating in a 'subordinate' manner while dealing with internationalised financial markets, and technological and financial superpowers of the Western transnational-cooperations? It has been suggested by the supporters of new trends in global capitalism of the 1990s that "no country can opt out of world economic integration because technological and tele-communications revolution has facilitated the creation and establishment of world-wide chains of production". The critical question is: Can Indian state maintain its 'relative autonomy' or get incorporated in the phase of financial centralisation and globalised phase of production? Our analysis is based on a correct observation of Rober Wade (1996) that one should look at the limits of Globalisation because the "Reports of the death of National Economy are greatly Exaggerated".[83]

Indian Democratic State: Sources of its Crisis in 1990s

A few facts may be mentioned which have helped creation of a qualitatively new social situation in India in the 1990s. First, universal adult franchise has played a revolutionary role in the consciousness of Indians who are demanding 'performance' from the leaders of the Indian state. The level of electoral participation in India has incrementally increased from about 45 percent in 1952 Lok Sabha election to over 60 percent to 65 percent in the 1990s. Second, new social groups have become politically and socially very active and they are demanding share in the fruits of economic development, and leaders of the Indian state cannot ignore this new social reality of the 1990s. Third, the share of power of different social classes and groups in state and society has become very unequal because newly emerging and socially assertive groups are witnessing that the capitalist classes, capitalist farmers, traders, merchant classes and entrepreneurial and professional middle classes alongwith the public bureaucracy and political leaders are appropriating the fruits of development and the Indian state is either incapable of protecting the poor and deprived or is integrally linked and incorporated with the dominant social and economic classes and groups.

The economic survey of 1998-99 of the Government of India enlightens us on the levels of inequality and poverty in India. It states that the poverty ratio declined from 56.4 percent in 1973-74 to 37.3 per cent in 1993-94 in rural areas and from 49.0 percent in 1973-74 to 32.4 percent in the 1993-94 in urban areas. For the country as a whole, the poverty ratio declined from 54.9 percent in 1973-74 to 36 percent in 1993-94.[84]

In such a situation of acute poverty and inequality, the role of democratic state has to be central, and crucial because voters expect performance and development with justice and equity. The Ninth Five-Year Plan Document (1997-2002), Volume I, of the Government of India enlightens us at least about the formal objectives of the role of the Indian state at the end of the Twentieth Century. The Economic Planners observe that "Encouragement of the private sector and reliance upon competition and market forces does not imply that the state has no role to play or even that its role in development may be reduced. What is involved is not so much a reduction in the role of the state as a reorientation."[85]

A few facts may be mentioned to substantiate the argument that the "so-called re-orientation of the role of the Indian state" as mentioned above has meant that opening of national economy and decision-making by the Indian state is subject to the pressures of the G-7 countries and global financial centers of power. The democratic state of India is becoming subservient to the powerful Western democratic states and we are moving towards a system of 'superior and subordinate' democratic states in the age of new globalisation of capitalism. A few facts may be mentioned to substantiate our central argument that Indian democratic state is becoming subordinate to western democratic state. First, the Indian state declares itself as "Nuclear Power" after the Pokharan-II of May 1998 and the superior Western democratic states impose 'economic sanctions' because India has violated the global norms of behaviour as decided by the sovereign capitalist states of the West. The Indian government has been actively lobbying before me US for the lifting of economic sanctions against India. The Nuclear Weapon States of the US or Russia or China never paid any attention to the opinions of other states. When President De-Gaulle of France opted for 'Independent Nuclear Status', the decision of the French state was quite autonomous and in opposition to the other nuclear Western countries. The Indian state had to explain to every western country about its decision to explode nuclear device in May 1998. When China of Mao-tse-tung decided to become Nuclear weapon state, the decision was of the Chinese state without any reference to other powerful states. A pillar of democratic state is its capacity to take its own decisions and its accountability is to its own citizens. In the case of India, accountability was shown to the western states. Second, India was involved in a war-like situation with Pakistan on Kargil during May-July 1999 and representatives of the Indian states were visiting every G-7 country to plead for the correctness of their stand towards Pakistan. The Indian state has been pleading with the United States to declare Pakistan a 'terrorist state' and India and US are trying to convince one another that they are confronted with a common enemy represented by Muslim fundamentalism and terrorism which Huntington identified as "clash of civilisations'.

By identifying Islamic fundamentalism as the main enemy of liberal democracies, the US and India are trying to come together on this common platform of common enemy strategy. The representatives of the Indian state have been celebrating that on Kargil dispute with Pakistan all the Western countries stood in support of India. Testimonial of good conduct from the west is considered a great asset by the Indian state functionaries of the 1990s. Third, the US Congress is superior to democratically elected Indian Parliament because India has to accept US Missile Regime Control, US Patent Laws and US Trade Laws. Indian democratic state is based on the 'consent' of the citizens. Yet, social and national consensus represented by the Indian state is fully exposed to 'conditionalities' of the Western capitalist democratic sidles in the field of trade, commerce and finance. Further, liberal-democratic state of India is 'accountable' to its own citizens for its acts of omission and commission, but the centers of capitalist West can impose 'political conditionalities' on the whole of India for the so-called violation of universal Human Rights or Rights of a Child or Women. Universal Rights are defined by the Western capitalist countries and the Indian state has to come up to the standards laid down by the Western societies and their governments because 'donor' countries can impose 'conditionalities' on the recipients of aid and capital from the West.[86]

The upshot of above description is that erosion of the real power of the democratically constituted state of India without a desire to protect its 'relative autonomy' while dealing with centers of capitalist power is a new reality of the 1990s. Indian state began its journey by asserting its autonomy in choosing its own path of development, but with the beginning of the 1990s autonomy of the developmental state began to erode and the model of market-led development was imposed on India by the Western capitalist countries as a reward for aid and trade. What are the social shifts within India which have made it possible to abandon the path of autonomous development in favour of Western prescribed and dictated model of market-led development. Why has the Indian state accepted dictations from the Western capitalist countries and why has the Indian state allowed to be dictated by the West in the areas of the so-called human rights or other social sectors of Indian development? Why is the Indian state retreating from the social areas of human development and allowing private sector to take over activities performed by the state?

The Indian crisis has emerged in a big way in the 1990s and the Indian state, its functionaries and strata and fractions of the dominant exploiting classes have opted to resolve this 'crisis of India' by linking themselves as 'junior partner' with the centers of capitalism. A sea change has occurred in India trading the path of economic development of the last fifty years. The capitalist classes, the capitalist fanners, the entrepreneurs of formal and informal sector, the upwardly mobile middle classes, are demanding a growing share in the fruits of economic development, and in this process of accumulation, they are linking themselves with global capitalists for joint ventures or any other related activity. Further, middle class state functionaries, political class and bureaucracy, have their autonomous interest in sharing the fruits of development, and these powerful social groups are expecting great benefits by linking themselves with transnational capitalist class. Public bureaucracy plays a critical role in the management of public affairs even under the regime of retreating and withdrawing state. A convergence of interests has emerged between the property owning classes—rural and industrial—and middle class state functionaries and they have collectively shifted their preferences in favour of foreign collaborations, deregulation and privatisation of economy. Global capitalism has found a powerful social constituency in India which expects economic and social benefits at the cost of state sovereignty. The IMF and the World Bank perform 'tutelage' functions in the aid-recipient countries by coopting powerful state bureaucracies of the third world. Harberger observes:

> "I hold the profound conviction that the World Bank and the International Monetary Fund have performed extremely important tutelage functions in ways that many people do not realise. I am referring to the upgrading of member country personnel through (a) the apprenticeships that many of them serve as staff members of the bank and fund; (b) the direct lessons learned by government personnel in member countries through dealing with missions from the two sister institutions; and (c) the similar but rather more specific lessons that member country cadres have learned by going through the Bank's process of project evaluation at various stages of a project is development. Each of the above entails a special kind of the job training that the Bank and the Monetary Fund are in my views uniquely qualified to impart".[87] It is not without reason that the main catalysts of New Economic Policy of Globalisation were powerful bureaucrats who had linkages with World Bank and IMF.

Max Weber has argued that the "national state which afforded to capitalism its chance of development—and as long as the national state does not give place to a world empire—capitalism will also endure."[88]

Similarly, John M. Keynes also observed that "let goods be homespun whenever it is reasonably and conveniently possible, and above all, let finance be primarily national."[89]

Weber, Keynes, Pandit Nehru and Indira Gandhi represented values of national economic sovereignty under the leadership of a national democratic state but the new dominant social formations of the 1990s in India are involved in the 'struggle for accumulation' with partnership of dominant global capitalism. It is the logic of shift within the Indian social groups which has facilitated the emergence of dominance of global capitalism over India with its ideology of market-led instead of state-led economic development. A social path is not abandoned midway unless social crisis is serious and new solutions are acceptable to powerful social constituencies in a country. This is the story of Indian state in the 1990s.

GLOBALISATION, MARKET AND STATE

Eric Hobsbawm, the most important historian of European capitalism, has warned that 'the specter of globalisation haunts us' in the last decade of Twentieth Century.[90] What is specific about globalisation of the decade of 1990s and the beginning of Twenty-First Century? Globalisation and internationalisation of world economy is the logical product of the growth of capitalism from the beginning of the Fifteenth Century to the end of Twentieth Century. Not only this. Industrial capitalism, differentiated from its predecessor feudal mode of production, needs global markets for raw material and finished products because industrialism means large-scale production of commodities for consumption. The history of five hundred years of growth and development of industrial capitalism is based on the emergence of nation-state or national capitalism, colonialism, imperialism and in spite of the Treaty of Westphalia, European countries fought wars among themselves for the establishment of colonies in Asia, Africa and Latin America. The only long period of peace in Europe has been from the end of the Second World War and up to December 1991 when the erstwhile socialist state system of Russia and other East European countries collapsed. President George Bush Sr. declared in 1991 the birth of a new global era and characterised it as New International World Order. The collapse of erstwhile socialist state systems from 1991 was interpreted by the Western, especially the American, State leaders and intellectuals as a victory for Western value system as opposed to one party socialist state system. Francis Fukuyamas' Essay '*The End of History*', published in *National Interest* of July 1989, stated that the values of 'liberal-democratic civilisation' have been globally vindicated and it has 'marked the end of the ideological evolution of mankind'. In 1991-1993 Samuel P. Huntington brought two books in which he, like Fukuyama, celebrated the victory of democracy over all other political systems and perceived the future faultiness based on religious hostilities and concluded that it will be an era of 'the West and the Rest'.[91] Huntington has interpreted the last decade of the Twentieth Century around the victory of Western democratic values; and the other motivating force according to him is 'religion' which is "perhaps the central force that motivates and mobilises people". American experience of September 11, 2001 confirmed the Western capitalist democracies and their scholars that 'Christian West' and 'Islam' are involved in struggle against one another as the new Twenty-First Century opens its account. It has led Sheldon Wolin, the Biographer of Tocqueville, to conclude that "Far from being valued as symbolising an aspiration towards the democratisation of power and a participatory society of political equals—democracy would come to be regarded by late-modern power elites as an indispensable yet valuable myth for promoting American political and economic interests among pre-modern and post-totalitarian societies. At home democracy is touted not as self-government by an involved citizenry, but as economic opportunity serves as the means of implicating the populace in anti-democracy in a politico-economic system characterised by the dominating power of hierarchical organisation, widening class differentials, and a society where the hereditary element is confined to successive generations of the defenceless poor."[92]

The specific and real meaning of the current phase of capitalist globalisation lies in the proclamation of the ideology of Western democratic values of individualism, liberalism, freedom for market, and free competition at global level. In concrete terms, instead of state activism in managing economies of the late developing countries, the shift is from state to market and to non-state civil society interventions especially by the non-government institutions. In the context of India, the decade of 1990s brings an end to Nehru-Mahalanobis model of economic planning and 'retreat of the state' from activities connected with major areas of Indian economy.

The central position which the state occupied in Indian national economy has to be vacated and it is replaced by free market economy both domestic and international. The new emphasis on market as a mediator in economic transactions is based on an indictment of planned economic development of India and of the four decades of post-independence struggle for nation-building. The inspiration for the New Economic Policy of liberalisation, privatisation, deregulation, disinvestment of public sector undertakings, and the opening of national economy to international players has come from the west-controlled global institutions. The World Bank, IMF, World Trade Organisation *et al* are selling the American Model of Capitalism of free market economy for the whole world, and it can be substantiated by just referring to the titles of annual publications of the World Bank beginning with its *World Development Report* (1991); *The Challenge of Development* (1995); *Bureaucrats in Business—The Economic and Politics of Pubic Ownership* (A World Bank Policy Research Report) (1996); World Development Report: *From Plan to Market* (1996). World Development Report. *The State in a Changing World (1997) et al.*[93]

The continuing focus of World Bank and other global agencies is to highlight the serious deficiencies of state-led planning model of economic development and promote global integration of economies by replacing and displacing the 'state' by the market. What is the new role for the state in the management of national economy under the new dispensation of neo-liberal classical economic ideology as propagated by the globalisers, liberalisers and deregulators? The state should regulate competition, regulate market, negotiate on behalf of the private corporate sector, promote the interests of domestic corporate interests, arbitrate in inter-corporate and intra-corporate disputes, manage inflation and interest rates and control fiscal deficit.[94]

A few statements from authentic sources may be mentioned here to firmly state the argument that the globalisers are projecting states and their bureaucracies as the real villain of the piece for road blocking economic growth which should be left to market forces and private corporate sector of the economy. The World Bank President James D. Wolfensohn while introducing the *World Development Report* (1996) states about the Report: "It drives home the utter necessity of both liberalising economies through opening trade and market opportunities and stabilising them through reducing inflation and practicing fiscal discipline—and then of sticking to these policies consistently overtime...the necessity of reforming enterprises and expanding the private sector, while restructuring social safety nets to deal with the social impact of the move to the market."[95]

The upshot of this Report is a total indictment of public sector and complete faith in free market and private sector. The World Bank President Wolfensohn further elaborates his views in the Twentieth World Development Report (1997):

> "For many, the lesson of recent years has been that the state could not deliver on its promises: transition economies have had to make a wrenching shift toward the market economy, and much of the development world has had to face up to the failure of state-dominated development strategies. Even the mixed economies of the industrialised world, in response to the failures of government intervention, have opted for a decisive shift in the mix in favour of market mechanism that development requires an effective state, one that plays a catalytic, facilitating role, encouraging and complementing the activities of private business and individuals. Certainly, state-dominated development has failed."[96]

It is no one's case that under the new ideology of free market economy the state will wither away. The argument is that national economies of developing countries will be fully integrated with world capitalist system in the absence of effective control of the national sovereign states over its own economic wealth. Further, this is new globalisation of the last decade of Twentieth Century which is premised on the denial of relative autonomy to the states of developing countries to manage their own public affairs as decided by their own democratically elected Parliaments and Political Executives. Hence, the issue is not about 'minimalist' versus 'maximalist state but it is about the role of the state in decision-making about national economic goals and strategies of economic development.

It is essential to have a brief look at a shift of nuances from 1991 World Development Report on '*The Challenge to Development*' to the Millenium goals of development based on Millenium Declaration adopted by 189 countries at the UN Millenium Summit in September 2000. Human Resource Development for economic growth has emerged as the new concern and a *mantra* of globalisers because 'labour as a factor of production' is a recognised pillar of industrial economy. From David Ricardo, Karl Marx to the Twentieth Century Welfare capitalist and socialist states, the conditions of industrial working classes have occupied a centrestage in the thinking and praxis of every industrial society of Western countries. The history of industrial capitalism clearly tells us that the concern for the social welfare of the labouring classes is in the enlightened self-interest of capitalist classes and their state systems. It also deserves to be stated that western industrial societies have different models of capitalist welfare states beginning with the minimalist welfare state of America with its 1935 US Social Security Law for retired and unemployed individuals to the maximalist Western European capitalist states like Norway, Denmark, Sweden etc. The Human Development Report of 2003 by the UNDP is only an attempt by the globalisers and believers of free market economy that human beings as 'capital' cannot be ignored and this brings back a truncated National State as the Report maintains: "The Goals must become a national reality, embraced by their main stake-holders people and governments."[97] In spite of this new concern for human welfare, the globalisers are not abandoning their commitment to free market economy; this tight rope dancing becomes clear when the Human Development Report 2003 states that: "In the 1980s and much of the 1990s many development efforts by international financial institutions and major donor countries were guided by the belief that market forces would lift all poor countries on to a path of self-sustaining economic growth. Globalisation was seen as the great new motor of world-wide economic progress. Poor countries were assumed to be able to achieve economic growth as long as they pursued good economic governance based on the precepts of macro-economic stability, liberalisation of markets and privatisation of economic activity… .

"Though this optimistic vision has proven hugely inadequate for hundreds of millions of poor people, it still has considerable merit for much of the world. Despite protest against globalisation in recent years, world market forces have contributed to economic growth…".[98]

The Other Side of Market-led Globalisation and Liberalisation Economic Model

The critics have faulted the centrality and primacy accorded to 'free market' and the demand for replacement and displacement of 'state-led' economic growth on many grounds. The first ground of indictment of the economic theology of the decade of 1990s is built on the argument that 'economics and politics' of the new globalism is directly beneficial to American capitalism, and the New Economic Policy and ideology of the liberalisation of financial markets and trade and the deregulation of capital markets in the name of 'macro-economic stability' is disastrous for the developing countries. Joseph Stiglitz, a former Chief Economist at the World Bank, makes it clear that the ongoing globalisation process is beneficial for the capitalist countries and it has disastrous social and political consequences for the developing countries Stiglitz observes: "When US Secretary of Commerce Ron Brown travelled abroad, he was accompanied by US business people trying to make contacts and gain entry into these emerging markets. Presumably, the chances of getting a seat on the plane were enhanced if one made significant campaign contributions."[99] Government of every western country is actively promoting the interests of its own capitalist classes by influencing the economic decisions of recipients of Foreign Direct Investments. Further, pressures are exercised by capital surplus countries on the capital deficit countries for securing 'unfair contracts'. Stiglitz observes: "The Foreign direct investment comes only at the price of undermining democratic processes. This is particularly true for investments in mining, oil, and other natural resources, where foreigners have a real incentive to obtain the concessions at low prices."[100] Stiglitz dramatises it by observing that the United States' national interests are equal to the Wall Street interests. A President of General Motors, Charles E. Wilson, was Secretary of Defence and it does not need any logic to maintain that "What's good for General Motors is good for the country."[101]

Consequences of the Phenomenon of the Retreat of the State

An important negative impact of the 'opening of national economy' to foreign capital has been the growth of speculative capitalism at the cost of productive capitalism because the Foreign Exchange Regulation Act of India has been debunked by the liberalisers without creating any capability of the Indian State to control speculators and 'fly by night capital' investors like George Soros and others. Stiglitz, while attracting attention to the menace of international speculator capital investors, warns that: "..., neither theory nor evidence supports the view that opening markets to short term, speculative capital flows increases economic growth. But there is considerable evidence and theory that it increases economic instability, and that economic instability contributes to insecurity and poverty. So, such forms of capital market liberalisation might in some ways increase 'globalisation'. But they do not enhance growth...".[102]

The second consequence of the policies of liberalisation and free market economies has been the emergence of regional disparities, income inequalities, disparities among social groups, widening of rural-urban gap and forced migration of the poor from their homes to unwelcome and inhospitable large cities and metropolitan cities. We have authentic evidence from the Human Development Report (2003) about economic and social distortions which have emerged in developing countries following the New Model of Free Market Economy. The Human Development Report (2003) informs:

> "But stark differences are emerging between regions, with some pulling ahead and reaching new levels of development—while others are left behind. The same pattern is occurring within regions: some countries are succeeding amid disappointing regional trends, while others are falling behind in regions making good overall progress".[103]

The Indian policy-makers are grappling with the problems of regional imbalances accentuated by the policies of the 1990s. During the period of Economic Planning, removal of regional imbalances was accepted as one of the most important goals by the Indian state and economic planners. This claim has been abandoned by the Central governments of the 1990s. Not only this. The Indian Constitution created a very important institution of Finance Commission for the task of distributing financial resources among the states of India on the basis of very objective criterion. Its recommendations were sacrosanct and never challenged except, for the first time, in the decade of 1990s when Chandrababu Naidu, the Chief Minister of Andhra Pradesh, raised the issue of 'developed' versus 'backward' states and asked that the Finance Commission should not punish the 'economically developed states' by conceding to the needs of 'backward states'. Is India moving towards 'islands of development' versus mainland of poverty? Can such an India be stable?

The most telling example of growing regional and sub-regional imbalances is reflected in the demand for the creation of new states like Chhattisgarh, Jharkhand, Uttaranchal, Telangana, Vidarbha because these sub-regions feel that they have been neglected by their own developed neighbouring districts. The Human Development Report (2003), on the basis of gender literacy, infant mortality and health concludes that India has 'progressive states' and extremely 'backward states'. While a few states have positively responded to the various aspects of Human Development, some others are laggards. What more evidence is required to substantiate the argument that many Indians are co-existing in the absence of an effective central planned growth model.

Another serious development which has disastrous social consequences is the growing gap between the developed and developing countries. The growing inequality among nations like the OECD countries and the others and also within the nations is likely to sharpen inter-nation and intra-nation conflicts. Milnovic, on the basis of his measurements of 'income inequality' informs that: "The richest 5 per cent of the world's people receive 114 times the income of the poorest 5 per cent. The richest 1 per cent receive as much as the poorest 57 per cent. And the 25 million richest Americans have as much income as almost 2 billion of the world's poorest people."[104]

A significant implication of the growing income inequalities among the nations is that the rich countries need global resources to maintain their standards of economic prosperity. How do developing countries protect their natural national resources from the greed and constant demands from the prosperous Western countries? The decade of 1990s has not only witnessed the collapse of the erstwhile European socialist state system, it has also seen the emergence of a 'unipolar world' under the supreme leadership of America, which has emerged as the sole military super-power and a global policeman. America and its European Union allies need to control global resources for the economic prosperity of the OECD countries. How can the vulnerable developing countries protect economic resources found in their recognised national geographical territories? Only a national state which is capable of protecting its national economy can bargain effectively with powerful western global players. Only a democratic state can act as an effective buffer between the capricious demands of the advanced capitalist countries and national interests. The ongoing process of globalisation is precisely aimed against the state systems and their capacities to manage national economies on the basis of relative autonomous relationships among the nation-states. The democratic nation-state is not only involved in a conflict situation with other powerful Western states, the growing national income inequalities and social disparities create serious conflict situations within these societies. How can any state manage its own domestic affairs without a positive response to the felt needs of the absolute alienated majority in an unequal society? The globalisers and liberalisers have to accept that it is only a democratic state and not a free market which can perform the role of resource allocation among regions, social classes and groups. And in the absence of an effective state intervention in favour of the deprived majority, social disorder will become an order of the day. Stiglitz observes that:

> "Civil strife in Africa has been a major factor setting back its development agenda. Studies at the World Bank show that such strife is systematically related to adverse economic factors,

including unemployment that can be produced by excessive austerity. Moderate inflation may not be ideal for creating an environment for investment but violence and civil strife are even worse."[105]

Such a warning deserves serious attention from the western public policy-makers. It can be reasonably stated that active state interventions are essential to control and contain serious distortions in economic development created by the market forces not amenable to state control. Bhanoji Rao offers an explanation on the basis of data of 50 economies that "(1) ...there is no convincing evidence that economic growth per se could lower income and wealth inequalities. (2) ..., with acceptance and emulation of socialism and/or welfarism on the decline, institutions that work for the decline of inequalities such as land reform and fully government funded public and social services get marginalised....[106] Eric Hobsbawm has also warned about the disastrous consequences of American-led free market model of capitalism. He states that: "It (US) has deliberately sabotaged the EU, and also aims at ruining another of the great world achievements since 1945: prosperous social welfare states."[107]

It is not market but only a democratic state with appropriate economic policies and strategies that can deal with social inequality and if it is not done, the state will be involved in fire-fighting operations to control violence and social anarchy.

Further, in developing countries, employment generation programmes have to be undertaken by the state because human resource planning is not the task of market. The market is not responsible for undertaking economic activities for providing employment opportunities to millions of people in labour-surplus populated developing countries. *Public Enterprises Survey, (1995-96)* mentions the following objectives of economic planning by the state:

"(a) To help in the rapid economic growth and industrialisation of the country and create the necessary infrastructure for economic development;

(b) To earn return on investment and thus generate resources for development;

(c) To promote redistribution of income and wealth;

(d) To create employment opportunities;

(e) To promote balanced regional development;

(f) To assist the development of small-scale and ancillary industries; and

(g) To promote import substitution, save and earn foreign exchange for the economy."

This comprehensive agenda of social and economic planning of India was arrived at by the democratic state on the basis of existing social realities of a diverse continental country. Employment crisis has emerged in the 1990s because generation of new employment opportunities has ceased to be public policy agenda. One of the consequences of growing unemployment is forced migration of the helpless and hapless labouring groups. According to Tushar Mahanti "*Waning job market makes 14 lakh Indians scurry abroad in last five years.*"[108] Migration within the country and outside the national territorial borders is a consequence of complex factors which can be positive as well as negative. Migration of labour is a welcome step if it is a product of expanding and booming economy. If economy is growing, migration is a 'pull' factor as it happened in the earlier stages of British industrialisation when the process of migration was 'from farm to factory'. Migrants are attracted towards new opportunities for gainful employment. Migration can be a consequence of negative factors when the labouring classes are pushed out of their 'home' because job opportunities nearer home are not available because of absence of economic growth. In Indian migration, both 'pull' and 'push' factors are at work because workers are migrating in search for new job opportunities in new places, both domestic and foreign, and there is large-scale 'distress' migration especially from backward regions and districts to relatively developed cities or towns. Every large metropolis has huge migrant working population in the slum areas and shanty towns.

Tushar K. Mahanti informs us that, "...India's job market has shrunk dramatically in the post-reforms years. Most of the big companies, both in the public and private sector, have introduced various separation schemes of late and reduced work force significantly".[109] He further informs that "The number of employed in the organised sector has fallen unchecked from 282.45 lakh in 1997 to 227.89 lakh in 2001. The fall was sharper in the public sector, where the number of employed has fallen by 4.20 lakh or 2.2 per cent during the period. The number of employed in the organised private sector during the same period has fallen by 0.4 per cent from 86.86 lakh in 1997 to 86.52 lakh in 2001."[110]

India is witnessing an inverse relationship between employment growth in the post-reform phase and the output growth. The National Sample Survey Organisation (NSS) confirms that the "growth rate of employment has declined from 2.7 per cent per annum during 1983-94 to 1.07 per cent during 1993-2000 when the growth of output, that is gross domestic product, accelerated from 5.2 per cent to 6.7 per cent." In such a gloomy employment situation, unskilled and semi-skilled working class migrants are moving from an inhospitable situation at home to a little less socially acceptable situation in new neighbourhood. Such a phenomenon has been described by Jermy Seabrook as 'creating economic migrants.' He observes that: "The International Monetary Fund has been criticised for imposing its uniform structural adjustment programmes upon every country that has fallen within its superintendence. In every case, they have included mechanism for making the poor even poorer: Cuts in government spending which have focussed on nutrition programmes, education, healthcare and welfare services, have compelled more and more poor people to seek a livelihood far from home".[111]

Social consequences of rising unemployment situation are giving rise to negativism and violence both within the country and foreign countries of the migrants. The 'village vagabonds' and the 'lumpen proletariat' of the early British industrial social history are the new phenomenon of the 1990s as a consequence of New Economic Ideology of neo-classical liberal variety. Advanced western countries are facing backlash against foreign migrants (immigrants) either in the form of race-riots or a demand to restrict migration. In the United States of America, unemployed workers are asking their political representatives to legislate against 'outsourcing' of production by American owned companies because establishing 'assembly lines' in foreign countries creates jobs for the workers of the host countries while it leads to joblessness in America. The Information Technology Association of America, a high power American industry body, has 'made a strong pitch for outsourcing the jobs so that the United States can remain competitive'. ITAA President, Harris Miller, says that: "This is the new global reality for US information technology companies and workers, and we must meet it with a new spirit of competitiveness". Since American IT companies are global, 'product or service localisation' is needed.[112] While high technology jobs through outsourcing are a drop in the ocean of growing unemployment, the Indian immigrants in America face hate campaigns. Public sector enterprises in India were assigned a goal to generate employment, but in the phase of the dismantling of state enterprises, employment as a public policy is confined to the corridors of policy makers and it has become a part of political rhetoric as shown by the NSS data of the Government of India.

Another socially adverse impact of New Economic regime is the emergence of great social disparities and the impact of these sharp social divisions of status are visible in the changing character of the consumer products.[113] The best example of the emergence of a socially narrow based Indian elite in the post-reform phase is provided by the availability of private cars by the global car makers, the General Motors, Ford, Toyota, Honda, Suzuki, Hyundai-Mitsubishi, Fiat *et al*. Not to be left behind, the new status symbol of the elite, BMW, is also planning to open shop in India. The management of Bayerische Morton Werke (BMW) announced the establishment of a Joint Venture car plant in India in 2003 which "can either be assembly or a manufacturing unit." The story does not end here. The government has opened financial sector of economy like banking, insurance and pension to foreign private investors because it is global capital which is a real player in the current stage of centralisation-cum-globalisation of economy and it is foreign banks and multinational corporations which want to open their shops in every developing country. This opening of Indian economy to foreign capital investors has been justified on the plea that India is capital-deficit and capital-surplus western countries deserve to be welcomed for accelerating the rate of economic growth. While the national financial sector is liberalised, deregulated and opened to foreign competition for the need for attracting Foreign Direct Investment for economic development; the opening of insurance sector and the market of milk products like yoghurt, cheese and butter to multinationals such as USA's Dean, Dairy Farmers of America, Scheiber and Land O Takes, and Europe based Arla, Parnalaat, Lactalis, and Compania can only serve the interests of a social minority of Indian elite. Nidhi Nath Srinivas observes: "With a market size of $2.5 billion for curd and curd-based products, and $375 million for *paneer* alone, MNCs are quickly realising the peril of ignoring these money-spinners."[114]

Even the opening of insurance sector to international insurance companies is to cater to the preferences of the status oriented elite because Life Insurance Corporation of India played a Yeoman role by creating the culture of insurance among the lower middle classes. The market is captured by foreign insurance companies because elite consider it as a status symbol. ICICI Prudential Life, a joint venture between ICICI and Prudential is first private insurance company to have crossed the Rs. 10,000 crore mark while premium income had already touched Rs. 680 crore on July 31, 2003. Shikha Sharma, Managing Director and CEO, ICICI Prudential said, "Among the private life insurance players we have captured a 38 per cent market share, while in the industry as a whole we have 3 per cent share. In fact, our market share for pensions is 23 per cent. The brand acceptance has been extremely positive".[115]

Another adverse consequence of the current phase of globalisation of the 1990s is that in an asymmetrical international political system, the state sovereignty of the developing countries is under threat from the real sovereign Western countries which are the headquarters of surplus capital for investments and superior technology. It deserves to be stated here that Nehru-Mahalanobis model of economic development based on import substitution industrialisation was not 'autarchic' or isolationist but it was an assertion of national interests being nationally defined by the Indian state and linkages with the world system were based on relative autonomy of the Indian state in conducting its inter-national relations. The best illustration to prove this point is that it was an Indian decision to establish steel plants in public sector and after arriving at this basic decision, the Nehru government started negotiations with foreign countries. The Americans were the first to be approached with a proposal for a steel plant for India but the American offer was declined because America was offering a steel plant to be managed by private entrepreneurs. The Russians, the Germans and the British agreed to India's request for steel plants in public sector and Bhillai, Rourkela and Durgapur steel plants were launched by foreign countries in India.[116] This situation of sovereign decisions by India does not exist any more in the trade regime of World Trade Organisation. A telling example of quasi-world government role of the WTO is the response of the Indian government on Indian Patent Law and meeting the demands of TRIPs[117] before 2005. The Patent Act of 1970 was first amended in 1999, the second amendment was made in 2002 and the third amendment to patent law is before parliament. The purpose of this third amendment is "the introduction of the TRIPs-mandated product patents regime in the country for food, drugs and pharmaceuticals and chemicals."[118] On the eve of discussion in Parliament, the Organisation of Pharmaceutical Production of India (OPPI) which comprises MNCs such as Pfizar, Glaxo-Smithkline, Novartis, Antra Zenera et al made a representation to the Government of India that 'not a single exclusive marketing right (EMR) has been granted by India's patent controller after its introduction in 1999, which shows that the country's EMR norms are flawed and not TRIPs compliant".[119]

It is not only that the MNCs are openly pressuring the Government of India for concessions, their powerful western nation-states also put pressure over the states of the developing countries to extend concessions to foreign-owned MNCs. Foreign and domestic capital many a time combine together to pressurise host country's government for favourable trade concessions. This new development of the globalised 1990s world has made some scholars, state leaders and foreign and domestic Big Business and global institutions like the World Bank, IMF and WTO to make unsubstantiated and fundamentalist statement that capitalist global market has 'an intrinsic tendency to transcend any national institutions.'[120]

The crux of the issue is not the logic of capitalist global market but the capabilities of a state to manage its own national affairs in a relatively autonomous inter-national global system where spaces for autonomy are available if the states have the intention to decide on their own and have the 'capability' to negotiate with Western capitalist countries. This is the reason that the decade of 1990s has created a situation in which middle classes of developing countries have been persuaded by the free market ideology that state-in-economy is a villain of the piece and public services should be either privatised or handed over to the institutions of civil society like the NGOs. The idiom of governance has changed in the 1990s and preference is for 'public-private partnership' and Non-Government Organisations providing public services and the consequence of this thinking is felt on the morale of public services whose capacity to govern is getting gradually eroded. The Indian state has greater competence than NGOs to regulate social aspects of economy, but it is made to surrender this role to the NGOs and in the process state's capabilities are getting eroded and making it more vulnerable to powerful foreign and domestic pressure groups.

The dramatic exposure of the states' unwillingness to manage and regulate the Big Business, external and internal, came from the Centre for Science and Environment (an NGO) on August 5, 2003, when "it rocked the corridors of Pepsi, Coca Cola MNCs by claming that their laboratory tests show traces of pesticide in the drinks sold in Delhi." This statement of Sunita Narain, the CSE Chicf, rattled the two MNCs and Parliament demanded an answer from the government, and till the answer was authoritatively given the parliamentarians demanded a ban on the sale of Pepsi, Coca Cola drinks.[121] The Indian state was put on the defensive by a NGO while it has institutions like Central Food Technological Research Institute, Mysore and Central Food Laboratory, Kolkata for performing tests on food stuffs and drinks. When the Health Minister Sushma Swaraj told parliament on August 21, 2003, that the tests conducted by government agencies 'clearly show that all the 12 samples do not have pesticide residues of the high order as was alleged by the Centre for Science and Environment (CSE) Report', it did not carry conviction because a sea change has taken place in the mindset of the elite including political class that somehow the state is not worthy of trust. The NGOs as voluntary agencies have won over the trust of the public which has developed a feeling of alienation from public services and public institutions. It deserves to be stated that the mushroom growth of the non-government organisations as voluntary bodies providing public services has been legitimised on the basis of an ideological myth that public services cannot deliver the goods. On the contrary, in a democratic country, accountability is imposed on public services and institutions and NGOs are not accountable to any public.[122] The government of India can be compelled to respond to public criticism for its acts of omission or commission but non-government voluntary agencies, funded by Indian or foreign donors, are not at all answerable to Indian public. Accountability of public services and institutions is built around constitutional arrangement of Indian democracy. The NGOs operate and function outside the preview of parliamentary or judicial accountability.

State and Social Justice

In a democratic country, citizens look towards the state and not free market forces or multinationals or global institutions for social justice and it is the sole responsibility of a democratic state to establish just social order. The ideology of liberalisation and globalisation by ejecting the state from its central role in the management of national economy leaves little space for the state to manage social inequities created by the New Economic Regime. Not only this. John M. Keynes had suggested public investments as the motor force of economic development for the generation of gainful employment in a country. It is not only Nehru-Mahalanobis model that has been discarded by the globalisers, Keynesian economics of public expenditure as the fountain source of economic and social growth has been also buried by the IMF, World Bank and neo-classical liberal economists who are concerned with 'fiscal deficit', 'fiscal balance' and structural adjustment. Since India is following the model of growth on the lines suggested by western global institutions and Western capital investors, it has followed their suggestion of structural adjustment and on July 29, 2003 the Rajya Sabha approved the Fiscal Responsibility and Budget Management Bill 2003. Finance Minister, Jaswant Singh, promised to implement schemes to control public expenditure and he also promised to regularly report to Parliament on the status of fiscal deficit. It is on the pattern of the Stability and Growth Pact of the European Monetary Union to cut spending.

The rise in government spending is a useful way to achieve national economic growth with justice in a developing country in spite of budget deficits. There is nothing automatic about fiscal 'stability' and democratically elected governments should have the autonomy to manage their own budgets and define their own social goals depending on the existing and prevailing social situation in a specific country. Even Americans do not do what they are prescribing to the Indians. J. Bradfold Delong observes that: "On the American side of the Atlantic, the usefulness of these automatic fiscal stabilisers is unchallenged. On the contrary, whenever recession threatens, political debate revolves around whether they need to be reinforced by *additional* stimulus via discretionary fiscal policy. No one considers how to put further downward pressure on the economy back on spending programmes. Neither Democrats nor Republicans have an interest in choking off economic activity. "This is not a partisan issue".[123] When a medicine is not acceptable to the most advanced capitalist country, a poor country can hardly accept the prescriptions of automatic 'fiscal stability' because it will cut expenditures from the welfare programmes of 500 million poor and labouring men and women in rural and urban areas. The poor of India look towards the state for programmes for the eradication of poverty, malnutrition, infant mortality and other social services. The ultra rich and newly emerging upwardly mobile middle and entrepreneurial classes of India have abandoned the state in favour of the ideology of free market, private enterprise and global market linkages. But the state can not be a private stock exchange company of the 250 million middle and upper middle classes who alongwith the Indian Big Business and global players are wanting to displace the centrality of state in economic management. The majority of Indians which include rural and urban poor, marginal and small farmers, unskilled and daily wage earners, lower middle classes—all look towards a democratic social welfarist state for economic development and social justice.

The upshot of above argument is that the prevailing ideology in favour of free market and non-government organisations providing public services to the community is premised on non-empirical reality of state's failures to provide public services to the multiple groups in society. The plea is not for statism. A democratic social welfarist state which is a jealous guardian of its own sovereignty and which can be effectively held accountable for the management of social problems is a preferred option over a state which is being marginalised both by foreign players and powerful domestic private interests. A poor country needs a Big Government which is democratically constituted and which is responsive to its own citizens and their welfare. The choice is clear—either a developmentalist state with an agenda of social justice or social disruption and chaotic violence under New Economic Regime of privatisation, liberalisation and globalisation.

NOTES AND REFERENCES

1. Law and State Focus: *Development Old Issue—New Problems*, Vol. 59/60, 1999, Tubingen: Germany.
2. See *Governance and Development*: World Bank, Delhi: Oxford University Press, 1992. Also see *The State in a Changing World, World Department Report*, Delhi: Oxford University Press, 1997.
3. P.S. Appus, *Land Reforms in India: A Survey of Policy*, Legislation and Implementation: New Delhi, Vikas Publishing House, 1996, p. 184.
4. Kirppa Shankar: Tenancy Reforms: Rhetoric and Reality, Bombay: *Economic and Political Weekly*, November 20, 1999, pp. 3264-65.
5. S.N. Eisenstadt: *Modernisation, Protest and Change*, (Englewood Cliffs, N.J. Prentice Hall; 1966).
6. George H. Sabine: *A History of Political Theory*: (London; George C. Harrap, 1951), edn. 3. p. 7.

7. *Ibid.*, p. 17.
8. Refer: Rajni Kothari: *Politics in India*, (Boston, Little Brown and Company, 1970).
9. Talcott Parsons, *Sociological Theory and Modern Society* (New York: Free Press, 1967), p. 125.
10. Daniel Bell, *The Coming of Post-Industrial Society: A Venture in Social Forecasting* (New Delhi: Arnold-Heinemann, 1974), p. 127:
11. S.M. Lipset, *Political Man: The Social Basis of Politics* (New York: Doubledey, 1960), p. 403.
12. Daniel Bell, *The End of Ideology: On the Exhaustion of Political Ideas in the Fifties* (New York: Collier Books, 1961), revd. edn. Also see Martin Seliger, *Ideology and Politics* (London: George Allen & Unwin, 1976).
13. Refer Bell, *The Coming of Post-Industrial Society, op. cit.*
14. Karl R. Popper, *Open Society and Its Enemies* (London: Routledge & Kegan Paul, 1962), 2 Vols, revd. edn. 4.
15. See Robert A. Dahl, *Pluralist Democracy in the United States* (Calcutta: Scientific Book Agency, 1969), Indian edn.
16. See Carl, J. Friederich: *Constitutional Government and Democracy*: (Bombay, Oxford IBH, 1966).
17. See S.N. Eisenstadt and Stein Rokkan, *Building States and Nation: Models and Data Resources* (London: Sage Publications, 1973), Vol. 1.
18. Dunkwart, A. Rustow and Robert, E. Ward, 'Introduction', in Ward and Rustow, eds., *Political Modernisation in Japan and Turkey* (Princeton, N.J., 1964), pp. 6-7.
19. Edward Shils, "On the Comparative Study of the New States" in Clifford Geertz, ed., *Old Societies and New States* (Delhi: Amerind Publishing Co., 1971), p. 21.
20. *Ibid.*, p. 21.
21. Samuel P. Huntington, *Political Order in a Changing Society* (New Haven, Conn., 1968).
22. Samuel, P. Huntington, "The Change to Change; Modernisation, Development, and Politics", *Comparative Politics* (USA), Vol. 3, No. 3, 1971, p. 316.
23. *Ibid.*
24. Alvin, W. Gouldner, *The Coming Crisis of Western Sociology* (New Delhi: Heinemann, 1971), p. 352.
25. Also see C.P. Bhambhri, "Functionalism in Politics", *Indian Journal of Political Science* (Delhi), Vol. 34, No. 4, October-December, 1973, pp. 455-70.
26. Irving Louis Horowitz, *Three Worlds of Development: The Theory and Practice of International Stratification:* (New York: Oxford University Press, 1966), pp. 47-48.
27. See C.P. Bhambhri, "Theoretical Framework for Comparative Politics: A Critique", *Indian Journal of Political Science*, Vol. 36, No. 4, October-December, 1975, pp. 414-30.
28. Isaiah Berlin; *Karl Marx: His Life and Environment* (London: Oxford University Press, 1963), edn. 3, p. 2.

29. See Nicols Poulantzs, "Classes in Contemporary Capitalism" *New Left Review*, 1975, p. 22.
30. For developments in the contemporary capitalist system, refer to: Paul, M. Sweezy, *The Theory of Capitalist Development: Principles of Marxian Political Economy* (New York, Modern Reader Paperbacks, 1968); and Paul, A. Baran, *The Political Economy of Growth* (London: Penguin Books, 1973).
31. Samir Amin, *Neo Colonialism in West Africa*, (Harmonds Worth); Penguin, 1973. A.K. Bagchi, *Private Investment in India, 1900-1939*, Delhi, Orient Longmans, 1975. R.P. Dutta: *India Today*, Bombay, PPH, 1947.
32. V. Pavlov, *et al.*, *Indian Social and Economic Development* (18th-20th Centuries): Moscow, Progress Publishers, 1975.
33. Eric Hobsbawm in conversation with Antonio Polito: *The New Century*: Little Brown and Company, USA, 1999: Translation Editori Laterza 2000, p. 52.
34. William, I. Robinson and Jerry Harris, Towards a Global Ruling Class? Globalisation and the Transnational Capitalist Class: *Science and Society*, Vol. 64, No. 1, Spring 2000: p. 12, See pp. 11-54.
35. See: George Soros, *The Alchemy of Finance: Reading the Mind of the Market,* John Wiley and Sons, New York, 1994.
36. Eric Hobsbawm, *The New Century,* 2000, p. 43.
37. Eric Hobsbawm, *The New Century, op. cit.*, pp. 77-78.
38. *Bureaucrats in Business*: Oxford University Press, New Delhi, 1995, p. XI.
39. *Bureaucrats in Business*: (1995) p. 50: SOE means State Owned Enterprises.
40. Eric Hobsbawm, *The New Century,* p. 74.
41. Harry Magdoff, *Essays on Imperialism and Globalisation,* Corner Stone Publications, Kharagpur, 2002, p. 278.
42. Yoshikazu Sakamoto (Ed.), *Global Transformation: Challenges to the state system,* United Nations University Press, Tokyo, 1994, p. 117, See the Chapter by Stephen Gill, pp. 169-99.
43. Also see: Karl Polanyi, *The Great Transformation: The Political and Economic Origins of Our Time:* Beacon Boston, 1957, (1994).
44. George Soros, *The Hindustan Times*, New Delhi, November 12, 2003, p. 12.
45. Strobe Talbott, An American Ideal I, *The Asian Age,* New Delhi, November 19, 2003, p. 16.
46. Strobe Talbott, *The Asian Age* II, New Delhi, November 20, 2003, p. 16.
47. Sripath Ramphal, '*Rage against the Machine*', *The Hindustan Times*: New Delhi, November 20, 2003, p. 10.
48. George Bush, *The Hindustan Times,* New Delhi, November 21, 2003, p. 13.
49. Robert, C. Angel, *E.plaining Economic Policy Failure*, Japan in the 1969-71 International Monetary Crisis, Columbia University Press, New York, 1991, quoted by Harry Magdoff, *Essays on Imperialism and Globalisation* 2002, p. 313.
50. See C.P. Bhambhri, *The Indian State Since Independence,* Shipra, New Delhi, 2000.

51. '*TISCO eyes Rs. 25,000 crore sales*', *The Business Standard,* New Delhi, November, 2002, p. 1.
52. *The Economic Times,* New Delhi, November 4, 2003, p. 4.
53. *Tata sign MOU to buy Daewoo Unit, The Hindustan Times,* New Delhi, November 6, 2003.
54. Sabarinath M. Abhinaba Das, '*——on Takeover spree abroad*', *The Economic Times,* New Delhi, November 27, 2003, p. 10.
55. *Going Global: Indian Multinationals Abroad, The Indian Express,* New Delhi, November 25, 2003, p. 10.
56. *The Economic Times,* New Delhi, November 4, 2003, p. 4.
57. T.N. Ninan, '*Globalised India*': *The Business Standard,* New Delhi, November 2003, p. 11.
58. Satish Deshpande, *Contemporary India: A Sociological View*, Vicking, New Delhi, 2003. Especially chapter 'The Centrality of the Middle Class. pp. 125-50.
59. One Crore is ten million.
60. *The Economic Times,* New Delhi, October 10, 2003, p. 3.
61. Garry Pursell, *The Indian Express,* New Delhi, October 17, 2003, p. 10.
62. Mukul G. Asher, '*Budgetary Resource Mobilisation in Asia: Growing Complexity*', *Economic and Political Weekly,* Bombay, August 30-September 5, 2003, Vol. XXXVIII, No. 35, p. 3642, See pp. 3639-46.
63. D.H. Pai Panandikar *7% growth may be a one-year wonder, The Hindustan Times,* New Delhi, D :cember 1, 2003, p. 17.
64. Alan Wheatly, *International Farm Economy, The Indian Express,* New Delhi, September 2, 2003, p. 10.
65. Lijee Philip, *Consuming 'n' very rich, a class apart in growth*, *The Economic Times,* New Delhi, September 9, 2003, p. 7.
66. *Demolishing myths*, *The Economic Times,* New Delhi, December 2, 2003, p. 6.
67. For the tragic consequences of the Reform Period of the 1990s on the labour market, See. Shuji Uchikawa (Ed.), *Labour Market and Institutions in India: 1990 and Beyond,* Manohar Publishers, New Delhi, 2003.
68. Jeremy Seabrook, Ironies of history, *The Statesman,* New Delhi, November 30, 2003, p. 9.
69. Quoted by Pantich, L. *Rethinking the Role of the State* in J.H. Mittesiman (ed.), *Globalisation: Critical Reflections,* (London: Lynne Rienner) 1996, pp. 83-113.
70. Anne O. Kruegger (ed.), "Introduction": in *The WTO as an International Organisation,* Oxford University Press, Delhi , 1999, p. 14.
71. Richard Blackhurst, "The Capacity of the WTO to fulfill its mandate" in Krueger (ed.), *n. 2,* p. 33.
72. WTO council bid to build consensus for Supachai as Director General: Sheila Mathrani (Geneva, May 9, 1999), *The Economic Times,* Delhi, May 8, 1999, p. 3.
73. United Nations Development Programmes, *Human Development Report,* 1996, New York. Also See-David Harvey, *"The Geography of Class*

Power", The Communist Manifesto, in Leo Panitch and Collin, Leys (Eds.) Socialist Register 1998, Calcutta K.P. Bagchi. 06,1998, p. 66.

74. *Human Development Report, 1999,* Oxford University Press, New Delhi, 1999, p. 3.
75. *Human Development Report, 1999.*
76. See Pearson Commission (Commission on International Development), *Partners in Development:* 1965, Praeger, New York.
77. See Lipset, S.M. (1959), "Some Social requisites of democracy: Economic Development and Political Legitimacy", *American Political Science Review,* 53(1), pp. 69-105. Also see Huntington, S.P. (1991), *The Third Wave: Democratisation in the late Twentieth Century,* (Norman University of Oklahome Press).
78. Huntington, *n. 9,* pp. 266-267.
79. A. Prizeworski, *Democracy and the Market,* Cambridge University Press, Cambridge, U.K., 1991, p. 10.
80. World Bank World Development Report, *The State in a Changing World,* Oxford University Press, New York, 1997.
81. See Bimal Jalan (ed.), *India's Economic Policy: Preparing for the Twenty-First Century,* Penguin, New Delhi, 1996 and Vijay Joshi and M.D. Little, *India's Economic Reforms: 1991-2001,* Oxford University Press, New Delhi, 1997.
82. See C.P. Bhambhri, *The World Bank and India,* Vikas Publications, New Delhi, 1980.
83. Robert Wade, *"Globalisation and its Limits"* in S. Beyer and R. Dore (eds.). *National Diversity and Global Capitalism,* Cornell University Press, Ithaca, New York, 1996.
84. *Economic Survey:* 1998-99, The Government of India: New Delhi p. 17.
85. *Ninth Five-Year Plan:* 1997-2002, *Volume I,* Planning Commission, New Delhi, 1999, p. 3.
86. See George Sorensen: (Ed.), *Political Conditionality: The European Journal of Development Research,* Volume 5, November 1, June 1993; London: French class.
87. Arnold C. Harberger, "Reflections on the Present and Future Role of the World Bank" quoted by Henne O. Krueger in "Whither the World Bank and the IMF?" *Journal of Economic Literature,* vol. XXXVI, December 1998, p. 11, *see* pp. 1983-2020.
88. Quoted by Stephen K. Sanderson, *Social Transformation: A General Theory of Historical Development,* Blackwell, Oxford, U.K. 1995, p. 235.
89. John Maynard Keynes, *"National self-sufficiency"* 236, Article in 1933 in England (the New Statesman), in USA (the Yale Review).
90. Eric Hobsbawm, *The Age of Extremes: A History of the World,* 1914-1991, Pantheon Books, New York, 1994.
91. See Samuel P. Huntington 1991, *The Third Wave: Democratisation in the Late Twentieth Century,* University of Oklahoma Press, Norman 1993. Also see his *"The Clash of Civilisations and the Remaking of World Order,* Simon of Seluestic, New York, 1993.

92. Sheldon Wolin, *Tocqueville Between Two Worlds, The Making of a Political and Theoretical Life*, Princeton: 2001; quoted by Tariq Ali in *The Clash of Fundamentalisms: Crusades, Jihads and Modernity,* 2003. Rupa and Co., New Delhi, pp. 311-312.
93. All Reports: Oxford University Press, New Delhi.
94. See Samir Amin, '*The Political Economy of the Twentieth Century*', *Monthly Review,* New York, June 2000, p. 9.
95. *From Plan to Market,* World Development Report 1996. Oxford University Press, New Delhi, 1996, p. 111.
96. *The State in a Changing World:* World Development Report 1997, Oxford University Press, New Delhi, 1997, p. 111.
97. *Human Development Report* (2003), UNDP, Oxford University Press, New Delhi, p. 1.
98. *World Human Development Report* (2003), UNDP, Oxford University Press, New Delhi, 2003, p. 16.
99. Joseph Stiglitz, *Globalisation and Its Discontents*, Penguin Books, New Delhi, 2002, p. 70.
100. *Ibid.*, p. 72.
101. *Ibid.*, p. 195.
102. Joseph Stiglitz, quoted in *Human Development Report*, (2003), Oxford University Press, New Delhi, 2003, p. 80.
103. Human Development Report (2003), op. cit. p. 34.
104. Branko Milnovic: "*True World Income Distribution,* 1988 and 1993: First Calculation Based on Household Survey Alone" *Economic Journal:* 2002, 112 (476), pp. 51-92. Also see Angus Maddison: *The World Economy: A Millennial Perspective:* Paris: Organisation for Economic Co-operation and Development, 2001.
105. Stiglitz: *op. cit.*, pp. 77-78.
106. Bhanoji Rao, "*Explaining Cross-Country variation in Income Inequality", Economic and Political Weekly*, Bombay, April 26, 2003, Vol. XXXVIII, No. 17, p. 1648.
107. Eric Hobsbawm, "*Empire State Building", The Guardian,* London, June 16, 2003, quoted from *The Hindustan Times*, New Delhi, June 18, 2003.
108. Tushar K. Mahanti, *Economic Times*, New Delhi, May 12, 2003, p. 10.
109. *Ibid.*, p. 10.
110. Jeremy Seabrook, *The Statesman*, New Delhi, 17, 2003, p. 9.
111. S. Rajagopalan, *"US tech backs out souring trends", The Hindustan Times*, New Delhi, August 21, 2003, p. 15.
112. See Satish Deshpande, *Contemporary India: A Sociological View,* Viking Penguin Books Ltd., New Delhi, 2002.
113. Nidhi Nath Srinivas, "MNCs to read the milky way in India", *The Economic Times,* New Delhi, July 18, 2003, p. 11.
114. "ICICI Prudential 1st Private Insurance to cross Rs. 10K-er Sum". *The Economic Times*, New Delhi, August 21, 2003, p. 8.
115. C.P. Bhambhri, *World Bank and India*, Vikas Publication Ltd., New Delhi, 1980. Also see Bhambhri, *The Indian State since Independence,* Shipra Publications, New Delhi, 2001.

116. Trade Related Intellectual Property Rights.
117. *The Economic Times*, New Delhi, August 6, 2003, p. 6.
118. *The Economic Times*, New Delhi, August 15, 2003, p. 11.
119. Immanuel Wallerstein and Etinne Balibar, *Race, Nation, Class: Ambiguous Identities*, Verso, London, 1991, p. 89.
120. *Hindustan Times,* New Delhi, August 7, 2003.
121. See Neera Chandhok, *The Conceits of Civil Society,* Oxford University Press, New Delhi, 2002.
122. J. Bradfold Delong, '*Herbert Hoover of the stability pact*', *The Economic Times*, Delhi, July 29, 2003, p. 10.
123. Incidentally, these classes also give birth to Ketan Parikhs and Harshad Mehtas, the speculators and adventurists in the Stock Exchange Market.

Index